MEDICAL OFFICE PROCEDURES

SECOND EDITION

COLLEGE SERIES

Miriam Bredow
Karonne J. Becklin
Edith M. Sunnarborg

GREGG DIVISION / McGRAW-HILL BOOK COMPANY

New York • Atlanta • Dallas • St. Louis • San Francisco • Auckland • Bogotá • Guatemala
Hamburg • Johannesburg • Lisbon • London • Madrid • Mexico • Montreal • New Delhi
Panama • Paris • San Juan • São Paulo • Singapore • Sydney • Tokyo • Toronto

The Authors

The late **Miriam Bredow** was associated with the Eastern School of Physicians' Aides, first as an instructor and then in the successive roles of dean of women, assistant director, and director. She was the author of five editions of the *Handbook for the Medical Secretary* and coauthored *The Medical Assistant*. Miss Bredow also worked as a medical secretary for three psychiatrists in New York City.

Karonne J. Becklin is the medical secretarial program coordinator at Anoka Area Vocational Technical Institute in Anoka, Minnesota. In addition to her administrative responsibilities, she teaches courses in the medical secretarial program as well as in the medical assistant program. Prior to her association with Anoka AVTI, she worked as a hospital medical secretary. Mrs. Becklin is a Certified Medical Assistant, Administrative, and is a member of the AAMA and the Minnesota State Society of AAMA.

Edith M. Sunnarborg, R.N., has a wealth of experience as a registered nurse, as an office manager in a medical office, and as a teacher. A registered nurse for over 25 years, she has been affiliated with several hospitals in a variety of capacities, including that of head nurse. Mrs. Sunnarborg also worked in a doctor's office as an office manager and staff nurse. For the past several years, she has taught in the medical secretarial program at Anoka Area Vocational Technical Institute in Anoka, Minnesota. In addition to her teaching responsibilities, Mrs. Sunnarborg serves as the coordinator of the medical receptionist program at Anoka AVTI.

Medical Consultant **Herbert S. Strait**, M.D., was graduated from the University of Minnesota School of Medicine and is board-certified in Family Practice. At present, Dr. Strait is in private practice with the Fridley Medical Center in Fridley, Minnesota.

Sponsoring Editor:	Barbara N. Oakley
Manuscript Editor:	Sheila Lalwani
Editing Supervisor:	Susan Goldfarb
Design Supervisor:	Eileen Kramer, Meri Shardin
Production Supervisor:	Lou DeMaglie
Art Supervisor:	Howard Brotman
Photo Editor:	Mary Ann Drury
Cover Photographer:	Will Nardelli
Technical Studio:	Burmar Technical Corp.

Credits: The part-opening photographers were Martin Bough: pages 1, 29, 76, 97, 125, 156, 187 and 203; Jan Lukas/Photo Researchers, Inc., page 175. Other credits will be found next to the forms and photographs supplied.

MEDICAL OFFICE PROCEDURES, Second Edition

Copyright © 1981, 1973, 1966, 1959 by McGraw-Hill, Inc. All rights reserved. Copyright 1954, 1948, 1943 by McGraw-Hill, Inc. All rights reserved. Printed in the United States of America. No part of this publication may be reproduced, stored in a retrieval system, or transmitted, in any form or by any means, electronic, mechanical, photocopying, recording, or otherwise, without the prior written permission of the publisher. Copyright renewed 1971.

NOTE: Reproduction of any material contained herein is expressly prohibited, except for the forms on WP 21 and WP 29, which may be reproduced without permission. This limited permission is granted provided the materials are only for classroom use and solely in conjunction with *Medical Office Procedures*, Second Edition, by Miriam Bredow, Karonne J. Becklin, and Edith M. Sunnarborg. Any other reproduction, for sale or other use, is expressly prohibited.

1234567890 WCWC 8987654321

ISBN 0-07-007441-0

Preface

The second edition of *Medical Office Procedures* is a revision of a well-known and widely accepted textbook used extensively in medical office programs at colleges and vocational schools. In revising the textbook, the authors have attempted to differentiate between the duties of the medical assistant, administrative, and the medical assistant, clinical. This differentiation has evolved through the American Association of Medical Assistants and their classification of medical assistants as administrative or clinical specialists. The responsibilities of the medical assistant, administrative, are emphasized in this edition. For the purpose of this text, the term *medical assistant* will be used to denote any medical assistant who has administrative duties.

Today the medical profession is so large and complex and the practice of medicine so specialized that the typical doctor rarely has enough time to attend to the administrative responsibilities of the office, let alone train an assistant in basic medical office procedures and practices. As a result, many medical assistants are expected to do more than they have ever done before; therefore, they require more extensive training than they did in the past.

Job opportunities in the field are constantly undergoing changes. Previously, the only jobs available were for medical secretaries. Now, in addition to the wide-ranging job of the medical assistant, there are specialized opportunities for various types of medical office assistants.

It was previously assumed that once on the job, the student would be able to pull together all his or her skills and knowledge of office procedures. This textbook allows for the integrated application of skills and knowledge in the classroom through the use of simulation techniques. The student learns to perform the duties of the medical assistant under realistic conditions—with realistic input from a variety of sources, with access to a variety of realistic records, and with a realistic set of pressures that require the student to organize the work and set priorities.

Although the major portion of the original *Medical Office Procedures* content has been retained, problem-oriented projects have been included to meet the current trend for competency-based performance. In addition, the *Instructor's Manual and Key* lists behavioral objectives for each chapter.

PROJECTS Within each chapter, integrating projects occur at frequent intervals so that the student can immediately put into practice the procedure just studied. Records and correspondence that the student creates in these individual projects are used later in the simulations, where they provide a complexity of experience.

SIMULATIONS Two-day simulations appear at the end of Parts 2, 3, 4, 5, and 6. In each of these five simulations, the student listens to taped conversations between Janet Owen (the doctor's medical assistant, with whom the student will identify) and the doctor, various patients, and other office callers. (*Note:* The recorded material, which is packaged in cassette form, may be used by the student individually or by the class as a whole. A complete transcript of the material appears in the *Instructor's Manual and Key.*)

REFERENCE SECTION

The reference section appearing at the end of the text includes a variety of information that the student will find helpful throughout the course. In addition, of course, the student should become aware of the importance of consulting both general and specialized dictionaries, handbooks, and other reference sources as the need arises.

WORKING PAPERS AND FORMS

The forms, medical histories, handwritten drafts, and incoming correspondence needed to complete the projects and the simulations are provided in the back of the book. There are a few forms the student will need to duplicate.

Karonne J. Becklin
Edith M. Sunnarborg

To the Student

You have chosen a truly fascinating, challenging profession—one that you will find extraordinarily gratifying and rewarding in all respects. And we join your instructor in welcoming you to a training program designed to prepare you for immediate and long-range success as a medical assistant. In this program, you will use *Medical Office Procedures* not only as a source of practical information but also as an instrument for realistic practice in applying what you have learned.

PRACTICAL INFORMATION

Every topic that you will study in this course is directly related to one or more of the many duties that you will be performing as a medical assistant. To put the technical information that you will acquire into its proper perspective, you will first learn about specific careers available to you and the qualifications that you should have in order to enter those careers and succeed in them. After absorbing the information in Part 1, you should be better able to set your sights on the job that is best suited to your interests, qualifications, and ambitions.

You will learn how to deal with a doctor's patients in an efficient, effective manner. Since dealing with patients is a responsibility that you will encounter immediately and continually in any medical office, all the information concerning handling telephone calls, making appointments, meeting patients, and preparing medical records is vitally important, regardless of the specific medical office job you choose.

Your work as a medical assistant certainly will require you to perform a variety of tasks involving financial and legal responsibilities in a doctor's office. Therefore, you will become thoroughly acquainted with such topics as billing, health insurance, and keeping medical records.

Like any other professional person, a doctor is involved in various activities outside the office. You will have frequent need for information concerning medical society meetings, professional reports, and travel arrangements.

The medical field offers many exciting opportunities other than those in a doctor's office. You will learn about the various medical specialties and the responsibilities you would have as a medical assistant, clinical, or as an assistant in a hospital.

Finally, you will be provided with guidance that you will find helpful in conducting your job-hunting campaign and in preparing yourself for advancement in the personally and professionally rewarding career you have chosen.

REALISTIC JOB TRAINING

At frequent intervals throughout each chapter, you will actually be asked to apply your knowledge of material you have just studied—not simply to tell how or why you would use the information on the job. And just as in a medical office, you will use the information you acquire repeatedly throughout the course.

As you complete the projects within the text, you will accumulate many of the medical records and much of the correspondence needed in the simulations of medical office activities that occur at the end of Parts 2 through 6.

You will be asked to assume the role of Janet Owen, a medical assistant. During each of these two-day simulations you will handle various requests made by the doctor, his patients, and other office callers.

Although the textbook gives you a brief description of each simulation and the way it will operate, as well as a list of the working materials you will need, you will be expected to listen carefully to recorded conversations between Janet Owen and the doctor, the patients, and other office callers and to perform duties—your duties—in the manner you think appropriate. (Your instructor will make the recorded conversations available to you; the medical forms, medical histories, correspondence, and other materials needed for the simulations will be found in the back of this book, as well as in the projects you prepared.)

In each of these simulations, just as in a medical office, you will be performing a variety of closely related tasks: transcribing dictation (from shorthand notes or from a transcribing machine), answering the telephone, making appointments, filing, duplicating, opening mail, greeting office callers, and so on. Thus you will gradually gain expertise in performing a wide range of medical office activities and in coping with a variety of problems and pressures. All of these activities will help you overcome some of the most serious and most common problems that many beginning office workers have: organizing work, setting priorities, seeing the relationship of one task to another, managing office time—in general, simply "putting it all together." Having completed these simulations, you will find the transition from school to office a fairly simple matter—and more important, you will find your employer both happy and grateful that you were chosen as the assistant.

The projects within each chapter and the simulations at the end of Parts 2, 3, 4, 5, and 6 are not the only activities you will encounter in this course, however. You will also find a variety of activities at the end of each chapter. These activities will involve you in thought-provoking questions that will help you understand your chosen profession and the work involved in it and in role-playing situations that will assist you in developing the tact, graciousness, and understanding needed to deal with patients, professional people, and your own boss.

REFERENCE MATERIALS

When you are working in an office, you will have available to you many outside references that will help you perform your work more effectively. In order to promote a more realistic atmosphere in this program, the reference section at the end of the text contains information you may need to refer to as you work on the projects and simulations. You may need to consult other reference sources for specific technical information.

SUPPLIES

To complete the projects and simulations, you will need a variety of supplies. As indicated previously, the back of this book contains all the medical forms as well as a number of the medical histories and notes that you will need. You will find specific instructions for removing and using them in the textbook directions.

In addition, you will need to provide the following supplies yourself: a box of typing paper, a box of carbon paper, 33 manila folders and file folder labels, a package of unlined index cards, a rubber band, a box of paper clips, a note pad, pens, pencils, and a loose-leaf binder. It is also recommended that you obtain an expandable portfolio file to house these supplies.

Good luck to you in this course and in the interesting and challenging career you have chosen!

Karonne J. Becklin
Edith M. Sunnarborg

Contents

Part 1
THE MEDICAL ASSISTANT'S CAREER

1 Career Opportunities 2
2 Career Qualifications 10
3 Medicolegal Communications 17

Part 2
SECRETARIAL RESPONSIBILITIES

4 Appointments 30
5 Meeting the Patient 38
6 Telephone Procedures 47
7 Records Management 56
8 Written Communications 64
   Simulation 1 74

Part 3
PATIENT RECORDS

9 Preparing Medical Records 77
10 Billing the Patient 85
   Simulation 2 95

Part 4
FINANCIAL RESPONSIBILITIES

11 Health Insurance 98
12 Financial Records 110
   Simulation 3 122

Part 5
PROFESSIONAL ACTIVITIES

13 Office Management 126
14 Medical Society Meetings 135
15 Professional Reports 140
16 Travel Arrangements 148
   Simulation 4 153

Part 6
SPECIALIZATION IN MEDICINE

17 Medical Specialties 157
18 Medical Assistant, Clinical 165
   Simulation 5 172

Part 7
FACING THE FUTURE

19 Your Job-Hunting Campaign 176
20 Preparing for Advancement 183

REFERENCE SECTION

Addressing Envelopes 188
Letter Styles 189
Medical Abbreviations 191
Metrics 192
Conversion Tables 193
Reading References 194

INDEX 197

WORKING PAPERS 203

1
The Medical Assistant's Career

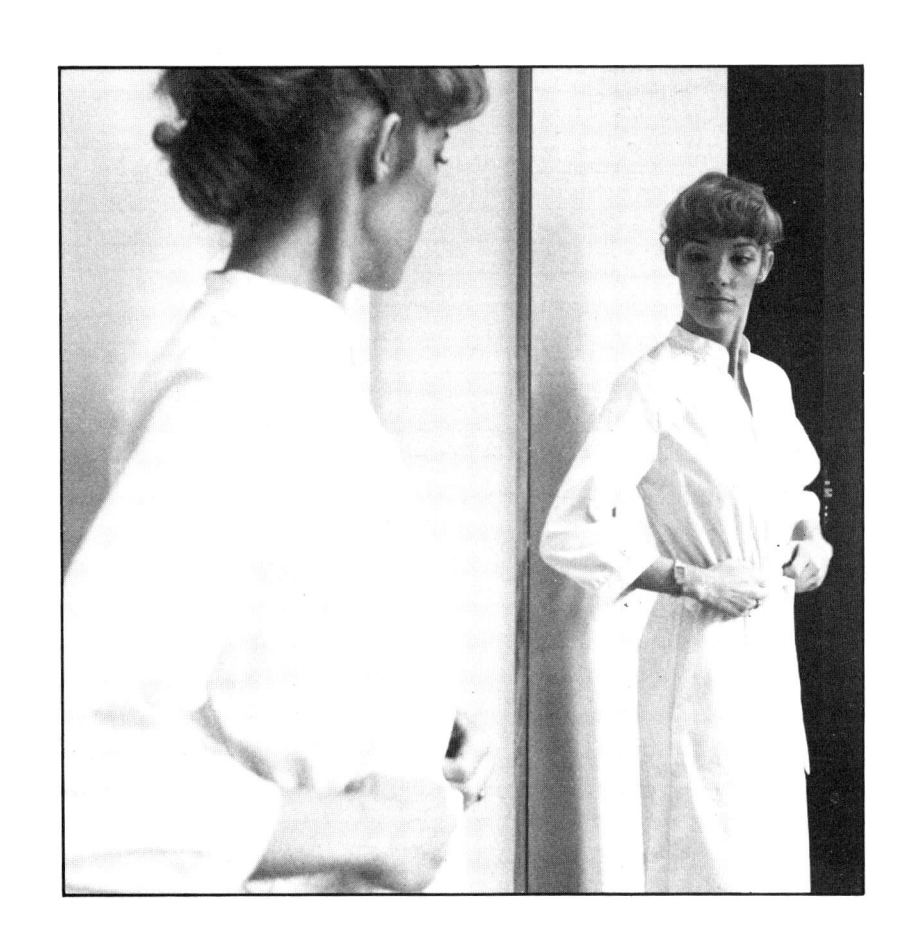

1

Career Opportunities

There are many opportunities today for a person who wants an office career. Jobs include clerk, receptionist, stenographer, secretary, and administrative assistant. Often the duties performed by a person holding one of the above job classifications are identical to the duties performed by a person holding a different classification. The jobs tend to vary only in the use of shorthand. Because duties overlap, the trend today is to call all office workers or secretaries "assistants"—clerical assistants, secretarial assistants, office assistants.

The assistant holds a key position, no matter what the specialty—law, science, medicine, international trade. A good assistant need never be without work, but to be a good assistant one must first attain and perfect necessary skills. This program will help you develop those skills and attitudes that will enable you to become a top-notch medical assistant.

DESCRIPTION OF A MEDICAL ASSISTANT, ADMINISTRATIVE

Many skills are needed to climb to the top of the career ladder as a good medical secretary—or, as the position is being increasingly called, *medical assistant, administrative*. One must be proficient in the use of English punctuation, grammar, style, pronunciation, and enunciation. One must be trained in office routines such as using the telephone, filing, and operating duplicating and other business machines. The assistant must know how to write routine business letters, where to look for sources of information, how to keep financial records, and how to order and keep a record of office supplies. He or she must have some knowledge of the particular field of work. Furthermore, one needs intelligence, systematic working habits, and willingness to take care of details. A person with these qualifications can move ahead easily.

A Day in the Doctor's Office

Few people—even those who have decided to become medical office assistants—realize how many and how varied are opportunities in that field. A doctor's life is a many-sided one, and in most of its phases a qualified assistant is needed. The assistant is the *receptionist* who greets patients, checks their appointments, and takes their names and addresses. The assistant is the *secretary* who prepares correspondence and types patients' records. The assistant is also the careful *accountant* who keeps a record of patients' visits and collects fees. Finally, the assistant is the *public relations agent* who knows patients by name, keeps the office running smoothly, and saves the doctor time and work.

The assistant may change into a white uniform after arriving at the office. Of course, one arrives a bit early so that the first patient will be greeted by a serene, composed, and properly dressed assistant. The morning mail must be sorted and distributed, and the records of patients who have appointments on that day must be taken out of the filing cabinet and placed on the doctor's desk. The sterilizer may have to be started. A quick tour of the office must be made to assure that everything is in order—fresh towels and sheets in readiness and no soiled equipment in view. If these things are done hurriedly, mistakes are more likely to occur. The assistant becomes flustered, the patient grows irritated, and the day starts all wrong. It is much easier to be on time and to attend to everything without haste.

2

In a doctor's office the telephone starts ringing quite early in the morning, for every day some appointments are made and others are broken, and these must be marked in the appointment book. A patient who has been awake all night with pain may wish to ask the doctor a question. There may also be an emergency call.

As patients arrive for their appointments, the assistant must give careful attention to each patient. If a patient has not been to the office before, part of the medical history may have to be taken before the patient sees the doctor.

Many doctors expect their assistants to handle routine correspondence, but important letters and medical histories will be dictated by the doctor, probably on tape or belts. Another duty is the filing of the previous day's mail and records. The assistant must also keep the doctor's books and record all income and expenses for tax and insurance purposes. Doctors are usually not concerned with the business aspect of the practice and are thankful to find employees who can relieve them of financial details.

There are always specialized tasks that keep the assistant aware of the word *medical* in the title *medical assistant*. Because of the scope and variety of duties, the position has crystallized into a distinct career. The routine of office work may be the same day in and day out, but there can be no routine in handling patients. Patients represent a cross section of humanity—each one different from the other. All persons coming to a doctor's office need attention of some kind, and so the assistant is constantly required to be tactful, gentle, understanding, firm, and patient.

WORK DELEGATED TO MEDICAL ASSISTANTS

Over the years many surveys have been made to ascertain how many doctors delegate work to their office personnel, and what type of work they delegate. The majority delegate all secretarial work, and many doctors delegate certain clinical tasks as well.

The following list is a composite of various lists that have been compiled. It is divided into two categories: duties expected of the *medical assistant, administrative;* and those duties performed by a *medical assistant, clinical.* The latter duties may also be performed by a registered nurse or a technician. However, the medical secretary is frequently asked to assist, or even to perform independently, the tasks listed under "Duties of Medical Assistant, Clinical."

DUTIES OF MEDICAL ASSISTANT, ADMINISTRATIVE

Handling telephone.
Making appointments.
Receiving patients.
Quoting fees to patients.
Recording patients' charges and payments.
Sending out bills.
Collecting bills.
Taking dictation and transcribing correspondence and medical histories.
Completing insurance forms.
Making hospital reservations for patients.
Procuring nurses for patients.
Filing histories and letters.

Keeping doctor's financial records.
Making deposits.
Reconciling bank statements.
Keeping payroll records.
Handling petty cash.
Supervising other personnel.
Using business machines.
Helping patients understand doctor's instructions regarding diet, prenatal care, exercises, and so forth.
Keeping track of dates for renewal of licenses, premiums due, membership fees, subscriptions, meetings.

PART 1: THE MEDICAL ASSISTANT'S CAREER

Checking medical journals for items of interest to doctor.

Proofreading doctor's articles, lectures, manuscripts.

Preparing records for doctor's use in court.

Ordering, handling, and storing supplies.

Planning trips for doctor.

Taking care of the office in doctor's absence.

DUTIES OF MEDICAL ASSISTANT, CLINICAL

Taking part of the medical history.

Taking patients' temperature, height, weight, and pulse.

Sterilizing instruments.

Preparing trays for injections.

Assisting with examinations, treatments, and office surgery.

Preparing patients for physical therapy and supervising treatment.

Taking routine laboratory tests.

Caring for surgical instruments and equipment.

Replenishing doctor's bag.

Dispensing medicines to patients on doctor's orders.

Taking basal metabolism tests.

Taking electrocardiograms.

Taking X rays.

Changing dressings and applying bandages.

DESCRIPTION OF A MEDICAL ASSISTANT, CLINICAL

The career of medical assistant, clinical, requires additional specialized training. Many administrative assistants working with a doctor become interested in the clinical aspect of office practice. The employer may be willing to train the assistant; or the assistant may take courses in these procedures. Requirements vary. A high school diploma is an almost universal requirement, and college training is frequently required.

Courses for this career are given by many colleges. Vocational schools may offer a course in clinical assisting, perhaps in the evening. In some instances the local county medical society may offer training to employed medical assistants. Information can be obtained from your state education department or from the local chapter of your state medical society. Training as an X-ray or laboratory technician also is available and would lead to a wider field of employment.

Project 1
Choosing a Medical Career

You have decided to become a medical office worker. Explain why you decided to specialize in the medical area. State your goals according to time periods: six weeks from now; one year from now; five years from now. Use plain paper. Be prepared to discuss your opinions. Beginning with this project you should set up a folder marked "Personal" in which you will keep all nonmedical-related tasks.

CAREER OPPORTUNITIES

Many tasks that medical office assistants are expected to perform are the same as those required of business office assistants. A thorough training in office routine, along with the ability to get along with people, will equip a person to be an excellent assistant in almost any field. Few assistants leave medicine voluntarily, for its fascination is great; but sometimes circumstances make a change necessary. A well-trained assistant will have no difficulty in changing jobs.

Kinds of Positions Available

There is a wide variety of positions available in the field of health care for an assistant specially trained in medical stenography, medical terminology, and medical procedures. A description of 18 different working environments from which one may choose follows.

☐ **The Doctor's Office.** Here, the assistant is the doctor's "right hand." One may work for a doctor who is in solo practice, handling all medical-secretarial work; or for an employer who has an associate (or who shares the office with another doctor) and may have a private consultation room but uses the same waiting and examination rooms. The assistant may thus do work for more than one doctor; if there are many patients, work may be shared with another assistant. There may be an office nurse or a clinical assistant who looks after patients. In such an arrangement responsibility for work may at times overlap.

☐ **Group Practice.** A rapidly developing form of practicing medicine is for specialists in different fields to take a suite of offices or a building together so that a patient can have the services of both a general practitioner and a specialist without delay, under the supervision of the referring doctor. Such a group needs an executive secretary to keep centralized records, to route patients to the different doctors, and to be responsible for billing and all other financial matters for the group.

☐ **The Dentist's Office.** Duties of a dental secretary are similar to those of a medical office assistant, and many persons trained in the latter capacity accept positions in dentists' offices. The chief difference is that the dental secretary has a knowledge of dental terminology.

☐ **Hospitals.** One of the widest fields for medical secretaries is in the hospital. Even a small hospital needs several secretaries for the chief of the hospital and the heads of different departments, for the administrative and business offices, and for the clinics and the record library. Large hospitals have many medical secretarial positions. Probably more medical office workers are employed in hospitals than in doctors' offices.

☐ **Clinics.** Many clinics are not connected with hospitals, but function independently. They may be privately owned by welfare agencies, or operated by state or municipal governments. Assistants are needed in these clinics to perform duties similar to those required in a private physician's office.

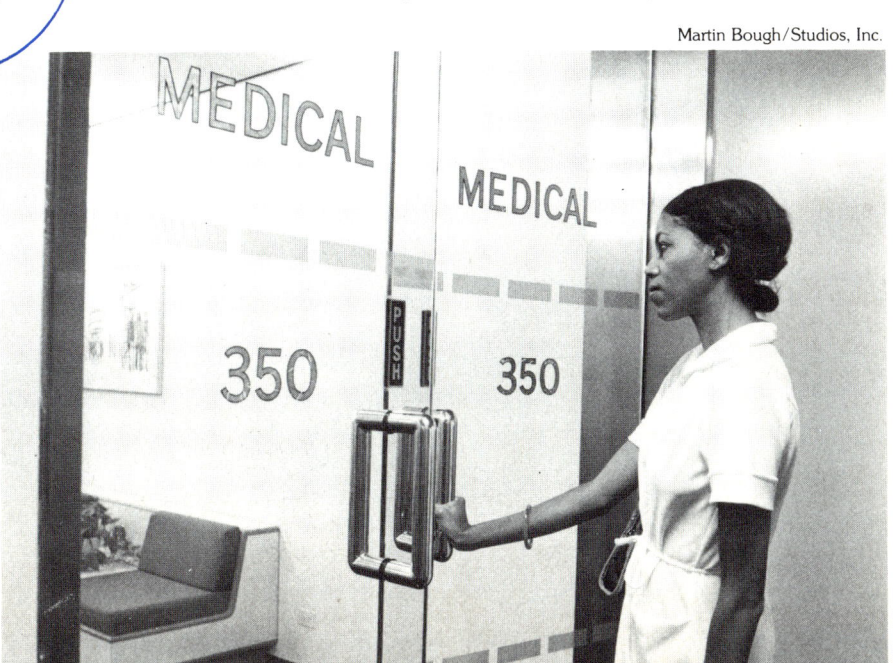

Martin Bough/Studios, Inc.

Martin Bough/Studios, Inc.

☐ **Public Health Departments.** Each state and almost every municipality has its own health department. Sanitation, supervision of public eating places and of the water supply, quarantining of contagious diseases, and vaccination are just a few activities of these departments. Trained persons are needed to take care of the office work. Some of these positions carry civil service status.

☐ **Foundations.** The United States boasts the largest number of foundations devoted to medical research of any country in the world. Some of them are concerned with a particular disease (the National Heart Foundation); some are concerned with standards of professional health care (Professional Standards Review Organization); some undertake specific research projects. Many office workers with medical training are employed in this fascinating field.

☐ **Institutions.** Convalescent homes; nursing homes; sanatoriums; homes for the aged, crippled, destitute, and terminally ill; children's homes; and many other welfare organizations and institutions all need office help. They prefer people who have had training in medical office procedures.

☐ **The Armed Services.** The Army, the Navy, and the Air Force have medical departments wherever there are military installations. In addition to routine medical services rendered to members of the Armed Forces, there are new specialties where work is often in the experimental stage. Among these are aviation medicine, space medicine, and nuclear medicine. Employees of the armed services may retain civilian status or may be offered the opportunity of enlisting. All Veterans Administration installations need medical office workers.

☐ **Nonprofit Health Insurance Companies.** There exist a great number of organizations whose members pay a monthly or annual fee, in return for which their hospital and doctors' bills are paid partially or in full. Among the best known of these nonprofit plans are Blue Cross and Blue Shield, Health Insurance Plan of New York (HIP), and Group Health Insurance of Washington, D.C.; but there are many other private programs operated by clubs, unions, and employees' associations. The operation of any of these plans requires a vast amount of clerical work: filling out and checking reports received from doctors, mailing out payments of claims, renewing contracts, and keeping records. Nearly every city or town will have openings in a prepaid medical care plan.

☐ **Commercial Health Insurance Companies.** There are many commercial health insurance companies. A person with medical secretarial training and skills could be employed to type insurance forms and to examine and process claims.

☐ **Medicare.** Administration of the Medicare program provides jobs for medical office workers at every level—in federal, state, and city agencies as well as in hospitals, clinics, nursing homes, and private practice.

☐ **The Business World.** There are many openings for medical assistants in offices of manufacturers and distributors of drugs, pharmaceutical products, surgical instruments, and hospital supplies. Most of these firms not only maintain production and sales departments, but engage in medical research as well. They will give preference to an assistant who is trained in medical terminology and can transcribe medical dictation.

☐ **Publishers.** To many people the publishing field is of particular interest. There are publishers devoted to medical books exclusively, and others that have a medical department as part of their operation. Some publish medical journals. The need for medical secretaries here is obvious. In this area there are opportunities for assisting in the varied aspects of producing a medical publication and perhaps moving on to editorial work.

☐ **Free-Lance Work.** For those with a flair for writing and an interest in editorial work, there are excellent opportunities for medical-editorial assistants. Many doctor-writers employ full-time secretaries; others require temporary help with a specific book or article. Advanced training is required. It is necessary to know how to use a library and how to prepare a manuscript, compile a bibliography, construct an index, and proofread. As a free-lance worker the secretary is not tied down to fixed hours. One can work at home and take time off between assignments—a freedom not often found in office positions.

☐ **Teaching.** Who would be a better teacher of medical office workers than one who has been employed in a medical office? Several years of experience are necessary for this career. In addition, the right educational background and an ability to teach are prerequisites.

☐ **Laboratories.** Working for a doctor who heads a medical laboratory is also a challenging career. There are daily reports on diagnostic tests to be prepared, appointments to be made for patients, and specimens to be received, stored, or routed to the right department.

Martin Bough/Studios, Inc.

8 PART 1: THE MEDICAL ASSISTANT'S CAREER

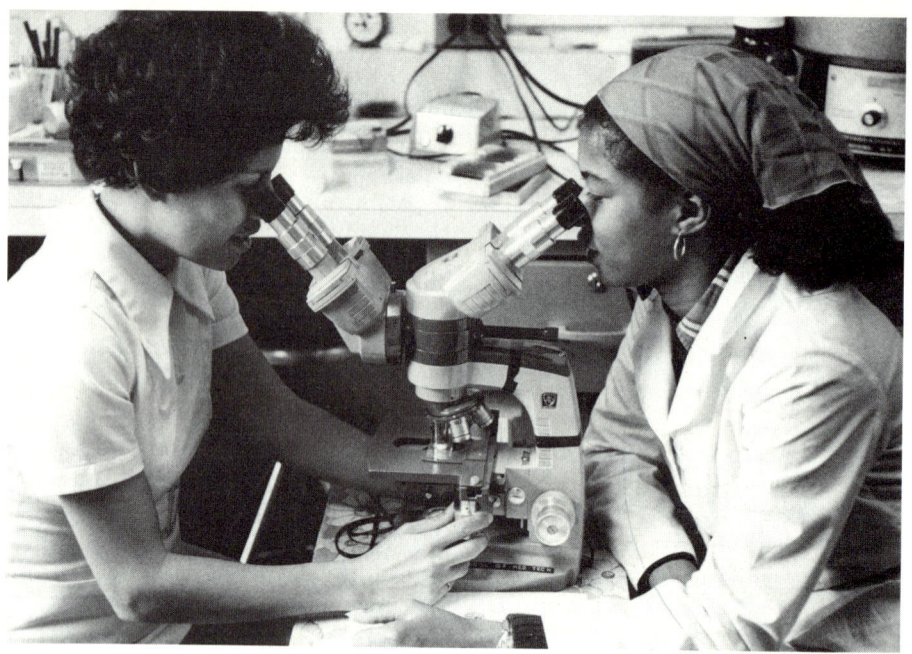

Michael Weisbrot and Family

☐ **Research.** Much medical research is being carried on today in a vast range of fields. Universities, hospitals, food industries, pharmaceutical concerns, and foundations have special departments devoted entirely to research, prevention, and cure of medical conditions. A requisite for a position in this field is a real interest in science and a background in biology and chemistry. Good English skills are also important, as many researchers are from foreign countries and may not be proficient in the language.

Project 2
Selecting a Medical Area

Consider the 18 working environments described in this chapter, and then select three in which you would prefer to work. Give at least three reasons for each choice. Use plain paper.

PROFESSIONAL STATUS

The successful assistant enjoys an enviable professional status. He or she is eligible to join several associations and can apply for certification in the particular field.

Associations

Any secretary with two years' practical experience may join the National Secretaries Association (International)—NSA. This organization has many chapters throughout the United States and overseas. Its aim is to "elevate the standards of the secretarial profession through a continuing program of educational and professional development," and to provide members with the benefits that come from contact and companionship among workers with mutual interests. Members receive copies of the official publication, *The Secretary*, and have the opportunity to attend meetings of local chapters, district conferences, and an annual convention. They may participate in residential seminars and share in a group insurance plan for retirement and income protection, as well as hospitalization and medical plans.

Examinations are held periodically for applicants who want to become Certified Professional Secretaries. The NSA actively promotes the designation *CPS* (Certified Professional Secretary) for those who have passed this examination, thereby setting a definite educational goal for secretaries. These examinations are open to nonmembers also.

CHAPTER 1: CAREER OPPORTUNITIES 9

Students taking secretarial courses may join the affiliated Future Secretaries Association (FSA). Members participate in various programs developed by the FSA and have the opportunity of associating with experienced secretaries.

Further information may be obtained from the National Secretaries Association (International), 616 East 63d Street, Kansas City, MO 64110.

Medical Affiliation The American Association of Medical Assistants (AAMA) is open to those who have worked under the direct supervision of a physician. The AAMA is patterned along the lines of medical societies; that is, local county societies are members of the state society. The state society in turn is a member of the national association. The state society has full autonomy, and the bylaws vary from state to state. Most chapters hold monthly meetings, offer seminars, publish a bulletin, and arrange social gatherings.

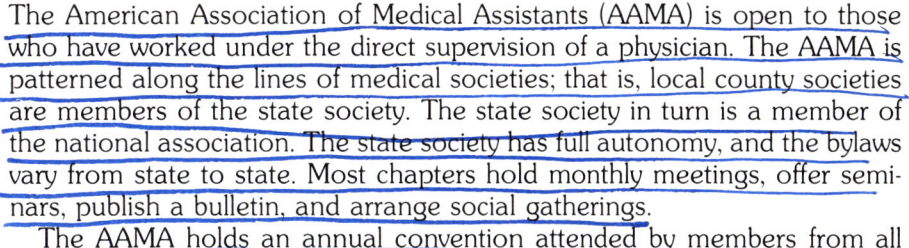

The AAMA holds an annual convention attended by members from all over the country. The program consists of scientific lectures, practical seminars, commercial exhibits, and various social affairs. The association also offers its members a group health insurance plan.

Through the AAMA it is possible to become a Certified Medical Assistant, Clinical, or a Certified Medical Assistant, Administrative, or both. Examinations are given each year during the annual convention. The designation Certified Medical Assistant is an esteemed one.

Courtesy American Association of Medical Assistants

Financial Benefits Financially, too, the assistant enjoys many advantages. The salary is in the top bracket for office workers. The assistant can also look forward to a pension. Under the Keogh Act, which became law on January 1, 1963, a doctor may put a certain amount into a personal retirement fund that is tax-exempt if all full-time employees who have been with the practice for three years are also covered. Some doctors choose to extend this benefit to all full-time employees, whether or not they have been with the practice for at least three years. The contribution to the employee's pension fund must be in addition to salary.

PERSONAL DEVELOPMENT PROJECTS

TOPICS FOR DISCUSSION 1. Bring in help-wanted ads from local newspapers. Discuss the job possibilities.

2. Compare the advantages and disadvantages of working in the medical field as opposed to working in the business world.

ROLE PLAYING 1. Your friend Janice works as a records clerk in the medical record room of a large hospital, and she wants you to accept a job there. You prefer a job with patient contact. Explain this to her.

2. Wednesday is your afternoon off because you will work Saturday morning. Another office worker asks to exchange hours with you. This is the third week you have been asked to exchange, and you already have plans for Wednesday.

2

Career Qualifications

Personality has been described as the evidence of one's character. In the following pages certain attributes of personality and character needed by a medical assistant are described.

PERSONAL ATTRIBUTES The doctor, like any business executive, requires certain personal attributes in an employee. Any employee with these attributes is an asset to the employer and helps the business function more smoothly and more profitably. It is particularly important for the medical assistant to have these qualities, as the doctor's work is with people, not products, and often involves life-or-death situations.

Accuracy and Dependability Some time ago a circular letter was addressed to executives in various industrial concerns asking them to list what they considered the prerequisites for a good employee. The two requirements that led the list were accuracy and dependability. If these qualities seem important in the business world, where negligence may mean at most a loss of money, it is easy to see how much more important they are in a medical office, where carelessness, negligence, or forgetfulness may cause physical harm to a patient, or even endanger life. Therefore, the phrase *accuracy and dependability* may well be adopted by the assistant as a motto.

The medical assistant may be required to give injections, administer treatments, or dispense medicines. The doctor issues exact instructions but cannot always be present to see that they are carried out. Almost daily the press reports cases where patients have been badly injured or have died as the result of an assistant's error or negligence. In one such case, a nurse gave the wrong drops to a baby, and the baby died. She had not read the label before dispensing the drops but had just taken the bottle that was standing in the accustomed place as the right one. Unfailing vigilance and constant attention to detail are imperative. If a patient is injured during a treatment as the result of an assistant's carelessness or ignorance, the physician is legally responsible. A doctor would be better off with no assistant at all than with one who is not reliable.

Punctuality One aspect of dependability is punctuality. If the office opens at 9 a.m., the medical assistant should be there and ready to start work at 9 a.m. He or she should allow a few minutes before the start of office hours to change into a uniform, if one is worn; to pull patients' charts from the file; and to attend to other routine duties before patients start arriving. Traffic delays, missed trains, and last-minute interruptions at home are no excuse for being late.

A patient who has an appointment at the hour the office opens may be in a hurry to get to work or may have had an uncomfortable night and therefore will be anxious to see the doctor right away. Such patients are quite likely to arrive even before the appointed time, and the receptionist should be there to receive them. In a busy doctor's office, the telephone often begins ringing at 9 a.m. sharp, as patients may have been waiting for hours to call the doctor for some advice or to make appointments for that day.

10

Project 3
Planning a Personal Schedule

On a plain sheet of paper, plan a personal schedule beginning with the alarm ringing and ending with your arrival at the office. Assume it takes you 20 minutes to travel from your home to the office door. Your office opens at 9 a.m.

Thoroughness   The virtue of thoroughness cannot be too highly extolled. Because many people are not thorough, it is necessary to check almost everything that is of any importance. To give an illustration of this, when an assistant telephoned a large hospital to inquire at what hours one of the clinics was open, the answer was, "The clinic is open all day." This did not inform the assistant at just what hours the clinic opened and closed. After further inquiry, the assistant was told that the clinic hours were from 8:30 to 11 a.m. and from 1 to 3:30 p.m., which certainly is not "all day." Had the assistant accepted the previous information and passed it on to the patient, the patient might have arrived at the clinic at 11:15 a.m. and then would have had to wait for nearly two hours before it opened again. It is far more practical to ask a question two or three times, or to check something at once, than to find out later that wrong information had been given to someone. Then, it will take longer to rectify the mistake, and people may have been inconvenienced.

Attending to a great many details is irksome and may seem to be a waste of time. It is surprising how often one will find out many weeks or months later that time was saved by making an extra notation or preserving some printed statement. A doctor is too busy to remember routine matters or office details. The assistant blessed with a good memory will be valuable. Memory can be trained, and a well-developed memory greatly facilitates work. It is dangerous to rely on memory alone when important matters are involved, however. Making a memorandum of everything is a good habit to cultivate, as is checking all facts and information before passing them on to others or acting on them.

Kindness and Sympathy Certainly the qualities of kindness and sympathy are prerequisites for a good assistant. Every assistant has probably been a patient at one time or another. There is no better guide to conduct in dealing with patients than to remember your own personal experience and to ask how you would like to be treated when visiting a doctor's office.

Tact Much of the assistant's work will require infinite tact. Tact is the ability, either instinctive or acquired, to speak and to act perceptively and effectively in difficult situations or with difficult people, in a manner that will not give offense but will create goodwill while still achieving the purpose at hand. The ability to be tactful can be developed if an individual is sensitive to reactions of others. He or she should keep in mind that one of the principal ways of being tactful is to avoid offending others and to put people at ease.

Accepting Criticism The assistant, like any other worker, must be able to take criticism. No matter how capable and efficient one is, the doctor may prefer things done in a way different from one's training. The doctor alone decides what is to be done and how it is to be done. By being shown and corrected, the assistant can learn the employer's ways. Tears or sulks are out of place in any office, especially in a doctor's office full of patients. No one is perfect; to possess the humility to recognize one's limitations and to accept this fact is a sign of maturity.

Other Qualifications The above are qualifications required by employers. But what about patients? What do they consider the most desirable qualities in an assistant? The periodical *Medical Economics* was interested enough in this subject to take an opinion poll to try to find the answer. The result was that 61 percent of the persons asked named a friendly, pleasant personality as the most desirable quality in a doctor's assistant. Patience, understanding, helpfulness, and efficiency came next. Qualities disliked in a doctor's assistant were inefficiency, appearing bored, and being "too nosy."

A cheerful personality will prove to be one of the assistant's greatest assets. Not even a well person wants to see a gloomy face, and it is certainly not any more acceptable to those who are ill. Patients want to know that at the doctor's office they will be greeted with a smile. No matter what worries, cares, or irritations there may be in one's personal life, the assistant must know how to suppress them and to show a serene and pleasant face. A grouchy, gruff office worker will quickly drive patients away, whereas a pleasant, tactful one can greatly help smooth out many of the difficulties that occur in every human relationship, in a doctor's office as well as elsewhere.

CHAPTER 2: CAREER QUALIFICATIONS 13

PERSONAL APPEARANCE Along with the qualities just discussed, the personal appearance of the assistant is very important. He or she must present a pleasing image to patients.

Grooming A well-groomed person is a pleasure to behold, no matter what one's age or one's share of good looks. Grooming implies much more than just cleanliness. The daily bath, frequent shampoo, and well-kept hands are indispensable, but so is a neat, tidy appearance. There should be no ripped seams, loose or missing buttons, or wrinkled clothes. Hair that flows about the wearer's head like a mane or that straggles in unmanageable straight ends is neither attractive nor sanitary and certainly is not appropriate for an assistant. Good grooming also includes freshly polished shoes or, if worn with a uniform, white shoes that are kept white. Shoes should be plain. Above all, they should be comfortable.

Cosmetics For women, discreet use of cosmetics is important. The purpose of cosmetics is to help a person look better and healthier, not to make one conspicuous. As for gaudy, vividly painted nails—let the reader consider how it might feel to be touched by a person whose fingernails seem to have been dipped in blood. Strong-smelling colognes are not recommended for assistants who come in contact with sick people.

Uniform In many offices the assistant wears a uniform. The advantage of wearing a washable uniform while in contact with patients, preparing medicines, and so forth, is obvious. A uniform also has a definite psychological effect. Many patients instinctively have more confidence in a uniformed assistant's ability to give a treatment or a test. Patients seem less embarrassed to disrobe or to give personal information and, in general, cooperate much more willingly when confronted with a uniformed attendant. Needless to say, a white uniform must be snow-white.

Courtesy Angelica Uniform

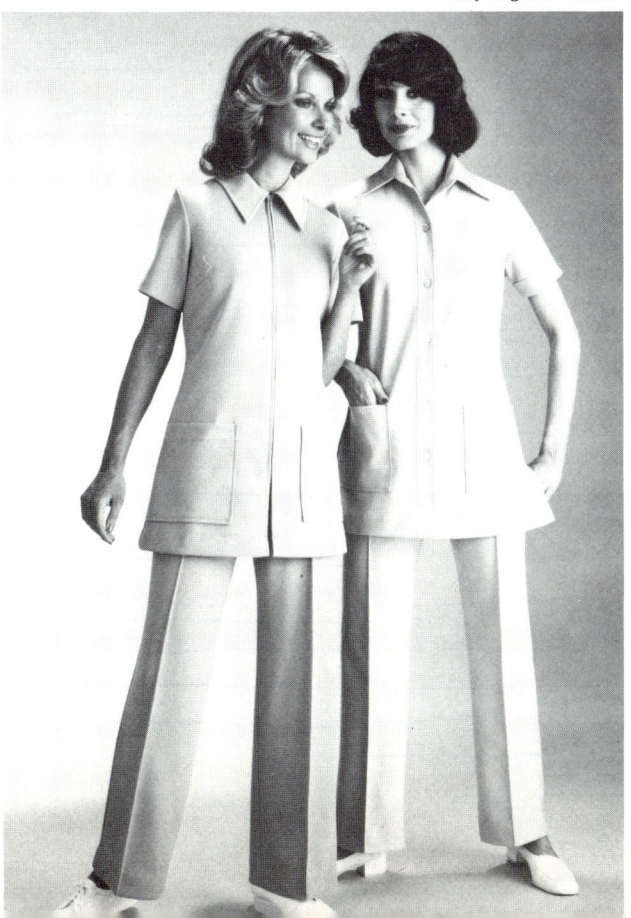

Martin Bough/Studios, Inc.

Martin Bough/Studios, Inc.

Street Clothes Wearing a uniform is not required everywhere. In fact, some doctors—pediatricians and psychiatrists, for example—like to have as little of the medical atmosphere in their offices as possible. In such circumstances, an assistant might avoid clothes that are too severe or unrelieved dark colors, which have a depressing effect. Although male assistants may wear dark suits, the effect can be relieved by colored or patterned shirts. In any event, street clothes should be simple and appropriate. Elaborate ornamentation, flashy patterns, and exotic jewelry do not belong in a doctor's office. Being well-dressed means being *appropriately* dressed. Being well-dressed helps one feel self-confident and poised.

PROFESSIONAL CONDUCT A doctor assumes the assistant knows how to act professionally. One must not abuse this trust. One must know when to be sociable, when to be professional, and when to be businesslike. Good manners—which means doing the right thing at the right time and not the wrong thing at any time—will be an invaluable quality for the assistant to possess.

Serenity A person who undertakes a career in a doctor's office must realize from the beginning that the working hours may be as irregular as those of the doctor. Patients become upset when they cannot choose a convenient appointment time. Delays are frustrating for the patient, the doctor, and the assistant. Even where office hours are regular, something is quite likely to cause a delay, and this can happen when the assistant has an important engagement. However, one must not show any disappointment but must be patient, gracious, and pleasant. Patients are very sensitive to the assistant's mood. If patients feel that the assistant resents their coming late or is in a hurry to get away, the patients may blame the doctor and may transfer to another doctor rather than make a return appointment.

CHAPTER 2: CAREER QUALIFICATIONS 15

Familiarity A word may be in order here for the assistant who works for a spouse, a relative, or a friend of the family. Regardless of the degree of familiarity, the assistant should address the doctor by last name and title, and it is advisable that the doctor call the assistant by last name. Nothing in their conversation before patients should indicate that any other but a professional relationship exists. Theoretically, it should not make any difference to patients whether the doctor and the assistant are married or related, but somehow it does; it gives rise to gossip, jealousies, imagined slights, and an air of familiarity, none of which belong in a doctor's office. Patients may believe that confidentiality is betrayed, and the doctor-patient relationship may suffer.

When talking to a patient, the assistant should refer to the doctor by name and title: "Dr. Taylor will see you now," or "Dr. Taylor is away at present." Referring to the employer as "Doctor" only—for example, "Doctor will see you now"—does not show proper respect.

Confidentiality The doctor's assistant must realize that medical information is of a highly confidential nature. Professional secrecy is a standard that the law demands and upholds. A doctor who divulges information about a patient without due authorization from the patient, except to another doctor, can be prosecuted under the law, and the doctor's license may be revoked. This naturally applies also to any person employed in a doctor's office. Everyone who works for a doctor assumes a personal obligation to adhere to the code of medical ethics. Employees will learn a great deal about the personal affairs of patients and doctors alike, but these should not become topics for conversation and gossip. Medical histories of patients yield much confidential information, not only regarding patients themselves, but also about other members of their families and perhaps their friends as well. Employees may not disclose any details of the patient's illness, personal history, or matters relating to the family.

A patient often questions the assistant about an illness, hoping to learn more than the doctor has told. It is not the assistant's place to tell the patient what the doctor's opinion is, either in regard to the diagnosis or the outlook of the case, even when knowing it. The doctor has reasons for what is or is not told to the patient. The doctor is the judge of what the patient should know about the condition. If the patient wishes to be more fully informed, he or she must ask the doctor, not the assistant.

Patients are often curious about other patients, especially those who seem to be suffering from similar afflictions. They may want to know how long another patient has been coming to the office, what the doctor prescribed, how much improvement there has been, and so forth. Friends or relatives of a patient may also—for the patient's own good, as they will say—ask the doctor's opinion, sometimes not quite daring to ask the doctor or sometimes wishing to check what they have heard. Patients and their friends alike may try to obtain information about the doctor personally or about routine matters in the office. In such cases the assistant must refuse information without giving offense. A tactful, courteous, but firm refusal will prevent further questioning.

Papers should be carefully guarded from prying eyes. No patients' histories, laboratory reports, letters, or other data should be left lying on the desk while the assistant is out of the room. A person may innocently walk up to the desk to borrow a pencil, for instance, and casually glance at some paper that may contain information of a most private and personal kind. Telephone calls that may reveal confidential information should not be made when other patients are in the same room. Patients who consult a doctor for a nervous disorder, venereal disease, or cancer may be more sensitive about having their visits known than are other patients. More discretion must, therefore, be exercised in the office of a psychiatrist, for example, than would be necessary in the office of an eye specialist.

Special care must be taken never to mention a patient's name outside the office. There may be a good reason why a patient wishes to keep from family or business associates the fact that medical care is required. The doctor's specialty may be an indication of the disease for which the patient is being treated, and the patient may not wish this to be known.

Nothing that happens in the office should be repeated at home or to one's friends, even without mentioning names. The arm of coincidence is long indeed, and more than once an indiscretion of this kind has had serious consequences because the persons concerned were identified from peculiar circumstances connected with the case. This does not mean, of course, that one should not speak of one's employer at all. If an assistant is loyal to the employer and enthusiastic about the work, he or she will know how to praise without exaggeration, how to tell of successes and of good work without taking the risk of giving away confidential information.

Maturity Emotional maturity is not dependent upon one's age. Many individual characteristics are a part of what is known as maturity. The mature person is able to work under authority and pressure, in conditions that are frustrating or unpleasant, and possesses the ability to stick with a job, giving more than is asked. To be able to make one's own decisions and follow through on them, to be independent, to have a determination to live and succeed—that's maturity.

Project 4
Evaluating Your Qualifications

On Working Paper 1 (WP 1, on page 1 of the Working Papers section at the back of this book) there is a checklist of qualities needed by a good medical office worker. Evaluate yourself on the characteristics listed, using Column 1 under the appropriate heading for each item. At the end of the semester, your instructor will rate you using Column 2. You will also have an opportunity to reevaluate yourself in Column 3 and compare the ratings.

Project 5
Modifying Your Behavior Pattern

Select one quality that you might improve from the checklist made in Project 4. Write a plan of action for improvement. List all possible choices of action and the expected results of each action; then choose one plan for improvement and begin working on it. Use plain paper and place your paper in your "Personal" folder.

PROFESSIONAL SECRETARIAL SKILLS One of the most important requirements for working in a medical office is a knowledge of medical terminology and abbreviations. Secretarial office aptitudes that prove to be real assets to the assistant are a good educational background in communication skills and proficiency in secretarial procedures such as typewriting, transcribing, filing, and keeping financial records. These skills will be discussed in detail throughout this book.

PERSONAL DEVELOPMENT PROJECTS

TOPICS FOR DISCUSSION 1. Many people have mannerisms or unconscious habits that could be annoying to patients in a doctor's office or on the telephone. Describe some of these mannerisms and explain why they would be annoying.

2. Patients waiting in a doctor's office often have time to observe the medical assistant. Describe some personal characteristics (both good and bad) that patients might notice.

3. Different kinds of jobs require people with different types of personalities. Discuss the type of personality needed by a medical office assistant in various kinds of medical offices as well as in business offices.

ROLE PLAYING 1. Arlene, one of your co-workers, has been coming to work lately in a wrinkled uniform, with uncombed hair. She appears to be very tired and distracted. You are concerned about her.

2. Dr. Taylor asks you to assist him with a sterile procedure. You are not familiar with the procedure, did not learn about it in school, and do not know what to do.

3
Medicolegal Communications

MEDICAL ETHICS Every organized field of human endeavor is governed by a code developed by its practitioners. Medicine is perhaps the oldest profession to have developed such a set of rules. These rules are not law, but are principles of right and wrong and are referred to as *medical ethics*. Ethics is defined as a "standard of conduct"; etiquette is "manners and customs." These two areas complement each other, and at times they overlap.

Etiquette Webster gives one definition of etiquette as "manners required in a certain profession"; medical etiquette includes good telephone techniques, greeting the caller, putting a smile in your voice, expressing consideration, and being courteous. Professional courtesy is shown when another doctor visits the clinic; rather than have the visiting doctor wait in the reception area, he or she is asked to wait in the doctor's private office. Usually, one doctor does not charge a fee when providing medical care to another doctor and the doctor's family. Professional discounts may be offered to pharmacists, members of the clergy, or nurses. Good professional etiquette results in good interpersonal communications.

The Hippocratic Oath Hippocrates was a Greek physician who lived in the fifth century B.C. He is called "the father of medicine," and the principles he devised to govern the conduct of physicians toward their patients and the public are incorporated in the *Hippocratic oath* that has been taken by physicians for centuries.

THE OATH OF HIPPOCRATES

I swear by Apollo, the physician, and Aesculapius, and Health, and Allheal, and all the gods and goddesses, that, according to my ability and judgment, I will keep this oath and stipulation, to reckon him who taught me this art equally dear to me as my parents, to share my substance with him and relieve his necessities if required; to regard his offspring as on the same footing with my own brothers, and to teach them this art if they should wish to learn it, without fee or stipulation, and that by precept, lecture and every other mode of instruction, I will impart a knowledge of the art to my own sons and to those of my teachers, and to disciples bound by a stipulation and oath, according to the law of medicine, but to none others.

I will follow that method of treatment which, according to my ability and judgment, I consider for the benefit of my patients, and abstain from whatever is deleterious and mischievous. I will give no deadly medicine to anyone if asked, nor suggest any such counsel; furthermore, I will not give to a woman an instrument to produce abortion.

With purity and with holiness I will pass my life and practice my art.

I will not cut a person who is suffering with a stone, but will leave this to be done by practitioners of this work. Into whatever houses I enter I will go into them for the benefit of the sick and will abstain from every voluntary act of mischief and corruption; and, further, from the seduction of females or males, bond or free.

Whatever, in connection with my professional practice, or not in connection with it, I may see or hear in the lives of men which ought not to be spoken abroad, I will not divulge, as reckoning that all such should be kept secret.

While I continue to keep this oath unviolated, may it be granted to me to enjoy life and the practice of the art, respected by all men at all times, but should I trespass and violate this oath, may the reverse be my lot.

Principles of Medical Ethics

Over the years many rules were added and then discarded concerning medical ethics, and confusion reigned. To guide physicians in this country, the American Medical Association (AMA) formulated its own principles of medical ethics. These principles are now accepted by the medical profession and are expected to endure for a long time to come. The revised principles shown below were adopted on July 22, 1980.

AMERICAN MEDICAL ASSOCIATION PRINCIPLES OF MEDICAL ETHICS

Preamble: The medical profession has long subscribed to a body of ethical statements developed primarily for the benefit of the patient. As a member of this profession, a physician must recognize responsibility not only to patients, but also to society, to other health professionals, and to self. The following Principles adopted by the American Medical Association are not laws, but standards of conduct which define the essentials of honorable behavior for the physician.

I. A physician shall be dedicated to providing competent medical service with compassion and respect for human dignity.

II. A physician shall deal honestly with patients and colleagues, and strive to expose those physicians deficient in character or competence, or who engage in fraud or deception.

III. A physician shall respect the law and also recognize a responsibility to seek changes in those requirements which are contrary to the best interests of the patient.

IV. A physician shall respect the rights of patients, of colleagues, and of other health professionals, and shall safeguard patient confidences within the constraints of the law.

V. A physician shall continue to study, apply and advance scientific knowledge, make relevant information available to patients, colleagues, and the public, obtain consultation, and use the talents of other health professionals when indicated.

VI. A physician shall, in the provision of appropriate patient care, except in emergencies, be free to choose whom to serve, with whom to associate, and the environment in which to provide medical services.

VII. A physician shall recognize a responsibility to participate in activities contributing to an improved community.*

The Assistant's Responsibility

The underlying principle of the physician's devotion to the profession is evident. While performing within the scope of employment, the assistant is considered an agent of the physician. A promise or commitment made by an assistant can be legally binding upon the doctor. A competent assistant plays an important role by applying these same standards of conduct to personal and professional life. Following are some guidelines:

☐ **Human Dignity.** Offer each patient the same respect and concern regardless of race, age, nationality, or social or economic background.

☐ **Confidentiality.** Keep everything you hear, see, and read about doctors or other health professionals to yourself. However, if you believe a doctor or other health professional is acting unethically or in a nonprofessional manner, discuss it with your employer. A physician is in a better position to decide whether questionable conduct should be referred to the AMA or to another disciplinary organization.

Never criticize *any* doctor to a patient, whatever the patient may say.

Keep everything you hear, see, and read about patients completely confidential. This includes information about a patient's personal life, illness, diagnosis, and treatment. Confidential papers, reports, and case histories should all be placed where they cannot be read by others; even telephone reports must be guarded against eavesdroppers. When information is requested by another doctor or by a hospital or agency, an authorization for release of information must be signed by the patient. An example is shown below.

*Reprinted with the permission of the American Medical Association.

Courtesy Little Press, Inc.

☐ **Disclosure of Information.** There are circumstances requiring legal disclosure of confidential information. Listed here are examples of circumstances usually reported to state departments of health or social services:

> Births and deaths.
>
> Blindness.
>
> Child abuse.
>
> Industrial poisoning.
>
> Vaccinations.
>
> Venereal and communicable diseases.
>
> Injuries resulting from violence, such as gunshot and stab wounds; in fact, any evidence of criminal violence.
>
> Requests for plastic surgery without apparent reason, such as changing fingerprints.
>
> Anything that would indicate that the patient is a fugitive from justice.

☐ **Selection of Patients.** The doctor is responsible for providing competent care but has a right to select patients. If you know a patient is being treated by another doctor or is not following the advice of or using the medication prescribed by your employer, it is your responsibility to report this information. Your employer may decide to withdraw from the patient's case. You would be responsible for preparing an appropriate letter. A sample is shown below:

> Dear Ms. McGrath:
>
> I find that I must withdraw from further professional treatment in your case, because you did not follow my advice and treatment plan. Your condition requires medical attention; I suggest you employ another physician without delay.
>
> After receipt of this letter, I will be available to attend you for no more than five days. With your written consent, I will make available to the physician of your choice your medical information.
>
> Sincerely,
> Warren Taylor, M.D.

☐ **Continued Education.** Take advantage of seminars, in-service workshops, and professional organizations to keep abreast of new developments.

☐ **Civic Responsibility.** Participate in community and civic activities and assist the doctor in carrying out his or her civic duties. Assisting the doctor will involve such duties as making arrangements, taking minutes, making telephone calls, and tactfully declining committee appointments.

☐ **Professional Conduct.** Remember that the assistant's conduct may be subject to the same scrutiny as the doctor's. Behavior should be above reproach when attending meetings of professional organizations and conventions and when participating in community activities.

"Patient Bill of Rights"

The assistant plays an important role in maintaining good rapport with the patient and the clinic. The patient should be informed of the communication process. The American Hospital Association (AHA) distributes a "Patient Bill of Rights" to its member hospitals. These same principles can be applied to a clinic. The patient has the following rights and responsibilities:

1. The right to be recognized and respected. The right to the same consideration and treatment regardless of beliefs, race, sex, or source

of payment. A right to be seen at the appointed time or an explanation if a wait is necessary.
2. A right to privacy in the interview, examinations, and treatment.
3. A right to confidentiality unless the patient gives permission to release information, or the information is ordered into court, or the information is necessary for the welfare of others. Before releasing information, the patient needs to know what information is being released and why.
4. A right to understand what the health problem is; what treatment is recommended and why; what the alternatives are; how much it will cost; and how long it may take.
5. A right to consent to or refuse medical care unless it is an emergency, or a law is involved, or the patient is not of legal age. Each state has laws regulating consent of a minor.
6. The responsibility to be honest with the doctor, to ask questions when uncertain, to follow the treatment plan, to report changes, to keep appointments, and to name other doctors involved.

MEDICAL LAW

Medical law—that is, the law as applied to the practice of medicine—holds many responsibilities for both doctor and employees. Lack of proper professional conduct on the part of the doctor or the office workers may cause the doctor to be sued.

Medical Practice Act

All activities in the field of health are regulated by the Medical Practice Act of each state. Exact provisions of this law vary slightly in different states, but the general principles prescribe who must be licensed to perform various procedures, the requirements for licensure, duties imposed by the license, grounds on which a license may be revoked, statutory reports that must be made to the government, and similar matters.

☐ **Licensing.** The license to practice medicine is granted by a state licensing board, known as the Board of Medical Examiners. License may be by examination, by reciprocity, or by endorsement. An applicant may be granted a license by endorsement after passing the examination of the National Board of Medical Examiners. The applicant for a license to practice medicine must meet other requirements which vary from state to state. Some states require United States citizenship. There are also requirements as to age, moral character, formal education, and residence. After the examination is passed, the license is issued and must be displayed in the doctor's office.

After a license is granted, periodic reregistration is necessary, either annually or biennially. This is accomplished by payment of a registration fee upon notification by the Board of Medical Examiners. The date and number of the original license should be readily accessible, as it is frequently necessary to refer to it. If the doctor is licensed to practice in several states, care should be taken that the annual registration is not overlooked; different states send out their registration forms at different times.

The license may be suspended or the local medical society may institute disciplinary action against a physician for various reasons: conviction of a felony, gross immorality, fee-splitting, or habitual, intemperate use of narcotics or alcohol. A doctor is liable to criminal prosecution for practicing without a license, fraudulently obtaining a license, or violating some of its provisions.

☐ **Narcotics.** A federal permit is necessary for a physician to prescribe or dispense narcotic drugs. A physician must register with the Registration

Branch Drug Enforcement Administration. This narcotic license is renewed annually. The physician is assigned a Narcotic Registration Number. Under federal law, a special narcotic record must be kept to show the narcotics that the doctor has administered or dispensed. This record is always open to inspection by a federal investigator.

Professional Liability

Not all patients are grateful for what the doctor is trying to do. If they are dissatisfied or if an accident occurs, as may happen in spite of vigilance and care, patients are likely to sue for damages. A hysterical person may sue for some imagined wrong, or a person who does not want to pay a large bill may try to avoid payment by bringing suit against the doctor. Doctors can protect themselves against financial loss by subscribing to medical malpractice insurance.

The number of malpractice suits increases every day. More malpractice insurance is paid out to prove there is *not* a justifiable case than to defend the physician in a court case. Physicians are looking forward to the establishment of a panel which will decide whether or not there is a case; if evidence shows possible malpractice, a case will be referred to the court system.

☐ **Physician-Patient Relationship.** The relationship between the doctor and the patient is legally considered a *contract*. While this is rarely put in writing, it is assumed that by consulting the doctor the patient has agreed to be treated by the doctor and has thus entered into a contract with the doctor, consideration for which will be the doctor's fee. The doctor thus assumes the obligation of treating the patient, and the latter of paying the doctor's charges.

The physician-patient relationship is not always a personal one. A pathologist who examines a biological specimen or a radiologist who interprets X rays may never see the patient.

☐ **Malpractice.** Negligence, as applied to the medical profession, is called *malpractice*. Malpractice is defined as the "doing of some act which a reasonable and prudent physician would not do, or the failure to do some act which such a person should or would do."

If a patient is injured during a doctor's treatment or if the patient develops pathological symptoms as a result of the treatment, the patient may sue the doctor for malpractice. It must be emphasized, however, that the patient must prove negligence or want of ordinary care or skill. Neither failure to effect a cure nor an error in judgment are causes for a malpractice suit.

The doctor is liable for any injury to a patient that results from a mistake of an employee. If the employee burns a patient while applying a diathermy (heat-producing) electrode, for instance, the patient can sue the doctor and collect damages.

For example, a patient was being given an ultraviolet light treatment, which was to last three minutes. The attendant went to answer the telephone. It was a personal call, and she chatted for a considerable time, forgetting all about the patient, who developed a severe sunburn. Had the patient sued, the doctor would have been liable. In this instance, the doctor only lost a patient—and the assistant, her job.

Formerly, the principle of *res ipsa loquitur* ("the thing speaks for itself") did not apply, and doctors had to be called in for their technical knowledge to help evaluate the situation. Recently, however, decisions have been handed down against doctors without expert testimony in such obvious cases as sponges left inside the body after an operation, the tip of a broken needle in the flesh, a diathermy burn, or giving out information without an authorization. Failure to make diagnostic tests or X rays or to administer prophylactic measures may be interpreted as "insufficient care" and may cause the doctor to lose a malpractice suit.

Frequently, the patient's own behavior contributes to poor results of the doctor's treatment, and the doctor's case is greatly helped if he or she can prove "contributory negligence." The patient's refusal to have tests, X rays, vaccinations, or failure to follow the doctor's instruction might be considered such negligence. However, the doctor must prove this by careful *written* evidence at the time of the patient's refusal. Any such incidence must be recorded for the doctor's file. The assistant can help the employer by describing the situation in detail, dating it, and preserving the report in the patient's file. Such a notation would protect the doctor against a later claim that reasonable precautions had not been taken.

☐ **Consent.** In entering into a contractual relationship, the patient's consent is implied. However, this applies to routine treatment only. In more complicated procedures, especially in surgery, diagnostic tests, and X-ray treatments, written consent is important to avoid later malpractice suits; or even more seriously, suits for assault and battery. It has, therefore, become standard practice to have the patient sign a special form before any procedure is instituted.

When consent is required of a patient, this must be an informed consent. The procedure should be explained to the patient, and the reason for the procedure, the consequences, the risk (if any), as well as any alternatives should be defined. In the case of a minor, consent of a parent or guardian must be obtained; for a person who is mentally incompetent, that of the guardian.

Printed consent forms for many different purposes are readily available. The booklet entitled *Medicolegal Forms With Legal Analysis* published by the American Medical Association shows many different samples. It is available to the doctor free of charge upon request. These samples can be either copied or paraphrased by the assistant. It must be kept in mind, however, that all such forms must be worded with extreme care, so that they will be admissible in court, if necessary.

If any of these consent forms are used frequently, a supply should be kept on hand. Once completed and signed by the patient, a consent form must be kept in the patient's folder.

Consents and donor cards are necessary when a person wishes to donate organs. In 1968, the National Conference of Commissioners on Uniform State Laws approved the Uniform Anatomical Gift Act. Details about organ and tissue donations may be obtained from the National Kidney Foundation, 315 Park Avenue South, New York, NY 10010.

☐ **Assault and Battery.** Strictly speaking, assault is when a person threatens another person with intention to hurt; battery is the actual hurting. However, under medical law this has been interpreted to include surgical and medical procedures performed without the patient's consent or extended beyond the consent given; for instance, if a surgeon removes an additional or a different organ from the one for which the consent was given. Battery has been claimed even in cases where the procedure was in the interest of the patient. Unless there is a severe emergency, a doctor may well lose a suit as a result of an incorrect consent.

☐ **Privileged Communications.** All information furnished to a doctor by a patient is considered confidential and may not be divulged to any unauthorized person. The assistant who processes the doctor's correspondence and medical histories is considered such an authorized person. However, the assistant must not pass on this information to anyone, not even to the patient, without expressed authorization from the doctor. Sufficiently strong warning on this point cannot be given. Time and again, a person will call the office and ask for confidential information, posing perhaps as a lawyer, a patient's spouse, or even another doctor. Such cases have happened. If the assistant becomes intimidated and answers the questions, this information may later be misused, and the doctor sued for invasion of privacy, which is a tort (a civil act of wrongdoing not involving a contract).

In some states doctors are not permitted to testify in court regarding examinations and treatments of patients without the consent of the patient involved.

☐ **Slander.** Slander, defamation, and libel all mean oral or written false information given with intent to injure the reputation of another person. Some situations where an assistant gave out confidential information have led to lawsuits for slander. A doctor may lose such a suit, even though the information was correct (in that case invasion of privacy may be claimed); or an assistant may give out incorrect information by mistake.

Any unfavorable criticism of another doctor or patient may be construed as defamation of character. In view of these legal considerations, it is easy to see why the assistant must at all times be aware of the obligation to be discreet and to keep doctors' and patients' affairs confidential.

☐ **Breach of Contract.** The doctor is liable for breach of contract if derelict in any professional duties. Another ground for breach of contract is provided if the doctor promises the patient results that do not materialize; that is, if the doctor promises to cure a patient of an affliction and does not succeed.

The assistant is especially alerted to heed this warning. If an assistant should assure a patient that the doctor will make the patient well and the patient does not recover completely, this promise by the assistant is binding on the doctor, as the assistant is considered to be the doctor's agent. Many of the assistant's acts are performed on the doctor's behalf and are, therefore, considered under the law as being done on the doctor's authority and approval.

If the doctor is engaged in a partnership practice, each doctor is liable for the acts of each partner and of each employee of the partnership. However, if a doctor attends patients in the hospital, the doctor is not liable for the acts of hospital personnel, except when they are working under immediate supervision of that same doctor.

☐ **Good Samaritan Acts.** The first Good Samaritan Act was passed in California in 1959, and most states have followed that example. The purpose of such acts is to protect the physician from liability for civil damages that may occur as a result of emergency care. Because there are minor variations in the state statutes, the assistant's role in emergency situations will need to be identified according to the individual state.

☐ **Statute of Limitations.** The statute of limitations applies to the time during which a patient can bring suit for malpractice. This time varies in different states, not only in its length, but also as to the time from which it dates. It may begin when the accident occurred, when the injury was discovered, or when the patient-physician relationship was ended. In practically all states, the statute of limitations begins after childhood; pediatricians and obstetricians, therefore, should keep records beyond this time.

☐ **Safeguards Against Litigation.** Most patients never consider starting legal action against their physician. The competent assistant plays an important role in the prevention of malpractice. Good patient rapport is essential, in addition to the following:

> Keep everything you hear, see, and read about patients completely confidential.
>
> Never criticize a doctor to a patient.
>
> Notify your doctor if you learn that a patient is under treatment by another physician for the same condition.
>
> If a referred patient mentions to you that he or she has no intention of returning to the referring physician, inform your doctor.
>
> Don't discuss a patient's conditions, diagnosis, or treatments with the patient.
>
> Don't ever diagnose or prescribe, even though you feel sure you know what the doctor will prescribe. (There may be additional circumstances. Prescribing constitutes the practice of medicine and is unlawful unless you are so licensed.)
>
> Keep complete and accurate records. The medical record should show if a patient fails to keep an appointment, discontinues treatment before completion, or fails to follow instructions.
>
> Obtain proper authorizations, releases, and consents.
>
> Be safety-conscious. Be alert for potential hazards. See that all equipment is in safe working condition.
>
> Be available to assist the doctor.

THE DOCTOR AND THE COURT

Doctors are frequently called to appear in court as witnesses; they may also be called to testify as defendants. Court appearances in both capacities are discussed below.

The Doctor as a Witness

Doctors are called as witnesses in the course of their practices for a great variety of reasons, depending, of course, on their specialties.

A doctor who gives testimony regarding the case of a patient is permitted to consult private records during the trial to refresh the memory. The doctor must, therefore, take to court all the papers on the case: the medical history, an account of the first examination and diagnosis, treatment and prognosis reports, the number of visits made both at the office and at the patient's home, the dates of all visits (this is very important), and the charges made and collected. Also, all X-ray and laboratory reports must be included. It will be the assistant's task to attend to the compilation of these records so that they are complete, up-to-date, in perfect condition, and in the proper sequence.

If the physician does not wish to testify, it is necessary that a subpoena be served to compel the physician to appear in court. (A subpoena is a court order requiring a person to appear and testify.) In most clinical cases, however, a deposition made by the doctor is accepted.

☐ **Damage Suits.** One of the most frequent occasions for a doctor to appear as a witness is in damage suits after accidents or in negligence cases where there is a claim for compensation. In order to pronounce judgment, the court must learn the type of injury from the physician who has treated the claimant, as well as the condition of the patient when first seen by the doctor, the progress of the patient's condition, the length and type of treatment, how much the patient has suffered, whether there is permanent or

John L. Lopinot/Black Star

partial disability, and to what extent earning capacity has been impaired. This information furnishes the basis for the decision.

☐ **Patient's Competency.** When a will is contested, the question of testamentary capacity may be involved. In such a case, the court is asked to establish whether the person who made the will was in a condition to use the judgment necessary to make a will. Testimony of the doctor under whose care the patient was at that time will be an important factor.

In cases involving mental competency or insanity, a psychiatrist as well as the family physician is called to testify. Suit may be brought by a relative of the patient to have the patient declared incompetent to handle business and financial affairs or to have the patient committed to an institution if unmanageable or dangerous. If a patient does not sign commitment papers voluntarily, the court has to make the decision and would not do so without the testimony of a qualified psychiatrist and the patient's regular physician.

☐ **Expert Testimony.** In addition to the above, physicians may be asked to give testimony as experts in their respective fields. In such instances, they are entitled to compensation. In criminal trials, for instance, if the defendant's lawyers bring in a plea of insanity, psychiatrists specializing in legal cases are called in by both sides for their expert opinion. If there is an accusation or suspicion of homicide, doctors may be required to testify as to the cause and the time of death.

The Doctor as a Defendant

When a malpractice suit is brought against the doctor, the doctor (and the doctor's lawyer) must appear in court to defend the case. The assistants may also be called to testify if they were present when the incident occurred or were in any way involved.

In order to collect damages, a patient must prove "want of proper care, skill, or diligence upon the part of the physician." The rights of the doctor are more easily established if carbon copies of written instructions are available, and if the records are kept in such a way that they are perfectly clear, even to an outsider.

CHAPTER 3: MEDICOLEGAL COMMUNICATIONS 27

Project 6
Understanding Legal Terms

Briefly define the following terms on plain paper: malpractice, slander, assault, privileged communication, litigation, subpoena, negligence, statute of limitations, testimony.

PERSONAL DEVELOPMENT PROJECTS

TOPICS FOR DISCUSSION 1. Locate a newspaper article about a malpractice suit and bring it to class for discussion. If an article cannot be found, discuss the pros and cons of malpractice suits.
2. Why have a "Patient Bill of Rights"?

ROLE PLAYING 1. A lawyer, Mr. Pierce, telephones and inquires whether a Mrs. Berquist is a patient of the doctor you work for.
2. Mrs. Burnett asks the assistant if cigarette smoking is harmful.

BUILDING OFFICE SKILLS

You now have a basic understanding of what opportunities exist in the medical field for well-qualified assistants. You have also seen what kinds of personal traits are necessary for a successful career. In the following chapters you will learn what office skills are necessary, and you will be given the opportunity to develop those skills.

Starting with Part 2, you will begin "working" for Dr. Warren Taylor. All the work you do in the chapter projects must be saved. This work will form the basis for your "office files." In the end-of-part simulations, you will draw on and add to the information in those files.

In order to make this program as realistic as possible, you have been provided with the preprinted forms you will need. Because of the quantity of letterheads and clinical data sheets you will need (approximately 35 letterheads and 22 clinical data sheets), you have been given a master for the letterhead and for the clinical data sheet. These masters may be reproduced in a variety of ways (through stencil, fluid master, or photocopy). If you prefer, you may design your own letterhead, or you may use plain paper. You will also need to provide the following supplies:

1. A pack of 100 index cards, bound by a rubber band.
2. Thirty-three file folders and file folder labels.
3. A ring binder or a file folder for your appointment book.
4. An expandable portfolio which can serve as your "file cabinet." All your working materials should be stored in this portfolio.

Before you begin Part 2, you will need to prepare two file folders. Label one folder "Supplies." This folder will be used to hold your letterheads, unused index cards, and other supplies you will remove from the Working Papers section of this book. Label the other folder "Miscellaneous." This folder will contain work that pertains to Dr. Taylor's practice but doesn't pertain to patients. (Use this folder for patient materials until you set up the files in Project 25.)

The information on page 28 provides the guidelines you need to have concerning Dr. Taylor's practice. Detach this page from the book and attach it to the inside front cover of the binder you will be using for your appointment book.

☐ **Office Hours.** Patient appointments should be made from 10:30 to 12 Monday through Thursday and 2 to 5 on Tuesday and Thursday. Hospital visitation (at University Hospital, 3388 South Sawyer Avenue, Chicago, IL 60623, telephone number 312 555-8200) is scheduled Monday through Friday from 8 to 10. Dr. Taylor teaches at the University Medical School on Monday and Wednesday from 12 to 5. On Fridays from 10:30 to 12, Dr. Taylor is at the office for dictation, messages, writing, and course preparation. He has the afternoon off. Dr. Taylor likes to plan lunch from 12 to 2 daily.

Dr. Taylor's office address is 2235 South Ridgeway Avenue, Chicago, IL 60623. The telephone number is 312 555-6022.

☐ **Appointments.** New patients and physical examinations require one-hour appointments. Otherwise, patients should be scheduled for 30-minute appointments. Patients who see the doctor for injections only will need a 15-minute appointment. Dr. Taylor prefers to make house calls after 5 p.m.

☐ **Telephone Calls.** A log should be kept of all telephone calls received. Memorandums should be made of all calls that must be relayed to Dr. Taylor. When a house call is requested, a house call slip should be given to the doctor instead of a memorandum.

☐ **Daily Routine.** Dr. Taylor prefers you to call the answering service and to process incoming mail before patients arrive. He likes his correspondence mailed the same day it is dictated; however, patient histories must be completed before patients arrive for another appointment.

☐ **Filing.** Correspondence referring to a patient should be filed under the patient's name. Material is filed alphabetically and chronologically. Clinical data sheets should be in the front of the file. All other material pertaining to the patient, such as reports and correspondence, is filed chronologically behind the history.

☐ **Charges.** Charges for operations, deliveries, X rays, injections, and laboratory tests vary according to the service performed. Dr. Taylor will indicate these charges in the dictation. Charges should be entered on the ledger cards or in the charge columns on the clinical data sheets.

☐ **Accounts.** The billing will be brought up to date in the chapter on billing.

2
Secretarial Responsibilities

4
Appointments

General practitioners often have fixed office hours rather than scheduled appointments, and patients are seen in the order in which they arrive. Physicians in larger cities and specialists, however, rarely see patients except by appointment. The arrangement of appointments is one of the principal duties of the assistant, and to do so efficiently and intelligently is one of the most important tasks. Appointments must be entered in an appointment book, and canceled appointments must be indicated and the time used for another patient whenever possible. The doctor's outside appointments must be listed, and, if necessary, the doctor must be reminded of them in advance.

The first thing to do when taking a new job is to find out what the doctor's schedule is and at what hours appointments with patients can be made. The doctor probably is on duty at one or more hospitals on certain days and at certain hours. Office hours, therefore, may vary on different days. Many people find it difficult to make appointments during the daytime, and so some doctors have office hours late in the afternoon or in the evening, perhaps once or twice a week. If there are several doctors in one office, the hours of each of them may be different. This is especially true if they use the office alternately. A chart should be drawn up to show at a glance the hours when the doctors are in the office and where they can be reached at other times. (During office hours not much routine work can be accomplished. This should be done at times when there are no patients in the office, if that is at all possible. As soon as an assistant assumes a position in a doctor's office, a program of work that will best fit the particular circumstances of the office should be made.)

It has been found that patients complain twice as much about waiting in the doctor's office as they do about any other cause, including high fees and unsuccessful treatment. If an appointment has been made for a specific time, it is indeed frustrating to have to wait an hour or perhaps even more. An appointment system must eliminate long waits if it is to function smoothly and efficiently.

APPOINTMENT BOOK All appointments should be entered in an appointment book or on an engagement calendar. A copy of the day's appointments may be given to the doctor to keep the doctor informed of the schedule.

Allotment of Time Appointment books vary in size and content, but the more popular styles contain a page for each day of the year, and each page divides the working day into hour, half-hour, and quarter-hour intervals. In this way the doctor can allot the necessary amount of time to the individual patient. For example, some doctors allow an hour for consultation and examination of new patients and 15 minutes for checkup visits. Such an appointment book is shown at the top of the next page.

Page Arrangements Larger appointment books showing six days on two facing pages are also available, so that an entire week's schedule will be visible at a glance. The right-hand page of such a book is illustrated at the top of the next page.

30

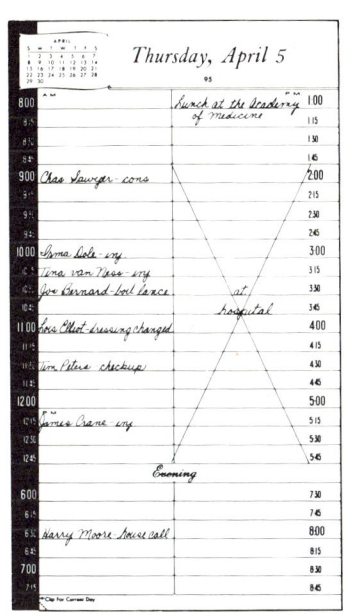

CHAPTER 4: APPOINTMENTS 31

Courtesy Sheaffer Eaton Division of Textron Inc.

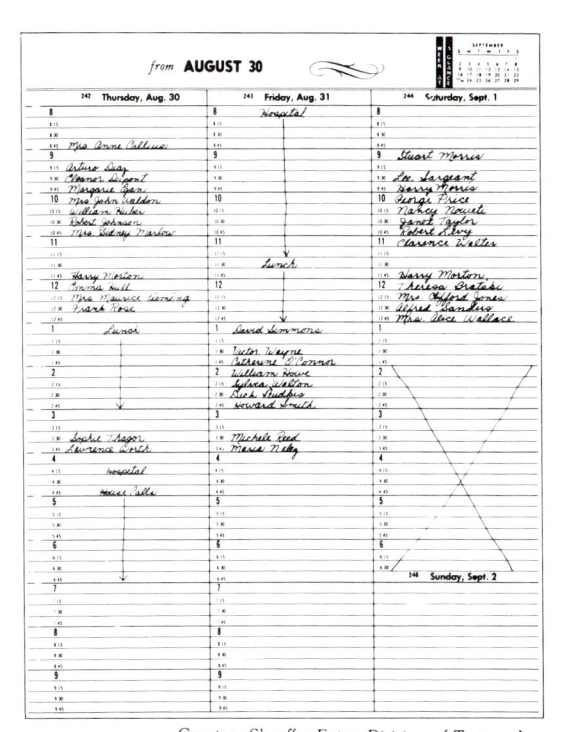

Courtesy Sheaffer Eaton Division of Textron Inc.

Recording of Data   The appointment book must provide space for recording all the data necessary, such as patient identification and description of the professional service to be rendered. This information helps the assistant estimate how much time to allot to each patient. A new patient coming in for consultation and examination will need more time than one who simply needs an injection or a blood test. When a patient is scheduled for an X ray or laboratory test, the doctor's time need not be reserved. It is in this area of making decisions that the assistant can best demonstrate the ability to manage the doctor's office. After knowing the purpose of each patient's visit and how long each procedure will take, one can schedule appointments so that there will be a smooth flow of patients and wise use of the doctor's time and energy. You may also wish to include the patient's telephone number and account number in the appointment book.

   The appointment book should be checked upon the arrival of each patient to make sure that no mistake has been made. Because entries are confidential, the appointment book should not be left where patients can see it.

Permanent Record   The appointment book may also serve as a record from which the number of visits is taken when bills are made out. It is therefore important that all appointments be carefully entered. Appointment books should be kept permanently, because they are acceptable records for tax purposes, and a legal record in case of court action.

GUIDELINES FOR SCHEDULING   Whenever a patient asks for an appointment without specifying the time, the patient should be asked "When would you like to come?" or "Could you come tomorrow at 2 o'clock?" or "Do you prefer a morning or afternoon appointment?"

   Should the patient wish to see the doctor on the day of the telephone call, only a certain hour may be available; the patient could be told: "The only time Dr. Taylor has open today is at 4 o'clock. Can you come at that time?"

On the other hand, the patient may state a time when the doctor is busy. To this the reply would be: "I am sorry, but Dr. Taylor is not available at that time. Could you come at 11 o'clock instead, or would 12 o'clock be more convenient for you?"

There may be no appointment time open for a week. A patient could then be told: "Dr. Taylor's schedule is filled for several days. I cannot give you an appointment until Tuesday of next week, unless it is an emergency. In that case, I would cancel the appointment of another patient." Such a reply shows that another patient would have to be inconvenienced. Most patients will cooperate and accept the first appointment available unless it really is an emergency. The assistant may then assure the patient, "I shall telephone you as soon as we have a cancellation," and, of course, do so if a cancellation occurs.

Remember that the patient must be made to feel that the doctor is available when really needed. The assistant should inquire sympathetically whether it is urgent that the caller see the doctor. One may also ask, "Can you tell me what is the matter?" Sometimes it is possible to tell a patient: "The doctor's schedule is full, but if you come promptly at 3 o'clock, the doctor will be able to see you for a few minutes. The doctor can then decide what the next step will be."

Of course, there will be special cases. For people who come long distances to see the doctor, for patients who must come during their lunch hour, and for those who are in pain the wait must be shortened. All such eventualities must be taken into account in making appointments.

When a new patient telephones, it is usually to make an appointment. The assistant may ask whether this is the purpose of the call and offer to make the appointment. A new patient often has to overcome a certain reluctance to see a doctor. For example, a patient may be calling at the insistence of a friend or of a referring doctor; he or she may be afraid of what the doctor will say about the condition. If the assistant senses this hesitation on the patient's part, expressed sometimes by saying that whatever hour is suggested for the appointment is not convenient, the assistant could encourage the patient to come to the office by asking what time would be best. It is well to explain where the office is located and to make sure the patient knows how to reach it, mentioning the nearest bus stop or subway station.

It is important for the assistant to consider the amount of time required for treatments so that ample time is given for each patient. The doctor can see a patient in one room while another patient is in a treatment room, and while a third perhaps is getting ready for an examination. Just how close appointments can be scheduled depends on the type of practice. In general, it is best not to make appointments so close together that there is a risk of crowding, but they should be consecutive. If there are only a few appointments on one day, the doctor may prefer to have an entire morning or afternoon free for other work rather than have one appointment in the middle of the morning and another in the middle of the afternoon. This, again, depends on the preference of the individual doctor.

No matter how carefully appointments are scheduled, however, sometimes crowding is unavoidable, and appointments fall behind schedule. Some assistants have found that by leaving a 15- or 20-minute free interval in the late morning, and again in the middle of the afternoon, they can straighten out a delayed schedule. If no delays occur, this time can be used to catch up with other work. This also allows time for the emergency patient or the unscheduled patient.

In an office devoted exclusively to the practice of physical therapy, a chart could be worked out which makes it possible to utilize all the equipment simultaneously without conflicting appointments. Two attendants give treat-

CHAPTER 4: APPOINTMENTS 33

ments, and as the hours are carefully assigned, there is no duplication or confusion. The chart can be adapted to other specialties. Where there are several examination and treatment rooms, these can be indicated. If different pieces of equipment are used by the doctor, these may be indicated in the various columns. Such a chart is shown here.

WEDNESDAY, SEPTEMBER 12

HOUR	Dr. Jones	Dr. Leppart	X ray	Whirlpool
8 00				
8 15				
8 30				
8 45				
9 00	Mary Randolph	Alice Smith		Donald Johns
9 15	George Birby			Mrs. Silverman
9 30		Mrs. F. Thomas		
9 45			Margarite Bossi	Mary Randolph
10 00	James Hume	Charles Groves	Jonathan Smith	Robert Barton
10 15				
10 30	Janet Moore	Mrs. R. Allen		James Hume
10 45			Charles Groves	
11 00		Grace Britt		
11 15			Trudy Lindsey	
11 30		Mrs. Deven		
11 45			Grace Britt	Janet Elder
12 00		Carl Rudd		
12 15				
12 30				
12 45				
1 00				

Courtesy Sheaffer Eaton Division of Textron Inc.

Where doctors have office hours instead of appointment times, it has been found that patients tend to arrive late, so the office may not be busy at the beginning of the morning or afternoon but will be crowded toward the end. One way to avoid this is to assign certain patients to certain office hours—for example, to tell about six patients to come between 9 and 10 a.m., the next six patients to come between 10 and 11 a.m., and so forth. Some doctors think that patients will not take up unnecessary time when they know others are waiting their turn but believe they are entitled to a great deal of time when they come by appointment.

In addition to hospital commitments and appointments with patients, the doctor will be attending special clinics, seminars, lectures, and medical meetings; the doctor may have an appointment with another doctor or a dentist or a luncheon engagement. All these should be entered in the appointment book so that patient appointments will not be entered for times when the doctor will not be in the office. Often it is helpful to give the doctor a memorandum ahead of time as a reminder of some especially important engagement.

Project 7
Setting Up the Appointment Book

You will find calendar pages dated Thursday, October 9, to Wednesday, December 10, on WP 3-19. Remove these pages and place them in the ring binder. You will work with these pages throughout most of the course, entering, canceling, and rescheduling appointments, as well as noting certain events that must be brought to Dr. Taylor's attention. Cross out the hours Dr. Taylor is on hospital rounds, teaching at University Medical School, and so forth. Don't forget to clip page 28 to the inside of the ring binder.

Project 8
Scheduling Appointments

On the calendar pages, enter the following appointments:

October 13, 11:00—Ellen Goldberg, recheck.
October 14, 2:00—Sheila Leslie, nausea.
           2:30—Jill Grimes, chest pain.
           3:00—Janis Provost, back problems.
           3:30—Jason Stephens, recheck fracture.
October 15, 10:30—Stanley Berndt, tired.
           11:00—Manuel Perez (new patient), back pain.
October 16, 11:30—Paul Grebowski, injection.

On the appropriate pages, enter the following commitments:

October 15, 4:00—Lecture by Dr. Dean Ashcroft at Memorial Hospital.
Second Thursday of every month at 8 p.m.—Local medical society meeting.
October 18, 10:30 a.m.—Ophthalmology appointment with Dr. Scott McIntosh.
November 4—Marvin Payne's birthday.

Registering Arrivals   It will be the assistant's duty to take the patient's name, address, and other information as soon as the patient enters the clinic. The assistant may do this personally or may provide a sheet of paper on which patients "sign in" when they arrive. Verify the spelling of each name. This daily patient register provides a record of who came first and prevents the cardinal mistake of ushering a latecomer into the doctor's office ahead of an earlier arrival. The list of patients' names and addresses also serves for posting the day's charges and collections and completing the patient's own record. The registration record can be periodically checked against the appointment schedule to make sure a patient has not arrived and forgotten to sign in.

Keeping to the Schedule   Making appointments carefully and accurately is only the first step in achieving an office schedule that runs on time. Frequently, the entire day is thrown out of balance because a patient is late. Patients who are late for appointments may have to be asked to wait until the doctor has seen the next patient or until a treatment room is free. It is not the assistant's place to reproach a patient for tardiness, but many doctors approve of a patient who is habitually late being made conscious of the fact that this is an inconvenience to other patients. If the doctor is late, the patients who are waiting should be told why the doctor has been delayed.

Another reason schedules fall behind is that either the patient or the doctor or both forget the time and go on talking. The assistant, therefore, must watch the clock, and if the consultation runs over the allotted time, the doctor may be notified on the interoffice phone or by buzzer; or the assistant may enter the room and either hand the doctor a slip with a message or say that Mr. Jones is ready for treatment. The doctor can then decide whether or not to conclude the interview with the patient.

Irregular Appointments   In general, patients should be given appointments during the usual office hours. When possible, patients who work should be accommodated during the hours convenient to them. If the doctor's office hours are at a time when the patient cannot come, special arrangements must be made, and these will depend on the convenience of the doctor. The doctor must be consulted if a patient cannot come during the regular hours.

Occasionally a patient will arrive without an appointment. If the doctor is busy, it should be explained that the doctor will see the patient for at least a few minutes. No doctor would let a patient leave the office without ascertaining whether there is need of any immediate attention. The assistant must use good judgment when deciding to take a walk-in patient if others who have made appointments are waiting. An emergency, of course, takes precedence over scheduled appointments; it should be explained to patients why they are being kept waiting.

CANCELING APPOINTMENTS Almost every patient will cancel an appointment at one time or another, and many patients make a habit of doing so. When a patient telephones to cancel an appointment, a new appointment time should be suggested. Patients who habitually cancel their appointments and thereby interfere with the doctor's treatment or undo many of its good effects should be persuaded to keep to the appointed time.

Most appointments are broken for trivial reasons. If it is pointed out to the patient that the treatment may be affected if the doctor's care is not received regularly, the patient will often keep the appointment.

When an appointment has been canceled, an appropriate entry should be made in the appointment book at once, such as a line drawn through the canceled appointment, or an erasure of the appointment if the appointment book is not a legal record. This will ensure that the visit will not be put on the bill. If the patient has canceled the visit, the time will be available for other appointments. The cancellation may also be entered in the patient's chart.

If a patient does not keep an appointment and does not notify the office, a notation to this effect should be made on the patient's chart. The doctor will decide what action to take if another appointment should be requested by the patient.

Project 9
Rescheduling Appointments

Ellen Goldberg telephones to say that she cannot be at the clinic for the 11 a.m. appointment on October 13. She would like to reschedule for 10:30, October 20. Make the appropriate change in the appointment book. Dr. Taylor's policy is to draw a line through canceled appointments.

There are times when the doctor will have to cancel an appointment. In an emergency, it may not be possible to notify the patient in time, and the circumstances must be explained to patients when they arrive at the office. New appointments should be made. If the doctor knows beforehand that there will be a delay, the patient can probably be notified by telephone. It is, therefore, important to know the patient's home and work telephone numbers.

If a patient cannot be reached by telephone, the doctor may send a telegram, or, if time allows, a letter modified to suit the particular circumstances can be sent by the assistant. Here is an example of a cancellation letter:

Dear Mr. Brown:

Dr. Taylor will not be able to keep his appointment with you at 11:30 on Tuesday, September 23. He has been called out of town until September 27.

We have scheduled you for the following Tuesday, September 30, at the same time.

If this is inconvenient, please telephone our office and another appointment time will be arranged.

Sincerely,
Medical Assistant

Project 10
Canceling Appointments

Dr. Taylor asks you to check his calendar for October 18 to see if he has anything scheduled. You inform him of his ophthalmology appointment; he asks you to cancel—to request another appointment at the same time on the following Saturday. He will be attending a seminar in Belleville, Illinois, on October 18. Compose a cancellation letter (date it October 13) to Dr. Taylor's ophthalmologist, Scott McIntosh, M.D., 2785 North Ridgeway Avenue, Chicago, IL 60647. Use blocked style on letterhead. (Duplicate the form on WP 21.)

NEXT APPOINTMENT

Before a patient leaves, the assistant should inquire whether another appointment is needed. If it is necessary, the appointment should be made for the patient. The routine varies in this respect in different offices: some doctors make the next appointment themselves; others tell the patient to arrange it with the assistant.

Since patients often ask to have the next appointment written down for them, regular printed appointment cards are being used by an increasing number of physicians. A supply of such cards on the assistant's desk will save a great deal of time and will help to avoid mistakes in the patient's next appointment. All professional stationery concerns sell cards of this type.

Specialty clinics may use a system of follow-up telephone calls to remind a patient of the appointment for the next day.

Project 11
Preparing an Appointment Card

Dr. Taylor wants to see Marion Wellman on Tuesday, October 14, at 4 p.m. for a recheck and a complete physical. Complete the appointment card using one of the forms on WP 189. Enter the new appointment in the appointment book.

OUT-OF-OFFICE CALLS

Some doctors will make house visits. A definite time each day may be set aside to make these visits. In such a case, the appointment book should be marked so that no appointments are made during those hours. It is important for the assistant to ascertain (1) the patient's name, (2) address (it is advisable to inquire how to reach the house if the neighborhood is unfamiliar), (3) telephone number, (4) condition, and (5) whether the person calling is the patient.

Each day the assistant should list in duplicate the patients whom the doctor expects to visit, in the order in which it will be practical to visit them, depending on the urgency of the cases or on locality. One copy is for the doctor, and the other is for the assistant. If, during the doctor's absence, a patient telephones requesting a house call, the assistant can quickly determine where the doctor is likely to be and how long it will take the doctor to contact the patient (at least by telephone). Very often a telephone call from the doctor quiets the patient or relatives sufficiently for them to wait calmly for the doctor's visit. If the doctor cannot be reached, the assistant can leave a message at the home of a patient the doctor is scheduled to visit, asking the doctor to telephone the office. Medical stationers carry a variety of forms for recording house call visits; a sample is shown at the top of the next page.

CHAPTER 4: APPOINTMENTS 37

```
DATE  May 3, 19—
PATIENT  Mary Murphy
ADDRESS  40 Lake Street
         Centerville, NY
CHARGE TO
ADDRESS

APPETITE_____ SLEEP_____ BOWELS_____
TEMP. 98  PULSE 80  RESP. —  BLOOD PRESSURE 125/80
SYMPTOMS  Still feeling weak

DIAGNOSIS

TREATMENT  Continue bed rest and antibiotic
```

House call form.

If a telephone call to the office concerns an emergency such as an accident, a heart attack, or a stroke, the doctor may have to leave the office, and the scheduled patients will have to wait. In such a case it must be explained to the patients that the doctor has been called out for an emergency, and the patients should be asked whether anyone would prefer to return another day. Undoubtedly there will be some patients who do not need to see the doctor immediately and who do not care to wait. They can be given other appointments as soon as time is available. The remaining patients will be seen after the doctor returns in the order of their original appointments.

Project 12
Completing a House Call Slip

Dr. Taylor hands you some handwritten notes that he made at the house call on October 9 for Paul Bachmann, 5503 South Perry Avenue, Chicago, IL 60621. He asks you to transfer the notes to a house call slip as he did not have any forms with him. Use the house call slip form on WP 157.

Father-John. 18-month boy. Poor appetite. Bowels appear normal. Temp. 102.4 rectal. Pulse-120 Respirations-30. Rhinorrhea, conjunctivitis, occasional cough, irritable. Exam is essentially negative. Dx—cutting teeth. Treatment, ASA gr 1 temp. over 101 (R). Encourage fluids. Office call if no improvement in 48 hr.

HOSPITAL ROUNDS

Hospital visits may be made at fixed hours before the doctor starts seeing clinic patients or during the midday hours before the doctor starts back to the clinic for afternoon appointments. The assistant may be responsible for recording daily hospital visits, operative procedures, or emergency calls. The doctor will need a daily record of hospitalized patients. This list of patients can be used by the doctor to jot notes for the assistant to post patient charges.

PERSONAL DEVELOPMENT PROJECTS

TOPICS FOR DISCUSSION 1. Discuss advantages and disadvantages of fixed appointment times as opposed to open office hours.

2. Is it advantageous to know the reason for a patient's appointment? If so, who benefits?

ROLE PLAYING 1. Explain to a patient that Dr. Taylor is going to be late because (a) he has been called to the emergency room for an emergency; (b) he is ill today; (c) he is still in surgery.

2. Jill Grimes arrives for an appointment an hour early. She is certain that she has arrived at the scheduled time.

3. Today's schedule is full. The following calls are received: a patient wants a complete physical examination; a patient wants an appointment sometime today.

5

Meeting the Patient

The key to a successful career as a medical assistant is the patient-assistant relationship. How the assistant talks to patients, attends to their requests, and handles personal relations with them will affect the entire atmosphere in the office.

THE RECEPTIONIST

Most doctors' offices are arranged so that when patients enter they are met by the assistant. The desk may be in the waiting room or in a small office near the entrance door. When patients arrive during office hours without appointments, the waiting room often becomes very crowded.

The doctor's public relations agent is the assistant. As a rule, he or she is the first person patients meet when coming to the doctor's office. The way the assistant receives, welcomes, and makes the patient feel at home will influence the patient's attitude toward the doctor and the treatment.

As has already been cautioned, if patients are seen by appointment, it is well to check the appointment book upon the arrival of each patient so as not to upset the schedule. If a patient arrives at the wrong time and the doctor has some time free earlier than the hour that had been arranged, the patient can be seen at that time. If the doctor is very busy and the appointment was for a later day, it would depend on the seriousness of the patient's condition whether the patient was seen on that day or asked to come back at the time originally set for the appointment.

When the office is busy, the assistant may be called upon to do many things at once. Both doctor and patients may want to speak to the assistant at the same time; the telephone may be ringing; a patient may be waiting for treatment. Under such trying circumstances it is difficult not to become flustered and nervous, but the efficient assistant remains calm and self-possessed. Nothing interferes more with the patient's confidence in the physician than the impression of being hurried through an appointment. No matter how difficult the situation, how many demands on the doctor's and the assistant's time, each patient must be made to feel important and believe that sufficient time is available to attend to wants. The patient should not get the impression that only superficial attention is given.

CHAPTER 5: MEETING THE PATIENT 39

Martin Bough/Studios, Inc.

Greeting Patients should be greeted by name if possible and made to feel welcome. If a patient enters while the assistant is away from the desk, the assistant should acknowledge the patient's presence by a smile or a hello. A friendly greeting will go a long way toward putting the patient into a pleasant frame of mind.

Often, friends or relatives accompany patients. If the waiting room is crowded, there is the problem of finding seats for all. It may be necessary to ask patients to remove coats or packages from chairs.

Handling Nonpatients All visitors to the doctor's office should be greeted courteously. Most will have legitimate business reasons for being there; for instance, representatives of manufacturers of medical instruments or drugs or of medical book publishers. The doctor may wish to see these callers personally in order to keep informed on latest developments in medical science. When the doctor is too busy to give the time, the assistant may be asked to obtain all the pertinent information and prepare a summary for the doctor. It will be helpful if the assistant is aware of new remedies, new instruments or equipment, and new publications that relate to the doctor's special field.

There are visitors who take up the doctor's time quite unnecessarily, and most doctors appreciate an assistant who will protect them from intruders. Unless the assistant has been definitely instructed that the doctor wishes to see personally all who call at the office—there are some doctors who do see everybody—all possible information should be obtained from the caller, saying that the information will be relayed to the doctor and asking the visitor to telephone in a day or two for an answer. If a person does not wish to state the nature of business and the assistant knows the doctor does not wish to be disturbed by such visitors, the caller should be asked to write a letter.

First Visit Patients coming to the office for the first time are usually required to give some basic information about themselves. The information requested will be the name, home address, business address, telephone number, and the name of the person who referred the patient to the office. The name and address of the person responsible for the bill should be obtained. It is wise to

40 PART 2: SECRETARIAL RESPONSIBILITIES

Patient introduction slip

MR. MRS. (MISS) MS.		
PATIENT: Persky, Barbara E.		
SOCIAL SECURITY NUMBER: 470-68-2239	DATE OF BIRTH: April 6, 19—	AGE: 23
ADDRESS: 2828 W. Pierce Ave.	CITY: Chicago	STATE: Il ZIP: 60622
HOME PHONE: 555-2525	SEX: F	MARITAL STATUS: Single	REFERRED BY: Dr. W. Manly
EMPLOYED BY: First National Bank	EMPLOYER'S ADDRESS: 1757 N. Talman Ave.	OCCUPATION: Teller	BUS. PHONE: 555-7000
NEAREST FRIEND OR RELATIVE: Robert Persky	RELATIONSHIP TO PATIENT: Father	PHONE: 555-1723
MEDICAL INSURANCE: Blue Shield 744-44-2874		
SIGNATURE: Barbara F. Persky		

Courtesy Little Press, Inc.

request the business address as well as the home address. (A business person sometimes pays no attention to bills sent to the home address but will pay promptly when the bill is sent to the office.)

This information should form part of the patient's record. A sample patient introduction slip is shown above.

The patient may be asked to pay for charges for the first visit.

The requested information appears on the patient's chart, but it is practical to enter the information also on an index card that can be kept in a filing box or a filing wheel. There will be many occasions when one will refer to this information, and it is more efficient to consult a card than to take the patient's chart out of its folder. Therefore, it is important to keep the information on the card updated. These cards should contain the following information when appropriate:

Name, date of birth, age.

Marital status and spouse's name.

Home address, telephone.

Occupation.

Name of person responsible for bill if other than patient.

Name of referring physician.

A sample card is shown on the next page. If the doctor wishes, cards may be printed to suit the practice.

CHAPTER 5: MEETING THE PATIENT 41

```
Gray, Kathy, DOB 1/5/--, 3 years old

1545 South 57th Avenue

Chicago, IL 60650                555-7982

Bill to John Gray (father)
```

Project 13
Registration of New Patient

You receive the following information for a new patient. Enter the appointment in the appointment calendar, and begin a new patient registration form (patient introduction slip) using WP 23.

Jane Burnett, telephone number 555-6702. Mrs. Burnett was referred by Dr. Benjamin Kaplan. She is complaining of nausea and tiredness. You give her an appointment on October 14, at 10:30.

Project 14
Typing Index Cards

The assistant must type an index card for each patient. This card contains pertinent personal information about the patient. Prepare the following index cards. To obtain the year of birth for each patient, subtract the age from the current year. For example, Marion Wellman is 52 years old. If the current year is 1982, her birthdate would be 4/2/30. These are current patients of Dr. Taylor's.

Put a rubber band around these index cards and keep them in a handy place. You may wish to keep them in your expandable portfolio.

Marion Wellman, DOB 4/2/—, 52
Widow
13405 South School Avenue
Chicago, IL 60627; 555-5034
Executive secretary

Rebecca Berquist, DOB 7/12/—, 25
Widow
4415 West 15th Avenue
Chicago, IL 60623; 555-5144
Teacher

Sheila Leslie, DOB 5/21/—, 17
Single
2525 South Sacramento Avenue
Chicago, IL 60623; 555-2255
Bill to Thomas Leslie (father)

Lois Curtiss, DOB 4/2/—, 3½
1515 North Talman Avenue
Chicago, IL 60622; 555-7251
Bill to Mrs. Ann Curtiss (mother)

Janis Provost, DOB 9/30/—, 15
4548 North St. Louis Avenue
Chicago, IL 60625; 555-4207
Bill to Joseph Provost (father)

Carl Logan, DOB 11/6/—, 86
Married. Spouse—Ethel.
729 North Wolcott Avenue
Chicago, IL 60622; 555-2365
Retired college professor

Stanley Berndt, DOB 10/2/—, 51
Married. Spouse—Janet.
527 North Springfield Avenue
Chicago, IL 60624; 555-5124
Lawyer

Jason Stephens, DOB 11/11/—, 51
Married. Spouse—Louise.
712 North Ridgeway Avenue
Chicago, IL 60624; 555-3265
Librarian

Jill Grimes, DOB 12/18/—, 49
Single
1022 West 63d Place
Chicago, IL 60621; 555-2102
Billing clerk

42 PART 2: SECRETARIAL RESPONSIBILITIES

Sharon McKinley, DOB 3/11/—, 42
Married. Spouse—Tom.
5910 West Park Avenue
Chicago, IL 60650; 555-1524
Housewife
Bill to Tom McKinley (husband)

Mario Grazzini, DOB 12/16/—, 53
Married. Spouse—Tina.
1315 South 53d Avenue
Chicago, IL 60650; 555-1273
Storekeeper

Paul Grebowski, DOB 3/25/—, 49
Married. Spouse—Greta.
1532 South 47th Avenue
Chicago, IL 60650; 555-1325
Assistant bank manager
Referred by Dr. A. Williams

William Malinsky, DOB 5/31/—, 32
Married. Spouse—Karen.
2929 West Pierce Avenue
Chicago, IL 60622; 555-2543
Foreman

Ellen Goldberg, DOB 7/2/—, 66
Married. Spouse—Lee.
3425 South 61st Avenue
Chicago, IL 60650; 555-3055
Retired mail clerk

Alice Kellogg, DOB 9/27/—, 67
Widow
4724 North Seeley Avenue
Chicago, IL 60625; 555-7244
Retired cook

Karen Knutson, DOB 1/7/—, 26
Single
533 North Ridgeway Avenue
Chicago, IL 60624; 555-0569
Self-employed

Paul Bachmann, DOB 3/27/—, 18 months
5503 South Perry Avenue
Chicago, IL 60621; 555-7024
Bill to John Bachmann (father)

Joseph Bachman, DOB 2/17/—, 34
Single
704 North Sawyer Avenue
Chicago, IL 60624; 555-7400
Lawyer

Referred Patients It is particularly important to know the name of the person by whom the patient has been referred. If the patient has been sent by another doctor, a note of thanks must be sent to the latter, giving a brief report of the results of the examination, the treatment prescribed, and the results expected. This letter should be written promptly, and the assistant should remind the physician to do so in each case. Likewise, whenever the doctor refers a patient to a colleague, a letter or a telephone call should go to the other physician advising of this fact, giving the name of the patient, the condition for which the patient has been referred, and results of any tests or X rays already performed. Thus, the other doctor knows that a patient is to be expected and has a brief history of the patient's problem. A release form should be signed by the patient (a sample was shown in Chapter 3).

Below is a sample letter referring a patient to another physician, and a second one thanking a doctor for referring a patient. They may serve as a guide in drafting such letters for the doctor's signature.

> Dear Dr. Whitman:
>
> I am referring Janet Schmidt, a four-year-old, to you. She has been a patient of mine for six months. Janet has had a heart murmur since birth and recently has had extreme pressure on her chest.
>
> Enclosed is Janet's complete medical history, along with the results of the latest tests.
>
> Janet's mother is to call you for an appointment within the next two weeks.
>
> I would appreciate receiving your consultation report.
>
> Sincerely,
> Warren Taylor, M.D.
>
> Enclosure

Dear Dr. Cassini:

I have just completed examining Frank Johnson, a patient you referred to me. Mr. Johnson was first examined by me on March 4. His diagnosis at that time was otitis external, bilateral; defective hearing, mixed type, bilateral. The results of the audiogram are enclosed.

In May, Mr. Johnson had another audiogram (results are also enclosed). At that time, a considerable loss of high tones indicated a beginning degeneration of the auditory nerve, associated with severe tinnitus.

Thank you for referring this patient to me.

Sincerely,
Warren Taylor, M.D.

Enclosure

Frequently, a communication announcing a patient is received, but the patient never appears. After a reasonable period of time has elapsed, a letter should be sent to the referring doctor explaining that the patient did not come to the office. The referring doctor will know it is not due to neglect on the part of the colleague that reports on the patient have not been received.

Project 15
Composing a Referral Letter

Dr. Taylor asks you to compose a letter referring Joseph Bachman to an allergist, Dr. Manuel Gonzalez, 2901 West Fifth Avenue, Chicago, IL 60612. Dr. Gonzalez's telephone number is 555-3581. Mr. Bachman's chart is WP 25. Today's date is October 13. This letter is to confirm a telephone conversation on October 2.

ATTITUDE TOWARD PATIENT

If the assistant has to spend considerable time with a patient, the patient should be the one to decide whether to start a conversation. If the patient wishes to talk, let the patient choose the subject. The assistant should listen courteously. One should never argue or try to persuade, and one should never under any circumstances offer advice. The patient identifies the assistant with the doctor, and the assistant carries the doctor's stamp of authority. Very few patients know anything about medicine, anatomy, or physiology and may easily misunderstand any remark. If an opinion regarding the condition, the treatment, or the prospects of a certain patient is given, the patient often distorts the information or finds a discrepancy between the assistant's statements and those of the doctor, and embarrassing situations may result. The assistant should quite firmly refuse any discussion of the patient's case, referring the patient to the doctor for information and limiting the conversation to generalities.

In an effort to be helpful or encouraging, an assistant may innocently say to a patient, "Oh, you should be well enough to return to work in a week." If not so able, the patient may reproach the doctor. Or an assistant may recommend some patent medicine, without knowing that the doctor had prescribed something quite different for the patient. This obviously is not helpful to either the patient or the doctor.

Neither should the assistant express an opinion or offer advice when a patient talks about his or her personal problems. Should the patient appear genuinely troubled about something, the assistant may suggest that the matter be talked over with the doctor.

General Talk Some patients like to be entertained, and, in such cases, some safe general subjects should be chosen for conversation: the weather, motion pictures, books. Controversial matters should be avoided—politics or religion, for instance. Of course, the assistant must not discuss any personal affairs with a patient, even if the patient seems interested or inquisitive. As has already been stated, the affairs of the doctor or of other patients are absolutely taboo. No more flagrant breach of confidence could be imagined than for an assistant to discuss with a patient the personal, private life of the employer and staff or to gossip about other patients. Any attempt on the part of a patient to engage in that type of conversation should be met with a tactful reply that will put an immediate stop to personal questions.

Routine Patients It is helpful to know something about the patient—profession, number of children, hobbies, and such. It will put any mother in a pleasant mood if, after an absence of three months, she is greeted with a question such as "How did Johnny make out in that debating team last April?" or "Is Mary still enjoying her singing lessons?"

Patients seen frequently should be greeted by name. They should always be treated in a courteous and friendly manner, even if they are grouchy and ill-tempered. An inquiry regarding a person's health is usually appreciated, but sometimes it is resented, especially if the patient has not felt the expected relief from the treatment given or prescribed by the doctor. If a patient has to wait a considerable time before being seen by the doctor, thus becoming restless or impatient, some little gesture of attention may be helpful: offering a magazine, adjusting a light for better vision, friendly conversation.

Difficult Patients There will be unreasonable and unpleasant patients. Their behavior must not be taken personally, and they should be treated with the same calm, pleasant consideration as the patient whom one likes to see. When several patients are waiting, tension sometimes develops. For instance, where several doctors share a waiting room, a latecomer may be taken into the consultation room of one doctor while the patient of another doctor is still waiting to see the physician. Not knowing that more than one doctor is in the office, the waiting patient may become angry. The assistant must immediately explain the circumstances in the most friendly, pleasant manner, even if the patient is abusive, as sometimes happens.

The hardest test of good public relations is met with the difficult or problem patient. It must be remembered that a person who is sick or in pain is more sensitive and more given to outbursts of irritation than a well person. A person's self-control may have been undermined by pain and worry. Others may be by nature disagreeable people, given to arrogant manners and rude behavior. Dealing with such individuals requires a great deal of understanding and restraint. If the patient complains or accuses the assistant of some wrongdoing, one very likely will react with anger. Yet under no circumstances must it be shown. The patient's outburst is seldom meant personally: the assistant is simply the nearest target. If the assistant shows no offense and continues to speak in a calm and pleasant manner, the patient will calm down. Arguments are useless and out of place in a doctor's office.

Public relations implies that the assistant create goodwill for the doctor without seeming to have this as the purpose. The patient should leave the office in a good mood. The patient may feel resentment or anger at the doctor over something the doctor did or did not do. If the patient shows

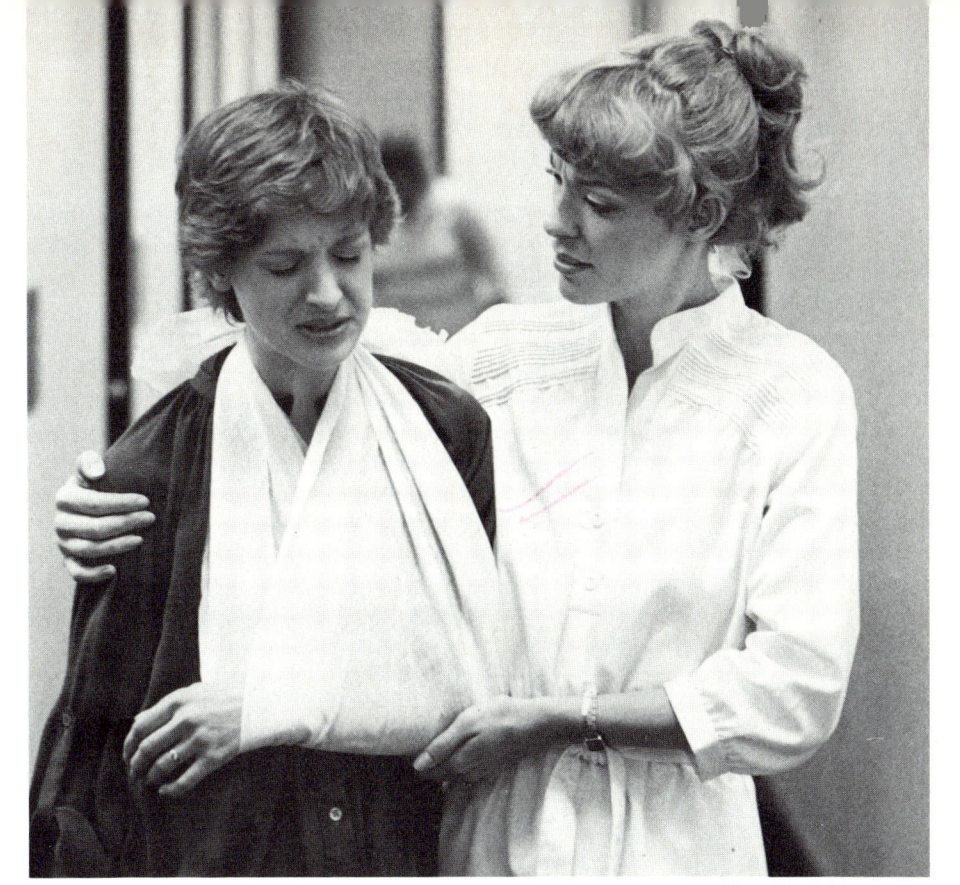

Martin Bough/Studios, Inc.

such resentment, the assistant may step in and try to create a good impression of the doctor. There is no foolproof formula for doing this. An assistant who is loyal to the employer and who respects the doctor's ability and dedication to patients will find the right thing to say to smooth over disagreements and send patients on their way feeling satisfied and in pleasant spirits.

Some patients who come to the doctor's office will be suffering from deformities and visible open wounds; others may exhibit peculiar behavior. The assistant must exercise self-control, showing no surprise or distaste toward such patients.

Social Relationships In the course of work, the assistant will meet men and women who come to the office frequently and with whom he or she becomes friendly. A real liking may develop, and patients may invite the assistant to go out with them or to visit their homes. Under no circumstances should a social engagement be made with a patient without first discussing this with the employer and obtaining permission to do so. Many physicians have a strict rule on this point, feeling that a social relationship between an assistant and a patient is not consistent with a professional atmosphere and may interfere with the proper medical management of the patient's case. An assistant should know the employer's attitude before accepting a social invitation from a patient.

Financial Status Almost all doctors adjust their charges to the financial status of the patient, and in every doctor's office there are patients who are being treated for a nominal fee only, or even entirely free of charge. Needless to say, the amount a person pays has no bearing whatsoever on the quality of the treatment received. In a doctor's office, people are perhaps more nearly equal than anywhere else in the world. For a physician there are only sick people and well people. When confronted with a sick individual, the physician's aim is to make that person well in the shortest possible time. The same obligation of disregarding social and financial distinction rests on the assistant. It would seem unthinkable to tell a patient, "You won't have to wait very long; the patient before you is only a compensation case," yet that has actually happened. A poor patient needs attention and sympathy even more than a wealthy one, for the poor person cannot afford to be sick and has worry added to pain.

A booklet published by the American Medical Association dealing with public relations between physician and patient may prove useful not only to the doctor but also to the assistant. The first part contains many helpful suggestions that pertain to the assistant's field. The title is *The Human Side and the Business Side of Medical Practice.* It may be obtained from the Chicago headquarters of the Association.

USE OF ROUTE SLIPS

It must be remembered that patients not only visit the doctor for a consultation but may have treatments, laboratory tests, or X rays by members of the doctor's staff. This means that after seeing the doctor in the examination room, the patient may be taken into the laboratory or X-ray room and then to another waiting area. Keeping this flow of patients running smoothly from room to room is the assistant's responsibility. If the doctor has an associate or if several doctors share an office, considerable planning and careful programming may be necessary. Patient flow may be controlled by using a route slip, as follows:

1. When the patient arrives, the route slip is clipped to the patient's chart as it is given to the doctor, before he or she sees the patient.
2. After examining the patient, the doctor indicates on the route slip which procedures have been performed and which procedures are still to be performed.
3. By glancing at the slip, the assistant knows what further action is needed. The patient may be taken to X ray, laboratory, or physical therapy. A medication may need to be administered.
4. The patient is given the route slip when ready to leave and is sent to the clinic cashier, where arrangements are made concerning the patient's charges. In a small office the medical assistant may take care of the financial arrangements.

RECOGNIZING EMERGENCIES

An assistant who has been with a doctor for some time and who is alert and interested in the work no doubt will soon learn to recognize many symptoms of the conditions the doctor sees most frequently and will know the remedies prescribed. In the doctor's absence or when the doctor is busy, the inclination will be, should the opportunity present itself, to tell the patient what to do. Under no circumstances must one yield to this impulse. One would be guilty of practicing medicine without a license. Nobody but a physician can know just what a symptom means and what treatment is indicated in each individual case. This does not mean, however, that an assistant who is alone in an office should not attend to an emergency case. If a patient arrives bleeding profusely from a cut, or if a patient faints or has just had an accident, the assistant should have some knowledge of first aid and enough presence of mind to apply it until the doctor's arrival. A course in first aid, such as that given by the American Red Cross, is invaluable for any doctor's assistant. A book of standard first aid should be readily available so that in an emergency the assistant may refer to the most important points.

The doctor should explain how much information the assistant should obtain in an emergency situation. The assistant should have at hand the telephone numbers of the local poison control center, hospital, ambulance service, and police station.

The assistant should know where to reach the doctor in case of an emergency, and the assistant must know the doctor's policy regarding the care of emergency situations when the doctor is not available.

PERSONAL DEVELOPMENT PROJECTS

TOPICS FOR DISCUSSION 1. Discuss emergency situations that students have experienced. Were patients sent to a clinic or hospital? Given first aid?

2. Wherever you go—to a restaurant, to a department store, to a doctor's or dentist's office—you make a snap judgment about the person who is there to greet you or help you. Relate first impressions you have received to the impression you think should be conveyed by a pleasant medical assistant.

ROLE PLAYING 1. Joseph Bachman, one of Dr. Taylor's patients, asks Janet Owen to have lunch with him.

2. Ellen Goldberg is in the waiting room, and she is crying. She is afraid she has cancer.

6

Telephone Procedures

The framework on which a doctor's practice is built consists of appointments with patients. As we have seen, making these appointments is one of the first duties of the assistant. Since most appointments are made by telephone, the telephone plays an important part in the office. Telephone technique in the medical office requires very specific skills governed by definite rules, some of which are set down in the following pages.

IMPORTANCE OF THE TELEPHONE

The main channel of communication between the doctor and the public is the telephone. Almost all patients make their first contact with the doctor by telephone. Usually, urgent and emergency cases are reported by telephone. In addition, there may be calls requesting house visits. The assistant must handle the telephone calls in such a way as to reassure the caller but not interrupt the doctor, who may be engaged with other patients' problems. There will be calls from other doctors about professional matters, as well as personal calls and business calls. People soliciting contributions or aid for some cause or other will call the doctor's office. There are calls from people who can be described only as intruders. The assistant must learn to recognize quickly the type of call and how best to represent the doctor when answering each call.

When the assistant is busy and the waiting room is overflowing with patients, the ever-ringing telephone can become a source of great irritation. The insistent ring may be from a patient in great distress, from a mother whose baby is having convulsions, or from someone whose neighbor is having a heart attack. There are less dramatic calls from patients who want to ask questions about medication the doctor has prescribed or to make or to cancel an appointment. To the person in need, the telephone is of the utmost importance.

Telephone calls may be incoming, outgoing, or interoffice. The telephone on the assistant's desk may have one or more call buttons, which, when pressed, will connect the telephone with the doctor's private office and allow the assistant to consult with the doctor without breaking an outside connection. This makes it possible for the assistant to ask the doctor a question and

Martin Bough/Studios, Inc.

relay the answer to the caller. If there is more than one doctor in the office, several buttons and interoffice connections may be installed on one telephone instrument.

TELEPHONE PERSONALITY The medical office assistant spends a great deal of time on the telephone. A favorable or an unfavorable impression of the doctor can be conveyed by the assistant and the skill or lack of skill with which he or she handles the telephone.

Promptness Courtesy begins with prompt attention to the call. If there is a delay, even a brief one, the caller may hang up or become irritated. When two lines ring simultaneously, answer line one and ask if the caller can hold. Answer line two and complete the call before returning to line one.

"Voice With a Smile" The telephone company has made everyone familiar with the importance of the "voice with a smile." The assistant should answer just as if face-to-face with the caller. In fact, it is a great help to visualize the person with whom one is talking—the voice will sound more alert, interested, and concerned. By all means, one should avoid a tone of voice that sounds monotonous, indifferent, or inattentive. The assistant should not indicate impatience or annoyance by the sound of the voice. The caller may sense this mood and react accordingly, making communication more difficult. The conversation should give the caller time to think and understand.

How to Answer Present custom is to answer the ring with the name of the physician—"Dr. Taylor's office." If several physicians share an office, "Doctors' office" is the best reply. The telephone company counsels medical office workers to identify themselves at the same time: "Dr. Taylor's office, Miss Owen," or "This is Stephen."

CHAPTER 6: TELEPHONE PROCEDURES 49

The usual response at the other end will be "Is the doctor in?" or "May I speak to the doctor?" The assistant will then say, "The doctor is busy with patients. May I help you?" As a rule, it is advisable for the assistant not to give any information or enter into discussion until the caller has given a name.

Verification of Information

When the assistant is not sure or has difficulty in understanding the speaker, the assistant may say something like this: "I want to get your name correct. Will you spell it for me, please?" Many names sound alike over the telephone—for instance, Wood and Worth, Mason and Payson—and if the doctor happens to have patients with similar-sounding names, embarrassing or even serious consequences may result from not making sure that the name has been rightly understood. The doctor may also have several patients with the same surname, and in such cases it is imperative to know the first name of the person.

People who are ill are sensitive, irritable, and sometimes unreasonable. Their attitude will depend to a considerable degree on the assistant's handling of the telephone call. When an assistant shows interest in the caller, the patient will be more willing to state the purpose of the call instead of just asking to speak to the doctor. A voice that carries authority without sounding curt will help to avoid much needless argumentation.

The following advice, so obvious as to be trite, is yet important enough to be placed in a special paragraph: Pad and pencil must always be kept at the telephone. Imagine yourself calling a doctor's office in an emergency and having an assistant say, "Wait a minute while I get a pencil to take your name and address."

Nothing is more annoying than to be told "Wait just a moment" and then to be left waiting for a long time. Minutes seem like hours. Never be guilty of this offense. If you must ask the doctor a question or look up some information, do it quickly or ask the caller if you may return the call. If a caller is on hold and there is a delay, return to the line and ask if the caller wishes to continue holding.

It is a good idea to repeat the date and time of the appointment. Say good-bye and use the caller's name. This will leave the patient with a pleasant impression. Finally, put down the receiver gently.

SCREENING CALLS

In general, a physician does not like to be interrupted unnecessarily and expects the assistant to handle as many telephone calls as possible. Much depends on the assistant's experience, judgment, and efficiency. Frequently, a new patient asks to speak to the doctor just to make an appointment. If the assistant asks, "Do you wish to make an appointment?" the matter can be settled then and there.

Most telephone calls concern matters that can be handled by a well-trained assistant. The assistant must be guided by the individual preference of the doctor. Many doctors will always speak to a patient, no matter what the circumstances. In some offices, a nurse is available to answer patient questions.

Management of telephone calls is often a difficult problem for the beginner, who may be afraid to assume the responsibility of making decisions. It is important to discuss this aspect of the job with the doctor at the very beginning and ascertain to what extent the assistant will handle calls alone, what medical information one should give out, when messages should be taken, and when to tell the patient that the doctor will return the call.

There will be telephone calls from patients who want to report on their condition or on the effect of medication or treatment; there will be those who want information; there will be still others who telephone for trivial or

Martin Bough/Studios, Inc.

Martin Bough/Studios, Inc.

perhaps even nonexistent reasons. The assistant must be guided by the doctor's wishes as to whether to take the call or transfer it to the doctor. The patient's record should be taken from the file so that accurate answers can be given. Sometimes the assistant may save the doctor's time by saying in a friendly manner, "Perhaps I can help you." The patient will sometimes respond to this by stating the purpose of the call.

If the doctor is out of the office and it is necessary to contact the doctor, tell the patient that you or the doctor will call back; then collect the necessary files and contact the doctor. For example, if you cannot reach Dr. Taylor, leave a message for him to call you; when he returns the call, you will have on your desk all the information he needs in order to speak to the patient. Whenever possible, know where the doctor is. It is the assistant's responsibility to locate the doctor.

One of the most difficult people to deal with over the telephone is the person who refuses to state the purpose of the call, saying that it is a "personal call" or a "personal matter." A personal friend does not hesitate to state that fact. If the caller is mysterious about the reason for calling, it is a pretty safe assumption that the matter is of more importance to the caller than to the doctor. Few doctors like to be called to the telephone only to be confronted with a solicitor of some sort, and this is one of the reasons why many physicians expect their assistants to find out a caller's business before asking the doctor to take the call. If such are the doctor's instructions, the assistant should explain that the doctor cannot be disturbed unless told the nature of the telephone call. If the caller still insists that it is a personal matter, it is well to ask whether the caller wishes to make a professional appointment. This usually prompts people to state their business, as they are afraid they may receive a bill if they make an appointment.

If the caller absolutely refuses to give any information to the assistant and the doctor does not wish to speak to strangers without knowing their business, it is permissible to suggest that a letter be written so that the doctor can become acquainted with the matter the caller wishes to present and then to decide whether to take time for further discussion.

It is a rather terrifying experience for the beginner who has been instructed by a doctor not to put a call through unless the purpose of the call is known to be told by an important-sounding individual that the caller must be connected with the doctor at once—or else. Take courage. A legitimate caller will give a name.

If the telephone call concerns some nonprofessional matter—for instance, an offer to give advice on financial matters, a request to buy tickets for a benefit, or an inquiry regarding the doctor's insurance—it usually is preferable to say that the matter will be presented to the doctor. In this way the message can be given to the doctor at a time when the schedule is not busy, and the doctor will have an opportunity to think over the proposition.

Project 16
Screening Calls

WP 27 lists 20 incoming calls an assistant may have to screen to determine what action to take. When you have completed the working paper, be prepared to discuss the situations with the class.

Emergency Calls

An emergency telephone call may come at any time, and the assistant must be able to cope with any eventuality. There may have been an accident, a patient may have had a stroke, or someone may have died. The person who telephones will probably be upset, and people who are excited often forget to give the most important information. It is imperative that the assistant remain calm and handle the call efficiently, reassuring the caller that help will come as quickly as possible. The importance of obtaining the name, address, and telephone number of the patient cannot be emphasized too strongly. The more information the assistant can obtain, the better.

If the doctor is in the office when an emergency telephone call comes through, he or she will speak to the patient. However, it is recommended that the assistant screen such calls and determine whether or not it really is an emergency. Great tact and excellent judgment are necessary to do this. One way to determine the urgency of the call is to ask the patient about the problem and how long it has been a problem. Frequently, in explaining the details, the patient realizes that the condition is not as serious as thought. The assistant should make it clear that the questions asked are on behalf of the doctor: "Dr. Taylor will want to know . . ." or "I shall want to tell Dr. Taylor just exactly what is troubling you."

RECORDING INCOMING CALLS

A record of telephone calls may be kept, since a message left on the doctor's desk sometimes gets lost. Misunderstandings do occur, and in such cases a note made at the time of the conversation will clarify the situation. Instead of writing duplicate messages, some doctors require their assistants to record all calls in a journal kept for this specific purpose. This telephone log should include the date and time of the call, the name of the caller, and a notation of the action taken.

The Message Form

The printed message form available for telephone messages is simple. Too much emphasis cannot be placed on the importance of making memorandums rather than relying on memory. No matter how firm the resolve to remember to do something, things will slip out of one's mind.

52 PART 2: SECRETARIAL RESPONSIBILITIES

The italics in the example below show information that would be supplied on a typical message form:

To: *Dr. Taylor.*
Name of caller: *Mrs. Dennis Hayes.*
Phone number, if return call requested: *555-0659.*
Message in detail or gist of conversation: *Reports she has been experiencing dizzy spells for three weeks. Please call her.*
Hour and date: *3:45 p.m. on 4/3.*

Some doctors have their own telephone message slips printed. Such a slip may contain some of the questions most frequently asked. For example, a pediatrician might ask "What is the child's temperature?" and "When was the last meal eaten?" Each doctor has standard questions that would be included if personalized telephone memorandums were used.

The Message The more explicit the memorandum, the better. The doctor can get a much clearer picture of the conversation if given a detailed report. Statements by patients, such as complaints of pain or discomfort, perhaps a chance remark regarding ability or inability to work, or a reference to illness in the family, may convey a very significant piece of information to the doctor. The assistant may also add a personal impression, such as "The patient seemed very tense and depressed," or, in the case of a new patient, "Mr. Brown spoke very rapidly and at great length."

The importance of keeping memorandums is not confined to telephone calls. When the doctor has an outside appointment or plans to go to a lecture or an exhibit or to do some errand—private or professional—a written reminder from the assistant will be most welcome.

Even memorandums to oneself are helpful. When the assistant knows that something should be done a few days or weeks hence, a memorandum may be placed where it cannot be overlooked—in the calendar or in a pending folder that is consulted daily.

Project 17
Taking Messages

While Dr. Taylor is busy with a patient, Mrs. Goldberg telephones to ask what laxative to give her elderly mother. Write out a telephone message for Dr. Taylor using one of the forms on WP 141-153. What additional information, if any, would you need to obtain from Mrs. Goldberg?

Remove all telephone message blanks from the working papers and place them in your supply folder for future use.

Following Through The responsibility of managing the telephone efficiently does not end with the taking of calls. The assistant must follow through on all requests and instructions. An incident in the office of an internist illustrates what could happen if the assistant does not carry out instructions to their completion. In this case, the doctor had ordered vitamin injections for a patient and had told the patient that arrangements would be made with the visiting nurse service for a nurse to come to her home regularly for this purpose. A few days later, the patient telephoned the doctor and complained that the nurse had not visited her. It was obvious to the doctor that the assistant had forgotten to carry out the instructions. Later the same day, after the assistant had made the necessary arrangements, the visiting nurse service called and inquired whether the injection material had been ordered. Additional calls to the doctor's office, the pharmacy, and the nurse service were necessary before the doctor could be sure that the injections would begin the following day.

CHAPTER 6: TELEPHONE PROCEDURES   53

OUTGOING CALLS   In the course of work, an assistant will have many occasions to make telephone calls for the employer to various people, institutions, or places of business. These calls may be either local or long-distance.

Planning   The alert receptionist plans the conversation before making outgoing telephone calls.

For example, if the assistant has to make a telephone call to schedule a patient for outpatient services such as laboratory or X-ray procedures, to secure a patient's admission to a nursing home or hospital, or to arrange an operative procedure, the basic information needed includes the name of the doctor requesting the procedure, the name of the patient, the name of the procedure, the date the procedure is to be performed, and the name of the facility (hospital) where the procedure will take place. Additional information may be required: patient age, diagnosis, special instructions. All information should be verified by the assistant. Likewise, if the assistant telephones someone to whom the employer wishes to speak, telephone etiquette requires that the person calling be on the line when the person who is being called answers.

In planning to relay a message, the assistant should have the information at hand. If questions must be asked, they should be outlined.

Project 18
Outgoing Calls

Dr. Taylor has been asked to speak at the in-service education meeting at University Hospital. He asks you to get specific details about the meeting when Mrs. Bateson calls from the hospital. On plain paper, write a list of questions to ask Mrs. Bateson.

Use of Directory   The assistant can use the telephone directory more quickly by remembering that names are listed in strict alphabetic order. For instance, MacAllister comes before Maccari, which is followed by McAllister. Many names that sound the same may be spelled in different ways. The telephone directory lists the different spellings under which to look. Identical surnames are listed according to first name and initials: Kelly, A. B.; Kelly, Arnold.

A great deal of valuable information is contained in the directory, and the assistant should become familiar with it. Telephone rates, emergency numbers, area codes, ZIP Code numbers for local areas, a map of time zones, and a list of telephone company services appear in the directory.

In addition to the alphabetic directory, most cities and towns have a classified directory. In small towns the two may be combined in one volume. In the classified directory, subscribers are listed according to the business in which they engage, under such headings as "Medical Supplies," "Electricians," and "Stationers." Thus, if the assistant wants to find the name and telephone number of a firm dealing in medical supplies, the appropriate heading would be "Medical Supplies."

After looking up a telephone number, the assistant should jot it down for future reference. If a number cannot be found in the directory, then consult the information number and ask the operator for help.

A personal telephone directory should be made for numbers that are frequently used. The telephone company will furnish indexed notebooks for this purpose. Various types of personal directories are available at stationery stores. These must be kept up to date, for addresses and numbers change. If the directory is used often, it soon becomes frayed and untidy and should be replaced.

54 PART 2: SECRETARIAL RESPONSIBILITIES

Numbers entered in personal directories can best be compiled from experience. They would probably include the following:

Hospitals	Western Union
Laboratories	Repair services
Pharmacies	Building superintendent
Referring doctors	Laundry
Surgical supply houses	Post office
Registered nurses	Bank
Specialists to whom the doctor refers patients	Fire department
	Police department

Project 19
Preparing a Personal Directory

Dr. Taylor asks you to prepare a directory of these frequently called places. Use your local telephone book for the telephone numbers of the following persons or services located nearest you:
Hospital
Dentist
Post office
Fire department
Registered nursing service
Ambulance service
Bank
Police department

Long-Distance Calls

Long-distance calls may be dialed direct almost anywhere in the United States. Even if the call is to be made person-to-person, it is more practical and economical to use direct-distance dialing. In some parts of the country, the prefix number 1 is dialed before the area code. In other areas, just dial the area code number before the regular seven-digit number—for example 212 555-9735. Telephone directories include a list of area code numbers for major U.S. cities. A booklet containing all area code numbers may be obtained on request from the telephone company. If you do not know the telephone number, you can obtain it from long-distance information by dialing the prefix number 1, if necessary, and then the area code plus 555-1212.

Before making a long-distance call, check the difference in time zones and place the call to arrive during business hours. Keep track of all numbers called and of the charges so that the telephone bill can be checked.

Project 20
Placing Long-Distance Calls

Dr. Taylor is on a committee for the AMA convention. The following is a list of people submitted to Dr. Taylor. The telephone numbers were not included. Place the names in the proper order so that Dr. Taylor would be able to start telephoning these people after 2 p.m. Explain how to obtain the telephone number of each person. Type your answer on plain paper.
Rev. Joshua Eller, La Jolla, CA
Dr. A. P. Collen, Charlotte, NC
Kathryn Leeman, Los Alamos, NM
Dr. Steve LaFran, Burnham, ME
Ellis Grant, St. Paul, MN
Olivia St. Steven, Fairhope, AL
Dr. Dennis deVictoria, Orlando, FL

CHAPTER 6: TELEPHONE PROCEDURES 55

TELEPHONE EQUIPMENT There is a variety of telephone equipment available; newer models are continually entering the market. There are several kinds of switchboard equipment, and there are automatic answering devices as well as answering services.

Switchboards A common switchboard is the Call Director, which monitors all telephones in the office. It can accommodate from 12 to 30 extensions. An operator takes all incoming calls, but outgoing and interoffice calls can be dialed directly from any extension. Incoming calls are connected or transferred by pushing a button. Completed calls are automatically disconnected. In a one-doctor office, there could be a telephone with only two or three incoming lines and an intercom or interoffice extension.

Several auxiliary services are available for the telephone. Some of these are listed below:

    Conference calls
    Connection to dictation instrument
    Loudspeakers
    Card dialers
    Rapidial
    Camp-on
    Automatic call-back

The telephone company will send a representative to explain the advantages of each type of service to a prospective subscriber. It also furnishes telephone training sessions for new employees.

Answering Service As a convenience to their patients, most doctors prefer to have the telephone answered day and night. They can subscribe to a commercial answering service, and they may also install an automatic answering service.

☐ **Commercial Services.** In larger cities there are commercial organizations that offer answering services on a monthly basis. Arrangements are usually made for after-office hours, nights, and holidays. Operators employed by a commercial service will answer telephone calls and take messages. The doctor or assistant may telephone the service at any time to inquire about any calls that were received. In emergency cases, the service will try to get in touch with the doctor.

☐ **Automatic Answering Devices.** The doctor's office may also be equipped with an automatic answering and recording service. One device consists of a record with no equipment for recording incoming messages. The recording, which can be made by the voice of the doctor or the assistant, is set off by the ringing of the telephone. It may be worded as follows: "This is a recorded message by Miss Owen, assistant to Dr. Taylor. Dr. Taylor's office hours are from 10:30 to 12 and from 2 to 5. Please call back during those hours." This would suffice for an office in which emergencies are unlikely to occur.

Telephone answering machines may be rented or purchased. The recordings can be changed according to circumstances. Some machines will also record a message from the caller. When the doctor or the assistant returns to the office, the recording is played back and the message is obtained. Remote devices will also enable the doctor to call the office and play back the messages over the telephone.

Project 21
Recording a Message

Write a message (less than one minute long) to be recorded for an automatic answering service. Explain that Dr. Taylor's office is closed for the weekend and give information for routine and emergency calls. Use plain paper.

If possible, use a tape recorder to record and listen to your message.

PERSONAL DEVELOPMENT PROJECTS

TOPICS FOR DISCUSSION 1. How would you handle two incoming calls at one time if one was an emergency?
2. A patient calls and insists upon talking with the doctor personally; she will not give a reason. The doctor is with another patient.

ROLE PLAYING 1. Mr. Bachman asks to use the desk telephone.
2. By phone, schedule a patient for an outpatient upper GI X ray; for outpatient lab work such as the SMA profile; for hospital admission.
3. By phone, refer a patient to a specialist.

7
Records Management

Efficient records management is essential in any medical office. The organization of the office is evident in its files. The assistant can learn how the office operates by observing its filing system and procedures. Therefore, an assistant must recognize the types of records, assist the employer in choosing suitable equipment and supplies, know the organization of the office files, and apply appropriate filing procedures.

TYPES OF RECORDS The various records in an office should be classified into categories according to the office's operation. In a medical office, records would be classified primarily into patient records, medical or general correspondence, and business and financial records.

Patient Records Patient records would include the clinical data sheet, medical reports, and correspondence pertaining to each individual patient. These records could be filed alphabetically or numerically with a cross-index file.

Medical or General Correspondence General correspondence pertaining to the operation of the office and medical correspondence unrelated to individual patients should be filed separately from patients' records. Medical correspondence could include articles from journals and so forth. These records would be filed by subject.

Business and Financial Records

These records pertain to management of the office. Patients' ledgers, which are the most active financial records, must be easily accessible and kept in one central location. These ledgers should be arranged alphabetically by name.

Examples of other business files include insurance policies (both professional and personal), income and expense records, financial statements, and tax records. These records should be filed chronologically within the subject area.

EQUIPMENT AND SUPPLIES

An assistant must be familiar with the kinds of filing equipment and supplies available in order to aid the employer in selecting suitable filing essentials for the office.

Card Files

Patient ledgers, patient indexes, telephone numbers, and various other records may be kept in card files.

Cards can easily be inserted and removed in a visible card file. This card file uses either a shallow metal tray or is in an upright stand; both styles show only the lower edge of each card, which denotes the patient's name or the title of the card.

In a vertical card filing system, cards are kept in a conventional file box or cabinet. A "tickler file" is an example of a system that may use vertical card filing. The "tickler file" is a monthly chronological arrangement which reminds the assistant that something needs to be done on a particular date.

The rotary card file system is the most space-saving system. The rotary wheel file is designed to rotate, permitting the use of both sides of each card.

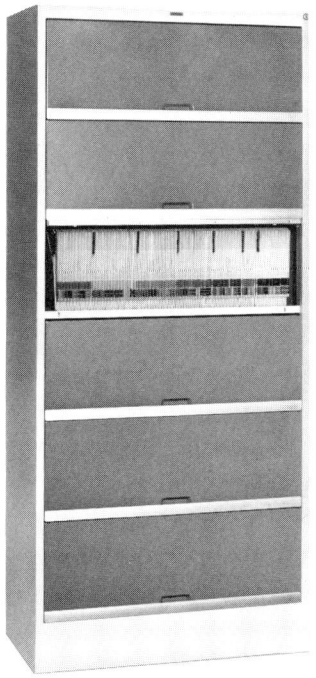

Courtesy Tab Products Company
Open shelf file.

Courtesy Business Efficiency Aids, Inc.
Rotary card file.

Courtesy Rubbermaid Commercial Products, Inc.
Vertical card file.

File Cabinets

The most common type of filing cabinet is the vertical file. Vertical files can range in drawer size, in number of drawers in a unit, in color, and in quality of material.

There is a trend toward open shelf files in offices with limited space. These shelves can extend to the ceiling and require less floor and aisle space. The folders are placed sideways with protruding tabs. Many clinics use open shelves for patients' charts.

Another file that saves space and is easily accessible is a rotary circular file. These files can hold a large volume of records and usually have push-button controls to revolve the files.

Microfilming

Microfilming is another way to reduce filing space requirements. The process transfers records to film; then the records can be destroyed or put in "dead" storage, and only the film has to be filed.

Microfiche Another version of microfilm is called *microfiche*. *Fiche* is a French word meaning card. Microfiche reproduces information, which is transferred onto a sheet of film (a card). These cards vary in size and, therefore, vary in the number of pages recorded on a card, depending on the microfiche machine and the viewer. The microfiche cards can be filed in a card file or a book-type binder.

Folders File folders can be purchased in various styles, weights, colors, and tab widths (tab cuts). Folders should be filed so that tab cuts are read in an orderly fashion from left to right.

Labels Folder labels varying in color and in width come in perforated rolls or self-adhesive strips and are used to identify the files following each guide. The larger the file, the more divider guides are needed. When a file becomes too cumbersome to locate records quickly, then the assistant uses extra divider guides.

Out Guides An out guide is a substitute for a folder which is temporarily removed. The name of the person who has the folder, the date the folder was removed, and what material the folder contained is recorded on the front so that others can locate the file. When the folder is returned, this notation is crossed out, and the out guide can be reused.

Cross-Reference Sheets A cross-reference sheet is used to indicate that material can also be filed elsewhere and notes where the original material is filed. This sheet can vary in color in order to be quickly recognized.

FILING METHODS Records are filed according to how information is sought and should be readily accessible. Therefore, several filing systems have been developed—alphabetic, geographic, numeric, subject, and phonetic. Each of them has certain advantages.

Alphabetic Filing Alphabetic filing is the most popular system. Before accurately filing and retrieving records in the alphabetic system, an assistant must thoroughly understand the following basic rules for alphabetizing and indexing:

1. Names of persons should be indexed (filed) by the surname (last name) first; given name (first name) second; and middle name or initial third. Each word is considered an indexing unit.
2. When comparing names, alphabetic order is determined by the first letter that is different. The standard is thus set: "Nothing comes before something."

NAMES	INDEXING ORDER
W. Luedenbeck	Luedenbeck/W.
Wesley Luedenbeck	Luedenbeck/Wesley
Thomas Luedenbock	Luedenbock/Thomas

3. Surnames with prefixes such as *D', Da, De, El, Fitz, La, Los, Mac, Mc, O', Van,* and *Von* are considered part of the name, not a separate unit. The prefix *St.* is alphabetized as though it were spelled out—*Saint*.
4. A hyphenated part of an individual's name is considered one indexing unit (*Ann Ames-Batte* is filed "AmesBatte, Ann").
5. Professional or personal titles, when followed by a complete name, are disregarded in indexing. A title with only a surname or a given name is the first indexing unit. Terms designating seniority such as *Jr.* or *Sr.* are only identifying elements, not indexing units.

CHAPTER 7: RECORDS MANAGEMENT 59

NAMES	INDEXING ORDER
Mrs. Janis Carlson	Carlson/Janis (Mrs.)
Father Blakely	Father/Blakely
Dr. Carl Frank	Frank/Carl (Dr.)
Sister Katherine	Sister/Katherine

6. When names are identical, their alphabetic indexing order is determined by their addresses in the following order: city, state, street name, direction (North, South, etc.), house or building number (with the lowest first).

NAMES	INDEXING ORDER
Adam Burke, Jr. 452 North Seeley Avenue Chicago, Illinois	Burke, Adam/ Chicago/IL/Seeley Avenue/North/452
Adam Burke, Sr. 862 North Talman Avenue Chicago, Illinois	Burke, Adam/Chicago/IL/ Talman Avenue/North/862

7. Abbreviated words are indexed as if spelled in full.

NAMES	INDEXING ORDER
Wm. Harris	Harris/William
St. Mary Hospital	Saint/Mary/Hospital
Spec Bros., Inc.	Spec/Brothers/Incorporated

8. When a firm name contains the full name of an individual, the surname is indexed first; then the given name; and finally the middle name or initial, followed by the word *Clinic, Hospital, Company*, etc. Articles (*a, an, the*), conjunctions (*and, but*), and prepositions (*in, of, for*) are disregarded and placed in parentheses.

NAMES	INDEXING ORDER
The Richard Grant Clinic	Grant/Richard/Clinic (The)
George Harris Hospital	Harris/George/Hospital
Brect and Sons, Inc.	Brect (and)/Sons/ Incorporated

9. All letters in a firm's name are considered separate units.

NAMES	INDEXING ORDER
B B Diaper Service	B/B/Diaper/Service

10. Words that are hyphenated in a business name are indexed as single units. An apostrophe is not considered in indexing.

NAMES	INDEXING ORDER
Self-Service Pharmacy	Self-Service/Pharmacy
South-East Clinic	South-East/Clinic
Tom's Bus Service	Toms/Bus/Service

11. A number in a business name is considered one unit, spelled out.

NAMES	INDEXING ORDER
54th St. Laboratory	Fifty-fourth/Street/Laboratory
9th Way Clinic	Ninth/Way/Clinic

12. The following businesses are indexed as written: banks and other financial institutions, hotels and motels, hospitals and religious insti-

60 PART 2: SECRETARIAL RESPONSIBILITIES

tutions, and educational institutions. If the words *Hotel, Motel, College,* or *University* appear at the beginning of a name, consider the distinctive part of the name first.

NAMES	INDEXING ORDER
Hotel St. George	Saint/George/Hotel
University of Iowa	Iowa/University

13. Names that pertain to the federal government are indexed under *United States Government* (first three units), then under the department name, and finally the name of the division, bureau, board, etc.

NAMES	INDEXING ORDER
U. S. Public Health Service	United/States/Government/Public/Health/Service

14. When a name pertains to a state or local government, such as state, county, city, or town, index it under the distinctive name, followed by the word *State, County, City,* etc., and finally the name of the division, bureau, board, etc.

NAMES	INDEXING ORDER
Chicago Public Library	Chicago/City/Public/Library

Project 22
Organizing Patient Index Cards

Alphabetize all the existing patient index cards. Wrap a rubber band around them; this will be the patient card file. When a new patient arrives, prepare an index card and add the card to the card file.

Geographic Filing Geographic filing classifies the records filed by particular regions. Divisions in this system involve a sequence such as nations, states, cities, and so forth. Files titled by regions are then filed alphabetically.

Project 23
Organizing Card Files

The following list represents persons or organizations Dr. Taylor may like to consult. He wants the names and the addresses typed on index cards and filed in geographic order according to states. Place the cards in your folder.

Fulton Publishers, 758 West Sherman Avenue, Phoenix, AZ 85007
John Johnson, M.D., Arizona Medical Society, 6975 East Sixth Avenue, Mesa, AZ 85208
Baker Book Company, 1575 Seiler Avenue, Savannah, GA 31404
Literary Medical Society, 778 Puritan Road, Boston, MA 02168
Ellis Grant, 1898 Burns Avenue, St. Paul, MN 55119
Fulton Book Store, 4899 North 63d Avenue, Phoenix, AZ 85033
Anthon's Antiques, 1157 Bay Drive, Miami, FL 33141
Leonard Tam, M.D., Treasurer, Iowa Medical Society, 2283 Butler Avenue, Waterloo, IA 50707
Taylor Publishing Company, 3297 Monroe Avenue, Rochester, NY 14618
Janis DeOlla, Ph.D., 680 North Niles Avenue, South Bend, IN 46617
The Honorable Lawrence Kelly, 4393 Maple Avenue, Baltimore, MD 21227
Carlton Publishing Company, Inc., 2692 Fox Avenue, Fort Wayne, IN 46807
Graham Binding Company, 4492 South Park Avenue, Buffalo, NY 14219
Professor Ward White, 1497 East 64th Avenue, Anchorage, AK 99502
Dr. Jeffrey Kane, 9559 College Avenue, Kansas City, MO 64137

Numeric Filing In numeric filing, files are numbered consecutively and filed in chronological order. Offices with a large volume of patients' records may use a numeric system. A new patient is assigned a number, and a cross-index is prepared to identify the number with a name. Numeric filing is considered the most accurate system; it is harder to lose files or to misfile them.

A numeric system is used in hospitals to file clinical data sheets in four categories: diseases, anatomical areas, operations, and treatments. This system is useful for research and statistical purposes.

Subject Filing Correspondence and other kinds of records which pertain to the same subject should be filed alphabetically by subject categories. This system is often used for a doctor's research materials and is referred to as "diagnostic filing." This allows a doctor to classify the material according to the disease or condition content.

Under what subject to file material will depend first on the specific needs of the doctor and second on the amount of material that has accumulated under each heading. A general practitioner may collect clippings and file them under general subject headings. A specialist will have the material filed under more specific headings.

A most valuable aid in setting up a scientific file is contained in a publication entitled *Medical Subject Headings,* which may be purchased from the United States Government Printing Office, Washington, DC 20402. The publication follows headings used in the *Index Medicus,* the monthly bibliography of articles that have appeared in medical journals.

Manuscripts are filed alphabetically under the title of the article or book. Abstracts, excerpts, and reviews may be typewritten or clipped from journals or newspapers. If they are typewritten, a carbon copy is made. The original is filed by subject, and the carbon copy is filed alphabetically, thus providing two ways of locating an article. Whether to file clippings by author or subject depends on how the doctor plans to use the items. All reviews of, and references to, the doctor's own writing should be filed together under the title of the article or the book.

Here are examples of headings for a subject file:

ACCOUNTING
APPLICATIONS
  Active File
  Inactive File
BUILDING
  Janitorial Service
  Maintenance and Repairs
EDUCATION
  Continuing
  In-service
  Patient
EQUIPMENT
  Business Office
  Examining Rooms
  Lab and X-ray
  Waiting Room
INSURANCE
  Accident
  Fire and Theft
  Health
  Liability
  Worker's Compensation

LICENSES
  Local
  State
SAFETY
  Inspections
  Miscellaneous
SUBSCRIPTIONS
  General
  Medical
SUPPLIES
  Medical
  Office
TAXES
  Federal Income
  FICA
  Property
  State Income
  Unemployment
UTILITIES
  Electricity
  Telephone
  Water

Project 24
Using Subject Filing

As Dr. Taylor's assistant, you must retain and file the following items. On a plain sheet of paper, indicate under what subject heading each would be filed. Be prepared to discuss your answers.

An order for supplies for the examining rooms.
A statement from the state indicating property taxes for Dr. Taylor's office.
A change in Dr. Taylor's professional liability coverage.
An application for a nurse.
An advertisement for a new drug.
The renewal card for Dr. Taylor's state license.
A requisition for a new office typewriter.
A brochure about a future AMA convention.
A copy of a purchase order for stationery materials.
A contract with a local collection agency.
Last month's electricity bill.
Recent research on heart transplants report in the *Journal of Medicine*.
Health benefits available for office personnel.
Subscriptions to magazines for the reception area.
A copy of a quarterly report of paid FICA taxes.

Phonetic Filing When the exact spelling of a name is not known, a Soundex filing system can be used. This phonetic system groups all names that are pronounced alike under a simple code, reducing each name to a letter and a three-digit code number. When applying the Soundex system, the following rules should be observed:

1. The first letter of the name remains unchanged and is not coded.
2. Vowels and the letters w, h, and y are not coded.
3. The following consonants are coded by these letter equivalents:

CONSONANTS	CODE NUMBERS
b, f, p, v	1
c, g, j, k, q, s, x, z	2
d, t	3
l	4
m, n	5
r	6

If there are not enough code consonants for a three-digit code, one, two, or three zeros are added as needed to complete the code.
4. Double consonants are treated as one consonant.
5. After the coding of the surname, arrangement between the letter guides should be alphabetic according to the given name.

The name *Martin* would be coded as follows:

M, not coded (initial or first letter)
a, not coded (vowel)
r, coded 6
t, coded 3
i, not coded (vowel)
n, coded 5

Thus *Martin* would be coded "M-635."

FILING PROCEDURES The following systematic steps for preparing materials for filing enable the assistant to do accurate and effective filing, and also allow for an efficient use of filing space.

Releasing	Before an item can be filed, it must bear a release mark showing that the material has been seen, acted on, and is now ready for filing. This release mark varies from office to office; it can be stamped, initialed, or coded.
Indexing	Indexing is the process of selecting the name or word under which an item will be filed and putting the units of that name or word in proper order.
Coding	Some form of code (a number, a letter, or an underlined word) must be on an item to indicate where it should be filed.
Cross-Referencing	A cross-reference sheet should be prepared and filed for any material that could be filed under more than one heading.
Sorting	Papers should be arranged in the filing order before they are actually placed in the folders.
Follow-Up File	So many patients need a follow-up of one sort or another that a special file, commonly called a "tickler file," is useful. Patients who wish a regular checkup once or twice yearly appreciate being reminded of it. A patient may also need to be reminded of a series of injections or a course of treatments. One reminder method is to employ colored index tabs which may be clipped to the patient's record. A colored tab would indicate that the patient has to be followed up for some reason. Different colors may be designated for different purposes. A more practical system is using a monthly chronological arrangement of index cards. Notations of actions to be taken are placed behind specific dates of the month. At the end of the month, cards are distributed behind the specific dates of the next month, and so on. A tickler file must be used daily in order to be effective.
Transfer of Files	Every office needs a system for regular transfer of files. The three classifications commonly used in a medical office are *active, inactive,* and *closed.* Active files include current patients; inactive, patients whom the doctor has not seen in six months or so; closed, patients who have died, moved away, or terminated their relationship with the doctor.

Project 25
Arranging Your Files

Prepare folders for all the patients from the index cards. Duplicate the form on WP 29 and prepare a clinical data sheet for each patient, using the information on the index cards. Each patient now has an individual "chart." Material pertaining to each patient should be filed in its respective folder. As additional information is obtained, it should be filed accordingly. Items within a folder should be in chronological order. Items that do not pertain to patients are filed in the "Miscellaneous" folder. Arrange all the folders in alphabetic order. Prepare folders, clinical data sheets, and index cards whenever a new patient has an appointment with Dr. Taylor.

RETENTION AND DESTRUCTION	Every office should establish a system of record retention. This includes replacement of outdated items. For example, when new fee schedules are obtained, destroy the old ones.
Case Histories	Case histories will probably be kept permanently, but this depends on the doctor's preference. Microfilming and microfiche are two means of solving the storage problem of old records if it is feasible for a doctor to have the necessary equipment.

Insurance Policies	Current policies are kept in safe storage. Professional liability policies are kept permanently.
Tax Records	These are kept indefinitely. Keep three current years in safe storage; keep the others in dead storage.
Canceled Checks	These are kept in safe storage for three years, then indefinitely in dead storage.
Receipts for Equipment	Receipts for both medical and office equipment are kept until they are fully depreciated.
Personal Records	Professional certificates and licenses are kept permanently in safe storage. Current bank statements and bank deposit receipts are kept in the files for three years, then transferred to dead storage. Some other personal items that should be kept permanently in dead storage are old partnership and other business agreements and old major property records.

PERSONAL DEVELOPMENT PROJECTS

TOPICS FOR DISCUSSION 1. Display various types of filing supplies.
2. Examine filing supplies in catalogs of local distributors.
3. Using the Soundex system, assign the correct file number to your name.

ROLE PLAYING 1. The file clerk has asked you to help file patients' charts. As you file, you notice that quite a few charts are misfiled.
2. A week after you have been instructed in file room routine, you think you have a more efficient method for filing reports. Discuss your procedure with the supervisor.

8
Written Communications

The assistant will find that writing letters and processing the mail is a major part of each day's work. A physician usually receives several dozen pieces of mail every day, and if two or more doctors share an office, the volume of incoming mail will be even greater.

PROCESSING THE MAIL The assistant should process as much of the mail as possible. Sound judgment and experience are necessary if the job is to be done well.

Incoming Mail The competent assistant will learn to distinguish quickly between the types of mail most frequently received. If several doctors share an office, mail for each is processed according to importance and then is placed on each doctor's desk.

Incoming mail should generally be sorted into the following categories:

> Special delivery, express mail, telegrams, and Mailgrams
> Doctor's personal mail
> Certified and regular first-class mail
> Periodicals and newspapers
> Advertising materials
> Samples of medications

☐ **Handling Procedures.** The assistant will probably open all letters except those marked "Personal." The assistant may even open the doctor's personal mail if prior authorization is given. If the sender's address does not appear on the letterhead, the assistant should check the return address on the envelope and copy it on the letter. In most offices, a date stamp is placed on each letter, or the date is written in pencil at the top. If there is an enclosure, clip it to the letterhead. Patients' checks must be carefully removed and put in a safe place until they can be recorded and deposited in the bank. Make absolutely sure that the envelope is empty before discarding it. If a letter mentions that material is being forwarded separately, write a reminder on the calendar or in the follow-up file.

If a letter requires an answer, the patient's chart or whatever other material is necessary for a reply should be attached to the letter. If the letter is in answer to one of the doctor's letters, clip the carbon copy of the original letter to the one received. Put aside those letters that can be answered without the doctor—payments that must be acknowledged, insurance forms to be filled out, bills to be paid.

Announcements of medical meetings and other medical society news are of importance. If the doctor plans to attend a meeting, the proper notation must be made on the appointment calendar. Requests for contributions may also be looked over by the doctor, unless the assistant knows the charities and other causes to which the doctor contributes regularly. Any advertising matter that pertains to the doctor's specialty or interests should be placed on the doctor's desk. General interest magazines should replace outdated magazines in the lobby.

Medical journals are valuable and should be placed on the doctor's desk. If the doctor desires an annual file of certain journals, a record should be kept of the receipt of each journal. Reprints can be obtained by sending in a printed card to the publisher.

Medical samples should be unpacked and placed in the doctor's supply cabinet if they are the type that can be used; if not, they should be collected and turned over to a charity when enough of them have accumulated. They should not be thrown into the trash where they can be picked up.

The assistant is responsible for processing all mail when the physician is absent from the office. Decisions must be made in regard to each piece of mail—whether to telephone the doctor about it, forward it to the doctor, answer it immediately, or just acknowledge receipt of the mail, explaining that the doctor is out of the office.

An assistant should keep a record of mail that arrives during a doctor's absence, noting when it arrived, what action was taken concerning the item, and if it was forwarded to the doctor. If an item is to be forwarded, a copy of the original should be sent, not the original.

Project 26
Processing Incoming Mail

The following pieces of mail arrived in the morning mail. On a plain sheet of paper, explain how each item should be processed. Be prepared to discuss your answers.

Letter from a consultant concerning one of the doctor's patients.
Announcement of a medical society meeting.
A drug sample that the doctor can use.
Letter and check from a patient.
Letter from a patient complaining about being overcharged by the doctor.
Open-house announcement for a new specialty practice.
Journal of American Medicine.
Field & Stream Magazine.

Outgoing Mail Outgoing mail in a doctor's office will consist of professional, business, and personal correspondence. Professional correspondence concerns patients, hospital matters, and research. Business letters are necessary to the management of the office. These may concern insurance companies, lawyers, supply houses, and bills to the patients. If the doctor is a writer, letters to publishers and manuscripts are dispatched. If the doctor publishes an article, reprints are sent to interested persons. Personal correspondence pertains to the doctor's personal rather than professional life; examples are letters sent to friends and to the doctor's broker or banker.

Martin Bough/Studios, Inc.

☐ **Equipment and Supplies.** In order to complete tasks connected with outgoing mail, the assistant needs a typewriter in good working order. The ribbon should produce neat, dark, easily read copy. The type must be cleaned periodically.

Stationery supplies are entirely the assistant's responsibility. It is desirable to have a special cabinet for them or a shelf or two reserved for these materials. The doctor probably needs not only letterheads and copy paper but also manuscript paper, onionskin paper, carbon paper, prescription blanks, patients' chart forms, and patients' ledger cards.

The following is a list of supplies every office should have on hand: envelopes, business (calling) cards, appointment cards, manila envelopes in assorted sizes, memorandum pads, notebooks, index cards, file folders, labels for file folders and printed ones for postal packages, pencils, pens, large and small clips, rubber bands, erasers, and blotters. For a busy office, a postage scale is essential. It should be fairly solid and of good quality.

Stationery must be ordered before supplies are exhausted. Sufficient time must be allowed for printing of letterheads, prescription blanks, billheads, and so forth.

☐ **Mail Classifications.** In order for mail to be dispatched efficiently, the assistant must know the various classifications of mail.

First Class. This class includes letters of any form (handwritten or typewritten messages), postal cards, postcards, business reply cards, and bills and statements of accounts. First-class mail is kept sealed against postal inspection.

Priority Service. This service provides first-class handling for items that weigh more than 12 oz (340 g). The rate is determined by weight and distance sent.

Second Class. Publishers and news agencies must obtain second-class privileges from the post office in order to use a special second-class rate for mailing newspapers and periodicals. The public can also mail unsealed newspapers and periodicals using the second-class category.

Third Class. Mail that cannot be classified into first or second class and weighs less than 16 oz (454 g) is classified into third-class mail. This includes circulars, books, catalogs and other printed matter, merchandise, keys, and identification cards. Items that weigh more than 16 oz (454 g) have to go by fourth class.

Fourth Class. Books, printed matter, merchandise, etc., weighing at least 16 oz (454 g) and not exceeding 70 lb (32 kg) are sent fourth class. The rate depends on the weight of the item and the distance it is transported.

☐ **Postal Services.** The following services are available through the post office:

Special Delivery. Any class of mail can be sent special delivery. This provides that an item will have immediate delivery to the addressee when it arrives at the post office. This service should be used when an item has to be delivered to the addressee the same day it arrives at the post office.

Registered Mail. Additional protection can be provided for valuable first-class mail if it is registered with the post office. The fee for this service will vary according to the declared actual value of the registered item. The post office keeps a record of the mailing. The indemnity limit for registered mail is $10,000.

Certified Mail. For a small fee, a person can obtain evidence of mailing for items with no intrinsic value, and a record of delivery is made at the post office. There is no insurance coverage with this service. Examples of items that should be certified because they are hard to replace include insurance policies, birth certificates, passports, contracts, deeds, and bank books.

Special Handling. For third- or fourth-class mail, special handling provides the fastest handling and transportation practicable. This does not include special delivery.

Express Mail. The postal service has instituted a service called *express mail,* which guarantees next-day delivery between major cities in the United States. Items received by 5 p.m. are guaranteed to be delivered by 10 a.m. the next day to a post office or by 3 p.m. to an address within the city. If express mail does not reach its destination by the required time, your money will be refunded.

Insured Mail. Mail may be insured against damage or loss. The post office will reimburse the sender for a lost or damaged item according to the amount of the insurance fee.

Return Receipts. For a small fee, a receipt from the addressee may be obtained on registered, certified, and most insured mail. This receipt service provides legal evidence that the addressee received the item. If the return receipt is requested at the time of mailing, it will show to whom the mail was delivered, when it was delivered, and the address where it was delivered. After an item has been mailed, a request for a return receipt will show to whom the item was delivered and when it was delivered.

Every post office has leaflets available concerning the latest information about domestic and international postage rates and fees information. Current leaflets should always be in the assistant's desk.

☐ **Dispatching Mail.** After letters have been composed, they are given, together with the carbon copies, to the doctor. Enough time should be allowed for the doctor to read and sign the letters.

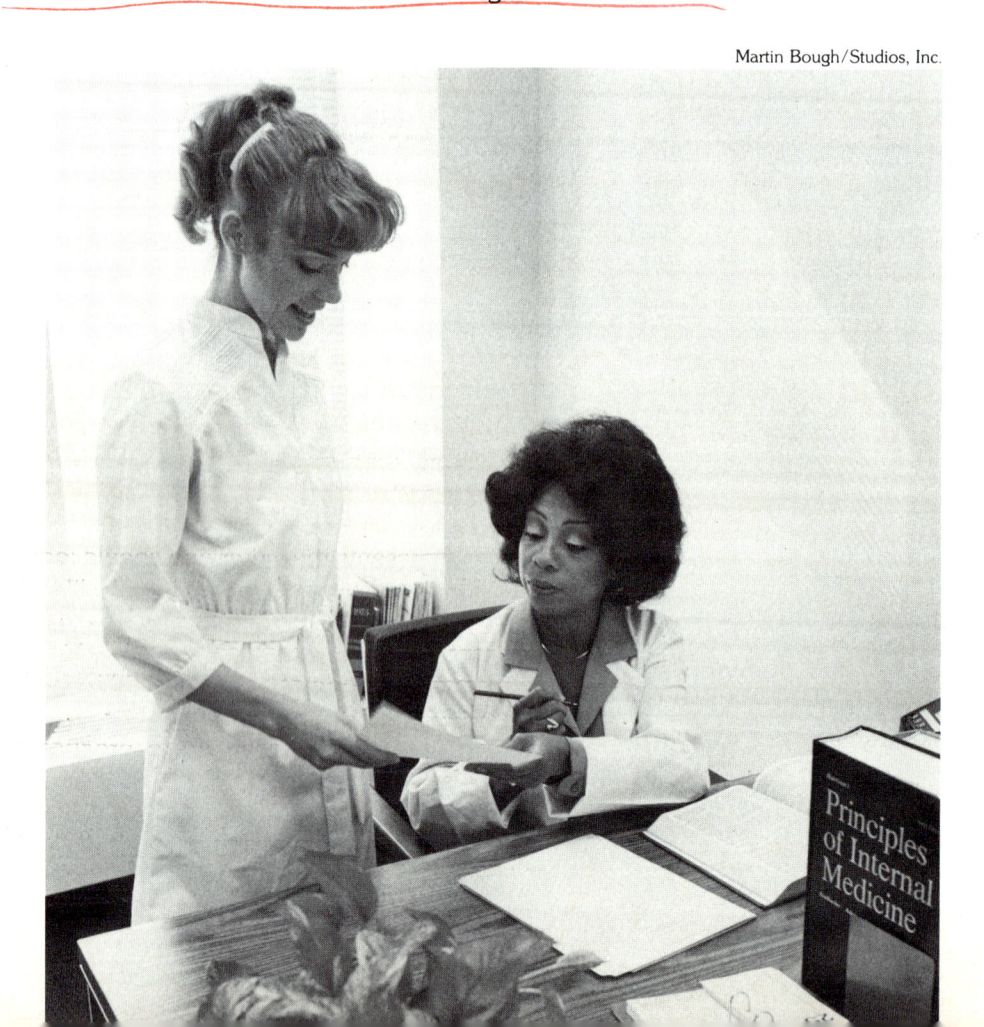

Martin Bough/Studios, Inc.

After letters have been signed, fold each for the size of the envelope. Letters are folded in half and then in thirds for a small envelope; for a large envelope, a letter is folded in thirds.

Check the enclosures listed in the letter. Make sure the right letter is in the right envelope. Seal the envelope securely. Affix postal service stickers when needed. Weigh the letter if necessary. Affix the proper postage.

☐ **Telegrams.** Western Union offers three types of telegraphic services. The fastest service is the *regular telegram*, which is based on a flat rate for the first 15 words and more for each additional word. The regular telegram is sent immediately and takes precedence over all other classes of service.

For lengthy messages which are not particularly urgent, an *overnight telegram* may be sent. This telegram can be sent anytime up to midnight and is delivered the next morning. The rate for an overnight telegram is based upon 100 words.

The third type of telegraphic service, the *Mailgram*, is also an overnight telegram. The message is sent electronically to the post office serving the area and is delivered with the regular day's mail. Mailgrams may also contain 100 words.

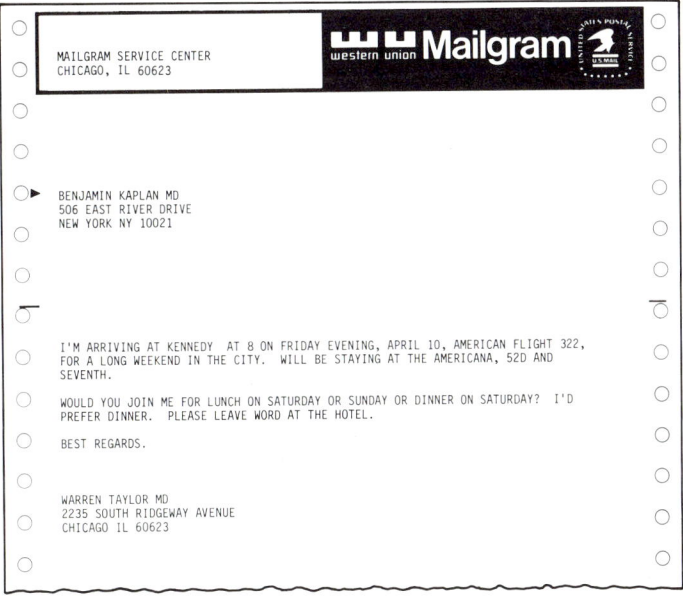

```
MAILGRAM SERVICE CENTER                    western union Mailgram
CHICAGO, IL 60623




    BENJAMIN KAPLAN MD
    506 EAST RIVER DRIVE
    NEW YORK NY 10021



    I'M ARRIVING AT KENNEDY AT 8 ON FRIDAY EVENING, APRIL 10, AMERICAN FLIGHT 322,
    FOR A LONG WEEKEND IN THE CITY. WILL BE STAYING AT THE AMERICANA, 52D AND
    SEVENTH.
    WOULD YOU JOIN ME FOR LUNCH ON SATURDAY OR SUNDAY OR DINNER ON SATURDAY? I'D
    PREFER DINNER. PLEASE LEAVE WORD AT THE HOTEL.
    BEST REGARDS.

    WARREN TAYLOR MD
    2235 SOUTH RIDGEWAY AVENUE
    CHICAGO IL 60623
```

Western Union Telegraph Co.

COMPOSING CORRESPONDENCE

In addition to the letters that the employer dictates, an assistant must compose letters. One must be able to produce letters that are pleasing in appearance and written in a professional style.

Appearance

A letter represents the writer and should look as professional as it sounds. It should be neat, properly spaced, and without any blemishes.

Some doctors do not permit a letter to be sent if any corrections are apparent. There are many commercial aids available for making corrections. No matter what kind of correction aid is used, the corrections should not be noticeable.

Proper spacing is necessary to produce a well-balanced and attractive letter. Use single spacing. Double-space between paragraphs. By experience, the assistant will learn how to judge the length of a letter and will be able to center it on the page properly. If the letter is longer than one page, a blank sheet is used for additional pages.

Martin Bough/Studios, Inc.

Style Letters must be dignified and faultless. The essence of good professional style is clarity, simplicity, and coherence. Sentences should be short, and their structure should vary. The same word should not be repeated too often, except for special emphasis. If possible, paragraphs in letters should not start with *I*.

When composing letters for the doctor's signature, the assistant should write as the doctor would. This will take a certain amount of experience and familiarity with the doctor's letters. It is essential that the assistant know the proper terms of address for the people to whom the employer writes. This is a courtesy that cannot be overlooked, and there are rules to guide those who may be in doubt.

The holder of a medical doctor's degree is addressed as *Doctor* in writing and speaking, but initials indicating type of degree should be placed after the signature and after the name on professional stationery—letterheads, envelopes, calling cards. The title *Dr.* and initials indicating the degree are never used together. The following examples will illustrate these principles:

>   Letterhead: Warren Taylor, M.D.
>   Address: Dr. Warren Taylor
>   Wrong form: Dr. Warren Taylor, M.D.

In writing to another doctor, to a university professor, or to any other professional person, it is customary to address the person by title—for instance, *Dear Professor Brown* or *Dear Dr. Murray*. In the absence of any professional title, the courtesy titles *Mr., Mrs., Miss* or *Ms.* must always be used. Dispensing with a title would be most discourteous unless the addressee's gender was not known and a professional title could not be used, in which case *Dear Leslie Brown* would be acceptable. Consult a reference book for commonly used forms of salutation.

Commonly used complimentary closings are *Sincerely, Sincerely yours, Cordially,* and *Cordially yours.*

The doctor may want to see a draft of a letter dealing with highly technical material. If a mistake was made in dictating, either in fact or construction, this can be corrected in the draft and the style improved.

Before each letter is given to the doctor for a signature, the assistant should proofread it for errors. Whenever in doubt about correct spelling of a word, consult a dictionary. An assistant must have a well-rounded education in English, but even so, reference books should always be available for use when necessary. A good general dictionary, a medical dictionary, and a thesaurus should be on every assistant's desk.

If any changes are made in the original copy of the letter, the carbon copy should also be corrected. Always fasten the carbon copy to the letter to which it is a reply. If a letter is answered by telephone or by a postcard, a notation giving the gist of the reply, together with the date, should be made on the original letter.

Letters From the Assistant

There are many letters the assistant may write over a personal signature. Examples are routine letters about appointments or reports of tests, requests for information, routine business letters, and, even more important, letters sent in the doctor's absence.

It would obviously be impossible to compose form letters to fit every occasion that an assistant might have to write a letter. Some situations are likely to occur in almost every office at one time or another. For these, the sample letters given throughout this book can be used as guides.

The assistant should have a reminder system for letters that require a reply. If a letter has not been answered within a reasonable time, a follow-up letter should be sent. It is one of the assistant's duties to remind the doctor to answer a letter. Some examples of follow-up letters are given here:

Dear Professor Brown:

Because Dr. Taylor has not heard from you, he wonders whether his letter of March 3 has reached you. In that letter he requested the name and address of a laboratory technician whom you recommended for employment.

Dr. Taylor would appreciate hearing from you as soon as possible.

Sincerely,
Medical Assistant

Dear Mr. Watts:

On April 3, Dr. Taylor wrote you a letter asking you to return the book that he loaned you on respiratory diseases. Dr. Taylor needs the book for an article he is writing and would appreciate it if you would return the book as soon as possible.

Sincerely,
Medical Assistant

Certain information may have to be sent to patients who are waiting to enter a hospital. Some sample letters for use in such circumstances are shown on the following page.

Dear Mrs. Thompson:

The Riverview Hospital has a private room available for you on Monday, July 21. Your surgery will be scheduled for the following morning. Report to the hospital by three o'clock on Monday.

Please notify us by July 14 if this is not satisfactory, and other arrangements will be made.

> Sincerely,
> Medical Assistant

Dear Mrs. Blake:

Because of a change in the hospital's operating schedule, Johnny's tonsillectomy has been postponed until Thursday, August 21, at 10 a.m.

Please admit Johnny to the hospital by 3 p.m. on Wednesday.

> Sincerely,
> Medical Assistant

Mistakes should not happen, but they do. The letter below might be used by the assistant when rectifying some oversight:

Dear Dr. Hershey:

Enclosed is the report that was inadvertently omitted from Dr. Taylor's letter of September 2.

I hope this has not inconvenienced you.

> Sincerely,
> Medical Assistant

Project 27
Composing a Letter

Dr. Taylor asks you to write a letter to Louise Merryweather, M.D., Medical Director of the Children's Home, 6452 North Ridge Boulevard, Chicago, IL 60626. He is requesting a reprint of an article by Dr. Merryweather on child abuse that appeared in last month's issue of *American Journal of Medicine*. Date the letter October 13. Address an envelope for this letter.

Dr. Taylor keeps index cards with the names of all doctors and businesses that he contacts. Check previous correspondence to obtain information for these index cards.

Using Dictation and Transcription Machines

Equipment for dictation and transcription makes it possible for the doctor to dictate letters, reports, or articles while the assistant is busy elsewhere. The dictation unit may be on the doctor's desk, in the doctor's home or car, or around the doctor's neck.

The recording device may be a plastic disk, a magnetic or plastic belt, magnetic tape, or wire. Machines come in various sizes: miniature, portable, and standard. Recording time will vary according to the recording device used and its size. All these have a switch allowing the dictator to play back the recording and make corrections.

Some machines are used for both recording and transcribing; in others, these functions are separate. Instruction booklets with each instrument explain how to place recorded material on the machine—whether disk, belt, or tape—and how to operate it. One can learn to operate such machines in a

CHAPTER 8: WRITTEN COMMUNICATIONS 73

few minutes, but a certain amount of practice is necessary before a transcriber can use the procedure smoothly.

Principles of transcription are the same regardless of the type of machine and recording device used. The machine, with either a headpiece or an amplifier, is placed next to the typewriter. Tone, volume, and rate of speed can be regulated to the assistant's own comfortable reception and rate of typing. A foot pedal switch is used for starting the machine and for reversing it. Another helpful item is an index counter, which makes it possible to locate a specific reference speedily and to indicate the length of a letter.

It is most important that the transcriber listen carefully for instructions and corrections. A good dictator will start out by explaining how many copies to make and stating preferences about setup and paragraphing.

If the transcriber is interrupted, the machine can be turned back to find the correct place for beginning again. The device that makes this possible is also useful in that dictation can be replayed.

The assistant's skill at spelling, knowledge of punctuation and capitalization, and familiarity with medical terminology will determine his or her efficiency in transcribing a doctor's dictation. On almost all machines, dictation can be erased and the recording material can be used over and over again. Plastic disks and belts cannot be reused, but it is often advisable to file them for later reference or to destroy them if that is office policy.

Project 28 Transcribing Correspondence

Transcribe a letter which Dr. Taylor has dictated to Dr. Monroe. (Your instructor will dictate the letter or provide you with the dictation material.) Use letterhead. Today is October 13.

Basic Reprographic Processes

It is sometimes necessary to make copies of certain papers—letters, bills, memorandums, announcements, or patients' histories. The assistant must determine which reprographic process to use for the duplication, or, when applicable, what duplicating equipment should be purchased for the office. Factors to consider in deciding which process to use or which machine to purchase include the quantity of copies needed, the quality of copy appearance, the time it takes to make copies, and the cost of duplication.

If the item is one that is being typed in the office, as many as 8 to 10 clear carbon copies can be made on a typewriter at one typing. This is a relatively inexpensive method to use—no additional equipment is needed and the copies can be made at the same time. However, only a limited number of carbon copies can be made at one time, and it may be time-consuming to correct the original and the carbons. The copy could be messy or even illegible if the assistant is not careful with erasures.

Other relatively inexpensive reprographic methods include stencil duplication and fluid (spirit) duplication. These two methods involve prepared masters that are mounted on drums of the appropriate machines. Reproduction can be multicolored. Anywhere from 11 to 300 copies can be made on the fluid duplicator, and 11 to 5000 copies can be made on the stencil duplicator. Various machines differ somewhat in their operation, but the principles are the same and they are easy to use. Masters are time-consuming to make but can be stored for reuse.

Offset duplicating equipment can inexpensively produce high-quality copies with full-color copy appearance. The number of copies that can be run on an offset depends on the type of duplicating master that is used: paper master, 50 to 1000 copies; plastic, 25,000; metal, 50,000 copies. Main draw-

Desk-top copier. *Courtesy 3M Company*

backs to offset duplication are the expense of the equipment and its complicated operation.

Photocopying machines can produce single-color or multicolor reproduction, depending on the type of copier. The cost per copy is a lot higher than costs of other reprographic processes for multiple copies but cheaper for one or two. No special master has to be prepared; the original copy or a copy itself can be used as the master. Photocopying equipment is relatively expensive but takes little training to operate.

PERSONAL DEVELOPMENT PROJECTS

TOPICS FOR DISCUSSION 1. Dr. Taylor is away on vacation. The following items arrive in the mail. Decide what must be done with each item.
  a. A letter marked "Personal."
  b. A request for a consultation on a patient.
  c. An electric bill.
  d. A check from a patient.

2. Decide how to send the following items in the mail:
  a. A four-pound box of candy to Dr. Taylor's grandmother in Chicago.
  b. A professional magazine.
  c. A set of surgical instruments weighing three pounds.
  d. A passport belonging to Dr. Taylor's son in New York City.

ROLE PLAYING 1. A secretary has asked you to photocopy correspondence from a doctor to a referring physician. While doing so, you notice a gross error in a letter.

2. You have learned the procedure for sorting, opening, and processing mail. The person presently doing this task doesn't follow the procedure, and thus spends twice the time to complete the task.

Simulation 1

Simulation 1 is the first of five simulations. These simulations will provide you with an opportunity to experience what it will be like to work in a doctor's office. You will discover how various tasks relate to each other. Your work will include making and canceling appointments, preparing medical forms, handling telephone communications, and following through on work left over from the previous day.

GENERAL PROCEDURES The following suggestions apply to all five simulations:
1. Review the contents of the chapters you have just finished to be sure you are familiar with all the procedures. You may refer to the text at any time during a simulation—just as in an office you would be free to use any reference source.
2. Prepare two folders—one labeled "Day 1," the other labeled "Day 2." Assemble the materials you will need; these are indicated in the specific directions for each simulation.
3. Set priorities each day—that is, organize your work in order of importance and complete it accordingly. Any work left over from the first day should be carried over to the second day and taken into account when new priorities are set for the second day. It is quite possible that you may have work left over at the end of the second day as well. The important thing is to make sure all the major tasks have been taken care of each day.
4. Be prepared for interruptions. These will occur frequently in the course of the simulation, just as they do in a doctor's office. No matter how carefully you plan your work, these interruptions will play havoc with your schedule. Do not let interruptions upset you, but rearrange your priorities accordingly.
5. Remember that on the job you will develop shortcuts, easier procedures, and better ways of doing certain things. Try to develop such improvements now.
6. Be sure your initials and the current date appear on each piece of material.

SPECIFIC PROCEDURES

Day 1 (Tuesday, October 14)
1. The simulation begins when the tape recorder is started. You will hear telephone conversations between the assistant and the answering service, the patients, and other callers. (You are

taking the place of Janet Owen, medical assistant for Dr. Warren Taylor.) You will hear the voice of Dr. Taylor giving you directions and dictation, and you will also hear the voices of patients as they enter, make appointments for rechecks, and so forth. (You will not hear the voices of all the patients, only those who ask you to do something.) Make appropriate notes as you listen.

2. On the basis of the material you have received, make a list of all the things you have to do, set priorities, and go to work. The doctor may give new directions; there may be additional telephone calls.

3. At the end of the first day, put all the completed work in the Day 1 folder. Using the checklist which your instructor will give you at the end of the period, check off the items you are enclosing and submit these with the Day 1 folder to your instructor. Transfer all unfinished work to the Day 2 folder.

Day 2 (Wednesday, October 15)

1. Go through the same procedure as in Day 1. In planning your work for Day 2, remember that some of the new things that occur may be more important than work left over from Day 1. Use good judgment in setting priorities.

2. At the end of Day 2, turn in all completed work. On the checklist indicate the work you are submitting by checking the appropriate boxes.

MATERIALS YOU WILL NEED The following materials will be needed to complete assignments in Simulation 1. If they are not already in the proper folders, obtain them from the sources indicated.

Appointment Book

Card File

Supplies Folder	Source
Telephone message blanks	WP 141–153
Appointment cards	WP 189
Records release forms	WP 153
Letterheads	You provide
Notepad	You provide
Plain paper	You provide
Index cards	You provide

Day 1 Folder

Rough draft letter to Dr. Anderson	WP 31

Day 2 Folder

Curtiss, Lois—house call slip	WP 155

Patients' Charts

The following patients' charts (folders) should contain the items given below:

Bachman, Joseph
Clinical data sheet	WP 25
Letter to Dr. Gonzalez	Project 15

Patients' Charts	Source
Bachmann, Paul	
Clinical data sheet	Project 25
House call slip	Project 12
Goldberg, Ellen	
Clinical data sheet	Project 25
Message	Project 17
Wellman, Marion	
Clinical data sheet	Project 25
Appointment card	Project 11
The following patients' folders should contain partially completed clinical data sheets	Project 25

Berndt, Stanley
Berquist, Rebecca
Curtiss, Lois
Grazzini, Mario
Grebowski, Paul
Grimes, Jill
Kellogg, Alice
Knutson, Karen
Leslie, Sheila
Logan, Carl
Malinsky, William
McKinley, Sharon
Provost, Janis
Stephens, Jason

Miscellaneous Folder

Letters: Dr. Scott McIntosh	Project 10
Dr. Louise Merryweather	Project 27
Dr. Milton Monroe	Project 28
Patient introduction slip for Jane Burnett	Project 13

If you have not completed all the projects and do not have all these records set up in advance, talk with your instructor.

EVALUATION You will be evaluated on the following basis:

1. In terms of the work you completed each day and the work you did not have time to do, did you use good judgment? Did you at least get the most important things accomplished?

2. In terms of all the work you completed, is it of good quality? Is it accurate and neat?

3. In terms of all the work you completed, does it represent a reasonable amount of work? Would a doctor be satisfied with your rate of accomplishment?

Remember: It is not likely that you will have completed all the work that comes in on Days 1 and 2. What counts most is (1) good judgment in establishing priorities, (2) good quality in the work you actually do, and (3) a reasonable quantity of work produced.

3
Patient Records

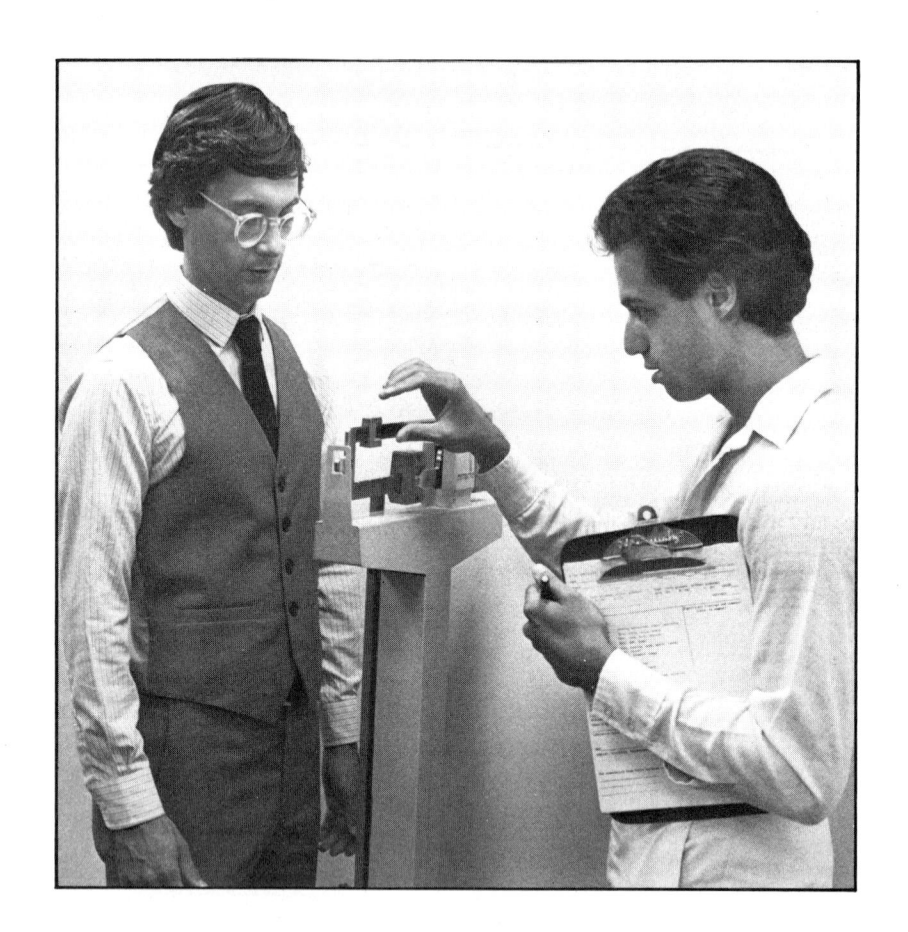

9

Preparing Medical Records

In the doctor's office, as in every other business and professional office, records of many types are needed. In a physician's office these papers are divided into two main categories: medical records of the patient's state of health, and business papers that consist of financial records and other documents necessary to the management of the doctor's office. The patient's medical record will be the topic of this chapter. Hospital records will be discussed in a separate chapter.

THE MEDICAL RECORD

Patients' records have been found among the earliest writings of Egypt and India, but until modern times no effort was made to keep such data in any systematic way. With the development of research and experimentation, patients' histories have taken on new importance. Every up-to-date hospital has a library devoted exclusively to patients' records, with an extensive index system under the supervision of a record librarian. Private physicians turn to one of the many systems devised to record and to file efficiently the medical data of their patients. These records are of the greatest importance to the doctor, not only while the patient is under treatment, but also if the patient returns after a number of years, as often happens. A patient's chart is the accumulation of data pertaining to that patient. It may include the history and physical examination, notes made by the doctor or nurse, laboratory and X-ray reports, special procedure reports, correspondence, and hospitalization summaries. The chart is used as a basis for planning care of the patient, as evidence of the course of the illness, as a record of treatment being used, and as an evaluation of medical care. Medical records have great statistical value as well—in evaluating a certain type of treatment or for ascertaining the incidence of a particular disease—or they may be used as the basis for preparing a lecture, an article, or a book. Patients' records may have to be produced in court, either to uphold the rights of the doctor if the doctor is involved in litigation or to substantiate the claim of the patient if the doctor is called as a witness.

When a doctor sees a patient for the first time, he or she obtains information necessary for diagnosing the case, prescribing treatment, and forming an opinion as to the chances for recovery. The doctor may write directly on the clinical data sheet, or the assistant may type the doctor's notes.

Content

Headings in records will vary slightly, but the basic content remains the same. A record usually begins by stating the reason the patient is seeking the physician's advice. This reason is sometimes stated as a symptom and is known as the *chief complaint*.

Information given by the patient is recorded under the heading *Subjective* and may include any or all of the next subheadings.

The *present illness* is an exact description of symptoms troubling the patient, the time when the symptoms were first noted, the patient's opinion as to the cause and possible influence by any external factor, any remedies the patient may have tried pertaining to the illness, and any medical treatment the patient may already have had.

Martin Bough/Studios, Inc.

The Health Insurance Plan of Greater New York/A. Robbins

The *past medical history* includes any illnesses the patient may have had in the past and treatments administered; any operations, accidents or injuries; any physical defects, congenital or acquired; any allergies to medications or other materials; and information about the person's habits.

The *family history* consists of facts about the health of the patient's parents, siblings, and other blood relatives. Such facts might be significant to the patient's condition and are especially important in all diseases in which heredity plays a part.

The *social and marital history* is included, if pertinent. Items such as eating, drinking, and smoking habits; occupation; and interests and hobbies may be questioned.

The doctor's examination comes under the heading *Objective*. A complete physical examination record is very detailed.

Results of the doctor's examination are incorporated in the *clinical data sheet*. Interpretations of the subjective and objective factors, plus any tests or X rays performed, are recorded under the heading *Assessment*. The disease or condition from which the patient is suffering is given a name, referred to as a *diagnosis,* which could be the assessment. Sometimes this is only tentative, pending further developments.

Under the heading *Plan* are listed special tests that need to be performed, medications prescribed, instructions given, and any notations about rechecks. Medications ordered are entered in detail with the name and strength of the medication, as well as the amount ordered.

Whenever an additional medication is prescribed, or the treatment is in any way changed, this notation is entered in the patient's chart, together with the date. If hospitalization, an operation, or bed rest at home are indicated, this is also included.

The patient's *prognosis*—the opinion of what the outcome of the illness will be; that is, the patient's chances of improvement or cure—is an important part of the record. This is often expressed simply as "good," "fair," or "poor."

After each visit, the doctor's observations—the *progress report*—are recorded in the patient's chart. Improvement or aggravation of the patient's condition, any change in treatment or medication, and the patient's own report about the condition, if relevant, are recorded. Each visit is, of course, dated.

When the patient is discharged—meaning the course of treatment has been completed—the date is entered on the chart, together with a final statement about the health at the time of discharge. Should the patient die, a statement describing the cause of death is entered in the patient's chart.

CHAPTER 9: PREPARING MEDICAL RECORDS   79

Obtaining Clinical Data Frequently, the medical assistant is delegated the task of obtaining data describing the patient's present complaint. Care must be taken to avoid asking personal questions in the presence of other patients, relatives, or friends accompanying the patient.

It is important not to overlook essential details. For instance, if a patient complains about pain in the arm, the assistant will need to ask which arm, how long the pain has been present, and the kind of pain. The assistant will gradually learn what pertinent questions to ask the patient. The following are examples of questions that might be asked if they are relevant to the complaints of the patient:

> When did you first notice this problem?
>
> Were the symptoms steady or at intervals?
>
> Is there pain? What kind—sharp, dull, soreness?
>
> Is the pain constant or brought on by moving?
>
> Where exactly is the pain?
>
> Do you have thirst, vomiting, dizziness, loss of appetite?
>
> Do you have diarrhea or constipation?
>
> Is there frequency or urgency of urination? Is is difficult? Does it burn?
>
> Did you take any medicine for the trouble or apply any treatments?
>
> Did you consult another physician?
>
> Have you had this or a similar condition before?

If the medical assistant performs some of the routine procedures, these are usually completed before the doctor examines the patient. The approved methods for taking pulse, respiration, temperature, blood pressure, and routine tests are given in a later chapter of this book.

Forms Many different types of printed forms are available for keeping patients' records. A physician who acts chiefly in the capacity of a consultant and would be unlikely to see the same patient again, may use a large card rather than an individual folder. An illustration of such a card appears below. Specialists may have their own forms printed to fit their specialty. The trend is generally toward using a letter-size form, which is filed in the patient's folder, together with all other material relating to the patient.

A completed form for a general practitioner may show small zeros placed after some of the questions. (An illustration of such a form is shown below.) These stand for *negative*, meaning there is nothing to report. A reaction or a symptom which shows that disease is present is called *positive*. The word *normal* usually means average. Sometimes illustrations are on the charts for the doctor's use to indicate the exact spot where a pathological condition was found.

Courtesy SCM Histacount Corporation

Project 29
Preparing Medical Records For Obstetric Patients

Dr. Taylor uses a special chart form for obstetric (OB) patients. He has started an OB chart for Mrs. Burnett on WP 33. Use this working paper and type in the following information: This was a complete physical. Family history: Mother, father, brother, living and well; sister died of tuberculosis at age 23. Personal history: Patient married two years. Present ailment: Nausea, vomiting, feeling tired for 3 to 4 weeks. Menses began at age 14, every 28 days for 3 to 4 days' duration. Last period was August 30. Remarks: Diagnosis is pregnancy of 6 weeks' duration; return for routine prenatal care. Laboratory: Plan is for blood type, antibody screening, rubella titer, RBC, WBC, Hgb, Pregnosticon. (When additional clinical data for Mrs. Burnett is given to you, type it on the back of this form.)

Clinical Data Sheets Clinical data sheets contain all the information necessary for diagnosing the case and prescribing treatment. When the problem-oriented medical record (POMR) format is used, there may be a special form on which the doctor lists each individual *problem* (complaint or symptom). This "problem list" is a continuing list and is referred to at each clinic visit. The doctor can, at a

CHAPTER 9: PREPARING MEDICAL RECORDS   81

glance, learn what problems the patient has had, how often, and the treatment prescribed. This list saves time, in that the entire clinical data sheet does not have to be studied before obtaining the same information. (On the clinical data sheet, subheads would be indented. Abbreviations may be used for major heads.)

Notice the correlation between the problem list and the notation on the patient's clinical data sheet in the illustration.

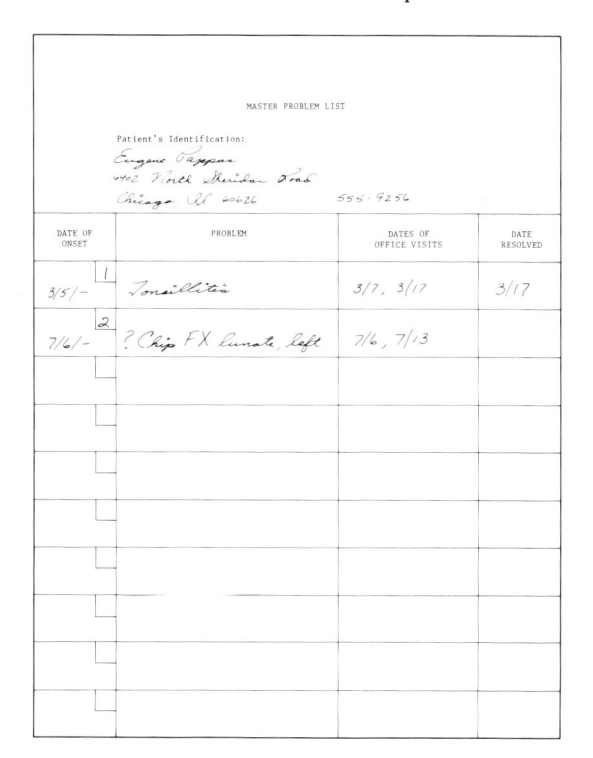

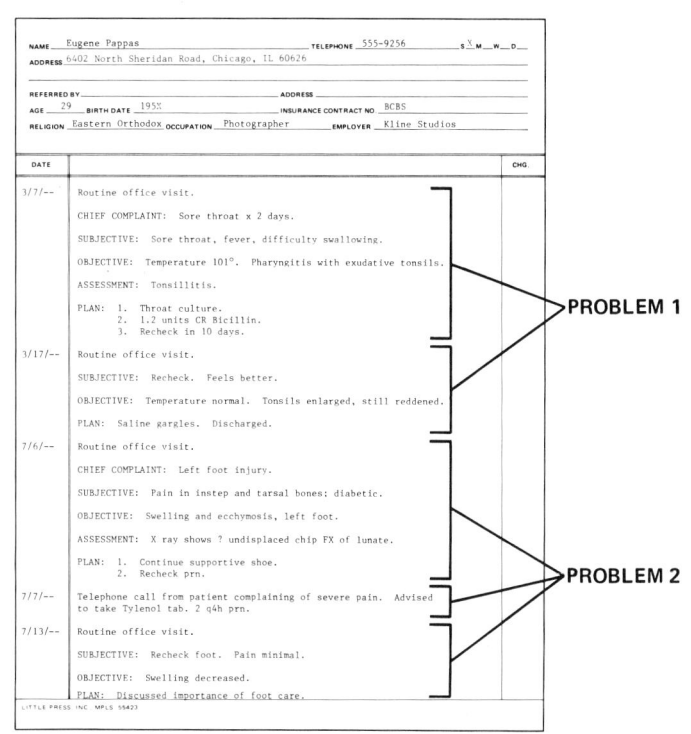

Courtesy Little Press, Inc.

Whether the doctor writes directly on the clinical data sheet or the notes are typed from the doctor's dictation, the arrangement should be clear and readable. Headings should be displayed and set off from the rest of the text. Different doctors will of course use their own method, and headings will vary according to what is the easiest way to assess the patient's problem or treatment.

Project 30
Completing Clinical Data Sheets

Today is Friday, October 17. Dr. Taylor has the afternoon off, which gives you time to take care of any pending work.

Dr. Taylor had written notes on Jason Stephens, Marion Wellman, and Ellen Goldberg after examining them. He asked you to prepare clinical data sheets for them, using the POMR method. Notice that Dr. Taylor does not use the problem list. You are to type the information exactly as given by Dr. Taylor. The notes are on WP 35 and WP 37.

Project 31
Transferring Information to Clinical Data Sheets

Dr. Taylor also asks you to transfer the information from the house call slips for Lois Curtiss and Paul Bachmann to their clinical data sheets using the POMR method.

Project 32
Preparing Clinical Data Sheets From Dictation

Today is October 20. Dr. Taylor calls you into his office for dictation. (You will need the information on WP 39 and 41; your instructor will provide the dictation.)

MEDICAL REPORTS In addition to the history, reports of tests and examinations are kept in the patient's file folder, except X rays, which usually are too large for standard manila folders. Special X-ray envelopes to fit the films are available, and these are filed in cabinets specially designed for that purpose. If the patient is sent to a radiologist for X rays, the latter keeps the films and sends only a report of the findings to the referring doctor.

Types of Reports The kind and number of medical reports depend on the patient's condition and the specialty of the attending physician. They include the types listed on the facing page.

CHAPTER 9: PREPARING MEDICAL RECORDS

☐ **Biopsy Report.** A biopsy is made for diagnostic purposes. The specimen is examined by a pathologist in a laboratory. Those results are sent to the referring doctor and then filed in the patient's chart.

☐ **Electrocardiogram.** This is a tracing of the heart activity. The entire tracing may be folded and retained in the chart, but that is cumbersome. Usually the tracing is cut into sections which are then mounted on a special chart form. The physician may write directly on that form or may dictate notes to be added to the clinical data sheet. The physician may request a specialized recording. Echocardiography is the graphic recording of ultrasound waves from the heart. The Holter monitoring test is a 24-hour continuous ECG of an ambulatory high-risk patient. Both tests are performed by a specialist. The dictated report and a copy of the ECG are sent to the referring physician and filed in the patient's chart.

☐ **Immunization Records.** These are permanent records on which each immunization for polio, diphtheria, pertussis, measles, and so forth, is entered each year. This record is sometimes found stamped to the inside of the patient's file folder. It is the assistant's duty to follow up any tests that have been ordered, make sure the report is received and seen by the doctor, and see that the results are entered in the chart.

Many schools require inoculations in order for students to enroll. The assistant will be responsible for preparing the notice for the school.

☐ **Laboratory Findings.** Results of laboratory tests may be written directly onto the clinical data sheet, or a special laboratory report may be sent from the laboratory to be inserted into the patient's chart. This applies to laboratory tests done in the clinic, in a special laboratory, or in the hospital. Reports are always given to the doctor, and then they are filed in the patient's folder.

Project 33
Entering Reports

You have received the opposite message from the laboratory and given it to Dr. Taylor. Dr. Taylor asks you to transfer the information to each patient's clinical data sheet. From now on, when you receive a laboratory report, enter the results on the patient's clinical data sheet and give the report to Dr. Taylor. (If the clinical data sheet takes more than one page, use plain paper for the second and all subsequent pages.)

TELEPHONE MESSAGE

To: Dr. Taylor

You Received a Call From:
Lab

Phone No. _____ Ext. _____
☐ Please Phone   ☐ Will Call Again

Alice Kellogg — UA, 100-150 WBC, few bacteria, moderate epithelial.

Sheila Leslie — Monospot, negative; throat culture, negative; WBC-10,500/cu. mm.

Jane Burnett — RBC-4,500,000/cu. mm. WBC-8,400/cu. mm; Hgb, 13.6 gm; Pregnosticon, positive.

TAKEN BY: J.O.   DATE: 10/15   TIME: 2:15

84 PART 3: PATIENT RECORDS

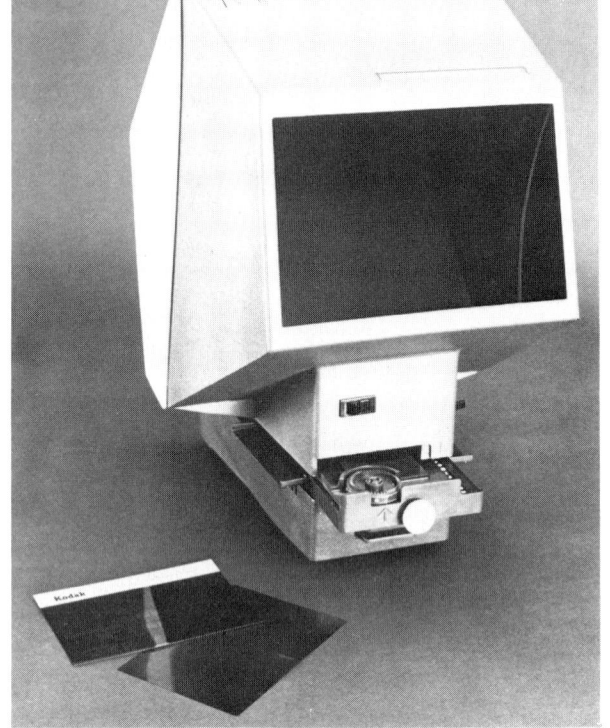

Martin Bough/Studios, Inc.

Courtesy Eastman Kodak Company

Protecting and Preserving Records

The patient's records—medical histories, laboratory or X-ray reports—are the property of the doctor and must not be given or shown to anyone without due authorization by the patient. However, they may be lent to a consultant who then assumes responsibility for them.

If a doctor wishes to keep records permanently, microfilming is a great space saver. The medical history may be useful later if a son or daughter consults the physician for a similar problem. All records should be kept until the possibility of a malpractice suit has passed. This depends on each individual state's statute of limitations.

PERSONAL DEVELOPMENT PROJECTS

TOPICS FOR DISCUSSION 1. Now that you know the contents of a patient's chart, discuss the importance of confidentiality, accuracy, and protection from loss even after a patient has been discharged.

2. Using a medical reference, explain these abbreviations:

| CC | PMH | MH |
| PI | FH | ROS |

TPR	DTR	Dx
LKS	LLQ	LMP
GI	ECG (or EKG)	H & P
GU	N & V	PE
CV	R/O	HEENT
ht.	VS	BP
wt.	PERLA	

ROLE PLAYING 1. Dr. Taylor has recorded some dictation. While transcribing it, you are unable to hear clearly the "plan" he dictated.

2. You have just finished typing the clinical data sheet for Rebecca Berquist when she telephones. She wants to know the results of her last visit. The doctor is out of the office and will not be back for three days.

10

Billing the Patient

One of the most important tasks of the assistant is to collect patients' fees and maintain the doctor's books. It is, therefore, necessary to know the amount the doctor charges for various procedures, how to discuss fees with patients, how to handle cash payments, and how to itemize bills.

Patients' accounts are handled differently from office to office, in accordance with the needs of each doctor's practice. A newly employed assistant should be informed immediately of the doctor's billing system. If the system does not seem practical, another method should be suggested, but the doctor must agree to any change in the system of handling patients' accounts. What has proved to be the best way in one office may be seriously wrong in another. Financial arrangements made by surgeons would not apply to a practice limited to office visits. Only general rules can be given. The doctor will usually allow the patient to pay in whatever possible manner, either in cash or by check.

DETERMINING THE FEE The subject of the doctor's fee should be handled with special attention and with a thorough understanding of the various problems that could be encountered. The doctor has to determine fees that are fair to the community and the profession. A doctor can check with the local medical society and other doctors in the community when establishing fees for a new practice. Each doctor must take into consideration the average prevailing rate in the area.

Fee Schedules A doctor may develop a fee schedule, which lists any procedures that the doctor performs and the cost for each procedure. This fee schedule is handy in determining the total cost for each patient's visit. It should be posted where it is easily accessible for both the doctor and the assistant. The doctor can also adjust the cost of any procedure when the need arises. Some insurance companies have established fee schedules that state how much they will cover for each given procedure.

Project 34
Typing a Fee Schedule

Dr. Taylor has composed a rough draft of a fee schedule (WP 43). Organize and type the fee schedule. Keep this schedule in your folder and use it to determine fees for performed procedures.

Discussion of the Fee Many misunderstandings develop and much dissatisfaction exists in the matter of the doctor's fees unless it is properly discussed in the beginning. Bad feelings can be prevented and collections are more easily made if the patient is told at the start of the treatment what the approximate cost will be and how payments can be arranged. The doctor, the assistant, or both of them together can discuss fees with the patient.

If the doctor alone settles the question of the fee with the patient, the assistant should keep an account of the patient's visits and attend to collection of the bill and, if necessary, make financial arrangements. The assistant must know the doctor's wishes regarding any financial arrangements: what the charges are, under what circumstances a reduction of the fee is possible, what the acceptable minimum fee is, and any other facts needed in order to deal efficiently with the problem of patients' payments. The better the assistant can handle financial matters, the more pleased the doctor will be.

It may be necessary for the assistant to explain why the fee is as high as it is, calling attention to the time involved, the cost of drugs administered, and, above all, the skill, knowledge, and experience of the doctor.

Most doctors have a fixed fee for home or office visits and for definite procedures (such as minor or major operations), but in some cases doctors' fees are adjusted to the financial status of the patient. An assistant should exercise good judgment about a person's ability and willingness to pay bills without having to bother the doctor. This must be learned from practice on the basis of an understanding of human nature and an ability to handle people. A book can serve only as a guide.

Patients who call to make a first appointment frequently inquire about the doctor's fee. The patient may be told that it is difficult to discuss such matters over the telephone, because the doctor will have to judge first what sort of examination or treatment is indicated. Another answer might be that it is impossible to state a definite fee without seeing the patient and determining the reason for the visit.

If the doctor does not wish the assistant to state a fixed fee over the telephone, this question must be dealt with tactfully. It is a fair assumption that a patient who inquires beforehand how much it will cost is concerned about the price and should be shown every consideration. If a definite amount is quoted and this seems to worry the patient, the assistant can reassure the patient by saying that arrangements can be made to facilitate payment.

When only small charges for office visits are involved, discussion of the fee is less likely to occur. Operations and maternity cases, on the other hand, are practically always discussed in advance and the fee agreed upon. In discussing the fee with the patient, it is important to point out exactly what the fee covers. Some obstetricians, for instance, include one postnatal visit, but no more. Some surgeons include all postoperative care, whether at home or in the office; others include office visits only.

Project 35
Composing a Letter Quoting Fees

Mrs. Burnett requests a letter quoting Dr. Taylor's fees for obstetrical care. Dr. Taylor's fees are explained on his fee schedule. Prepare the letter and an envelope. Date the letter October 20.

ARRANGING FOR PAYMENT

Many doctors like to have the assistant arrange the method of payment on a patient's first visit. Weekly payments are especially advisable for persons who are paid by the week if the treatment may extend over a long time or if the patient cannot pay the whole fee before termination of treatment.

In surgical cases, or whenever the cost of the entire treatment is set in advance (for a course of injections, for instance) and involves a considerable sum, the patient may not be able to pay the fee at once and might have to seek financial assistance. The assistant should be acquainted with the facilities in the locality to which a patient can be referred when financial assistance is needed.

There are several different ways in which patients' accounts are handled:

  Patients pay cash, that is, money or its equivalent.
  Bills are sent out monthly or at the end of the procedure.
  Health insurance covers a given amount.
  Patients pay a fixed amount weekly or monthly, regardless of charges incurred in that week or month.

Some doctors may use only one system in the office. For instance, some doctors work on a cash basis only, but in most offices different methods will be used, according to the preference of each patient; and the same patient may want to settle an account in different ways, according to the cost of the treatment involved. Any system of accounting, therefore, must be elastic enough to make it possible to handle each account.

Cash Payments

The assistant must be careful to enter each cash payment both in the patient's ledger (which is a record of charges, payments, and balances) and in the daily journal. The daily journal records daily fees charged and payments received. It should contain space for the patient's name, the cost of medical service, and the amount of cash received. It is preferable that the patient make cash payment to the assistant, not the doctor. The doctor may forget to make a record of the payment. A receipt must be given to the patient who pays cash. Carbon copies of receipts are permanent records, and the entries on the patient's account can be made from them.

The patient should be advised to keep the receipt for income tax purposes. These receipts will form the basis for claim deductions for medical expenses. If the patient is given a prescription, the prescription number, the name of the medicine (if possible), and the cost may also be written on the back of this receipt for the same purpose. If the patient pays by check, the canceled check will be the receipt.

Certain rules must be observed to safeguard money received. Cash, checks, and money orders should be kept in a locked metal box or drawer. Currency should be separated by denominations. Checks should be endorsed with a restrictive endorsement immediately (see Chapter 12 for a discussion of the different types of endorsements). To minimize the danger of theft, money received should be deposited in the bank daily. The total deposit should equal the amount in the bank book.

Sending Bills

Although most bills are sent out once a month, a patient's bill may be sent at the end of the procedure, or, occasionally, a doctor will send a statement immediately after the visit. It is more efficient to send out bills monthly so that the doctor's bill will be paid along with the patient's other bills. In large practices, however, cycle billing may be advantageous. Under this system, all accounts are divided alphabetically into groups, with each group being sent on a different date. If this system is used, the patient should be told on the first visit approximately when the bill will be mailed out. A definite pattern for sending bills should be established and adhered to.

A patient may request that the assistant not send any bills or other correspondence to the home or business addresses. A notation to this effect should be made on the patient's ledger card and index cards so this request will not be overlooked.

Health Insurance

Today the large majority of patients carry some sort of health insurance that provides payment of medical expenses. Such health insurance may be a commercial insurance policy, a nonprofit plan such as Blue Cross–Blue Shield, or a government insurance policy. The details and the assistant's responsibilities in this area will be discussed in Chapter 11. At any rate, ask a new patient who has health insurance to show you the membership card to ascertain what type of insurance it is and whether the contract is in force. This information must be entered in the patient's clinical data sheet.

Fee Adjustments

Every doctor may have many patients who are not charged for services. Medical etiquette prescribes that physicians treat colleagues and their immediate families free of charge. If a doctor's spouse or relative, or a nurse, who is also treated free of charge, asks for a bill, it is perfectly proper to send one. This should not be done without such a request, and the bill should be marked "By Request."

Since the advent of health insurance, this rule has been somewhat relaxed. Doctors carry medical health insurance, which pays for their medical expenses. As a result of this development, doctors have started to charge each other for various services, and especially for materials used (injection medication, X-ray films, laboratory materials). Just what amount to charge another physician or which members of the family are to be given professional courtesy is something the doctor must decide in each case. The doctor's staff and members of the clergy may also be treated free of charge, or the doctor may allow a professional discount.

Patients who are not able to pay the doctor's fee may be referred to a free clinic. The assistant should be familiar with free medical and professional services in the area. It is best to ask the doctor whether to refer a patient to a free medical service.

A doctor must be careful in the decision to reduce or cancel a fee; for example, for a patient who cannot pay or for services to a patient who dies. This decision to reduce or cancel a fee may be misinterpreted and, therefore, may lead to a malpractice suit. If a doctor does decide to reduce or cancel a fee, it must be in writing in order to protect the doctor.

Patient Credit Information

Arranging a method of payment does not ensure the doctor's collection of the fee. Doctors sustain losses from rendering services to patients who turn out to be bad credit risks. Each doctor, therefore, should take precautions to ensure collections.

What precautions can a doctor take? First of all, the assistant should get as much information about a new patient as possible. The patient's address, occupation, business affiliation, business address, and telephone number must be ascertained. It is also important to record the name of the person who referred the patient. A person's credit standing is also indicated by bank references and charge accounts. If the doctor's fee is likely to be a large one and the patient is not known to the doctor, these data should be a part of the information obtained on the first visit.

Handling credit arrangements should be done tactfully and in a routine manner. Doctors are entitled to payment for their services, just as any other professional or business person is. If the matter is presented to the patient in the right spirit, no fair-minded patient will object. It is important, however, that the amount of the fee be agreed upon and that it be clearly understood what this fee covers.

Third-Party Liability

If a person other than the patient assumes responsibility for the bill, this information should be obtained. Frequently relatives, particularly children of aged parents, say they will be responsible for payment of the doctor's bill; but in many of these cases, it is later found that the bill cannot be collected because the promise to pay was not in writing. Oral promises are not legally binding. Once the patient is well, the relatives may forget the obligation to pay. A signed promise will greatly reduce the credit risk. A third party is not obligated by law unless the signature has been obtained, denoting responsibility.

RECORDING TRANSACTIONS

The doctor, no doubt, gets great satisfaction when the patient becomes well through medical skill and knowledge. But if a doctor is to earn a living from the practice, services must be paid for, and to collect bills it is necessary to keep a careful record of accounts. No worker in any other profession or business goes without payment for services rendered as often as does a doctor; a doctor cannot shut off the service as a utility company can when bills go unpaid. The responsibility of keeping proper patients' accounts is the assistant's.

Whenever a patient consults the doctor, there is a charge, but not necessarily a payment. It is, therefore, necessary to keep track of all charges that the patient incurs for consultation or for any other services—X rays, laboratory tests, physical therapy treatments—and of any payments the patient has made, on account or in full.

The doctor's charges represent the *earnings*, whereas *income* is determined by payments received from patients. The two must be clearly distinguished, for income tax is paid on income only, not on earnings.

Every time a patient visits the office, the amount of the charge incurred is entered in the daily journal (see p. 112) unless the doctor has made arrangements for the patient to pay one amount for the entire course of treatment or for an operation. As the patient pays, the entry is made on the record. All ledger cards (see p. 91) should be brought up to date at the end of the day or the following morning. It is advisable to set aside a definite time for this task. Also, the assistant must check with the doctor to see if additional charges, such as home visits, should be entered on the accounts.

Jane Hamilton-Merritt

PART 3: PATIENT RECORDS

Charge Slips An efficient method of keeping track of the doctor's charges is by the use of charge slips. These steps are followed when using a charge slip:

1. The assistant clips the slip to the patient's folder.
2. The doctor indicates the services rendered and the fee charged (unless the assistant knows the fee for each service). The patient then gives the slip to the assistant (who may indicate the charge).
3. The assistant tactfully suggests that the patient might want to pay in cash. (The charge slip is a known incentive to pay immediately.)
4. At the end of the day, the amount on the slip is recorded onto the patient's account.

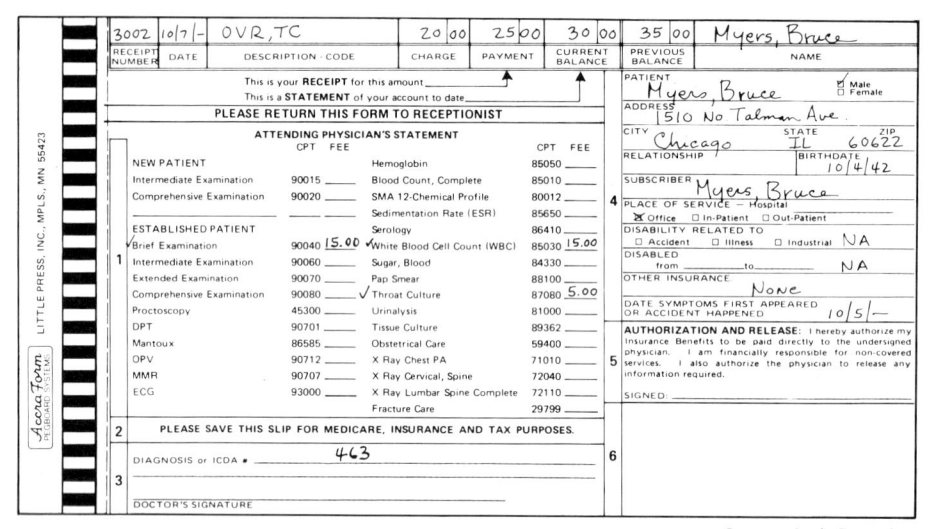

Courtesy Little Press, Inc.

Printed charge slips similar to the one illustrated above may be obtained from any medical stationer. They save time, since the doctor needs only to check each item performed. Some doctors have their own charge slips printed with additional headings; they may also desire to have their regular charges for each service added to these slips.

A charge slip may be used to refer a patient to another doctor for treatment or for tests, or to a surgical supply house for medical supplies. If the doctor has indicated such a referral, the assistant must give the patient the name, address, and telephone number of the person or place to contact.

Superbills Many medical stationers sell an item generally referred to as a "superbill." This bill contains blanks for the following information: a checklist of procedures that the doctor performs, along with proper codes for the procedures; patient's charge, payment, and balance of the account; space for the patient's signature to allow direct payment from the insurance company to the attending physician; the patient's insurance information; and the doctor's name and address. This item in triplicate provides for accurate billing; the original copy stays with the doctor, one copy is sent to the insurance company or other responsible third party, and the last copy is for the patient.

Patient's Ledger The patient's ledger is a record that shows charges, payments, and balances owed by each patient. All such fees and payments for professional services are posted daily to the patient's ledger and extended so that each account is always current. There are many forms of patients' ledgers: index cards filed in boxes, on wheels, or in visible sliding trays; loose-leaf or bound books; and individual ledger sheets in post binders. Some printed forms for patients'

		WARREN TAYLOR, M.D.			1 Alison
TELEPHONE 312-555-6022		2235 SOUTH RIDGEWAY AVENUE CHICAGO, IL 60623			2 George 3 4 5

Mr. George Ganders
13495 South School Avenue
Chicago, IL 60627

LITTLE PRESS, INC., MPLS. 55423

NO	DATE	DESCRIPTION — CODE	CHARGE	PAYMENT	CURRENT BALANCE
		Previous Balance			50 00
2	8/21	OVR	15 00	–0–	65 00
	8/28	ROA		50 00	15 00
2	9/3	OVR	15 00	30 00	–0–
1	9/15	OVE	20 00	–0–	20 00
1	9/15	ECG	45 00	–0–	65 00

PLEASE PAY LAST FIGURE IN THIS COLUMN ←

BP—Blood Pressure
BS—Blood Sugar
CON—Consultation
CP—Complete Physical Exam
ECG—Electrocardiogram
ER—Emergency Room Call
HC—House Call
HV—Hospital Visit

HGB—Hemoglobin
INJ—Injection
IOA—Insurance on Account
LAB—Laboratory
MIS—Miscellaneous
OVB—Office Visit, Brief
OVE—Office Visit, Extended

OVR—Office Visit, Routine
PS—Pap Smear with Physical
PEPS—Pelvic Exam & Pap Smear
ROA—Rec'd on Account
SPE—Short Physical Exam
TC—Throat Culture
UA—Urinalysis-Chem. or Full

Courtesy Little Press, Inc.

histories provide space for charges and payments, as shown above. These forms may be posted by hand, typed, or prepared on a posting machine that produces a ledger record and monthly statement in one operation.

Itemized Bills   The trend today is definitely toward itemized bills instead of bills marked only "For professional services." Patients prefer to have a detailed account, and collections are speeded up when the bill is itemized. Patients are likely to forget how often they visited the doctor and what services were rendered. When their bills are itemized, they often realize that the charges are more reasonable than they expected.

An itemized bill should show a detailed list of all services rendered: doctor's house visits, night visits, office visits, injections, examination, laboratory tests, X rays, physical therapy, and any other special procedures. The charge slips mentioned above will prove their value, for not only has the patient seen what the different services cost, but the assistant can take the details from these slips for the records.

A popular method of itemizing bills is to have a billhead on which all the different services are listed in code. The code letters are entered opposite the charge, and the explanation of the code is printed at the bottom of the form, as illustrated here. The number in the upper right-hand corner indicates the family member receiving the services.

Many different forms are used for bills. All of them show the doctor's name and address.

Timesaving devices have been introduced to cut down the work of sending out monthly bills. The most popular one is the photocopy of the ledger card. One type consists of billheads printed on a continuous sheet. The bills are typed consecutively and later torn off along a perforated line, which separates the billheads from one another. Time will be saved if they are mailed in window envelopes, then it is not necessary to type the name and address on the envelope.

Another form is the self-mailer. The bill is typed on a form that becomes the return envelope when folded properly. The patient can enclose payment with the bill and mail both of them in the same envelope. The doctor who uses this type of mailer usually has a business reply mail permit and pays the postage when the envelope is returned.

Project 36
Preparing Patient Ledgers

Prepare ledger cards for each patient who has a folder, using the index cards. Use the ledger forms on WP 159-187.

The name and address of the person to be billed should be typed in the space provided at the top. The patient's name is also written in the upper right-hand corner. Note that sometimes the patient may be other than the person billed (and it is for this reason that Dr. Taylor has had special ledger cards made up). After examining the patients' records, Miss Owen has recorded the following information to update the patients' ledgers:

Joseph Bachman — previous balance $55.50; 10/1 OVE; 10/6 ROA $75.50.
Paul Bachmann—10/9 HC; 10/14 ER visit.
Stanley Berndt—previous balance $50.25; 10/15 OVR.
Rebecca Berquist—10/20 OVE.
Jane Burnett—10/14 CP; 10/15 LAB $40 charge.
Lois Curtiss—previous balance $15; 10/14 HC.
Ellen Goldberg—10/1 CP; ROA $25; 10/07 surgery-$1500, five HV; 10/20 OV-no charge; ROA $25.
Jill Grimes—previous balance $10; 10/14 OVR.
Gail Hayes—10/16 new patient OVB, cortisone injection-$8.50.
Alice Kellogg—previous balance $30; 10/14 OVR; LAB $15 charge.
Sheila Leslie—previous balance $85; 10/14 OVR; LAB $29 charge.
William Malinsky—previous balance $75; 10/3 ROA $75.
Janis Provost—previous balance $132; 10/7 ROA $100.
Jason Stephens—previous balance $125; 10/7, 10/14 fracture care-charge $225; 10/17 ROA $100.
Marion Wellman—previous balance $40.75; 10/6 ROA $40.75; 10/14 CP, penicillin injection-$8.50; sputum culture.
Martin Whitfall—10/16 new patient OVB; ROA $35.

Itemize the ledgers, using the fee schedule. Post the charges and payments daily to keep the accounts up to date. You may keep the ledger cards separately or file them in the patients' charts (folders).

Computerized Billing Many commercial systems of computerized billing are available for the medical practice. The system can be designed for each doctor's specialized practice. The following features are a few of the items that are available through a computerized billing system: daily reports, itemized patient statements, patient ledgers, monthly reports summarizing the operation of the practice, and insurance claim forms. The doctor must take into account the number of bills that will be sent, the cost of the operation, and the system's usefulness and efficiency with regard to the doctor's practice.

COLLECTING ACCOUNTS

It is a regrettable fact that patients are often slow and even delinquent in paying doctors' bills. There are various reasons why a patient might not pay the bills. The patient may unintentionally or intentionally ignore a bill; the patient may not have any money to pay the bill; or he or she may be unwilling to pay the bill for some reason, such as disagreement with the amount of the bill.

The assistant must know how to properly handle patients' accounts to cut down losses from unpaid bills. The first step is to watch each account. Payments, in full or in part, must be entered in the patient's ledger, so that at billing time there is no question about any balance due. Each month delinquent accounts should be "aged" to show the status of each account in the collection process.

Customs vary on how many reminders (notes reminding the patient that money is owed to the doctor) should be sent and how to send them out; some doctors attach reminders directly to the bill (for example, a sticker saying that the bill is three months overdue); others may send such reminders separately.

Collection by Letter

The longer a bill remains unpaid, the less likelihood there is of collecting it. A bill should be followed up more vigorously after three months. A letter over the assistant's signature should be sent. If this is unanswered, additional letters of greater urgency are sent. The doctor should establish a set system of collection follow-up that will determine when to send out statements, reminders, and letters.

Writing collection letters that bring results is an art, and many articles on the subject have appeared in professional journals. A collection letter should be personal, not a form letter. The letter should show that you are interested in the patient's problem and want to work out a solution; it should be brief with short sentences; it should appeal to the patient's sense of pride, fair play, and desire for a good credit rating; the amount due should be stated; and it should ask the patient to telephone you. Below are examples of collection letters that have proved effective:

Dear Mr. Jones:

After reviewing our accounts, I find that your bill of $35.50 for an office call and a blood test is two months overdue.

Is there some reason why we have not heard from you?

Please contact our office immediately or send in your check for $35.50 today.

Sincerely,
Medical Assistant

Dear Mrs. Walters:

It is unlike you to let your account of $140.20 remain unpaid. Payment is now four months overdue, and yet we have not heard from you.

It is our policy to give patients every opportunity to pay their bills; but it is also our policy to turn accounts over to our collection agency if the account is six months overdue.

Therefore, we must have payment from you by May 1.

Send in your check today, or contact our office immediately and credit arrangements can be made.

Sincerely,
Medical Assistant

Project 37
Writing a Collection Letter

After checking your ledgers, you find that Mr. Berndt has not paid his bill for three months. Write a letter over your own signature requesting payment. Use letterhead. Today is October 20.

Collection by Telephone

One way to effect collections is for the assistant to telephone the patient. Tact and experience are necessary to obtain results. Also, as most patients are out during the day, evening is the best time to make these calls. Never call a patient at a place of business to inquire about an unpaid bill.

When you call the patient, your manner should be pleasant, reflecting your confidence that the problem can be solved. Ask to discuss the bill to determine whether any questions exist on the patient's part. This should elicit some response, which is your cue to the rest of the conversation. The patient may either plead hardship or launch into complaints. Listen carefully and say that you will discuss the matter with the doctor. Never show irritation in your voice or appear to be scolding the patient. You simply want to find out why the patient has not paid or answered the collection inquires. If the patient promises to pay, ask when you can expect the check. Then make a note of the conversation.

Some management consultants advise strongly against the telephone technique. The doctor will decide whether you are to use it.

Collection by Agencies

If the patient has not paid the bill after a reasonable time, the doctor has two ways of attempting collection. The doctor can sue the patient and go to court. This is a time-consuming and costly procedure. The other method is to use a collection agency. When to turn a delinquent account over to an agency is up to the doctor. Approximately 40 to 50 percent of the amount due will be lost when the account is turned over.

There are various types of collection agencies, and a doctor should thoroughly investigate a collection agency to determine the agency's reputation. The doctor can check with the local medical society, the local Better Business Bureau, and other doctors in the area to help in the investigation. Once an account has been turned over for collection, there is no further contact with the patient concerning billing.

Collection from Estates

When a patient has died, a bill should be sent to the estate after a short interval. Contact the probate department of the local government if you need the name and address of the person responsible for the patient's debts. It is wise to keep records of deceased patients long enough to be sure there will be no malpractice suit or other legal complications.

Statute of Limitations

If the doctor fails to collect a fee within a certain time, under the statute of limitations it becomes outlawed and no further claim is possible. Each state sets its own time limitation.

PERSONAL DEVELOPMENT PROJECTS

TOPICS FOR DISCUSSION 1. Invite a speaker from a local collection agency to speak on collection techniques.

2. Examine local supply catalogs and compare billing supplies.

ROLE PLAYING 1. Rebecca Berquist asks you why office visits to Dr. Taylor cost more than visits to other clinics.

2. When Martin Whitfall makes an appointment, he asks what his visit will cost him.

Simulation 2

Today you will begin your second two-day simulation in Dr. Taylor's office. The days will be Tuesday, October 21, and Wednesday, October 22.

PROCEDURES Review the general directions on pages 74-75 for handling simulations. Follow the same procedures for Day 1 and Day 2 as in Simulation 1.

MATERIALS YOU WILL NEED

Appointment Book

Card File

Supplies Folder	Source
Telephone message blanks	WP 141-153
Appointment cards	WP 189
Letterheads	You provide
Notepad	You provide
Plain paper	You provide
File folders and labels	You provide
Index cards	You provide

Day 1 Folder

Letter drafted to Dr. Jones	WP 45
Handwritten patient introduction slip for Marlene Stillman	WP 47
Handwritten notes on Sharon McKinley	WP 49
Handwritten patient introduction slip for Manuel Perez	WP 51
Lab report for Marion Wellman	WP 155

Day 2 Folder

Patients' Charts
The following patients' charts (folders) should contain the items given below:

Bachman, Joseph	
Ledger card	Project 36
Clinical data sheet	Project 15
Letter to Dr. Gonzalez	Project 15
Bachmann, Paul	
Ledger card	Project 36
Clinical data sheet, updated	Project 32
House call slip	Project 12
Message	Simulation 1
Berndt, Stanley	
Ledger card	Project 36
Clinical data sheet	Project 32
Collection letter	Project 37
Berquist, Rebecca	
Ledger card	Project 36
Clinical data sheet	Project 32

Patients' Charts	Source
Burnett, Jane	
Ledger card	Project 36
OB form, updated	Project 33
Letter about fees	Project 35
Records release and letter to Dr. Kaplan	Simulation 1
Patient introduction slip	Project 13
Appointment card	Simulation 1
Curtiss, Lois	
Ledger card	Project 36
Clinical data sheet	Project 31
House call slip	Simulation 1
Goldberg, Ellen	
Ledger card	Project 36
Clinical data sheet, updated	Project 32
Message	Project 17
Grazzini, Mario	
Ledger card	Project 36
Clinical data sheet	Project 25
Messages—2	Simulation 1
Grebowski, Paul	
Ledger card	Project 36
Clinical data sheet	Project 25
Letter rescheduling appointment	Simulation 1
Grimes, Jill	
Ledger card	Project 36
Clinical data sheet	Project 32
Appointment card	Simulation 1
Hayes, Gail	
Ledger card	Project 36
Clinical data sheet	Project 32
Patient introduction slip	Project 32
Kellogg, Alice	
Ledger card	Project 36
Clinical data sheet, updated	Project 33
Message	Simulation 1
Leslie, Sheila	
Ledger card	Project 36
Clinical data sheet, updated	Project 33
Stephens, Jason	
Ledger card	Project 36
Clinical data sheet, updated	Project 32
Wellman, Marion	
Ledger card	Project 36
Clinical data sheet	Project 30
Appointment card	Simulation 1
Appointment card	Project 11
Whitfall, Martin	
Ledger card	Project 36
Clinical data sheet	Project 32
Patient introduction slip	Project 32

Miscellaneous Folder
Letters:

Dr. Stanley F. Anderson	Simulation 1
Dr. Alan Andrews	Simulation 1
Dr. Scott McIntosh	Project 10
Dr. Louise Merryweather	Project 27
Dr. Milton Monroe	Project 28

PART 3: PATIENT RECORDS

Miscellaneous Folder   **Source**
Messages:
  Mrs. Taylor   Simulation 1
  Mrs. Bateson   Simulation 1
  Dr. Alan Andrews   Simulation 1
  Marlene Stillman   Simulation 1

In addition to the above, clinical data sheets and ledger cards with the patient's name typed on them should be in the following folders:

Knutson, Karen
Logan, Carl
Malinsky, William
McKinley, Sharon
Provost, Janis

If you have not completed all the projects and do not have all these records set up in advance, talk with your instructor.

MEDICAL TERMINOLOGY

_____ aerating
_____ angina
_____ Australian antigen
_____ bilirubin
_____ CHF
_____ compression rootlet
_____ conjunctivae
_____ dorsum
_____ DTR
_____ duodenoscopy
_____ enteric isolation
_____ fiberoptic
_____ fundi
_____ gastroenterology
_____ Grade IV/VI
_____ hemivertebrae
_____ insidious endocarditis
_____ lipping
_____ mitral stenosis
_____ palpable
_____ petechiae
_____ prophylactic
_____ pruritus
_____ rheumatic carditis
_____ Roth's spots
_____ RSR
_____ Schmorl's nodule
_____ scoliosis
_____ subacute bacterial endocarditis
_____ systolic

4
Financial Responsibilities

11

Health Insurance

Health insurance refers to insurance protection against medical care expenses. Because health insurance is a complex field, this chapter is meant only as an introduction to the assistant's role. The assistant must be well informed on this subject, because duties will include many phases of health insurance. Patients ask many questions and expect the assistant to know the answers.

Most patients do not pay doctors directly; the doctors are paid by insurance companies. It is the assistant's responsibility to see that the doctor receives compensation for services. This is partly fulfilled by processing insurance claim forms.

TYPES OF INSURANCE COVERAGE There are two major classifications of insurance—group and individual. Under group insurance, one master policy is issued to an organization or employer covering the eligible members or employees and their dependents. Thus, all the members or employees have the same basic insurance coverage. Group insurance provides better benefits with lower premiums. Individual insurance covers only the person taking out the policy and that person's dependents. Because it is not obtained at a group rate, the cost is higher than group insurance.

The following pages list major types of health insurance coverage. Blue Cross, Blue Shield, and the government-sponsored insurance programs will be discussed later in the chapter.

Hospital Hospital insurance provides protection for the costs of hospital care. It generally states a room allowance—such as $100 a day for a semiprivate room—with a maximum number of days per year. The hospital expense section will also include special provisions for operating room, laboratory, X rays, and drugs. The term *inpatient* refers to a patient in a hospital or skilled nursing facility.

Medical Medical insurance covers benefits for outpatient medical care, including physicians' fees for hospital visits and nonsurgical procedures. The word *medical* should always be related to physician's costs.

Surgical Surgical insurance provides protection for the physician's fee for surgery. Charges for anesthesia are usually covered by surgical insurance.

Outpatient Outpatient insurance usually provides protection for emergency room visits and other outpatient divisions in a hospital, such as X-ray, pathology, and psychological services. It can also cover office visits and surgical procedures performed in the doctor's office.

Major Medical In order to have protection for large medical expenses that go above and beyond the maximum set in the regular health insurance policy, a person must obtain major medical expense protection. There is usually an added cost factor for this type of insurance coverage.

Disability Disability insurance can be purchased to provide regular income for a person who is unable to work because of medical reasons.

Martin Bough/Studios, Inc.

INSURANCE TERMINOLOGY	The assistant must be familiar with basic insurance terminology in order to process insurance claims. The terms explained below should be understood by the assistant.
Carrier	An insurance *carrier* is an insurance company that provides the insurance benefits.
Provider	Whoever provides the health care for the patient is considered the *provider*. This may include the doctor, a clinic, and a hospital.
Coverage	Each policy must state the extent of health benefits, and how much payment is provided for each procedure. This is known as *coverage*.
Subscriber	In individual insurance, the *subscriber* (also known as "the insured") is the person who takes out the insurance policy. The policy is in the subscriber's name and can cover both the subscriber and the subscriber's dependents. In group insurance, the subscriber is the company that takes out the policy, which covers the subscriber's members or employees.
Contract	An insurance *contract* is a formal written agreement between the subscriber and the carrier stating the coverage. A *family contract* would cover the subscriber and the subscriber's unmarried dependents with some limitations, such as age of the dependents. A *single contract* provides coverage for the subscriber only.
Premium	The rate charged for the insurance policy is known as the premium.
Deductible	Many types of insurance coverage have *deductibles*. This means that the subscriber must incur a certain amount of medical expense before the insurance carrier will pay. For example, with a $100 deductible for outpatient

insurance the subscriber would pay the first $100 of outpatient expenses for the current year.

Usual, Customary, and Reasonable Fees

An insurance carrier can state in an insurance contract that it will pay "usual, customary, and reasonable fees." These may be referred to as "UCR fees."

☐ **Usual.** A *usual* fee is what an individual provider charges for a certain procedure. For example, a general practitioner may consistently charge $20 for brief office visits.

☐ **Customary.** A *customary* fee is a rate that is within the usual range of fees for a given procedure. The usual range of fees is determined by doctors of similar training and experience in a geographic locality. For example, the range for an appendectomy performed by general practitioners in a certain area is $375 to $450. Therefore, one general practitioner's charge of $425 would be considered a customary fee and would be covered by insurance. Another general practitioner who charged $485 for the same procedure could only receive $450 in payment from the insurance carrier.

☐ **Reasonable.** If there are any special circumstances involved in a given procedure, the fee is said to be *reasonable* and is accepted as justifiable by the insurance carrier. Thus, a reasonable fee would be covered by the insurance. For example, if a general practitioner performs an emergency appendectomy for $485, the fee would be labeled "reasonable" and the insurance could cover the amount because of the special circumstances—emergency.

Coinsurance

Coinsurance exists when the subscriber and the insurance carrier share in covering costs of medical care. Most major medical health plans have coinsurance plans. In an 80/20 coinsurance plan, the insurance carrier pays 80 percent of the costs and the subscriber pays 20 percent.

Assignment of Benefits

If the doctor agrees to work with an insurance company, the patient signs an *assignment of benefits*. This authorizes the insurance company to make direct payment to the doctor. If the doctor does not accept assignment, the patient collects from the company and then pays the doctor.

Coordination of Benefits

Some insurance companies have a *coordination of benefits* clause, a non-duplication provision. This provides that the patient's maximum benefit can only be 100 percent of health expenses. If a person has policies from two insurance companies, one must be designated the primary carrier. The primary carrier pays first on the claim, and the second insurance company can cover the remaining costs. Therefore, the patient does not benefit financially from being ill.

Release of Information

The patient must sign a *release of information* authorizing the release of medical information to an insurance company in order to process the claim. A sample release is show here:

12. PATIENT'S OR AUTHORIZED PERSON'S SIGNATURE *(Read back before signing)* I Authorize the Release of any Medical Information Necessary to Process this Claim and Request Payment of MEDICARE/CHAMPUS Benefits Either to Myself or to the Party Who Accepts Assignment Below
SIGNED   DATE

INSURANCE INFORMATION

Whenever a patient comes into the doctor's office, the assistant must obtain complete and accurate information. Not only is this information helpful to facilitate the care of the patient, it is necessary in order to process insurance claims. Most doctors use a new patient registration form or patient introduction slip, as described in Chapter 5. This information should be kept in the patient's chart and updated when necessary.

Identification Cards If a patient has a health insurance coverage plan, the assistant should ask to see the identification card. This card states the name of the insurance policy, such as Blue Cross; the subscriber's name; and the insurance policy number, group insurance number, and/or individual subscriber number.

Essentials for Completing Claim Forms It is of the utmost importance to complete forms accurately. If they are incomplete, they will be returned for correction. The basic information that is required on most claim forms includes the following items:

> Contract numbers—group number and subscriber contract number. Copy from current ID card.
>
> Patient's complete name, date of birth or age, sex, and relationship to subscriber.
>
> Subscriber's complete name and address.
>
> Whether the condition is job-related, maternity-related, and whether illness or injury.
>
> Patient account number (if your facility assigns numbers to patients).
>
> Complete diagnosis with ICD-9-CM diagnosis code.
>
> Provider information—name, address, and identifying codes.
>
> Statement of services rendered, which should include dates, names of procedures and procedural codes, charges, total charges, and necessary signatures.
>
> If the doctor accepts assignment, the patient/subscriber should sign an assignment of benefits.

Type all claim forms. Keep a copy for the files. Complete all blanks, using dashes (two hyphens) or "N.A." ("not applicable") for items which will not contain any information. This indicates that the item was not overlooked.

The assistant should use standard nomenclature for the procedures and diagnoses and the corresponding codes. A book published by the American Medical Association, *Current Procedural Terminology,* lists codes for diagnostic and therapeutic procedures. These codes are used by insurance companies to identify services rendered. Diagnosis codes are obtained from the *International Classification of Diseases,* 9th edition, *Clinical Modification* (ICD-9-CM). When a form has been completed and the claim submitted to the insurance company, the medical assistant should mark this fact on the patient's ledger. This is best shown by marking the date and writing "Submitted to insurance" after the last entry. A copy of the ledger is still to be sent to the patient for billing. The patient (responsible party) is still responsible for the complete charge, even if insurance is involved.

Keep a generous supply of insurance forms used in the office. Know the various companies' time limits for submitting claims.

Universal Claim Form Although each insurance company has its own insurance form, the Health Insurance Council (HIC) and the American Medical Association (AMA) have devised a form to standardize insurance claims and eliminate the great difference in claim forms and procedures. A Universal or Uniform Claim Form (also called Health Insurance Claim Form) was approved by the AMA in 1975. This standardized form, which is shown on the following page, can be used for both group and individual claims and must be accepted by all insurance carriers except government-sponsored plans.

102 PART 4: FINANCIAL RESPONSIBILITIES

HEALTH INSURANCE CLAIM FORM
READ INSTRUCTIONS BEFORE COMPLETING OR SIGNING THIS FORM

TYPE OR PRINT ☐ MEDICARE ☐ MEDICAID ☐ CHAMPUS ☒ OTHER

Northern Medical Insurance
1397 South 55th Avenue
Chicago, IL 60650

PATIENT & INSURED (SUBSCRIBER) INFORMATION

1. PATIENT'S NAME: Charles L. Knoll
2. PATIENT'S DATE OF BIRTH: 8 | 5 | 47
3. INSURED'S NAME: Charles L. Knoll
4. PATIENT'S ADDRESS: 1572 North Talman Avenue, Chicago, IL 60622
5. PATIENT'S SEX: MALE X FEMALE
6. INSURED'S I.D. No or MEDICARE No: 475-75-4755
7. PATIENT'S RELATIONSHIP TO INSURED: SELF X
8. INSURED'S GROUP NO: 7525B
9. OTHER HEALTH INSURANCE COVERAGE: --
10. WAS CONDITION RELATED TO
    A. PATIENT'S EMPLOYMENT: YES ___ NO X
    B. AN AUTO ACCIDENT: YES ___ NO X
11. INSURED'S ADDRESS: 1572 North Talman Avenue, Chicago, IL 60622
12. PATIENT'S OR AUTHORIZED PERSON'S SIGNATURE
    SIGNED: Charles L. Knoll DATE: 8/7/--
13. SIGNED (Insured or Authorized Person): Charles L. Knoll

PHYSICIAN OR SUPPLIER INFORMATION

14. DATE OF ILLNESS/INJURY/PREGNANCY: 8/7/--
15. DATE FIRST CONSULTED YOU FOR THIS CONDITION: 8/7/--
16. HAS PATIENT EVER HAD SAME OR SIMILAR SYMPTOMS? YES ___ NO X
17. DATE PATIENT ABLE TO RETURN TO WORK: no disability
18. DATES OF TOTAL DISABILITY: FROM -- THROUGH --
    DATES OF PARTIAL DISABILITY: FROM -- THROUGH --
19. NAME OF REFERRING PHYSICIAN: --
20. FOR SERVICES RELATED TO HOSPITALIZATION: ADMITTED -- DISCHARGED --
21. NAME & ADDRESS OF FACILITY WHERE SERVICES RENDERED: --
22. WAS LABORATORY WORK PERFORMED OUTSIDE YOUR OFFICE? YES ___ NO X CHARGES --
23. DIAGNOSIS OR NATURE OF ILLNESS OR INJURY:
    1. Acute bursitis--right shoulder, 726.10 (ICD-9-M)
    2.
    3.

24. A DATE OF SERVICE	B PLACE OF SERVICE	C PROCEDURE CODE	FULLY DESCRIBE PROCEDURES	D DIAGNOSIS CODE	E CHARGES	F
8/7/--	3	90040	Office visit, brief	1	15 00	
8/7/--	3	90782	Cortisone injection	1	8 50	

25. SIGNATURE OF PHYSICIAN OR SUPPLIER: Warren Taylor, M.D. SIGNED DATE 8/15/--
26. ACCEPT ASSIGNMENT: YES X NO
27. TOTAL CHARGE: 23 50
28. AMOUNT PAID: -0-
29. BALANCE DUE: 23 50
30. YOUR SOCIAL SECURITY NO: 345-94-2942
31. PHYSICIAN'S OR SUPPLIER'S NAME, ADDRESS, ZIP CODE & TELEPHONE NO:
    Warren Taylor, M.D.
    2235 South Ridgeway Avenue
    Chicago, IL 60623
    I.D. NO. T-74820 312/555-6022
32. YOUR PATIENT'S ACCOUNT NO: --
33. YOUR EMPLOYER I.D. NO: --

PLACE OF SERVICE CODES
1 — (IH) — INPATIENT HOSPITAL
2 — (OH) — OUTPATIENT HOSPITAL
3 — (O) — DOCTOR'S OFFICE
4 — (H) — PATIENT'S HOME
5 — DAY CARE FACILITY (PSY)
6 — NIGHT CARE FACILITY (PSY)
7 — (NH) — NURSING HOME
8 — (SNF) — SKILLED NURSING FACILITY
9 — AMBULANCE
0 — (OL) — OTHER LOCATIONS
A — (IL) — INDEPENDENT LABORATORY
B — OTHER MEDICAL-SURGICAL FACILITY

APPROVED BY AMA COUNCIL ON MEDICAL SERVICE 6/74

Courtesy Medical Arts Press, Minneapolis, Minnesota 55427

Project 38
Processing Universal Claim Forms

Dr. Taylor uses the Health Insurance Claim Form for all claims except Medicare and Blue Shield. Prepare a Health Insurance Claim Form for Jill Grimes, who has a private policy with Northern Medical Insurance, 1397 South 55th Avenue, Chicago, IL 60650. Jill's ID number is 473-62-7282. Insurance companies often ask for various identification numbers from providers in order to process claims more effectively. Dr. Taylor's provider number is T-74820 (his state license number), and his social security number is 345-94-2942. Make a notation of Dr. Taylor's provider and social security numbers on the fee schedule and use them in processing insurance claims. You will have to obtain the diagnosis codes from the *International Classification of Diseases*, 9th edition, *Clinical Modification* (ICD-9-CM). If this reference book is not available, ask your instructor. Submit the claim for services performed on 10/14 and 10/21, dating the claim 10/23. Use WP 53. Mark Ms. Grimes's ledger.

CHAPTER 11: HEALTH INSURANCE   103

INSURANCE PLANS To provide protection for hospitalization and medical expenses, various prepaid medical care plans have been established. Some are private, such as Blue Cross and Blue Shield, and some are government-sponsored, such as Medicare, CHAMPUS, and so on.

Blue Cross and Blue Shield Blue Cross and Blue Shield plans or combinations of both are nonprofit prepaid medical care plans that provide medical, surgical, and hospital benefits. The National Association of Blue Shield Plans provides guidance and membership standards for the plans. These plans vary from state to state, so the assistant should contact the local representatives to obtain information about types of contracts and how to process claims.

Blue Cross and Blue Shield forms can be obtained from a local state office. Check with a local directory to obtain the necessary information. Each local Blue Cross and Blue Shield plan has its own claim form. The one shown below is representative.

Courtesy Blue Cross and Blue Shield of Illinois

Both plans provide health care to their subscribers through participating providers who agree to accept the plan's payments for services. The Blue Shield plan mainly covers medical services, whereas Blue Cross covers hospitalization expenses. Their coverages may cross lines in various states. The Blue Cross and Blue Shield plans have merged to form one organization in a few states.

Contracts available include service, indemnity, and usual, customary, and reasonable (UCR) fees. Service contracts are determined by the subscriber's income, and the participating provider accepts the insurance payment as payment in full. An indemnity contract has a specific allowable schedule for each procedure. The doctor may bill the patient for the difference. UCR fees must be accepted as payment in full, and payment is sent directly to the participating provider.

Project 39
Processing Blue Shield Forms

Janis Provost is covered by her father's Blue Shield insurance—Group No. 4736, Contract No. 472-77-8411. Janis's father works for the Amiway Truckline. Complete a Blue Shield form using the patient's file and WP 55. Submit the claim for Janis on 10/23. Mark the ledger to show that the claim was submitted to insurance.

Medicare

In 1965, Congress passed the Medicare health insurance bill to provide medical care for persons 65 or over.

Medicare is divided into two parts—Part A, hospitalization insurance, and Part B, medical insurance.

☐ **Hospitalization Insurance.** Hospitalization insurance provides coverage of *medically necessary* services for an inpatient in a hospital, an extended care facility, and home health benefits from an approved home health agency.

Inpatient Hospitalization. Medically necessary services for a Medicare inpatient include such items as semiprivate room, operating room, drugs, and laboratory and X-ray tests.

The Medicare patient is responsible for some costs in each benefit period (spell of illness). A benefit period has a maximum of 90 days and ends when a person has been a nonpatient for 60 days in a row. The inpatient costs include the following items for each benefit period.*

    A deductible of $180 covering 1 to 60 days.

    For the 61st to 90th day, the patient must pay $45 daily.

If a patient is hospitalized for more than 90 days, a person will go into Lifetime Reserve, which contains 60 nonrenewable days. A patient must pay $90 daily for Lifetime Reserve days.

    Patient A has been hospitalized for 72 continuous days. Assuming all the charges are medically necessary, the patient's share of the expense is as follows:

Deductible covering 1-60 days	$180
Coinsurance—$45 for 12 days (61st-72d day)	540
Patient's total expense	$720

*Note that the amounts given must be updated annually. Figures cited are for 1980.

Extended Care Benefits. After a person has been an inpatient for at least three days, he or she can be transferred within 14 days to a skilled nursing facility for further medical care. This includes 20 days covering all the medically necessary services and 80 additional days costing the patient $22.50 daily.

> Patient B, after being in the hospital for 17 days, is transferred to an extended care facility for 22 days. Assuming all the charges are medically necessary, the patient's expense would be as follows:
>
> | | |
> |---|---|
> | 1-20 days | no cost |
> | 21st and 22d day—$22.50 daily | $45 |
> | Patient's total expense | $45 |

Home Health Benefits. Medicare will pay for medically approved skilled nursing care after a three-day hospital stay. A person could receive 100 home health visits with each benefit period. These benefits further treat the condition after hospitalization. A patient must also receive these benefits within 14 days after discharge.

☐ **Medical Insurance.** Part B, Medicare's medical insurance, helps the patient pay for doctor's services, outpatient services, medical services and supplies, home health benefits, outpatient physical therapy, outpatient speech therapy, and ambulance services.

Each year the patient must incur a deductible, the first $60 for covered services. After the deductible, Medicare will cover 80 percent, and the patient is responsible for 20 percent.

> Patient C, who sprained an ankle, went to visit the doctor for medically necessary services. The patient had not been in to see the doctor since the previous year. The following charges were the result of the visits for the sprained ankle: February 2, total $45; February 9, total $22; February 16, total $45; and February 23, total $16.
>
> Patient C paid deductible and coinsurance on February 23.
>
> | | |
> |---|---|
> | Total bill | $128.00 |
> | Less patient's deductible for the year | −60.00 |
> | | $ 68.00 |
> | Less patient's coinsurance—20% | −13.60 |
> | Medicare's share—80% after deductible | $ 54.40 |

Patient thus had to pay a total of $73.60 ($60 deductible + $13.60 coinsurance).

A doctor who accepts assignment on Medicare cases agrees to receive direct payments from Medicare and to charge only reasonable charges for medical services.

Some of the items that Part B does not cover include routine physicals, eye checkups, routine foot care, immunizations not related to injury or immediate high-risk infections, cosmetic surgery for beautification, self-administered drugs, eyeglasses, and false teeth.

Reasonable charges for radiology and pathology are covered 100 percent for services received as an inpatient in a hospital. Ambulance services must meet certain conditions for Medicare; other transportation that might endanger the patient, such as taxis, cannot be used.

Home health benefits similar to those received under hospitalization insurance are available. The doctor must state that they are necessary for the patient; the agency must participate in Medicare; and the patient must be confined to the home.

106 PART 4: FINANCIAL RESPONSIBILITIES

REQUEST FOR MEDICARE PAYMENT	Form Approved OMB No. 72-R0730

MEDICAL INSURANCE BENEFITS—SOCIAL SECURITY ACT (See Instructions on Back—**Type or Print Information**)

NOTICE—Anyone who misrepresents or falsifies essential information requested by this form may upon conviction be subject to fine and imprisonment under Federal Law.

PART I—PATIENT TO FILL IN ITEMS 1 THROUGH 6 ONLY

Copy from YOUR OWN HEALTH INSURANCE CARD (See example on back)

1 Name of patient (First name, Middle initial, Last name)
Ellen J. McDugan

2 Health insurance claim number (Include all letters)
3 9 7 2 2 7 1 0 4 B
☐ Male ☒ Female

3 Patient's mailing address City, State, ZIP code
2942 West Pierce Avenue, Chicago, IL 60622
Telephone Number 555-3422

4 Describe the illness or injury for which you received treatment (Always fill in this item if your doctor does not complete Part II below)

Was your illness or injury connected with your employment? ☐ Yes ☒ No

5 If any of your medical expenses will be or could be paid by another insurance organization or government agency (including FEHB), show below
Name and address of organization or agency — Policy or Identification Number —

Note: If you **Do Not** want information about this Medicare claim released to the above upon its request, check (X) the following block ☐

6 I authorize any holder of medical or other information about me to release to the Social Security Administration or its intermediaries or carriers any information needed for this or a related Medicare claim. I permit a copy of this authorization to be used in place of the original, and request payment of medical insurance benefits either to myself or to the party who accepts assignment below.

Signature of patient (See instructions on reverse where patient is unable to sign)
SIGN HERE ▶ *Ellen J. McDugan*
Date signed 8/14/—

PART II—PHYSICIAN OR SUPPLIER TO FILL IN 7 THROUGH 14

7 A. Date of each service	B. Place of service (*See Codes below)	C. Fully describe surgical or medical procedures and other services or supplies furnished for each date given	Procedure Code	D. Nature of illness or injury requiring services or supplies (diagnosis)	E. Charges (If related to unusual circumstances explain in 7C)	Leave Blank
8/14/—	O	Comprehensive exam	90080	Coronary artery disease,	$ 55.00	
8/14/—	O	Chest X ray, single view, posteroanterior	71010	" " "	22.50	
8/14/—	O	Electrocardiogram and interpretation	93000	" " "	45.00	
8/21/—	O	Office visit, limited follow-up	90050	" " "	25.00	

8 Name and address of physician or supplier (Number and street, city, State, ZIP code)
Warren Taylor, M.D.
2235 South Ridgeway Avenue
Chicago, IL 60623

Telephone No. 555-6022
Physician or supplier code T-74820

9 Total charges $ 147.50
10 Amount paid $
11 Any unpaid balance due $ 147.50

12 Assignment of patient's bill
▶ ☒ I accept assignment (See reverse) ☐ I do not accept assignment

13 Show name and address of person or facility which furnished service (if other than your own office or patient's home)
—

14 Signature of physician or supplier (A physician's signature certifies that a physician's services were personally rendered by the physician or under the physician's personal direction)
▶ *Warren Taylor, M.D.* / Warren Taylor, M.D.
Date signed 8/21/—

*O—Doctor's Office H—Patient's Home (If portable X ray services, identify the supplier) SNF—Skilled Nursing Facility OL—Other Locations
IL—Independent Laboratory IH—Inpatient Hospital OH—Outpatient Hospital NH—Nursing Home

FORM SSA 1490 (11-75) Department of Health, Education, and Welfare
Social Security Administration

Project 40
Processing Medicare Forms

Mrs. Ellen Goldberg is covered by Medicare insurance number 090-02-3436A. Submit the claim for Mrs. Goldberg's surgical care; services performed from 10/1 through 10/20. Her surgery (bilateral salpingo-oophorectomy and hysterectomy) was performed at the University Hospital, 3388 South Sawyer Avenue, Chicago, IL 60623. Use WP 57, dating it 10/23. Prepare the form for Dr. Taylor's signature. Mark Mrs. Goldberg's ledger.

☐ **Medicaid.** Title 19, a separate section of the Medicare law, provides assistance for health care free of charge or at a low rate for the indigent (people who already receive some type of categorical aid). Each state formulates its own program, following some federal guidelines. The program is financially sponsored by both state and federal governments. Because pro-

CHAPTER 11: HEALTH INSURANCE 107

grams vary in coverage and benefits from state to state, the assistant must contact the Medicaid state office through his or her state department of health or welfare.

CHAMPUS The Armed Forces has a comprehensive insurance program to provide for the health care of service families in the following eligible categories: active duty, retired, or survivors. The Civilian Health and Medical Program of the Uniformed Services (CHAMPUS) provides medical care and hospitalization in civilian hospitals and from civilian physicians when there are no available government medical facilities. Participation by providers is voluntary. The provider must submit the claim and accept CHAMPUS's reimbursement of reasonable charges as payment in full.

CHAMPUS is a cost-sharing program. The patient's share depends on the patient's eligibility category. Each category has a deductible and coinsurance. For example, dependents of active duty personnel have an outpatient deductible of $50 per patient or $100 per family. After the deductible, the patient is liable for 20 percent; CHAMPUS, 80 percent. The same category only has to pay $1.75 daily or $25 altogether (whichever is greater) for hospitalization charges.

If the assistant needs additional information about CHAMPUS, he or she must contact the state office.

Government-sponsored programs such as Medicare and CHAMPUS change from time to time; therefore, the assistant must obtain current information on each program.

WORKERS' COMPENSATION INSURANCE

Each state has its own workers' compensation laws to guarantee that an employee who is injured or who becomes ill in the course of employment will have adequate medical care and adequate means of support during the period he or she is unable to work. The employer must obtain insurance against workers' compensation liability and is liable no matter whether the employee is at fault through carelessness or not. The operation of workers' compensation insurance usually comes under the jurisdiction of the Department of Labor of each state, or under some special industrial commission.

Courtesy Workers' Compensation Board of New York

The assistant must verify with the employer that a patient claiming workers' compensation was indeed injured or became ill in the course of employment. The doctor must submit a report, usually within 48 hours, to the insurance carrier, which notifies the Workers' Compensation Board. The report must include the case history, the patient's symptoms, complete medical findings, tentative diagnosis, prescribed treatment, and length and extent of disability. There are different categories of disabilities, such as permanent, temporary, or partial. These are defined by the state and are administered by the Department of Labor.

After a set time, a progress report is sent to the same offices, and regular reports are sent thereafter until the patient is discharged by the doctor. The final report must be designated as the final report.

Forms are available at all insurance carriers. The assistant must always keep these forms on hand.

Typing these reports is one of the duties of an assistant who works for a doctor with a compensation practice. It is essential to make carbon copies of such reports, filing them for future reference. Litigation between doctor and insurance company regarding the number of treatments given, the amount of the bill, or the question of liability for compensation is common. Carbon copies of reports are necessary to prove the rights of the doctor if the dispute comes before an arbitration board or the court.

A workers' compensation initial (48-hour) report is shown on the opposite page. (Although the form is headed "Workmen's Compensation Board," the term *workers' compensation* is now preferred and is being substituted for *workmen's compensation* as forms are reprinted.)

Project 41
Processing Workers' Compensation Records

An initial report (WP 59) that was submitted concerning Jason Stephens established that Jason Stephens' fracture from the 10:30 a.m. accident on 10/7 qualifies as workers' compensation. Complete the compensation progress report on WP 61 for the fracture care only. Date the form 10/23. The WCB case number is 80-7342. Mark Mr. Stephens' ledger that the progress report was submitted. (Note that whereas the initial report is headed "Workmen's Compensation Board," the newer progress report reads "Workers' Compensation Board.")

HEALTH MAINTENANCE ORGANIZATIONS

An alternative to traditional insurance programs are health maintenance organizations (HMOs), which are medical centers that provide medical services to subscribers for an annual fee. The subscriber to an HMO plan is able to obtain health care on a regular basis with unlimited medical attention and no deductible expenses. Thus, HMOs provide preventive health care services.

PERSONAL DEVELOPMENT PROJECTS

TOPICS FOR DISCUSSION 1. Contact your state's Department of Health or Welfare to obtain current information on the Medicaid program for your state.

2. Invite a representative of the local Blue Cross and/or Blue Shield organization to speak on processing claims.

3. Define the following insurance terms:

Provider
Subscriber
Deductible
UCR
Coinsurance
Assignment of benefits

> **ROLE PLAYING** 1. Ellen Goldberg does not understand her hospital bill. She asks you to look at it and explain it to her.
>
> 2. Joseph Provost asks if you have received payment from his insurance company. (The form was mailed; payment is to be made to the patient.)

12

Financial Records

Government regulations make it mandatory for each business, including the physician's, to keep accurate records. By keeping accurate records, the doctor will have a record of all transactions, be able to prepare tax records, and determine whether the practice is operating at a profit or a loss.

A doctor can do the accounting on a cash basis or an accrual basis. When charges for services are not recorded as income until payment is received and expenses are not recorded until paid, the doctor is operating on a cash basis. Under the accrual method, income is recorded when earned, whether or not payment is received, and expenses are recorded when they are incurred.

Records must be available to the Internal Revenue Service at all times, and all source documents must be kept for tax purposes. The assistant must, therefore, have a working knowledge of tax regulations and of the accounting process in order to be responsible for the recording portion of accounting.

TYPES OF ACCOUNTING SYSTEMS

The type of accounting system a doctor uses depends on various factors such as the size of the practice, whether the practice is incorporated, whether an accountant is employed, and so forth. No matter what system is used, it should provide a record of daily earnings and expenses and total annual income and expenses.

Single-Entry Systems

A single-entry system requires the use of a daily journal (or daysheet) listing each transaction once; the patient's ledger showing each patient's outstanding balance; and a checkbook recording all cash disbursements. The daily journal is a record of the fees charged and the payments received for a given day.

Double-Entry Systems

A double-entry accounting system shows both sides of a transaction. This system involves recording transactions in the daily journal, posting them to a general ledger, doing adjusting and closing entries, and preparing financial statements. Besides the journal and general ledger, the system involves records for petty cash, patients' ledgers, employees' earnings, and a checkbook.

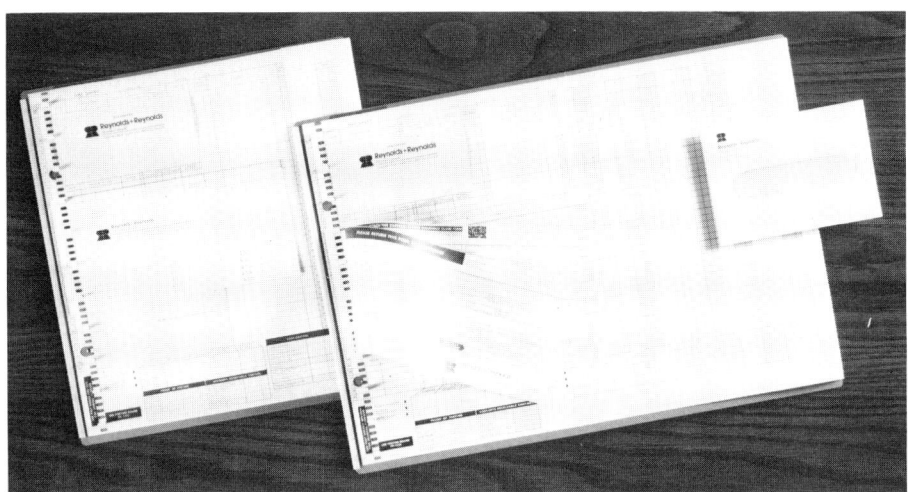

A pegboard

Reynolds & Reynolds

Write-It-Once Systems One of the most popular write-it-once systems in a doctor's office is the pegboard. Forms for the pegboard are made with holes on the left side to fit over pegs. Three forms are essential in order to operate the pegboard system: numbered charge/receipt slip, the patient's ledger, and the daily journal—the record of accounts receivable and cash receipts.

Each day a new daily journal is used. The charge/receipt slips are shingled over the daily journal. The patient's ledger is aligned between the daily journal and the charge/receipt slip. The information (patient's name, services rendered, charge, payment, and balance) is written on the charge/receipt slip, which transfers to the ledger card and the daily journal. The information is transferred using carbon paper between the forms or by using no-carbon-required forms.

Because of the way the system operates, ledger cards can be posted in the patient's presence, the patient can receive the bill immediately, statements are ready for mailing after they are taken from the pegboard (the assistant only needs to prepare the ledgers for patients who have not been in the office during the billing cycle), every charge/receipt slip is accounted for because they are in numeric sequence, and a daily accounts receivable control is provided.

PREPARING ESSENTIAL RECORDS The financial records necessary in a doctor's office include the appointment book; the daily journal for recording all income and disbursements; patient ledgers; monthly and yearly summary sheets for all accounts to show the summary of the office—its assets, liabilities, income, and expenses; employee earning records (for payroll, which will be discussed later in the chapter); and trial balance sheets to prove that the accounts' debits and credits balance. (The trial balance sheet is usually prepared by an accountant.)

Daily Earnings The journal used to record daily fees charged and payments received is referred to as a *daily journal* in the physician's office and is considered the journal for accounts receivable and cash receipts. It is also known as a *daysheet* or a *daily earnings record*. Fees charged and payments received must be recorded promptly on the daily journal.

Daily journal information should correspond to the patient's ledger.

If an office has a computerized billing service, the service provides computer printouts that usually show a daily journal, accounts receivable control, patients' ledgers, and so forth.

PART 4: FINANCIAL RESPONSIBILITIES

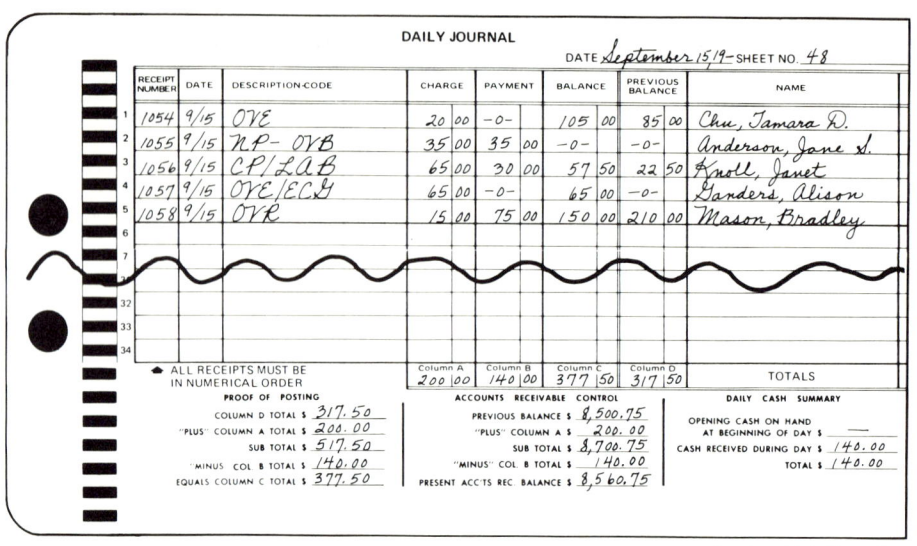

	DAILY JOURNAL					
RECEIPT NUMBER	DATE	DESCRIPTION-CODE	CHARGE	PAYMENT	BALANCE	PREVIOUS BALANCE	NAME
1054	9/15	OVE	20 00	-0-	105 00	85 00	Chu, Tamara D.
1055	9/15	NP-OVB	35 00	35 00	-0-	-0-	Anderson, Jane S.
1056	9/15	CP/LAB	65 00	30 00	57 50	22 50	Knoll, Janet
1057	9/15	OVE/ECG	65 00	-0-	65 00	-0-	Sanders, Alison
1058	9/15	OVR	15 00	75 00	150 00	210 00	Mason, Bradley

DATE September 15/9— SHEET NO. 48

ALL RECEIPTS MUST BE IN NUMERICAL ORDER

Column A: 200 00 Column B: 140 00 Column C: 377 50 Column D: 317 50 TOTALS

PROOF OF POSTING
- COLUMN D TOTAL $ 317.50
- "PLUS" COLUMN A TOTAL $ 200.00
- SUB TOTAL $ 517.50
- "MINUS" COL B TOTAL $ 140.00
- EQUALS COLUMN C TOTAL $ 377.50

ACCOUNTS RECEIVABLE CONTROL
- PREVIOUS BALANCE $ 8,500.75
- "PLUS" COLUMN A $ 200.00
- SUB TOTAL $ 8,700.75
- "MINUS" COL B TOTAL $ 140.00
- PRESENT ACCTS REC BALANCE $ 8,560.75

DAILY CASH SUMMARY
- OPENING CASH ON HAND AT BEGINNING OF DAY $ —
- CASH RECEIVED DURING DAY $ 140.00
- TOTAL $ 140.00

Courtesy Little Press, Inc.

A typical daily journal is shown above. The first column is for the number of the charge/receipt slip, which was discussed in Chapter 10. The daily journal also contains columns for description of services rendered, the charge, the amount of payment, the current balance of the patient's account (including the transaction), the previous balance, and the patient's name.

It is necessary to have an accurate balance of accounts, and this is obtained through the accounts receivable control, which is shown on the bottom of the daily journal. The charge, payment, balance, and previous balance columns are totaled daily. The charges are added and the payments are subtracted from the balance of the previous day to get the current accounts receivable balance. Balancing the journal should be done at the end of the day, or as early as possible the next day.

There is also a section in the daily journal to prove the daily posting balances. The daily cash summary is used to account for daily cash flow.

Project 42
Preparing Daily Journals

You are to complete daily journals for October 21 and 22, using WP 63 and WP 65 and following these instructions:

1. Enter patients' names on the daily journal as they are listed in the appointment book.
2. Obtain the previous balance from each patient's ledger.
3. Enter the following payments, which were made by check: 10/21, Mrs. Ann Curtiss—$50; Thomas Leslie—$85; Alice Kellogg—$30; 10/22, Manuel Perez—$25. In the receipt number column, Dr. Taylor would like you to enter the number of the receipt or the word *check*, depending on the kind of payment.
4. Compute the current balances from the day's charges.
5. Enter the money received on the appropriate ledger.
6. After completing a line for each patient on the daily journal, total columns A, B, C, and D.
7. Enter those total amounts in the proof-of-posting section.
8. After the proof-of-posting balances, compute the current accounts receivable balance and post onto the next daily journal.
9. Complete the daily cash summary section.

File the daily journals in a folder labeled "Financial Records."

Monthly Summary Sheet A monthly summary can consist of records such as those shown on the facing page (Parts A and B). Part A shows daily charges and payments for an entire month, enabling the assistant to have a yearly total to date. Part B shows the distribution of disbursements into various common categories. By using forms such as these, the doctor can determine monthly and yearly expenditures.

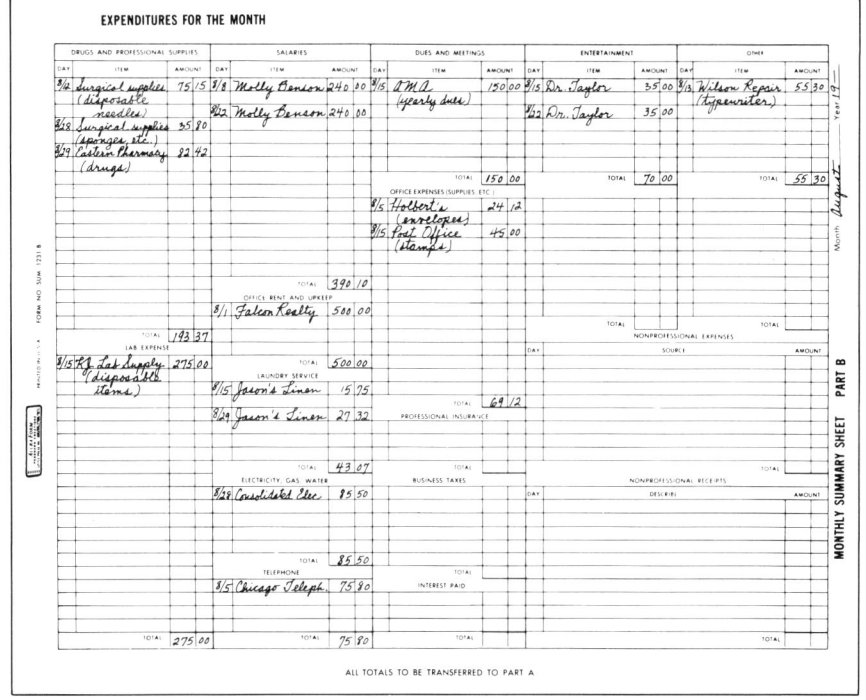

Project 43
Preparing a Monthly Summary Sheet

The following disbursements have been made for the month of October. Transfer them to the partially completed monthly summary sheet (WP 67).

Date	Item	Amount
10/1	Falcon Realty (rent)	$500.00
10/6	Surgical Supplies, Inc. (tongue depressors)	100.00
10/7	Chemical Company (drugs)	35.50
10/10	KJ Lab Supply (disposable items)	255.75
10/15	Eastern Pharmacy (drugs)	24.32

114   PART 4: FINANCIAL RESPONSIBILITIES

Date	Description	Amount	Date	Description	Amount
10/15	United Medical Supply (instruments)	54.00	10/21	Dr. Taylor (dinner with a colleague)	25.00
10/17	Chicago Telephone Company	65.90	10/22	Jason's Linen Service (laundry)	47.50
	Consolidated Electric Lights	55.25			
10/21	Holbert's Stationery (typing paper)	22.35			

Insert the total charges and payments from the daily journals completed in Project 42 in Part A of WP 67.

Yearly Summary Another necessary record is a yearly summary that provides columns for all monthly charges, totals of income, and totals of deductible and nondeductible expenses. On this form, the doctor can also keep accurate records of personal property, real estate, securities, professional travels, and so on. Such a form is illustrated here.

YEARLY SUMMARY

MO.	TOTAL BUSINESS	TOTAL INCOME	TOTAL DISBURSEMENTS	OFFICE EXPENSE	WAGES	AUTO & TRAVEL	MAINTENANCE	MISC. EXPENSE
JAN.	4,375 00	3,750 00	4,111 70	112 75	440 00		72 50	27 50
FEB.	4,020 00	2,860 00	1,656 25	93 50	440 00		37 75	66 50
MAR.	4,560 00	4,775 00	1,534 00	86 25	550 00		89 00	54 25
APR.	3,875 00	4,660 00	5,292 85	81 25	440 00		64 35	178 00
MAY	3,950 00	3,300 00	1,571 65	75 50	440 00		125 25	28 00
JUN.	3,765 00	3,440 00	4,696 50	125 00	550 00		57 50	36 50
JUL.	1,550 00	2,660 00	1,204 80	94 30	440 00		39 50	45 75
AUG.	2,680 00	1,500 00	1,203 00	97 75	440 00		45 75	68 50
SEP.	4,250 00	3,990 00	4,863 25	76 00	550 00		98 00	77 50
OCT.	4,965 00	4,885 00	1,575 25	87 50	440 00		72 25	47 25
NOV.	4,880 00	4,050 00	1,344 35	89 35	440 00		88 50	42 25
DEC.	4,100 00	4,010 00	1,438 25	135 50	550 00		105 25	62 50
AA TOTALS	46,970 00	43,880 00	30,491 85	1,154 65	5,720 00		895 60	734 50

BB	OTHER THAN PRACTICE INCOME COL. 32, LINE W LAST MONTHLY SHEET BK-32B	1,600 00
CC	TOTAL INCOME ADD LINES AA & BB	45,480 00
DD	LESS NON-DEDUCTIBLE DISBURSEMENTS COL. 21, LINE F, LAST MO. DISB. SHEET BK-31C	2,637 15
EE	TOTAL DEDUCTIBLE DISBURSEMENTS FOR PRACTICE LINE AA MINUS LINE DD	27,854 70
FF	OTHER THAN PRACTICE DEDUCTIBLE DISBURSEMENTS COL. 26, LINE L, LAST MO. DISB. SHEET BK-31A	— —
GG	TOTAL DEDUCTIBLE DISBURSEMENT FOR THE YEAR (PERSONAL & PRACTICE) ADD LINES EE & FF	27,854 70

THE YEARLY SUMMARY CHART ABOVE BRINGS TOGETHER ALL OF THE FIGURES FOR EACH OF THE 12 MONTHS FOR QUICK COMPARISON, AND PROVIDES MANY OF THE TOTALS NEEDED TO PREPARE YOUR COMPUTATION OF NET INCOME FOR THE YEAR - ON THE CHART BELOW.

DRUGS & SUPPLIES	LABORATORY	RENT	TAXES	INSTRUMENTS	INTEREST FEES	PROF. FEES		PERSONAL	EQUIPMENT
52 20	110 00	375 00	2,500 00	135 00		45 00		93 50	148 25
48 50	205 00	375 00				60 00		111 20	218 80
30 00	117 00	375 00						87 50	145 00
65 00	83 50	375 00	3,517 50	87 25	—	75 00		228 00	98 00
55 50	75 00	375 00						92 40	305 00
37 50	80 00	375 00	3,250 00					185 00	
75 25	—	375 00				75 00		60 00	
40 00	—	375 00						58 00	78 00
35 50	150 00	375 00	3,250 00	58 00				108 00	85 25
69 00	185 00	375 00		76 50				132 75	90 00
56 75	60 00	375 00						81 00	111 50
50 00	40 00	375 00						120 00	
615 20	1,105 50	4,500 00	12,517 50	356 75		255 00		1,357 35	1,279 80

Courtesy SCM Histacount Corporation

CHAPTER 12: FINANCIAL RECORDS 115

BANKING All money, whether cash or checks, that is received in the office should be deposited in the bank promptly; and all payments for supplies, equipment, services, salaries, or any other purpose should be made by check. This ensures that there are complete, accurate records of any money that is received and disbursed.

Endorsements Any checks or money orders received from patients should be endorsed immediately, so that there is no possibility of their being lost, stolen, or forgotten. An endorsement is written on the back of a check on the left side. There are three types of endorsements that can be used.

A blank endorsement has only the signature of the person to whom the check is payable. Once a check is endorsed in this way, it can be cashed by anyone. Therefore, blank endorsements are not used in business.

A full endorsement indicates the person, company, or bank to whom the check is being transferred, followed by the payee's name.

A restrictive endorsement is the safest and most commonly used type of endorsement in business. It specifies to whom the money should be paid and the purpose of the money, such as "Deposit only." This endorsement limits the purpose to deposit in the account of the payee. All business checks should be endorsed "For Deposit Only" immediately upon receipt. The restrictive endorsement is convenient for business use, since the assistant can rubber-stamp the check and deposit it without obtaining the doctor's signature. A blank endorsement cannot be made by rubber stamp; it requires the actual signature of the payee.

Deposits Before the cash and checks received during the day can be deposited in the bank, a deposit ticket like the one shown below must be prepared. Deposit tickets furnished by a bank are preprinted with the depositor's name and account number. The amount of currency—bills and coins—is entered on the first line. Then each check is separately listed. (Some banks prefer to have each check identified by a number or bank name.)

116   PART 4: FINANCIAL RESPONSIBILITIES

The total amount of checks and currency is entered on the appropriate line. This amount should be the same as the total shown in the daily journal for that day's receipts. The amount of the deposit is then written on the first unused stub in the checkbook or the checkbook register.

Project 44
Preparing a Deposit Ticket

Prepare a deposit ticket (WP 191–193) for the receipts of October 21 and October 22 (Project 42). All payments were made by check. Remove all deposit tickets (WP 191–193) and place them in your supplies folder.

Writing Checks

Checks must be very carefully written in order to prevent fraud or error. It is easy to forget to fill in the stub or check register or to enter the wrong amount. For this reason, the check stub or register should always be filled in before the check itself.

The date and name of the person to whom the check is made out (the payee) is entered on the stub or register. Then the purpose of payment is recorded. The previous balance and any deposits made since the last check was written are added and the total entered on the proper line. The amount of the check being issued is subtracted from this total, and the new balance recorded.

Note the following special points about writing the check itself. The name of the payee should be written in full starting at the extreme left of the line provided for the name. After the name has been entered, draw a line from the end of the name to the dollar sign. The amount in figures is written on the same line after the printed dollar sign. The first figure should be as close as possible to the dollar sign so that no number can be inserted before the amount (changing the amount of a check from $25 to $125, for example). When the check is handwritten, the cents amount is written as a fraction; thus, 25 cents is written "25/100." In this way, there can be no mistake about placement of the decimal point. When the check is typed, the amount in cents follows the decimal point. Circle amounts under one dollar.

Next, the amount is written in words. Again, it should be written beginning at the extreme left end of the line provided. After the dollar amount, the word *and* is written, followed by the cents amount as a fraction, in figures. If the check is for an even dollar amount, "00/100" is written. Draw or type a line from the fraction to the word *Dollars*.

CHAPTER 12: FINANCIAL RECORDS 117

The check can only be signed by an authorized person. Never sign the doctor's name yourself, even in an emergency situation. The bank will not honor the check, and you will be guilty of forgery. In order to save time, you may fill out the stub and check, but the doctor should sign.

Project 45
Preparing Checks

Prepare checks for Project 43. Use checks from WP 193, WP 195, WP 197, WP 199, and WP 201. Start numbering with 360. The balance is $1,745.65. Include the following deposits in the computations: 10/1, $25; 10/3, $75; 10/6, $116.25; 10/7, $100; 10/16, $35; 10/17, $100; 10/20, $25. Also include the deposit made in Project 44.

Bank Reconciliation

Each month the bank submits a statement of the checking account such as the one shown here. This statement includes all checks that have been paid out of the account (canceled checks) and also shows the beginning balance, deposits added during the month, any service charges that were involved, and the ending balance. The statement balance must be compared with the

First National Bank
Chicago, IL 60623

WARREN TAYLOR, M.D.
2235 SOUTH RIDGEWAY AVENUE
CHICAGO, IL 60623

STATEMENT OF ACCOUNT NUMBER
242 027720
CLOSING DATE   ITEMS
JUNE 25   12

PERSONAL CHECKING ACCOUNT STATEMENT

BEGINNING BALANCE	(+) TOTAL CREDITS	(−) TOTAL DEBITS	(−) SERVICE CHARGE	(=) NEW BALANCE
1,592.74	1,030.00	919.06		1,703.68

CHECKS & OTHER DEBITS		DEPOSITS & OTHER CREDITS	DATE	BALANCE
2.54		165.00	6/2	1,755.20
		100.00	6/4	1,855.20
97.00			6/5	1,758.20
450.00			6/6	1,308.20
		120.00	6/9	1,428.20
29.37			6/11	
13.00				1,385.83
		85.00	6/12	1,470.83
7.00		210.00	6/16	1,673.83
15.62			6/17	1,658.21
		90.00	6/18	1,748.21
37.98		185.00	6/23	
65.12				1,830.11
145.00			6/24	
15.00				1,670.11
41.43		75.00	6/25	1,703.68

SYMBOLS

AD = LOAN ADVANCE   CM = CREDIT MEMO   LS = LIST POSTED   RI = RETURN ITEM
BV = BACK VALUE   DM = DEBIT MEMO   OD = OVERDRAFT   SC = SERVICE CHARGE
C = CORRECTION   IP = INSTALMENT LOAN PAYMENT PY = PAYMENT TO LOAN

checkbook balance to determine whether there is a difference between the checkbook and the bank's balance. This is known as *reconciling the bank statement,* or *bank reconciliation.*

The first step in this process is to compare the canceled checks returned by the bank with the items listed on the bank statement. Some deductions, such as service charges, are explained on a debit memorandum included with the canceled checks.

When it has been determined that there is a canceled check or debit memorandum for *every* deduction listed on the bank statement, the canceled checks are arranged in numerical order and compared with the checkbook stubs or register. Any checks written but not yet paid by the bank (and therefore not included with the statement) are called *outstanding checks.* In comparing the canceled checks with the stubs or register, make certain that the amount and the payee are correctly entered on the stub or register.

Then the deposits are compared with the bank statement. A deposit entered in the checkbook but not recorded by the bank at the time the statement was made is called a *deposit in transit.*

The last step is to prepare the bank reconciliation statement. Many banks print a reconciliation form on the reverse side of the bank statement, like the one shown here.

CHANGE OF ADDRESS ORDER

TO CHANGE YOUR ADDRESS PLEASE COMPLETE THIS FORM;
THEN CUT ALONG DOTTED LINE AND MAIL OR BRING TO THE BANK

NEW ADDRESS:

NUMBER AND STREET _____

CITY _____ STATE AND ZIP CODE _____ NEW PHONE NUMBER _____

DATE _____ CUSTOMER'S SIGNATURE _____

| OUTSTANDING CHECKS ||
NUMBER	AMOUNT
	125 00
	18 65
	22 19
	48 90
TOTAL	214 74

TO RECONCILE YOUR STATEMENT AND CHECKBOOK

1. DEDUCT FROM YOUR CHECKBOOK BALANCE ANY SERVICE OR OTHER CHARGE ORIGINATED BY THE BANK. THESE CHARGES WILL BE IDENTIFIED BY SYMBOLS AS SHOWN ON FRONT.

2. ARRANGE ENDORSED CHECKS BY DATE OR NUMBER AND CHECK THEM OFF AGAINST THE STUBS IN YOUR CHECKBOOK.

3. LIST IN THE OUTSTANDING CHECKS SECTION AT THE LEFT ANY CHECKS ISSUED BY YOU AND NOT YET PAID BY US.

TO RECONCILE YOUR STATEMENT AND CHECKBOOK

LAST BALANCE SHOWN ON STATEMENT	1,703 68
PLUS: DEPOSITS AND CREDITS MADE AFTER DATE OF LAST ENTRY ON STATEMENT	130 00
SUBTOTAL	1,833 68
MINUS: OUTSTANDING CHECKS	214 74
BALANCE WHICH SHOULD AGREE WITH YOUR CHECKBOOK	1,618 94

If the two amounts on the reconciliation statement do not agree, compare the monthly statement with the checkbook again. Look for the following possible sources of error:

1. Recheck the deposits entered on the bank statement with the ones entered in the checkbook.
2. See that all service charges shown on the statement are entered in the checkbook and properly deducted.
3. Make sure no check has been drawn that has not been recorded in the checkbook.
4. Compare all checks with the stubs to make sure the amounts agree.
5. Go over the list of outstanding checks to ascertain whether an old check is still outstanding.
6. Go over all addition and subtraction.

When you find that the checkbook balance is correct, make a notation to that effect in the checkbook on the last-used stub or register line.

Any service charges or other debit memorandums that have not been recorded in the checkbook should be entered on the stub or register and subtracted from the balance.

Project 46 — Reconciling a Bank Statement

Reconcile the bank statement which appears on WP 69, using your checkbook stubs for October. The checks that are outstanding include Nos. 365, 368, and 370. The reconciliation form is on the back of the statement.

PETTY CASH

Some small purchases and expenses, such as cab fare, stamps, payment to a messenger, and the like, cannot readily be paid by check. Records still must be kept of these expenses. For this purpose, a petty cash fund is established.

For each payment from the fund, a petty cash voucher should be filled out. This provides a record of expenses and ensures that only authorized payments are made from the fund. Often, a petty cash register is also used so that disbursements may be properly recorded.

The amount of petty cash required over a short period of time, such as a month, is estimated. Let us assume that the doctor decides $100 will be sufficient. A check for this amount is drawn payable to the person responsible for the petty cash fund. The check is cashed and an assortment of small bills and coins is obtained. This money is put in a container and kept under lock and key in a safe place.

At the end of the month, or when the amount of cash is low, the fund is replenished. First, the total disbursements are determined; then the cash left in the fund is counted. The two amounts should total the original amount of the fund (this is called "proving the petty cash fund"). A check is then drawn to bring the petty cash back to its fixed amount. Assume that the original amount was $100 and that expenses were $89.75. This means that there should still be $11.25 in cash. By drawing a check for $89.75, the amount of petty cash on hand is again $100. The expenses should be recorded in the appropriate columns on the monthly summary sheet. They may be entered as petty cash.

Notice that even small expenses must be recorded on the petty cash register. Cab fare amounting to $5 or $10 a week may seem like an insignificant amount; however, in the course of a year $500 may be involved.

Project 47
Handling Petty Cash

Use a petty cash voucher (WP 155) to obtain $12 for stamps. Number it 52 and date it October 29. Petty cash must be balanced and replenished. The original amount was $100. The following expenses are disbursed: stationery supplies, $17.75; stamps, $13; pencil sharpener, $25.10; postage due, $1.05; and miscellaneous office supplies, $13.40. Prepare a check to replenish the fund and enter the amount on the monthly summary sheet as office expenses for October 29. Put the extra petty cash voucher in your supplies folder.

PAYROLL Federal regulations require that an employer withhold taxes from an employee's gross earnings and that the employer also pay certain payroll taxes. Employers must withhold amounts for federal and state income taxes and social security (Federal Insurance Contributions Act—FICA).

Income Tax Withholding Each employee must complete an Employee's Withholding Allowance Certification (Form W-4), which states the number of claimed exemptions. Actual amounts to be withheld for federal and state income taxes are determined by using wage-bracket tables supplied by the Internal Revenue Service; the amount withheld depends on the amount earned, on the number of claimed exemptions, and on the current tax rate. The IRS can provide the wage-bracket tables for various payroll cycles, such as daily, weekly, biweekly, semimonthly, or monthly.

FICA Tax In addition to income tax, the federal government requires that employers deduct a certain amount for social security. This amount is a percent of the employee's gross pay, regardless of the number of claimed exemptions. For example, the law could set this at 6.13 percent of the first $22,900 earned by an employee during the year. (The IRS, its publications, or the doctor's accountant will be able to advise you of the current rate. Congress can change this amount, so you must obtain current information yearly.)

Payroll Records The government requires that each employer keep records of the amount paid to each employee and the amounts withheld for tax purposes. A typical format for these records is shown on the facing page.

CHAPTER 12: FINANCIAL RECORDS 121

					INDIVIDUAL EMPLOYEE'S EARNINGS RECORD				

Name _Molly Benson_ Social Security No. _301-48-7122_ Position _M.A. (part-time)_
Address _5985 West Park Ave._ Marital Status _Single_ Monthly Rate ____
City _Chicago, IL 60650_ No. of Allowances _1_ Weekly Rate _$120_
Telephone _555-4251_ Birthdate _5/29/52_ Overtime Rate _$10/hour_

Period Ending	Hours Worked	Gross Earnings			Deductions							Net Pay	Accumulated Earnings (Gross)
		Regular	Overtime	Total	FICA	Federal Withholding	State Withholding	City Withholding	Insurance	Other	Total		
June 13	40	240 00		240 00	14 71	25 20	5 04				44 95	195 05	2,400 00
June 27	40	240 00		240 00	14 71	25 20	5 04				44 95	195 05	2,640 00
July 11	40	240 00		240 00	14 71	25 20	5 04				44 95	195 05	2,880 00
July 25	40	240 00		240 00	14 71	25 20	5 04				44 95	195 05	3,120 00
Aug 8	40	240 00		240 00	14 71	25 20	5 04				44 95	195 05	3,360 00
Aug 22	40	240 00		240 00	14 71	25 20	5 04				44 95	195 05	3,600 00
Sept 5	40	240 00		240 00	14 71	25 20	5 04				44 95	195 05	3,840 00
Sept 19	40	240 00		240 00	14 71	25 20	5 04				44 95	195 05	4,080 00
Oct 3	40	240 00		240 00	14 71	25 20	5 04				44 95	195 05	4,320 00

An employee's earning record must contain the social security number, address, number of claimed exemptions, gross salary earned, net salary paid, income taxes withheld, FICA taxes, and state and local income taxes deducted, if applicable. The "Other Deductions" column is used to indicate certain other deductions that are required by law or that might be made under agreement with the employee. For example, some states require that an amount be withheld for disability insurance or unemployment insurance. Many employers will deduct, with the employee's permission, amounts for savings bonds, hospital insurance, union dues, or other purposes. All amounts deducted are held in trust by the employer and must be remitted to the proper authority. When the payroll check is written, it is entered in the proper column of the monthly summary sheet.

Depending on the amount involved, the employer must remit amounts deducted from employees' retained earnings to the government each month, or at least each quarter (every three months). In addition to the amount kept from the employees' pay, the employer is obligated to contribute the same amount for FICA taxes.

When an employer remits money to the government, a report is filled out. Details for filling out such reports should be obtained from the Internal Revenue Service; the reports are subject to changes in detail from year to year.

Project 48
Preparing Salary
Checks and Records

Prepare Janet Owen's salary check (supplies folder) for the two weeks ending October 24. Dr. Taylor pays biweekly on the Wednesday following the biweekly pay period. Janet Owen's salary is $220 a week. Her federal income tax can be found on WP 73. State withholding is $10.04. FICA is 6.13 percent of her salary. Add this information to her individual earnings record (WP 71). Add the total amount of her biweekly salary to the monthly summary sheet.

PERSONAL DEVELOPMENT PROJECTS

TOPICS FOR DISCUSSION 1. Obtain samples of local bank statements; compare them in class.
2. Invite a representative of a local supply company to display and demonstrate a pegboard billing system.
3. Define the following financial terms:

   restrictive endorsement
   bank reconciliation
   outstanding checks
   single-entry accounting
   blank endorsement
   deposit in transit
   petty cash

ROLE PLAYING 1. Dr. Taylor has asked not to be disturbed while he is in his office preparing lecture notes. Mrs. Taylor telephones and wishes to know if the doctor will meet her for lunch.
2. While having lunch with some office employees, you learn that the newest employee, doing a job similar to yours, is receiving a higher salary than you. This information makes you angry.

Simulation 3

Today you will begin your third two-day simulation in Dr. Taylor's office. The days will be Thursday, October 30, and Friday, October 31.

PROCEDURES Review the general directions on pages 74-75 for handling simulations. Follow the same procedures for Day 1 and Day 2 as you did in Simulations 1 and 2.

MATERIALS YOU WILL NEED

Appointment Book

Card File

Supplies Folder	Source
All the usual supplies *plus*	
Petty cash voucher	WP 155
Bank deposit tickets	WP 191-193
Checks	WP 193-201
Receipts	WP 201-207

Day 1 Folder
Daily journals	
October 28	WP 75
October 29	WP 77
October 30	WP 79
"To Do" list	WP 157

Day 2 Folder
Medicare form for Carl Logan	WP 83
Daily journal	
October 31	WP 81

Patients' Charts
The following patients' charts (folders) should contain the items given below:

	Source
Bachman, Joseph	
Ledger card	Project 36
Patients' Charts	**Source**
Clinical data sheet	Project 15
Letter to Dr. Gonzalez	Project 15
Bachmann, Paul	
Ledger card	Project 36
Clinical data sheet, updated	Project 32
House call slip	Project 12
Message	Simulation 1
Berndt, Stanley	
Ledger card, updated	Simulation 2
Clinical data sheet, updated	Simulation 2
Collection letter	Project 37
Appointment card	Simulation 2
Berquist, Rebecca	
Ledger card	Project 36
Clinical data sheet	Project 32
Burnett, Jane	
Ledger card	Project 36
OB form, updated	Project 33
Letter about fees	Project 35
Records release and letter to Dr. Kaplan	Simulation 1
Patient introduction slip	Project 13
Appointment card	Simulation 1
Curtiss, Lois	
Ledger card, updated	Project 42
Clinical data sheet, updated	Simulation 2
House call slip	Simulation 1
Goldberg, Ellen	
Ledger card, updated	Project 40
Clinical data sheet, updated	Project 32
Medicare form	Project 40
Message	Project 17
Grazzini, Mario	
Ledger card	Project 36
Clinical data sheet	Project 25
Messages—2	Simulation 1
Grebowski, Paul	
Ledger card	Project 36
Clinical data sheet	Project 25
Letter rescheduling appointment	Simulation 1
Message	Simulation 2

Patients' Charts	Source
Grimes, Jill	
Ledger card, updated	Project 38
Clinical data sheet, updated	Simulation 2
Letter to Dr. Margaret Whitman	Simulation 2
Health insurance claim form	Project 38
Card with Dr. Whitman's address	Simulation 2
Appointment card	Simulation 1
Hayes, Gail	
Ledger card	Project 36
Clinical data sheet	Project 32
Patient introduction slip	Project 32
Kellogg, Alice	
Ledger card, updated	Project 42
Clinical data sheet, updated	Simulation 2
Message	Simulation 1
Message	Simulation 2
Knutson, Karen	
Ledger card	Project 36
Clinical data sheet	Project 25
Message	Simulation 2
Leslie, Sheila	
Ledger card, updated	Project 42
Clinical data sheet, updated	Simulation 2
Appointment card	Simulation 2
Logan, Carl	
Ledger card	Project 36
Clinical data sheet	Project 25
Malinsky, William	
Ledger card, updated	Simulation 2
Clinical data sheet, updated	Simulation 2
Message	Simulation 2
Appointment card	Simulation 2
McKinley, Sharon	
Ledger card, updated	Simulation 2
Clinical data sheet, updated	Simulation 2
Handwritten notes	Simulation 2
Perez, Manuel	
Ledger card, updated	Project 42
Clinical data sheet	Simulation 2
Patient introduction slip	Simulation 2
Letter to Dr. Andrews	Simulation 1
Message	Simulation 1
Provost, Janis	
Ledger card, updated	Project 39
Clinical data sheet, updated	Simulation 2
Letter to Dr. Lillian Bradford	Simulation 2
Blue Cross-Blue Shield form	Project 39
Stephens, Jason	
Ledger card, updated	Project 41
Clinical data sheet, updated	Project 32
Workers' compensation reports	Project 41
Stillman, Marlene	
Ledger card	Simulation 2
Clinical data sheet	Simulation 2
Patient introduction slip	Simulation 2
Message	Simulation 1

Patients' Charts	Source
Wellman, Marion	
Ledger card, updated	Simulation 2
Clinical data sheet, updated	Simulation 2
Appointment card	Simulation 1
Appointment card	Project 11
Appointment card	Simulation 2
Message	Simulation 2
Whitfall, Martin	
Ledger card	Project 36
Clinical data sheet	Project 32
Patient introduction slip	Project 32

Miscellaneous Folder

Letters:

Dr. Stanley F. Anderson	Simulation 1
Dr. Allen Jones	Simulation 2
Dr. Scott McIntosh	Project 10
Dr. Louise Merryweather	Project 27
Dr. Milton Monroe	Project 28

Messages:

Mrs. Taylor	Simulation 1
Mrs. Bateson	Simulation 1

Financial Records Folder

Daily journals	Project 42
Monthly summary sheet, updated	Project 48
Deposit slip	Project 44
Checks	Project 45
Bank statement	Project 46
Petty cash voucher	Project 47
Check	Project 47
Salary check	Project 48
Employee earnings record	Project 48

If you have not completed all the projects and do not have all these records set up in advance, talk with your instructor.

MEDICAL TERMINOLOGY

_____ antibody screening

_____ arcus senilis

_____ bronchovesicular

_____ bruit

_____ callus

_____ cholecystectomy

_____ cholelithiasis

_____ Codman exercises

_____ conjunctival injection

_____ contracted gallbladder

_____ cor pulmonale

_____ CVA tenderness

_____ emphysema

PART 4: FINANCIAL RESPONSIBILITIES

_____	epigastrium	_____	oncologist
_____	gravitation traction	_____	pedal pulse
_____	hypothyroidism	_____	rhonchi
_____	immune	_____	rubella titer
_____	infiltration	_____	serous drainage
_____	laminectomy	_____	trigone
_____	multifaceted	_____	trophic skin changes
_____	murmur	_____	wheezes

5
Professional Activities

13

Office Management

The medical assistant may add the roles of office manager and maintenance supervisor to the list of varied duties to be performed. Professional help is available in planning the practical side of the medical office.

MEDICAL MANAGEMENT CONSULTANT

Doctors might not give much time or thought to the business side of their practice; they may leave that to the assistant. Accountants, lawyers, and insurance agents have all been asked for advice concerning the business side of a medical practice. Over the years some of these advisers came to devote their entire time to this work. As a result, the profession of *medical management consultant* emerged.

The national society to which all reputable consultants belong is the Society of Professional Business Consultants, with headquarters at 221 North LaSalle Street, Chicago, IL 60601. This society will furnish names and addresses of consultants in the doctor's area.

The scope of activities of these consultants is very wide. They are most frequently engaged in analyzing accounting systems, surveying methods of handling appointments and keeping patients' records, and studying the work habits of the doctor's staff.

If patients have to wait too long for an appointment, if more patients are scheduled than can be properly accommodated, if collections are poor, if receipts and bank deposits do not tally, or if expenses of running the office seem too high, the professional consultant will come to the office, study every detail of operation, and make recommendations. The consultant will also train the assistant in recommended procedures—and if there is a change in personnel, train the replacement. The consultant is also available for conferences whenever the need arises.

Martin Bough/Studios, Inc.

By cooperating with the consultant, the assistant can gain valuable help. Problems can be discussed with the consultant. Often, consultants have designed their own forms for patients' referrals, instructions to patients, and insurance forms, thus simplifying the assistant's work. They may also offer investment counsel, give advice on the advantages or disadvantages of renting or buying office space, incorporate group practices, make tax surveys, and do estate planning.

OFFICE PROCEDURES MANUAL

An adjunct to efficient office routine is an office procedures manual, which can be made up by the assistant. This manual serves as a reminder of the various tasks that have to be done and how to do them. It helps to keep the office running smoothly during the assistant's temporary absence for illness or vacation, and it aids in training a substitute or successor.

The best way to keep the manual is in a loose-leaf binder with tab divisions. This makes it possible to write the different sections as each job is defined and mastered. Revisions are easily made by substituting a new page.

First, an outline should be made to determine what subjects should be included in the manual. Then the headings under which different tasks are to be listed should be decided. Subheadings may also be made and cross-referenced, if necessary. Below are suggestions for a manual as it might be set up for an office shared by several doctors with a number of employees.

Daily Routine

The first page may be a list of the duties that have to be performed regularly every day and would serve as a checklist. Here is an example:

DAILY ROUTINE

1. Call answering service.
2. Sort mail.
3. Check appointment book and pull charts for each patient.
4. Start sterilizer (if used in the office).
5. Complete yesterday's charts and file.
6. Bring financial records up to date.
7. Complete insurance forms.
8. Type letters.
9. Tidy treatment rooms.
10. Tidy magazines and ashtrays in waiting room.
11. Take care of used instruments (if indicated).
12. Balance accounts before leaving.
13. Lock up all files and desk, leaving no patient files in view.
14. Cover equipment.
15. Advise answering service.

Doctors

Make a page for each doctor by putting the doctor's name and specialty at the top of the page. List the hours during which the doctor is at the office, as well as any fixed hours at the hospital. If there is a department or extension at the hospital or college, give that information. Add the doctor's home address and telephone number. (This information is for office use and is generally not given out to the public.) On each page write down any special instructions for that doctor. Each may have a preference regarding telephone procedure, scheduling patients, or quoting fees. The doctor's charges would be cross-referenced in a separate section, under "Fees."

Licensing

All licenses (state, narcotic, workers' compensation registration, social security, and/or identifying numbers) should be entered for each doctor. Items to also note include original date when first issued, date when each renewal is due, the amount of fee to be paid, and where to send the renewal.

Medical Societies Include the names of all societies to which each doctor belongs; for example, the American Medical Society, all three doctors; American Radiological Association, the radiologist; and so forth. State the date when the doctor joined each society, the amount of dues, the date when due, and any office the doctor may hold.

Hospital Affiliation For quick reference, all hospitals with which the doctors are affiliated should be listed with addresses and telephone numbers, extension number of the admission office, visiting hours, hours when patients must be checked in, and whatever information may be needed to make a reservation.

Personnel List the name and title of each employee, such as receptionist, secretary, clinical assistant, X-ray technician, laboratory technician, and so forth. Indicate working hours, lunch hours, holidays, and vacation times. It is wise to include the duties and responsibilities of each employee, stating especially if some of the duties overlap or if employees substitute for one another during absence. Place the home telephone number of each employee after the name. If any personnel have professional registration numbers, these numbers should be noted. Here is an example of one employee's entry:

PERSONNEL

Alice Ann Watkins, Clinical Assistant (CMA-C)
Telephone Number: 555-0923
Working Hours: 8-5.
Lunch Hour: 11:30-12:30.
Vacation: Prefers first two weeks in August.
Duties and Tasks:
1. Assist the doctor as needed.
2. Clean examination rooms after each patient.
3. Replenish supplies in examination rooms as needed.
4. Prepare patients for examinations and treatments.
5. Make a monthly inventory of clinical supplies.
6. Order clinical supplies as needed.

Filing Describe the method of arrangement that is being used, different filing sections (active, inactive, closed, transient), and where located. Indicate the follow-up system, annual transfer file, and the length of time records are kept. If color is used as a filing aid, indicate what each color designates.

Billing A sample ledger and the method of billing should be explained. The name, address, and telephone number of any billing service used and a description of its type of service should be noted.

Health Insurance Detailed instructions should be included, telling how to handle each account, how to complete each form, and how to bill the patient. The name, address, and telephone number of each organization should be given. If a particular insurance company employee is usually consulted, include this person's name. An example of instructions on how to handle payments from insurance is given here:

PAYMENTS FROM INSURANCE

1. Verify payment against submitted claim. If correct, remove claim from pending insurance claim file.
2. Enter payment on daily journal and patient's ledger. Balance patient's ledger.

3. Patient is responsible for the balance, if any, and should be notified promptly.

Medicare This section should set forth the exact procedure the doctor wishes to have followed in processing claims, whether the doctor accepts assignment, and the custom in completing forms.

Forms List each form by number and title; include a sample of each. Forms can be punched to fit the binder or pasted on standard size paper. Give the name and address of the firm from which the forms must be ordered, where to send each completed form, the number of copies that must be made, and any other pertinent information.

Equipment and Supplies List names, addresses, and telephone numbers of manufacturers, dealers, and local repair services. List the supplies the doctor uses and any brand names preferred, the quantity usually ordered, and the last price paid.

Under "Stationery Supplies," give the name of the firm and the name and number of the paper used for letterheads, copy paper, manuscript paper, and carbon paper; indicate whether stationery is printed or engraved; and note how long it takes to have orders filled.

Other headings will occur to the assistant as the routine becomes familiar. While the initial time consumed in setting up such a manual may seem considerable, it will be found that it is a great time-saver in the end. To be of value, it must be kept up to date.

Project 49
Starting a Procedures Manual

Prepare several pages for your office procedures manual. Some of the information you need can be obtained from previous chapters. Headings for pages may be chosen from the list given below. You may add any other pages you choose at any time.

1. Daily routine for medical assistant. List tasks in proper sequence.
2. Task list. Prepare a task list for each position: medical assistant, medical secretary, receptionist, bookkeeper.
3. Periodicals. Make a list of professional journals and a list of magazines for the lobby; include subscription prices (and renewal dates, if known).

OUTSIDE SERVICES Every doctor has occasion to refer patients to outside agencies for some sort of service or for the purchase of medical supplies. Patients themselves often ask for the name of an individual or an organization where they may obtain such services. Names, addresses, and telephone numbers of those to whom the doctor might refer patients must be kept in such a way that the assistant can consult them quickly. This special file might also include the doctor's personal services (bank, garage, etc.).

A card file may be the most practical. Subjects may be written on the card file tabs, behind which names are then filed alphabetically. Following are some of the services that will probably be needed:

Cancer detection clinics	Government agencies
Dentists	Health food stores
Funeral homes	Health insurance organizations

Homes—convalescent, nursing, for the aged, for the chronic invalid
Hospitals—general and specialized
Laboratories
Laundry
Nurses
Optometrist
Pharmacies
Physical therapists
Podiatrists
Sickroom supplies
Social security office
Social workers
Specialists
Surgical appliances
Visiting nurse service
Welfare agencies

Project 50
The Outside Service File

In your local directory, look up names, addresses, and telephone numbers for the following list of outside services. Prepare index cards for each of them. Add these cards to the present group of professional outside services used by Dr. Taylor.

Laboratory
Surgical supplies
Welfare assistance
Pharmacy
Independent radiology clinic
Public health department
Blue Cross and Blue Shield office
Medicare information
Social security office
Workers' compensation office

ANNOUNCEMENT CARDS

When a doctor opens an office, moves, or becomes a specialist, he or she usually sends announcement cards to colleagues and patients. The list of patients' names may be taken from patients' ledger cards. The Christmas card list of personal or professional friends may be useful. An example of such an announcement is shown here.

Joseph Mills, M.D.
announces the opening of his office
at
215 East 38 Street
New York, New York 10016

Practice limited to Dermatology

Office Hours: Telephone:
4 to 7 p.m.   555-5678

ORGANIZATION

The assistant's desk and filing cabinets should be organized in such a way that they suit the needs of the clinic and also facilitate the work of the assistant.

The Assistant's Desk

One drawer should be set aside for personal items such as purse or briefcase, hand lotion, and tissues. An adequate supply of all stationery items should be found in the desk. Pencils, erasers, clips, memorandum pads, rubber bands, envelopes, appointment cards, and whatever else is needed for daily use should be placed neatly and methodically in the drawers and kept in the same place at all times. Letterheads, copy paper, and carbon paper will probably have a special arrangement in a desk drawer or a "desk organizer." Insurance forms, patients' introduction slips, clinical data sheets, and ledger cards should also be kept in a desk organizer, within easy reach. The top of the desk should remain neat and clear of all unnecessary items. Nothing that does not belong there should be allowed to accumulate in the filing baskets. A littered desk makes it hard to work efficiently.

Office Records Patients' charts should be kept in filing cabinets. Remember that patients' records are confidential material and should never be left in a place where other patients can see them.

In addition to patients' medical records, there are also documents and papers pertinent to the running of the office, such as leases, insurance policies, canceled checks, tax reports, and bills. An office safe is advisable for these papers. Bills should be placed in a folder as soon as they are received. When merchandise is delivered, an invoice usually accompanies it. For regular deliveries, a monthly statement or bill is sent. Both should be checked carefully—the invoice with the merchandise received and the bill with the invoice. If supplies are returned, a credit memorandum should be requested. This also must appear on the monthly statement.

Paid bills may be placed in a folder marked "Paid Bills" and filed chronologically by the month, or they may be filed alphabetically. In any case, they should be placed in separate folders and not filed with correspondence. Bills may have to be produced at an income-tax audit.

The Doctor's Bag Doctors calling on patients need to take instruments and medications with them. The assistant should see that the bag is kept stocked. It is a good plan to keep a list of items the doctor wants kept in the bag, check the contents of the bag each day, clean used articles, and restock supplies daily. Here is a typical list of supplies:

INSTRUMENTS

Blood-pressure apparatus	Ophthalmoscope
Head mirror	Otoscope
Hypodermic syringe and needles	Scalpel
	Stethoscope
Pencil flashlight	Thermometers (rectal and oral)
Percussion hammer	Tourniquet
Probes	

MEDICATIONS (AMPULES, VIALS, CAPSULES, OR TABLETS)

Antibiotic	Local anesthetic
Aspirin	Narcotic
Barbiturate	Skin sterilizer
Cardiac stimulant	Tranquilizer
Eye drops	

ACCESSORIES

Adhesive tape	Prescription pad
Alcohol	Safety pins
Aspiration equipment	Scissors
Bandages of various sizes	Slides (6)
Container for specimen	Stain
Cotton	Sterile dressings
Fixer solution	Sterile gloves and lubricant
Fountain pen	Tongue depressors
Gauze	Wood applicators

MAINTENANCE It may be the assistant's duty to attend to all the details involved in keeping the clinic tidy and clean, though he or she does not actually perform the work. Generally, a cleaning contractor is responsible for daily cleaning and special weekly, monthly, or annual jobs. The assistant may observe the cleaning personnel to see that no laxity develops. At the end of the day, the office should be left looking neat and clean. Electrical appliances may have to be turned off. Following are suggested daily, weekly, and periodic tasks:

DAILY

Wash ashtrays	Wash enamel tabletops
Empty trash baskets	Wash sinks, basins, and toilets
Dust	Clean floors

WEEKLY

Polish furniture	Brush lampshades; wipe parchment
Dust open bookshelves	Clean mirrors and pictures
Vacuum rugs	Scrub and wax floors
Vacuum upholstered furniture	

PERIODICALLY

Clean windows	Clean draperies
Polish metal fixtures and apparatus parts	Clean upholstered furniture
Wash venetian blinds	Wash slipcovers
Wash window curtains	Check and clean air conditioner

In addition, there are other details that must be attended to frequently:

Throw away old and torn magazines	Replace light bulbs
Discard broken items or have them repaired.	Supply paper towels, toilet tissue, and soap

Waiting Room The assistant is not expected to do the actual cleaning but may be responsible for the supervising. The waiting room is the first place a patient enters, and first impressions are important. If the waiting room looks inviting, cheerful, and well-kept, the patient gains a feeling of confidence toward the clinic or office. Plants help to create a pleasant atmosphere but must be properly tended. There should be a good supply of reading matter, and magazines should be up-to-date. As soon as they begin to fray, discard them. Sofas and chairs in the waiting room should be placed in such a way as to provide some privacy for the patient and make the wait more pleasant. There should be reading lamps and a separate smoking area if smoking is permitted. If the doctor has children among the patients, a few toys and games will help to keep them occupied.

Things that produce a bad effect, even if the room is otherwise clean, are burned-out light bulbs, soiled ashtrays, torn curtains, finger marks on panes, pictures hanging askew, dead plants, and spotted tables.

**Project 51
Adding to the
Procedures Manual**

Add a sheet to your procedures manual, giving the routine for daily, weekly, and periodic cleaning.

Safety Guidelines The doctor most likely carries personal liability insurance to cover any personal injuries that occur in the office as a result of an accident. Malpractice insurance does not cover accidents caused by slipping, falling, or other injury not connected with medical treatment. Here are some guidelines that should be followed:

☐ **Floors.** Floors should never be so highly polished that they are slippery. If small rugs are on the floor, they should be anchored by rubber pads. Large rugs or carpets must be securely fastened to the floor, and any tear must be mended. If anything is spilled, it must be mopped up quickly.

☐ **Electric Cords.** Cords must not be strung across an aisle or block the way between desks or tables. Tripping over cords causes many accidents.

☐ **Fire Hazards.** Wall sockets must not be overloaded, or short circuits may occur. Fire alarm systems may be required; fire extinguishers should be strategically located.

☐ **Furniture.** Lack of space may cause people to bump into corners of tables and desks. Open drawers invite mishap. Pulling out file drawers too far can result in the entire cabinet tipping over unless it is bolted to the floor. If children visit, additional safety rules must be observed. Keep all sharp instruments and all medicines out of reach. If there are toys, be sure that they do not have sharp edges and that they cannot be swallowed.

Laundry Linen may consist of doctors' white coats, nurses' uniforms, examination gowns, sheets, pillowcases, towels, and drapes. They may be clinic property, sent out to a laundry to be washed, or they may be rented from a linen-supply company. Many clinics now use disposable items rather than the washable linens. These are used once and thrown away. The cost compares favorably with the purchase and upkeep of conventional linen.

SUPPLIES In every office, there are many different kinds of supplies. It may be the assistant's duty to order these supplies, store them, and monitor their use, cost, and quality.

Maintenance Supplies Efficient housekeeping requires many supplies: cleanser, paper towels, toilet tissue, deodorizer, light bulbs, and detergent.

Medical Supplies These supplies include chemicals, solutions, lotions, cleaning solutions, rubbing alcohol, disinfectants, cotton, bandages, adhesive tape, tongue depressors, swabs, dressings, gloves, and so forth. All supplies should be stored

Martin Bough/Studios, Inc.

methodically. All bottles should be plainly labeled. Supplies should be ordered when the stock runs low, not when the supply runs out. It is a good plan to place the order for an item as soon as the last box is opened.

Project 52
Ordering in Quantity

Supplies for the medical office can be very costly. To emphasize how wise purchasing procedures can save the doctor much expense, do the following math problems.

1. If hypodermic needles cost $4.95 per 100, 300 needles would cost $_____, and 700 needles would cost $_____.

2. If purchased in large lots of 1,000 or more, the hypodermic needle manufacturer allows a discount of 15 percent. Therefore, 3,000 needles would cost $_____, and 14,000 needles would cost $_____.

3. If a doctor uses 200 needles a month, he or she would save $_____ in a year by making a single purchase for a year's supply rather than 12 monthly purchases.

Project 53
Ordering Supplies

Write a letter on letterhead to the Medical Supplies Service, 255 Second Avenue South, Minneapolis, MN 55401. Order the following items: appointment cards, Style Y, No. 325, on white vellum with regular printing, 4,000 for $25.50; tongue depressors, No. 7280, 1,000 for $9.45; and latex sterile gloves, medium size, No. 7545, 100 (1 box) for $25.30. Enclose one of Dr. Taylor's appointment cards. Compute the total cost, including a 4 percent sales tax and request that the items be sent by priority mail. Today's date is November 3.

PERSONAL DEVELOPMENT PROJECTS

TOPICS FOR DISCUSSION 1. Discuss the advantages of having a task list when giving directions to new personnel.
2. Examine catalogs from medical supply companies, comparing equipment, materials, and prices.
3. Visit your local fire department for a demonstration on the use of fire extinguishers.

ROLE PLAYING 1. The assistant telephones a commerical cleaning service to obtain fees for their services.
2. Mrs. Leslie complains because it takes so long to get the charges on laboratory work.

14

Medical Society Meetings

Most physicians hold memberships in several professional societies. This provides them the opportunity of meeting with colleagues, furthering their education, and keeping informed of new developments in the medical, political, and manufacturing fields.

MEDICAL SOCIETIES

There are national, state, and local medical societies, and most doctors will maintain membership in medical organizations at all three levels.

The national federation of regional medical associations is the American Medical Association (AMA). It is an organization that promotes the advancement of medicine and health care, sponsors medical and scientific research, maintains medical and health care activities, and promotes medical education. The AMA publishes one of the most widely distributed medical journals in the world, the weekly *Journal of the American Medical Association (JAMA)*.

The AMA holds a general convention yearly. The program consists of business meetings at which members discuss and vote on matters of policy and scientific sessions devoted to the presentation of medical reports. Also, commercial exhibitors—manufacturers of drugs, instruments, nutritional products, medical stationery, books and related items—display their wares. If the opportunity presents itself, the assistant is urged to visit such a commercial exhibit. It will prove fascinating and informative.

In addition to the AMA, there are a number of national societies representing special interests or medical specialties, such as the American College of Physicians, the American College of Surgeons, and the American Psychiatric Association.

The national societies publish their membership lists annually. The current membership list is a useful reference book, which will be consulted often and should be kept easily accessible for the doctor and the assistant.

If the doctor is an officer of a medical society or a member of a special committee, a great deal of work is involved. The secretary of a society, for example, prepares the agenda, compiles the membership list, and attends to publicity and many other details. The treasurer collects the membership fees and handles all disbursements. The program for each meeting is planned by

Courtesy American Medical Association

the program committee. The publication committee arranges for the publication of manuscripts read at the society meetings. Other committees investigate conditions in the community as they affect the specialty of the member physicians. This participation by the physician will involve much correspondence with other members, government agencies, and institutions. The assistant will be expected to do much of the detail work, such as sending out notices of meetings, mailing bills and receipts for membership fees, and depositing money received—in short, handling all nonprofessional work.

MEDICAL SOCIETY MEETINGS

National societies hold meetings once or twice a year, but local societies usually hold monthly meetings.

The date and place of the next meeting of a national society is decided at every meeting. This information, which is published in medical journals or a special bulletin, should be entered on the doctor's appointment calendar.

Meetings of local societies are usually held in the same location on certain days of the month. Dates and programs of these meetings are published in local medical journals, but even so, the dates should be marked on the calendar and a memorandum given to the doctor a few days in advance.

Occasionally, a special meeting may be called to discuss some important business or new development. In this case an announcement of the meeting must be mailed to each member.

```
              THE CHICAGO MEDICAL SOCIETY
                   November 13, 19—



                 General Business Meeting
                          8 p.m.



                  597 South Dearborn Street
                      Chicago, IL 60605
```

Project 54
Preparing an Announcement

As Dr. Taylor will be at the University Medical School most of the time from November 6 to November 19, he has asked you to take care of a number of tasks in his absence. You are to compose and type an announcement of the December 11 Chicago Medical Society dinner meeting at the Langdon Hotel, 597 South Dearborn Street, Chicago, IL 60605, at 7 p.m. The program will be a lecture in neurology by Dr. Steven Cassini. This announcement will be published in the Society's journal. Use a half sheet of plain white paper. Prepare a folder for local meetings of the Society.

Preparing for Meetings   Either the secretary or the chairperson of the program committee is responsible for making the necessary arrangements for the meeting. This involves the following arrangements:

> Selecting and reserving the meeting site (speaking with managers of several possible sites, then confirming the reservation).

Obtaining speakers (inviting, confirming, and obtaining information about a speaker's credentials).

Arranging the luncheon or dinner, if necessary (obtaining sample menus, selecting the appropriate menu, and confirming the number of luncheon or dinner reservations).

Preparing the program (obtaining items of interest from colleagues).

Preparing the agenda (order of business).

The agenda is typed and copies are made for members. A sample agenda is shown here.

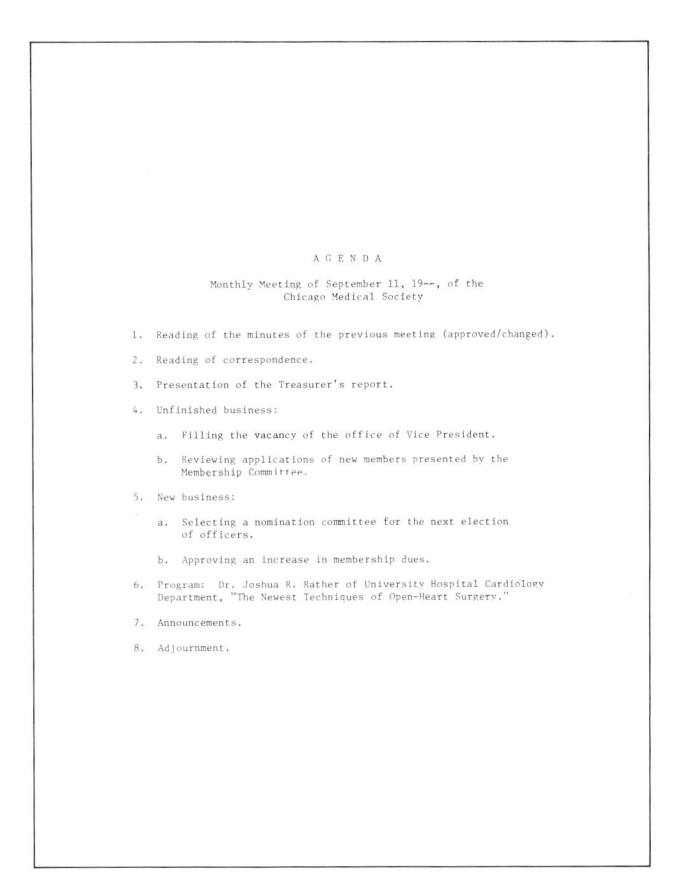

```
                         A G E N D A
            Monthly Meeting of September 11, 19--, of the
                      Chicago Medical Society

    1. Reading of the minutes of the previous meeting (approved/changed).
    2. Reading of correspondence.
    3. Presentation of the Treasurer's report.
    4. Unfinished business:
          a. Filling the vacancy of the office of Vice President.
          b. Reviewing applications of new members presented by the
             Membership Committee.
    5. New business:
          a. Selecting a nomination committee for the next election
             of officers.
          b. Approving an increase in membership dues.
    6. Program:  Dr. Joshua R. Rather of University Hospital Cardiology
       Department, "The Newest Techniques of Open-Heart Surgery."
    7. Announcements.
    8. Adjournment.
```

Before the meeting, the assistant should make sure that the room is ready for the meeting. The speaker may need a podium, a microphone, audiovisual equipment, and fresh water. Pens, notepads, pencils, agendas, and handouts should be ready and available for distribution. The assistant may even be called upon to greet guests.

Project 55
Preparing an Agenda

Prepare the agenda for the business session of the December 11 meeting. The order of business is as follows: reading of the minutes of the previous meeting, a report by the treasurer of the annual financial statement and a budget for the coming year, and voting whether to increase the annual membership dues from $75 to $100. Under new business there will be a consideration of whether to renew the lease of the present meeting site for another year, and the chairperson of the program committee will outline the program planned for the coming season. After that, the meeting can be adjourned. Prepare the agenda for duplication. Remember to include the program (Project 54).

138 PART 5: PROFESSIONAL ACTIVITIES

Project 56
Preparing Meeting Arrangements

You are to prepare a letter for Dr. Taylor's signature, thanking Dr. Cassini for accepting the invitation to speak at the Chicago Medical Society meeting in December. Also inquire as to the exact title of the lecture and whether any audiovisual equipment will be needed. Invite Dr. Cassini to the dinner. Dr. Cassini's address is the Professional Building, 8672 South Ridgeway Avenue, Chicago, IL 60652.

Dr. Taylor has made tentative arrangements with the hotel to serve dinner before the meeting. He has chosen the chicken Kiev specialty at $10.50 per person for 56 people, and he wants you to confirm this by writing to the hotel. Today's date is November 6. Dr. Taylor will be in the office on Monday and will sign the letter.

Recording the Minutes

During a meeting, *minutes* (an official record) are kept of the proceedings. The assistant may be asked to take down the proceedings during the meeting or to type the minutes from the recording secretary's notes. Meetings are conducted according to parliamentary procedure. Minutes typed in the formal style are shown here. Some employers may prefer the informal style, which dispenses with heads.

```
                        Minutes of the Meeting
                      CHICAGO CARDIOLOGY SOCIETY
                          November 14, 19--

The Call           The monthly meeting of the Chicago Cardiology Society
to Order           was held on November 14, 19--, in the office of the
                   County Medical Society. It was called to order at 8 p.m.
                   Dr. M. F. Watson presided.

Attendance         The following members were present:

                       Dr. Ernest Dodd      Dr. Morris Levine
                       Dr. Louise Fischer   Dr. Janis Potter
                       Dr. Richard Fisher   Dr. Joshua R. Rather
                       Dr. F. L. Gaither    Dr. Arthur Smith

Reading of         Upon motion made, seconded, and unanimously passed, the
Minutes Waived     reading of the minutes of the last meeting was waived.

Applicants for     The Chairperson of the Membership Committee reported the
Membership         names of three physicians who made application for member-
                   ship. These were Drs. John Adams, Alice Crawford, and
                   David Green. After a brief discussion of the eligibility
                   of each individual, a motion was made, seconded, and
                   unanimously carried to admit the three applicants to
                   membership. The Chairperson was instructed to so notify
                   the applicants.

Office of          The next matter of business was filling the vacancy of the
Treasurer          office of Treasurer. In view of the fact that elections
                   will be held shortly, it was decided after discussion that
                   the Secretary would take over these duties until new elec-
                   tions are held.

Nomination         The meeting then proceeded to the election of a nomination
Committee          committee. Nominations were proposed by the President and
                   also from the floor. After a voice vote was taken on each
                   name, the following committee was appointed by the President:

                       Dr. Richard Fisher, Chairperson
                       Dr. F. L. Gaither
                       Dr. Arthur Smith

Adjournment        There being no further business on the agenda, the meeting
                   was, upon motion, adjourned.


          _____        _____
            Recording Secretary                 President
```

If it is the assistant's duty to record the minutes, care should be taken to have the necessary supplies available: pens, pencils, and notebooks, or recording equipment if verbatim minutes are recorded. The assistant should read and refer to previous minutes. The following facts should be recorded for the minutes:

Date, location, time, and purpose of meeting.
Name of presiding officer.
Names of present members.

CHAPTER 14: MEDICAL SOCIETY MEETINGS 139

Order of business (obtained from agenda).

Motions made, whether approved or rejected, and names of those who made the motions.

Summaries of discussions.

Minutes are signed by the recording secretary, and usually also by the presiding officer. They are kept in an official book of minutes and are taken to every meeting. Sometimes copies are sent to each member or to each person who attended the meeting.

Project 57
Typing the Minutes

Dr. Taylor was recording secretary for the November 13 meeting of the Chicago Medical Society. He has drafted the minutes on WP 85. Type the minutes on plain paper, preparing them for Dr. Taylor's signature.

PROGRAM PARTICIPATION

A doctor may be asked to participate as a program speaker by invitation, by the doctor's submitting a desire to report some new developments or research, or by a "call for papers" by the society sponsoring the program. There usually is a deadline for submitting the title of a lecture and an outline or a summary, which is sent to the program committee.

Preparing for the Lecture

After the doctor has been notified of the acceptance of a paper for a program, various tasks must be completed by the assistant. A folder, labeled with the title of the lecture, should be made, and all notes and correspondence pertaining to the lecture should be kept in this folder. If photographs, charts, slides, or films are to be shown, it is imperative to assemble them in time, check them against the manuscript, and arrange them in the order in which they will be needed.

As soon as feasible, the committee should be informed of the following information about the lecture:

Correct title of lecture.

Approximate length of lecture.

Whether or not any audiovisual equipment is needed.

Biographical credentials of speaker.

Biographical credentials may be needed by the chairperson to introduce the speaker, for printing in the program, or for publicity purposes.

Project 58
Confirming Speaking Arrangements

Dr. Taylor has been asked to speak at the January 8 meeting of the Chicago Medical Society. Write a letter dated November 14 to Dr. M. F. Watson, President, Chicago Medical Society, 8672 South Ridgeway Avenue, Chicago, IL 60652. Tell Dr. Watson that Dr. Taylor's speech, entitled "The Role of Science and Research in Medical Practice," will be about 15 minutes long. No special equipment is needed. Enclose a biographical sketch of Dr. Taylor, which you should prepare on a separate sheet of paper. The following information should be included: date and place of birth—Albany, New York, June 3, 1943; medical degree—Johns Hopkins University, 1969; internship—University Hospital, Chicago, 1969 to 1971; Resident in Family Medicine, University Hospital, Chicago, 1971 to 1974; in private practice since 1974; resident instructor, University Medical School, Chicago, since 1977; memberships—AMA, Illinois AMA, Chicago Medical Society; office address.

Typing the Lecture

The length of time allowed for reading a paper varies at different meetings. A paper should be carefully planned to conform to the time limitation. As a rule, a typewritten page of 250 words takes about two minutes to read at medium speed. If the author speaks freely or uses only notes, care should be taken to watch the time while lecturing. If the paper is read, the type should be especially clear and dark. Doctors who read many papers might prefer to have a typewriter with very large type.

The draft of any speech or report is typed in standard manuscript style—double-spaced on a 60-space (Pica) or 70-space (Elite) line. The final copy of a speech is typed with triple spacing (it makes it easier to read) and with side margins of 20 to 25 spaces. This extra space provides for easier reading, and it allows space for the doctor to make notes and indicate where charts, slides, or transparencies are to be used.

If the material is to be published, it will be handled somewhat differently. Writing for publication is discussed in the next chapter.

PERSONAL DEVELOPMENT PROJECTS

TOPICS FOR DISCUSSION 1. Some doctors' husbands or wives participate in the running of the office. They check accounts, supervise the assistant's work, and watch expenses. As an assistant, what would you do to ensure a smooth relationship with the doctor's spouse?

2. One of the patient's folders is missing. Where could you look for it?

ROLE PLAYING 1. The Langdon Hotel telephones and asks what menu Dr. Taylor has chosen for the dinner meeting. You were not aware that a menu had to be selected.

2. Dr. Taylor frequently prepares handwritten correspondence at home for you to type at the office. His handwriting is difficult to read, and you need to discuss the matter with him.

15

Professional Reports

Many physicians are involved in writing articles, books, and speeches. A medical history of particular interest or reports of some special investigation may be presented to the doctor's colleagues. A doctor engaged in research work may do extensive writing in order to communicate findings to the scientific world. Whether it is for a lecture, an article, or a book, the assistant will be required to assist in assembling information, preparing the manuscript, and, in the case of publication, assisting with editorial duties.

ASSEMBLING INFORMATION

The term *research* can mean work the doctor has done for publication, such as investigations of clinical material or experiments or the study of pathological conditions. It can also mean work accomplished in the library. This is where the assistant becomes involved in obtaining materials for the doctor's reports.

Using the Library A doctor who is writing an article on a certain topic should first make a survey of work already published on the same subject. A doctor may need a research worker who can locate the literature and provide summaries or abstracts of pertinent information.

Physicians and other health workers have access to medical libraries. The librarian is one of the best sources of information. The assistant should talk to the librarian to obtain information about what type of material is available in the library.

Materials are systematically organized in any library to make information easily obtainable. The card catalog is an index of book contents available in the library and helps the researcher locate materials quickly. Cards are alphabetized by subject, author, and title. An example of a card is shown here.

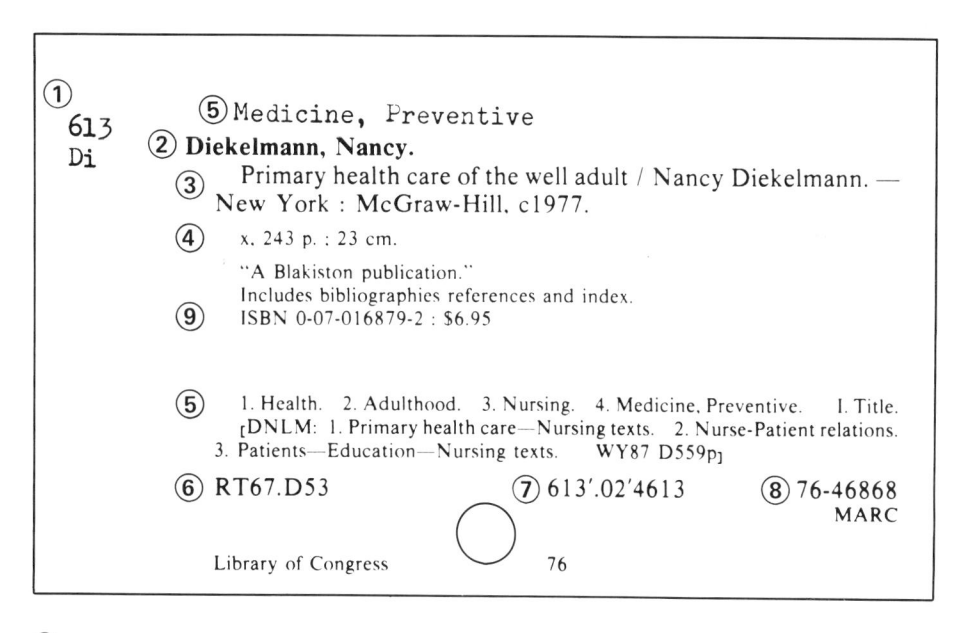

```
①                ⑤ Medicine, Preventive
  613            ② Diekelmann, Nancy.
  Di             ③    Primary health care of the well adult / Nancy Diekelmann. —
                      New York : McGraw-Hill, c1977.
                 ④    x, 243 p. : 23 cm.
                      "A Blakiston publication."
                      Includes bibliographies references and index.
                 ⑨    ISBN 0-07-016879-2 : $6.95

                 ⑤    1. Health.  2. Adulthood.  3. Nursing.  4. Medicine, Preventive.  I. Title.
                      [DNLM: 1. Primary health care—Nursing texts.  2. Nurse-Patient relations.
                      3. Patients—Education—Nursing texts.   WY87 D559p]
                 ⑥ RT67.D53              ⑦ 613'.02'4613        ⑧ 76-46868
                                                                    MARC
                   Library of Congress           76
```

① Classification and book number.
② Author's name.
③ Book title, coauthor(s) (if any), edition (if other than first), publisher, and publication date and place.
④ Number of text pages and size of book in centimeters.
⑤ Subject classification.
⑥ Library of Congress call number.
⑦ Dewey decimal classification number.
⑧ Card serial number.
⑨ International Standard Book Number (ISBN)

Medical journals and periodicals contain most of the current medical literature. In order to obtain information from these sources, the assistant must use the indexes available in a medical library. The *Index Medicus*, published by the National Library of Medicine, contains a monthly bibliography of medical reviews. The American Hospital Association, in cooperation with the National Library of Medicine, publishes a quarterly, *Hospital Literature Index*, pertaining to all specialty areas in a hospital. The *Cumulative Index Medicus*, also published by the National Library of Medicine, is an annual index volume containing both a subject and an author index, besides a list of recently published medical books.

The National Library of Medicine has a computer-based retrieval system, MEDLARS, which is available at medical centers, hospitals, universities, government centers, and commercial organizations. Terminals at the various institutions are connected by telephone lines to the computers at the National Library of Medicine. Besides having access to references in books as well as articles in health science journals, MEDLARS terminals have access to MEDLINE (biomedical references), TOXLINE (toxicology information), CHEMLINE (dictionary of chemical substances), CANCERLIT (cancer literature), and several other data bases.

Abstracts The *Journal of the American Medical Association* and most of the other medical and scientific journals contain abstracts of articles. An abstract is a summary of an article, book, or case history. It denotes the purpose of the item and summarizes the main ideas and conclusions. *Biological Abstracts* and *Psychology Abstracts* are journals that contain only abstracts of published work in these respective fields. By reading an abstract, the doctor can decide whether the article needs to be studied more thoroughly.

PREPARING THE MANUSCRIPT

Steps leading to the typing of a manuscript will vary according to each doctor's preference. Some authors make voluminous notes, and then either dictate from these notes or hand them to the assistant for typing. Most writers start by making an outline, jotting down main headings, and subheadings, and perhaps breaking these down still further. At any rate, the first complete and consecutive typing is in the form of a draft.

Drafts The assistant should double-space or triple-space the draft, leaving generous margins on both sides. This spacing leaves ample room for additions and corrections. (The most common proofreader's marks for typewritten drafts are shown at the bottom of the page.) A very practical system is to type drafts on different-colored paper. This greatly helps to keep different versions separated and aids in identifying them quickly.

Final Drafts The final copy submitted to the publisher should be typed on good-quality standard-sized white bond paper. At least one photostat or carbon copy must be made, but a second copy is advisable. Authors frequently wish to send copies of manuscripts to friends or colleagues for suggestions and advice. The text should be double-spaced and have a margin of at least 15 to 18 spaces on all sides. All pages should contain the same number of lines.

The title is typed in capital letters, followed by the name and degree of the author and possibly an official title and the institution where the doctor is employed. A statement as to the auspices under which the article was written or the experimental work done may be given in a footnote. If the article has been presented at a meeting, exact information regarding the name of the medical society and the date of the meeting is also included in a footnote.

> THE ROLE OF SCIENCE AND RESEARCH IN MEDICAL PRACTICE
> Warren Taylor, M.D.
>
> In many quarters there still exists the attitude that medicine is an art and not a science. Yet, without science—and research, which is the handmaiden of science—patients would not enjoy the vast improvements in diagnosis and treatment that today they take as a matter of course. To prove my point, I would like to outline for you some of the modern developments that have benefitted medical practice and have resulted in our being able to save patients' lives or at least relieve some of their symptoms.
>
> Outstanding, of course, are defenses against infectious diseases. These scourges, such as typhoid fever, diphtheria, tuberculosis, and the plague, which formerly laid low whole populations, have been almost eradicated because of our knowledge of the bacteria involved and of methods to combat their effects.
>
> Several lines of attack were required to conquer these bacterial infections. It was necessary to study the biology of the organism in order to understand what caused the virulent reaction, to learn the meaning of immunity, to develop methods of immunization, and to predict the pattern of epidemics of a disease and its movement through a populated area. Finally came the development of drugs that killed the bacteria without harming the patient. This research produced the drugs called antibiotics.
>
> However, some viral diseases are resistant to antibiotics. One of these is poliomyelitis. The virtual disappearance of this disease is one

Most typewriters are equipped with a line scale to guide the typist to make sure that the margin at the bottom of the page is correct throughout the manuscript. Uniformity of page length and width helps in estimating the number of words in the manuscript.

No number is placed on the first page; subsequent pages are consistently numbered at the top in the center, at the top right-hand corner, or at the bottom in the center beginning with page 2. Pages are numbered consecutively, not by chapters.

Project 59
Typing From Rough Drafts

A rough draft of the beginning of a manuscript appears on WP 87. Retype this draft in final form. In addition to the corrections shown, there are a number of errors in spelling and punctuation that must be corrected. The title of the manuscript is "Loving Hands—A Page From the Past."

Martin Bough/Studios, Inc.

Headings   Headings are used throughout the text to alert and guide the reader to new subjects. Main headings should be flush with the margin so that they will not be overlooked. Subheadings may begin with the paragraph indention and be underlined. Words that are to be printed in italics are underlined once, and boldface type is indicated by a wavy underscore. Foreign words are underlined, but not medical terms in common use.

Quotations   When published material is quoted in an article or a book, it must be either enclosed in quotation marks or indented to set it off from the text. If the quotation is brief, quotation marks are acceptable.

Footnotes   Footnotes and references that are to be printed at the bottom of the page may be indicated by typing the footnote after the line where it is mentioned and separating it from the rest of the text by solid lines across the page. Another way is to type all footnotes at the end of the manuscript on a separate page.

Some authors prefer still another method; that is, to have footnotes typed at the bottom of the page, just as they will appear on the printed page.

Illustrations   If photographs, tables, or graphs accompany the article, they should be handled carefully. Do not paste or mount any illustrative matter in the manuscript. Keep the illustrations separate, keying each to the appropriate page of the manuscript. Photographs must be glossy prints, and notations should be typed on separate paper, not on the prints.

Bibliographies

Practically every scientific article or book refers to other publications. These references are placed either at the bottom of the page in a footnote, at the end of the article under the heading *References,* or, in the case of a book, at the end of each chapter or at the end of the book as a bibliography.

A complete reference contains all the necessary information enabling the reader to find the book or article quickly. A book reference contains the surname of author or editor, followed by first name or initials, title of book, name of publisher, place of publication, and year of publication. Bibliographic entries are listed alphabetically by author. If there is no author, alphabetize by title. The words *The* and *A* are disregarded in determining this alphabetic sequence. If there are two or more authors, only the first author's name is inverted. If there is more than one entry by the same author, the author's name is replaced by a long dash (six hyphens) in all the entries for that author. The entries for this author are then alphabetized by title. A periodical reference requires the name of author, title of article, name of journal in which the article appears, volume number of journal, page numbers on which the article begins and ends, and date of issue.

BIBLIOGRAPHY

Bredow, Miriam, Karonne Becklin, and Edith Sunnarborg, *Medical Office Procedures,* 2d ed., Gregg Division, McGraw-Hill Book Company, New York, 1981.

Sabin, William A., *The Gregg Reference Manual,* 5th ed., Gregg Division, McGraw-Hill Book Company, New York, 1977.

Stewart, Marie M., Frank W. Lanham, and Kenneth Zimmer, *College English and Communication,* 3d ed., Gregg and Community College Division, McGraw-Hill Book Company, New York, 1975.

――――, *Communication Problems Correlated With College English and Communication,* 3d ed., Gregg and Community College Division, McGraw-Hill Book Company, New York, 1975.

West, Judy F., and Daniel R. Boyd, "Mail Processing Updated," *The Secretary,* February 1978, pp. 16-17, 26-30.

The sequence of information varies somewhat with different publishers. Consult the publisher for the style that is desired.

Project 60
Preparing a Bibliography

Prepare a bibliography in alphabetic order of all books you are using in your present course. Include at least one magazine article. Type it on plain paper.

ASSISTING WITH EDITORIAL DUTIES

If a manuscript has been accepted for publication, the author is notified and a new set of tasks begins.

Proof

After a manuscript has been set in type, the proof is sent to the author for corrections. Galley proofs are long, narrow sheets on which material is printed consecutively, without page divisions. This proof must be carefully read for typographical errors and checked against the original manuscript. The manuscript may then go into page proof, where it is again checked for errors and also checked for proper pagination, insertion of footnotes, page makeup, and so forth.

Corrections of both galley and page proof are always made in the margin and never in the text. The place where the correction should be made is indicated in the text by a caret (for insertions) or a slash (for changes or deletions). Standard proofreading symbols are illustrated in most dictionaries. Corrections should be made in ink of a different color from that used by previous proofreaders. Publishers usually give authors guidelines for making changes on proof.

Whenever a correction has been made on the galley proof, check the whole line, for the entire line may have been reset and other mistakes may easily have crept in. Make only changes and additions that are absolutely essential, especially on a page proof; if a page is overrun, all the remaining pages must be remade. If a correction seems imperative, new material should take up approximately as many letters as there were in the deleted type.

Index Every modern technical book has an index, and frequently there are separate author and subject indexes. The more complete the index, the more valuable the publication, especially if it is to be used as a reference book.

The indexer usually works with page proof. Starting with the first page, each subject mentioned is written on a separate slip or index card. If there is a possibility that material might be sought under another heading, a second card is made. For instance, when indexing a passage about the patients' ledger, one card would be marked "Patients' ledger," and a second card "Ledger, patients'." Whenever different topics are discussed under one main heading, a secondary entry is made, "Clinical data, filing" and "Clinical data, forms." The page numbers where the entry occurs are entered on each card.

It is a good practice to arrange the cards alphabetically as they are made. Subheadings are arranged alphabetically under the main heading.

The index of this book can be consulted for an example of how an index should look in its final form. Meticulous checking of cards against proof is necessary. Copy for the index should be sent to the publisher as soon as possible after proofs are returned.

MEDICAL JOURNALS

Most medical societies publish their own journals. The American Medical Association publishes about a dozen periodicals on special subjects in addition to the official organ of the society, the *Journal of the American Medical Association*, which includes articles relating to the entire field of medicine. Other medical journals are published by hospitals, by universities, or independently.

Journals are often bound annually for permanent reference, since they contain much valuable information. Most journals publish an index for the entire volume in the last number of each volume (volumes do not always correspond to the calendar year and may vary in the length of time covered). The journal should not be sent to the binder until the index has been received, so that it can be bound together with the appropriate volume.

Subscribing to Medical Journals In an office where many journals are subscribed to, a detailed record is necessary. A card should be made for each journal, indicating frequency of publication, subscription price, and expiration date. Cards used for this purpose may be filed in a small box. Cards especially printed for use in a periodical file are obtainable.

Project 61
Composing Subscription Letters

Dr. Taylor wants you to cancel his subscription to the *Journal of Family Practice,* Appleton-Century-Crofts, 292 Madison Avenue, New York, NY 10017, which expires at the end of next year. He wants to subscribe to the *American Family Physician,* American Academy of Family Physicians, 1740 West 92d Street, Kansas City, MO 64114. Date both letters November 14.

Reprints The only way a doctor can inform colleagues and other scientists about work accomplished is by lecturing and writing about it. If the doctor reads a paper at a medical meeting, it is usually published in the official publication of the society or in another medical journal. However, the article may be submitted to a journal without having first been read at a meeting.

Doctors may receive a limited number of reprints free from the publisher; additional copies are available at cost. These reprints are sent by the doctor to other professionals interested in the same or allied fields. The assistant has to handle both incoming reprints received by the office and reprints sent out by the employer.

Incoming reprints should be stamped with the date of receipt and promptly acknowledged on a printed form (made for this purpose) or by letter.

Sometimes a doctor may want a reprint of a designated article. Then the doctor must write a letter requesting a reprint from its author. A second note, acknowledging receipt of the reprint, should be sent after it has been received.

The filing of reprints presents a very special problem because of their size and bulk. One system for filing is to prepare an index card for each reprint with the name of the author, the title of the reprint, and a notation indicating where the reprint is filed. These cards are filed alphabetically, while the reprints are kept in boxes, in filing drawers, or on shelves, by subject. A designated filing area should be set aside for these reprints, such as in a certain location in the file room or storage area.

**Project 62
Requesting Reprints**   Dr. Taylor would like to obtain a reprint entitled "Continuing Education for Family Physicians." This topic is of special interest to Dr. Taylor. Dr. Milton Monroe is the author and the article was published in the May issue of this year's *Journal of the American Medical Association (JAMA)*. Date the letter November 14.

If the doctor has had an article accepted for publication in a medical journal, reprints should be ordered at the time corrected proof is returned to the publisher.

The list of those to whom reprints are sent is compiled from directories and membership lists. A record should be kept in the general correspondence file of reprints sent and of acknowledgments received. Individuals who have not acknowledged two or three reprints may be removed from the list. New names can always be added and changes of address made.

REFERENCES AND RESOURCES   An educated person must have the ability to know where to find varied information. The assistant should be familiar with a variety of reference books. Below is a list of the five kinds of books most commonly in use. All these references must be revised periodically; the most recent edition should always be consulted.

1. *Dictionaries,* both general and medical, should be consulted to obtain information about spelling, pronunciation, definition, syllabication, capitalization, hyphenation, and noun plurals.
2. *Synonym and antonym references,* or *thesauruses,* should be used to obtain exact terminology, as many words have approximately the same meaning, but a certain shade of difference may exist.

3. *Secretarial reference books* will provide the assistant with information on grammar, punctuation, style, letter closings, salutations, legal forms, and other subjects.
4. *Drug and medicine references* give up-to-date information on all drugs and medications on the market, their trade names, manufacturers, indications, contraindications, and recommended dosages.
5. *Biographical directories* provide credential information about medical colleagues and other prominent persons. These may also be used to compile a list of specialists in one field or another.

PERSONAL DEVELOPMENT PROJECTS

TOPICS FOR DISCUSSION 1. Visit a medical library to see what resources are available to physicians and other professionals.
2. Use the local library to make a list of the current books available in the following categories:
   a. Medical dictionaries
   b. Synonym and antonym references
   c. Secretarial reference books
   d. Biographical directories
   e. Indexes to publications

ROLE PLAYING 1. You notice how cluttered Dr. Taylor's desk is becoming. He has a stack of journals with markers in them, and he indicates he is interested in those articles. Offer your assistance.
2. Dr. Taylor is not in the office when the pharmaceutical sales representative visits. The representative asks if you would spend a few minutes with her.

16

Travel Arrangements

When the doctor travels for professional or social reasons, the assistant will be involved in preparations for the trip and has many obligations while the doctor is away.

PREPARATIONS FOR THE TRIP

In preparing for the doctor's trip, the assistant must consult the doctor, carefully noting date and time of departure, destinations, length of stay at each destination, and time of arrival at and departure from each destination.

A folder should be kept for any information about the trip. After the doctor returns, some of this material can be discarded, and the rest filed in the usual manner.

Travel Arrangements

The doctor may travel by airplane, railroad, ship, bus, or car. In the latter case, no advance ticket arrangements are necessary. For travel by any other means, advance reservations are advisable. The earlier they are made, the better. If it is the assistant's responsibility to attend to this, the assistant must know what class of travel the doctor prefers and the chosen travel carrier.

Airlines and railroads operate various plans which enable members of the passenger's family to travel at reduced rates. It is also advisable to inquire

from OCTOBER 9

NOVEMBER

S	M	T	W	T	F	S
						1
2	3	4	5	6	7	8
9	10	11	12	13	14	15
16	17	18	19	20	21	22
23/30	24	25	26	27	28	29

Thursday, Oct. 9
- 8:15–10 Hospital rounds
- 12–1:45 Lunch
- 5:30 Paul Bachmann – HC
- 8 Local medical society meeting

Friday, Oct. 10
- 8:15–9:45 Hospital rounds
- 10:45 Dictation
- 12:15–4:45 Afternoon off

Saturday, Oct. 11

Sunday, Oct. 12
COLUMBUS DAY

from **OCTOBER 13**

OCTOBER

S	M	T	W	T	F	S
			1	2	3	4
5	6	7	8	9	10	11
12	13	14	15	16	17	18
19	20	21	22	23	24	25
26	27	28	29	30	31	

WEEK AT A GLANCE

Monday, Oct. 13 287	Tuesday, Oct. 14 288	Wednesday, Oct. 15 289
8 COLUMBUS DAY OBSERVED	8	8
8 15	8 15	8 15
8 30	8 30	8 30
8 45	8 45	8 45
9	9	9
9 15	9 15	9 15
9 30	9 30	9 30
9 45	9 45	9 45
10	10	10
10 15	10 15	10 15
10 30	10 30	10 30
10 45	10 45	10 45
11	11	11
11 15	11 15	11 15
11 30	11 30	11 30
11 45	11 45	11 45
12	12	12
12 15	12 15	12 15
12 30	12 30	12 30
12 45	12 45	12 45
1	1	1
1 15	1 15	1 15
1 30	1 30	1 30
1 45	1 45	1 45
2	2	2
2 15	2 15	2 15
2 30	2 30	2 30
2 45	2 45	2 45
3	3	3
3 15	3 15	3 15
3 30	3 30	3 30
3 45	3 45	3 45
4	4	4
4 15	4 15	4 15
4 30	4 30	4 30
4 45	4 45	4 45
5	5	5
5 15	5 15	5 15
5 30	5 30	5 30
5 45	5 45	5 45
6	6	6
6 15	6 15	6 15
6 30	6 30	6 30
6 45	6 45	6 45
7	7	7
7 15	7 15	7 15
7 30	7 30	7 30
7 45	7 45	7 45
8	8	8
8 15	8 15	8 15
8 30	8 30	8 30
8 45	8 45	8 45
9	9	9
9 15	9 15	9 15
9 30	9 30	9 30
9 45	9 45	9 45

Directions: It is 1 p.m. The appointment book has two 15-minute openings for this afternoon. Dr. Taylor is now busy with the afternoon appointments. The schedule for tomorrow is almost filled. When someone telephones, you must choose what to do about the call. The left-hand column lists some incoming calls. The right-hand column lists the choices you have regarding each call. Indicate what action you would take for each call by putting the appropriate letter from the right-hand column before each situation in the left-hand column. Letters may be used more than once.

Incoming Call

_____ 1. Insurance company representative telephones.

_____ 2. Dr. Andrew Jones telephones.

_____ 3. Patient complains of chest pain.

_____ 4. Patient requests a pap smear.

_____ 5. Social worker asks for Dr. Taylor.

_____ 6. Lab technician has a report.

_____ 7. Patient has difficulty breathing.

_____ 8. Patient has abdominal pain.

_____ 9. Child has temperature of 104° — no transportation.

_____ 10. Patient has a rash; is on no medication.

_____ 11. Child has been walking with a limp for several days.

_____ 12. Two-year-old cries when she walks.

_____ 13. Personal friend of Dr. Taylor asks to speak with him.

_____ 14. Emergency room nurse calls to talk with Dr. Taylor about patient in emergency room.

_____ 15. Patient wishes to have a wart removed.

_____ 16. Hospital administrator's secretary asks to speak with Dr. Taylor.

_____ 17. Pharmacy calls for prescription refill.

_____ 18. Patient complains of voiding frequently, with burning sensation.

_____ 19. Three-year-old has aspirin bottle in hand; may have ingested some aspirins.

_____ 20. High school athlete wants physical today so that he can play football tomorrow.

Course of Action

a. Take a message.

b. Make appointment for today.

c. Make appointment for tomorrow, or as soon as an opening is available.

d. Transfer call to Dr. Taylor.

e. Give advice.

WP 27

about excursion fares, economy fares, and group rates. These reduced rates usually are valid only on certain days of the week, are good for a limited duration, and may not be applicable during peak travel seasons. Different kinds of plans are offered by passenger lines, and the latest information about each should be carefully checked. It is also advisable to compare services of several lines. Timetables are available free of charge. The assistant should obtain several timetables and become familiar with them.

If reservations are made by telephone, tickets may be sent to the office or may have to be picked up at a certain location. After receiving the tickets, carefully check them. Also, note any additional information given by the travel carrier, such as luggage limitations.

A passport must be obtained in advance for travel abroad. A passport picture and application must be submitted to a passport agent's office or an issuing office. A passport is only valid for five years; if the doctor has one already, it should be checked to see if it is still valid. For certain foreign countries, a visa must be obtained. Certain vaccinations and immunizations may be necessary for travel in various countries. It is well to check these points, either with the consulate in question or the travel agency.

The best resources for travel information are skilled agents at a reputable travel agency. They are trained to assist in almost every aspect of travel—making travel and hotel reservations, issuing tickets for travel, renting cars, assisting in obtaining necessary documents for foreign travel, and even helping obtain tickets for entertainment.

Hotel Reservations   As soon as possible, hotel accommodations should be reserved. Most resort hotels and hotel chains have offices in the larger cities or have toll-free numbers one can call to obtain reservations by telephone. The *Hotel and Motel Red Book* lists leading hotels and motels in the country, together with their rates and facilities. It is necessary to know the type of accommodation to reserve. Some hotels require a deposit. Confirmation of reservations in writing should always be requested. This must be given to the doctor before departure.

Martin Bough/Studios, Inc.

```
                              ITINERARY
        Warren Taylor, M.D.                                    April 19--
                     (Chicago, New York City, Boston)

        Friday, April 10
        (Chicago-New York City)

            5:00 p.m., CST       Depart Chicago, O'Hare International,
                                 American Airlines, jet coach (Y) nonstop
                                 flight 104, 707.  Dinner.

            8:00 p.m., EST       Arrive New York, Kennedy International
                                 Airport.

                                 Accommodation:  Americana Hotel, 52d Street
                                 and Seventh Avenue, New York, NY 10019.

        Sunday, April 12
        (New York City-Boston)

            7:00 p.m., EST       Depart New York, La Guardia Airport,
                                 American Airlines, jet coach (Y) nonstop
                                 flight 526, 727.

            8:01 p.m., EST       Arrive Boston, Logan International Airport.

                                 Accommodation:  Sheraton-Boston Hotel,
                                 Prudential Center, Boston, MA 02199.

        Monday, April 13

            Reminder             Make dinner reservations.

            7:30 p.m., EST       Dinner with Dr. and Mrs. Charles Whitfield.

        Tuesday, April 14
        (Boston-Chicago)

            6:45 p.m., EST       Depart Boston, Logan International Airport,
                                 American Airlines, jet coach (Y) nonstop
                                 flight 157, D10.  Dinner.

            8:12 p.m., CST       Arrive Chicago, O'Hare International.
```

Project 63
Changing Hotel Reservations

Dr. and Mrs. Taylor will be visiting Mrs. Janis Boeker, Mrs. Taylor's sister, at 785 West Sherman Avenue, Phoenix, AZ 85007, from November 21 to November 29. They will then be in San Diego until December 3. Dr. Taylor had previously made a reservation for a single room at the San Diego Heights Hotel from November 28 to December 2. Write a letter, dated November 14, to change the reservation dates and room accommodations. Dr. and Mrs. Taylor would like a double deluxe room at poolside for the nights of November 29 through December 2. Confirmation should be sent by the hotel to Dr. Taylor while he is in Phoenix. The hotel address is 11199 Berry Knoll, San Diego, CA 92126.

Prepare a travel folder.

Itinerary If the doctor plans to visit several places, an itinerary must be prepared. Travel agencies will provide an itinerary as part of their services. An itinerary consists of a list of each place where the doctor will stay, the name and address of the hotel, and the date of arrival and departure. A number of copies should be made: one for the doctor, one for the assistant, and other copies for persons who might have to get in touch with the doctor at any time. Itineraries may include a person's schedule at a convention.

Project 64
Typing an Itinerary

Dr. Taylor has used the Best Travel Agency for the trip to Phoenix and San Diego. The agency has prepared the itinerary shown in WP 89. Dr. Taylor has corrected the meeting schedule for the convention on WP 91. Dr. Taylor would like you to combine the prepared itinerary with the meeting schedule into one itinerary that he can follow. Use plain paper and make three carbons: one for Dr. Taylor, one for Mrs. Taylor, and one for the office.

Travel Funds It is necessary for the doctor to have travel funds. One of the most practical methods is the use of traveler's checks. Traveler's checks come in denominations of $10, $20, $50, and $100 and may be purchased at most banks for a small charge. The purchaser signs each check at the place of purchase and then countersigns it in the presence of the person cashing it. In case of loss, the money is refunded.

Another popular method is the use of credit cards. People who travel can charge purchases, hotels, meals, and transportation. Some cards are universally accepted and provide the user with a quick method of payment for any necessary purchases or services.

If the doctor attends a medical convention, or if the trip is somehow otherwise connected with the doctor's practice, travel expenses may be deducted for income-tax purposes. It is necessary, however, to retain receipts for every expenditure. The doctor should keep an accurate and detailed record of expenses. After the doctor's return, all expenses can be tabulated, entered in the appropriate accounting records, and the receipts filed.

WHILE THE DOCTOR IS AWAY The assistant has a double responsibility, when left alone, to look after the employer's affairs in addition to regular duties. Everything must be taken care of, and the doctor must be informed of details.

Financial Duties Arrangements need to be made beforehand with the doctor about paying bills during the doctor's absence. Sufficient petty cash should be available to last while the doctor is away. The doctor may arrange with a lawyer or a bank to take care of all expenses. It is important to have a clear understanding of what will be done about these matters.

Appointments As soon as dates for the doctor's trip have been decided upon, the appointment book must be marked accordingly, so that no patients will be scheduled to visit the doctor at that time. Patients who have regular appointments may have to be notified that the doctor will be away, and new appointments should be arranged.

The doctor should select another physician to provide for patients' care during the absence. The name, address, and telephone number of the substituting doctor should be available at all times so that the assistant can give the information without any delay if a patient telephones. This information may also be included in the letter notifying patients that the doctor will be away. A sample letter is illustrated at the top of the next page.

Dear Mrs. Jackson:

Dr. Taylor will be away from the office from June 15 to August 30. During his absence, Dr. Albert Cronklin, 3399 South Sawyer Avenue, telephone number 555-3550, will look after Dr. Taylor's patients. Therefore, if you need a physician, please telephone Dr. Cronklin.

I have rescheduled you for an appointment with Dr. Taylor for Tuesday, September 9, at 10 a.m.

Sincerely,
Medical Assistant

Telephone Calls Telephone calls are handled in the same way as when the doctor is in the office. The important point is to follow through on as many calls as possible so that as few matters as possible will be left pending. A telephone log should be kept of all calls. A memorandum should be made of important calls, with a brief summary of the conversation and the action taken.

Since it may be necessary in an emergency to telephone the substitute doctor, the telephone number where the doctor can be reached should be noted at all times.

Mail Mail must be handled with special care. Whether or not to forward letters depends on the length of time the doctor will be away, on the urgency of the matter, and on the assistant's ability to handle the problems involved. If a reply must wait until the doctor's return, receipt of the letter should be acknowledged. A sample letter that will serve in most instances is shown below:

Dear Dr. Green:

Your letter of March 24 was received during Dr. Taylor's absence and will be brought to his attention when he returns on April 7. You will receive a reply from him as soon as possible.

Sincerely,
Medical Assistant

Reports Reports should be sent to the doctor regularly regarding happenings in the office, especially if the doctor is absent for a month or more. These reports should be frequent and specific. It is the responsibility of the assistant to send the doctor such a report, if so directed. In order not to forget anything, it is best to keep a daily log, jotting down each telephone call and letter received and the action taken in each instance.

Spare Time With the doctor away, the assistant may find free time. This is a good time to do the many things for which there is little opportunity when the doctor has a busy appointment schedule. Here are a few suggestions:

Clean out files and replace worn folders.
Make new labels for all types of containers.
Straighten out supply cabinets.
Update procedures manual.
Have curtains, rugs, and draperies cleaned.

Some more extensive work can be done at this time, such as sending apparatus or furniture for repair, having the offices painted, or having floors scraped and waxed. These details would have to be discussed beforehand with the doctor.

PERSONAL DEVELOPMENT PROJECTS

TOPICS FOR DISCUSSION 1. A serious problem arises with the office nurse when Dr. Taylor is out of town at a convention. Should you telephone him?

2. When some doctors go on vacation for two or more weeks, they close their offices and require the assistants to take their vacations at the same time. How do you feel about this sort of vacation arrangement?

ROLE PLAYING 1. When Dr. Taylor is away, a patient telephones to say that her husband is having difficulty breathing and feels very sick.

2. When Dr. Taylor is away, a colleague telephones and wants to know whether Dr. Taylor has decided to speak at the February meeting of the Chicago Medical Society.

Simulation 4

Today you will begin your fourth two-day simulation in Dr. Taylor's office. The days will be Thursday, November 20, and Friday, November 21.

PROCEDURES Review general directions provided on pages 74-75 for handling simulations. Follow the same procedures for Day 1 and Day 2 as you did in the other simulations.

MATERIALS YOU WILL NEED

Appointment Book

Card File

Supplies Folder
All the usual supplies

Day 1 Folder	Source
Daily journal	
November 20	WP 93
Check from Ann Curtiss	WP 207

Day 2 Folder	
Daily journal	
November 21	WP 95
Workers' compensation form	WP 97
Coding sheet	WP 99
Checks from Ellen Goldberg, Joseph Provost, and Thomas Leslie	WP 207-209

Patients' Charts
The following patients' charts (folders) should contain the items given below:

	Source
Bachman, Joseph	
Ledger card	Project 36
Clinical data sheet	Project 15
Letter to Dr. Gonzalez	Project 15
Bachmann, Paul	
Ledger card, updated	Simulation 3
Clinical data sheet, updated	Project 32
House call slip	Project 12
Message	Simulation 1
Berndt, Stanley	
Ledger card, updated	Simulation 3
Clinical data sheet, updated	Simulation 3
Collection letter	Project 37
Appointment card	Simulation 2
Message	Simulation 3
Berquist, Rebecca	
Ledger card	Project 36
Clinical data sheet	Project 32
Burnett, Jane	
Ledger card	Project 36
OB form, updated	Simulation 3
Letter rescheduling appointment	Simulation 3
Letter about fees	Project 35
Records release and letter to Dr. Kaplan	Simulation 1
Patient introduction slip	Project 13
Appointment card	Simulation 1
Message	Simulation 3
Curtiss, Lois	
Ledger card, updated	Project 42
Clinical data sheet, updated	Simulation 3
House call slip	Project 31
Message	Simulation 3
Goldberg, Ellen	
Ledger card, updated	Simulation 3
Clinical data sheet, updated	Simulation 3
Medicare form	Project 40
Message	Project 17
Receipt	Simulation 3
Grazzini, Mario	
Ledger card	Project 36
Clinical data sheet	Project 25
Messages—2	Simulation 1
Grebowski, Paul	
Ledger card	Project 36
Clinical data sheet	Project 25
Letter rescheduling appointment	Simulation 1
Message	Simulation 2

Patients' Charts	Source
Grimes, Jill	
Ledger card, updated	Simulation 3
Clinical data sheet, updated	Simulation 2
Letter to Dr. Whitman	Simulation 2
Health insurance claim form	Project 38
Card with Dr. Whitman's address	Simulation 2
Appointment card	Simulation 1
Hayes, Gail	
Ledger card, updated	Simulation 3
Clinical data sheet, updated	Simulation 3
Patient introduction slip	Project 32
Receipt	Simulation 3
Appointment card	Simulation 3
Kellogg, Alice	
Ledger card, updated	Simulation 3
Clinical data sheet, updated	Simulation 3
Message	Simulation 2
Message	Simulation 1
Knutson, Karen	
Ledger card	Project 36
Clinical data sheet	Project 25
Message	Simulation 2
Leslie, Sheila	
Ledger card, updated	Simulation 3
Clinical data sheet, updated	Simulation 3
Appointment card	Simulation 2
Message	Simulation 3
Logan, Carl	
Ledger card, updated	Simulation 3
Clinical data sheet, updated	Simulation 3
Medicare form	Simulation 3
Message	Simulation 3
Malinsky, William	
Ledger card, updated	Simulation 3
Clinical data sheet, updated	Simulation 3
Appointment card	Simulation 2
Appointment card	Simulation 3
Receipt	Simulation 3
Message	Simulation 2
McKinley, Sharon	
Ledger card, updated	Simulation 3
Clinical data sheet, updated	Simulation 3
Messages—3	Simulation 3
Perez, Manuel	
Ledger card, updated	Simulation 3
Clinical data sheet, updated	Simulation 3
Patient introduction slip	Simulation 2
Letter to Dr. Andrews	Simulation 1
Message	Simulation 1
Provost, Janis	
Ledger card, updated	Project 39
Clinical data sheet, updated	Simulation 2
Letter to Dr. Lillian Bradford	Simulation 2
Blue Cross-Blue Shield form	Project 39
Stephens, Jason	
Ledger card, updated	Simulation 3
Clinical data sheet, updated	Simulation 3
Workers' compensation reports	Project 41

Patients' Charts	Source
Stillman, Marlene	
Ledger card	Simulation 2
Clinical data sheet	Simulation 2
Patient introduction slip	Simulation 2
Message	Simulation 1
Wellman, Marion	
Ledger card, updated	Simulation 3
Clinical data sheet, updated	Simulation 3
Appointment card	Simulation 1
Appointment card	Project 11
Appointment card	Simulation 2
Message	Simulation 2
Whitfall, Martin	
Ledger card	Project 36
Clinical data sheet	Project 32
Patient introduction slip	Project 32

Miscellaneous Folder

Letters:

American Family Physician	Project 61
Dr. Stanley F. Anderson	Simulation 1
Dr. Allen Jones	Simulation 2
Journal of Family Practice	Project 61
Dr. Scott McIntosh	Project 10
Medical Supplies Service	Project 53
Dr. Louise Merryweather	Project 27
Dr. Milton Monroe	Project 62

Messages:

Mrs. Taylor	Simulation 1
Mrs. Bateson	Simulation 1

Financial Records Folder

Daily journals	Project 42
Daily journals	Simulation 3
Monthly summary sheet, updated	Simulation 3
Deposit slip	Project 44
Deposit slip	Simulation 3
Checks	Project 45
Bank statement	Project 46
Petty cash voucher	Project 47
Check	Project 47
Salary check	Project 48
Employee earnings record	Project 48

Local Society Meetings Folder

Announcement	Project 54
Agenda	Project 55
Letter to Dr. Cassini	Project 56
Letter to Langdon Hotel	Project 56
Minutes of the meeting	Project 57
Letter to Dr. Watson, including Dr. Taylor's biographical sketch	Project 58

Travel Folder

Letter changing reservations	Project 63
Itinerary	Project 64
Dr. Milton Monroe	Project 28

If you have not completed all the projects and do not have all these records set up in advance, talk with your instructor.

MEDICAL TERMINOLOGY

_____ analgesia
_____ anesthesia
_____ anorexia
_____ aspiration
_____ atelectasis
_____ atresia
_____ atrophy
_____ contracture
_____ coronary
_____ diastole
_____ febrile
_____ gangrene

_____ hemostasis
_____ in situ
_____ lavage
_____ meatus
_____ necrosis
_____ nevus
_____ prophylaxis
_____ pruritus
_____ somatic
_____ syncope
_____ systole
_____ verruca
_____ vertigo

6
Specialization in Medicine

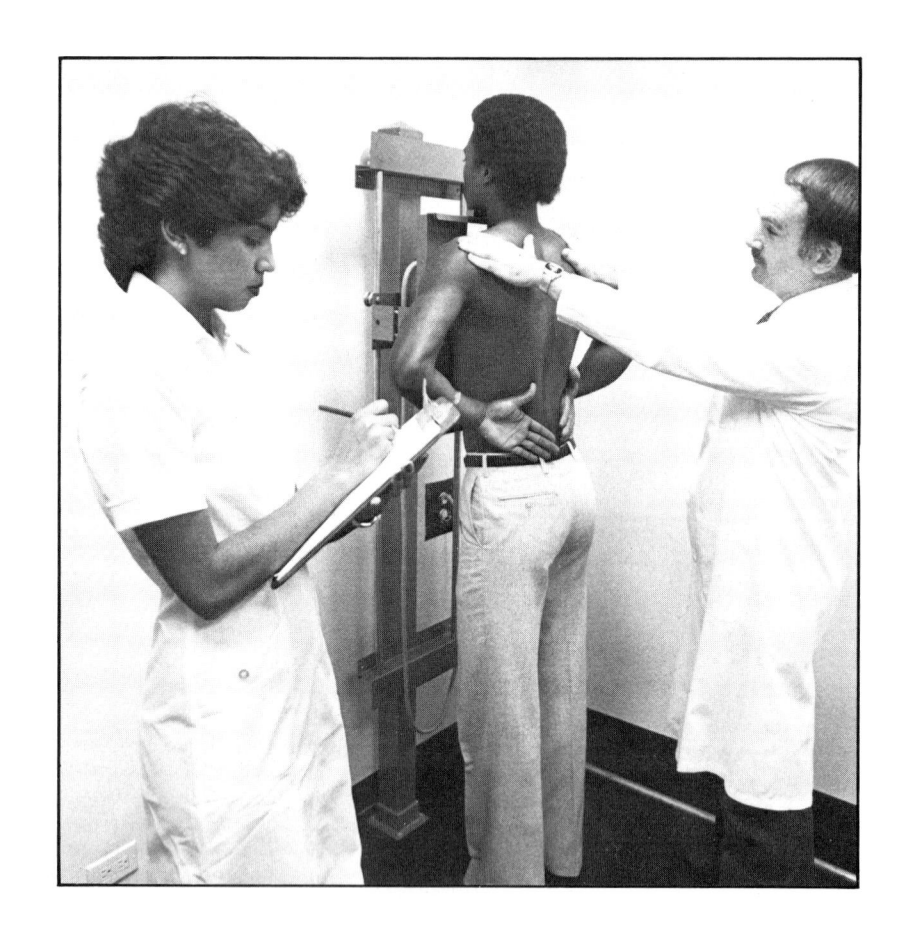

17
Medical Specialities

A variety of job opportunities awaits the medical office worker. Chapter 1 listed 18 possible working environments for the medical assistant. This chapter discusses opportunities for work in the various branches of the medical profession, whether in private practice or in a hospital setting.

THE MEDICAL SPECIALIST

The medical assistant should have a basic understanding of the education required of the physician, especially if the physician has specialized in a particular field of medicine.

Education

In order to obtain a license, the doctor must fulfill certain educational requirements. Education will include graduation from high school and college. The college degree will frequently be in biology, organic chemistry, physics, or mathematics.

After passing a medical college admission test, the student spends four years at a medical school associated with a hospital. The first two years are devoted to theory. In the third and fourth years, the student begins practical work, both in the laboratory and with patients, under the supervision of the physician-instructor. The student receives the M.D. *(Medicinae Doctor)* degree upon graduation.

License to Practice

In order to practice, the graduate must obtain a state license. Requirements include at least one year's internship in a hospital in addition to the M.D. degree. The intern cares for patients under the supervision of the resident or attending physician, helps out in emergencies, assists with operations, and performs other duties.

Doctors must continue their education and keep abreast of new developments by taking postgraduate training and refresher courses throughout their professional life. In many states, these continuing education courses are required for license renewal.

If the doctor wishes to become a specialist and apply for certification, two to five years of additional training in an approved residency program and two years of practice are required.

BRANCHES OF MEDICAL PRACTICE

The assistant who chooses to work for a doctor in private practice has a variety of job opportunities. The assistant should have a general knowledge of the work performed by medical specialists, because the type of work will depend largely on the specialty. The commonly practiced specialties are discussed in this chapter. Some of the specific routines required in the offices are briefly described. The emphasis is mainly on the duties of the medical assistant, administrative; but some of the tasks of the medical assistant, clinical, are also mentioned.

Family Medicine

Many doctors start out with general family practice before entering a specialty. The general practitioner may lance a boil, give injections, remove an appendix, or deliver a baby. The assistant may assist with clinical duties.

Allergy

Because of the frequency of allergic reactions, the allergist treats all kinds of problems. Hay fever is one of the most common.

Dermatology	The dermatologist is concerned with the care of the skin in health and its treatment when affected by disease. Because skin problems usually don't require extensive examinations, the appointment scheduling may be more hectic. Most of the patients will be referrals.
Gynecology and Obstetrics	Gynecology is the study of women's diseases. Obstetrics is concerned with conditions of pregnancy, prenatal care, and childbirth and its aftermath. It is to the assistant's advantage to understand the processes of pregnancy and childbirth. It may be the assistant's role to explain how often the patient is to visit the doctor and the purpose of the visits, to discuss financial arrangements for obstetric care, and to outline what the doctor's fee includes.
Internal Medicine	The greatest share of the internist's practice is diagnostic workup of patients that have been referred. Many patients are examined and treated in hospitals and never make a visit to the internist's office. Branches of internal medicine include the following specialties:

☐ **Cardiology.** This branch of medicine deals with functions and disorders of the heart.

☐ **Endocrinology.** The endocrinologist is concerned with the ductless glands, their functions and disorders. The adrenal, thyroid, and reproductive glands are a part of this study.

☐ **Gastroenterology.** The study of disorders of the digestive system belongs to the gastroenterologist. Diagnostic studies include X ray, endoscopy, and laboratory work.

☐ **Oncology.** The oncologist studies tumors and their treatments. Because this is a subject of great interest today, the assistant may be asked to assist increasingly with statistics, research studies, and speaking engagements.

Neurology	Disorders of the nervous system caused by congenital defects, organic disease, and trauma are dealt with by the neurologist and neurosurgeon. Every neurosurgeon is a neurologist, but not every neurologist performs neurosurgery. Most patients are referred, and many are first examined in the hospital. The neurosurgeon performs emergency examinations and operations.
Ophthalmology	The physician who examines eyes, prescribes glasses, and treats eye diseases is the specialist known as the ophthalmologist. Many times the assist-

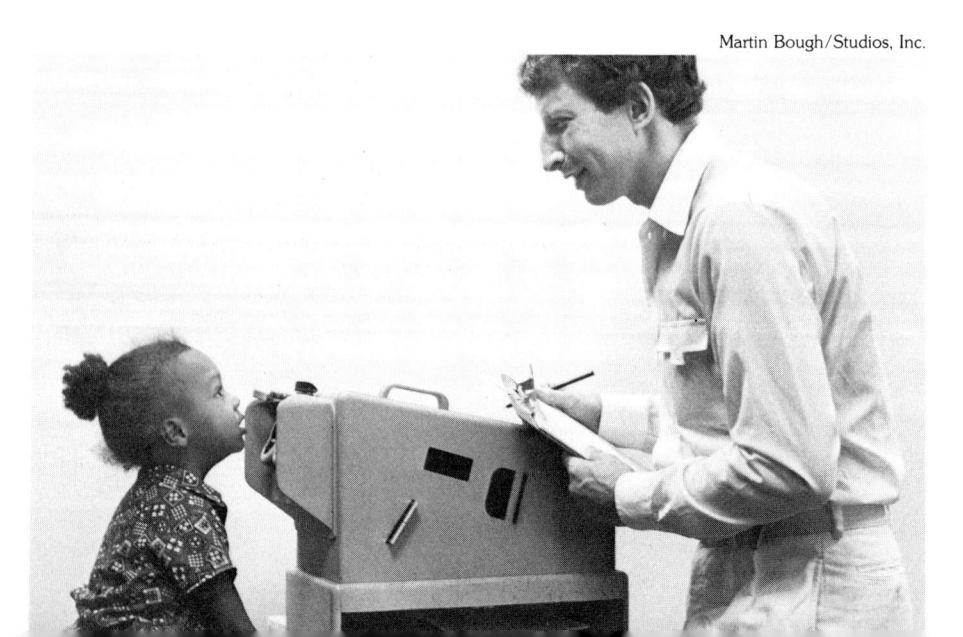

Martin Bough/Studios, Inc.

ant is trained to perform the routine eye examination and administer eye drops in preparation for the ophthalmologist's more extensive examination. The ophthalmologist sees many emergency patients.

Orthopedics This classification is concerned with the treatment of muscular and skeletal diseases, such as fractures and sprains, and with the correction of deformities. The assistant may be asked to order braces, assist patients in wheelchairs and on crutches, and may also be asked to assist the orthopedist with the application of casts.

Otorhinolaryngology The commonly used abbreviation ENT refers to otorhinolaryngology, the specialty concerned with the structure, function, and disorders of the ear, nose, and throat. The assistant may be trained to perform hearing tests before the patient is examined by the otologist. Patients who are hard-of-hearing may present a special problem in communications.

Pathology The pathologist in private practice usually is in charge of a medical laboratory. A patient may have blood work done at the office. More often, specimens are obtained in another physician's office and delivered to the medical laboratory for analyzing. The assistant may also be responsible for specimen pick-up arrangements with individual clinics, handling specimens when delivered, transcribing the pathologist's reports, and sending reports to clinics.

Pediatrics The pediatrician is responsible for treatment of children and their diseases. An assistant who chooses this specialty must have a special talent for dealing with children, particularly when they are ill, in pain, or afraid. A good assistant will know how to play and laugh with children, distract them, and allay their fears. Subspecialties include pediatric allergy, pediatric cardiology, and pediatric surgery.

Martin Bough/Studios, Inc.

Physical Medicine	Physiatry includes the treatment of conditions or rehabilitation by the use of water, heat, electricity, light, and mechanical devices as distinct from medicinal means. The physiatrist may have a complete range of modalities in the office—ultraviolet, diathermy, and ultrasound. A physiatrist may apply or prescribe medical massage and exercises. A registered physical therapist may be employed in the clinic. The physiatrist may have certain days scheduled for visits to nursing homes, convalescent homes, or hospitals for consultations.
Proctology	Diseases of the rectum and colon are included under this heading. Patients with hemorrhoids, fissures, polyps, and tumors are referred to the proctologist. Examinations, including proctoscopy, are performed in the office.
Psychiatry	The specialist caring for patients with mental health disorders is the psychiatrist. It is useful for the assistant to have a basic knowledge of psychology and mental health, as well as an understanding of mental illnesses.
Radiology	This specialty refers to the diagnostic and therapeutic application of radiant energy from roentgen rays (X rays) and radium. In private practice, the radiologist usually limits the practice to diagnostic purposes. An X-ray technician is employed to take and develop X rays. The assistant may be required to assist a patient, schedule X-ray appointments, and transcribe dictation concerning patients and X rays sent from other clinics to be "read" by the radiologist. Therapeutic radiology is usually confined to the hospital.
Surgery	A surgeon may specialize in any one branch or may be a general surgeon who operates for a variety of conditions. Over the years, surgery has split into several branches, each requiring special skills and techniques. Some of these branches are general surgery, abdominal surgery, thoracic surgery, plastic surgery, vascular surgery, and orthopedic surgery. Only so-called minor surgery can be performed in a doctor's office. The person assisting in office surgery will need special training, such as that possessed by a medical assistant, clinical.
Urology	The urologist is concerned with disorders of the genitourinary system of the male and the urinary system of the female. This includes kidney and bladder conditions. The assistant may be trained to assist with procedures done in the office, such as minor surgery, catheterizations, and cystoscopy.

Project 65
Recognizing the Specialties

On WP 101 you will find a list of specialties. In the appropriate columns, write the name given to the specialist and briefly describe the type of problem for which the specialist is consulted.

RELATED SPECIALTIES	In addition to the above specialties, whose practitioners hold an M.D. degree, there are other specialties practiced by persons who hold a doctor's degree other than an M.D. in their particular specialty.
Optometry	An optometrist is skilled in refraction, that is, measuring a patient's vision and prescribing glasses. Eye exercises, called orthoptics, may be advised to improve vision or correct visual defects. The optometrist is a graduate of a School of Optometry and upon graduation becomes a Doctor of Optometry (O.D.).

CHAPTER 17: MEDICAL SPECIALTIES

Osteopathy and Chiropractic

Osteopaths practice medicine and manipulation of the skeleton, especially the spine, as a therapeutic measure. It is this manipulation which sets them apart from an M.D., although some osteopaths also hold an M.D. degree. An osteopath must attend a School of Osteopathy, which includes six years of medical studies. Upon graduation, a degree of Doctor of Osteopathic Medicine (D.O.) is received. A chiropractor (D.C.) is trained in manipulation but does not prescribe drugs or perform surgery.

DIPLOMATES

M.D. specialists have the option of applying for certification in their particular specialties. At present, there are 20 American Boards of Specialties. Members of these boards are elected from among outstanding physicians. A doctor who applies for certification must fulfill certain requirements regarding education, training, and practical experience, and must pass an examination. When the examination is passed and the doctor is accepted, a diploma is issued stating that the physician is a Diplomate of the Board of that specialty. Because of the strict requirements and rigid examination, the standing of a diplomate is correspondingly high. A directory of diplomates is published periodically.

THE HOSPITAL ASSISTANT

Most persons, when they think of a hospital, picture a room where the patient is staying, but few individuals know anything of the tremendously complex organization of a large modern hospital. The hospital represents a wide-open field for the medical assistant seeking employment.

There are three types of hospitals: public hospitals, which are owned by the federal government, the state, or the city; voluntary hospitals, which are nonprofit organizations maintained by private contributions, bequests, and endowments; and private hospitals, which are profit-making institutions. Many hospitals are associated with a medical college, and the doctors connected with the hospital teach medical students in the hospital clinics and the college classroom.

In a hospital, there are several departments where clerical and secretarial help is needed. There is, first of all, the administrative department, which directs the function of the hospital. An assistant may work for the administrator and is usually called an administrative assistant. Shorthand ability as well as proficiency in all office-related skills are necessary; experience is generally a requirement for employment in this highly skilled position. Nonmedical hospital departments may include personnel, purchasing, housekeeping, finances, patient accounts, insurance, security, and public relations.

This chapter will briefly discuss some of the different medical departments. Opportunities for advancement are excellent. A capable and ambitious person who is willing to acquire the necessary training may become an administrative assistant in one of many hospital departments. Salaries and fringe benefits compare favorably with those of industry.

Admitting Office

Work in the admitting office involves not only admitting patients and directing them through the prescribed routine, but also directing patients to the proper departments. In certain cases, a reservation may have been made and processed for admission, and this must be checked. In the private hospital, some payment is usually required on admission, even if the patient carries hospitalization insurance. Statistical data must be obtained. The patient's name must be entered on the register, and an admission number assigned. Valuables may have to be checked. Most hospitals use carbon pack forms which are completed in the admitting office. Sheets of various lengths are attached to the carbon pack so that confidential information is not reproduced on every copy of the form.

In every hospital today, automation plays a large part. A great variety of data are gathered for statistical research. Data include such items as the number of patients admitted; how many are male and how many female; age groups; incidence of diseases, operations, recoveries, and deaths; financial status; and accommodations used. Computers may be used to enter, add, and retrieve information. The admitting office may become very busy. It requires workers who can manage their time, handle stressful situations, and show concern for patients. Emergency room services are frequently coordinated with the admitting office. The assistant will learn how to assess situations requiring immediate medical help and may be needed to assist in transporting a patient. This worker will be exposed to many illnesses and will witness lesions, injuries, and trauma.

Medical Record Department

The heart of every hospital is the department in which all the patients' records are kept, the medical record department. Depending upon the size of the hospital, this department will have several levels of workers, none of whom will be in contact with patients. Instead, there will be daily contacts with doctors, lawyers, and insurance carriers.

There is usually a receptionist to greet doctors and assist them in obtaining charts. Employees are constantly on the telephone, answering questions, taking messages, and dispensing information. The department will have file clerks to store and retrieve information.

A medical transcriber will transcribe all dictated material, making copies for patients' charts and doctors' offices. This transcriber must have excellent knowledge of medical terms, as most of the job is transcribing medical admission notes, consultation reports, and discharge summaries. A medical transcriber may be salaried according to production. Thus, the more efficient the transcriber is, the greater the monetary reward.

A registered medical record librarian is in charge of the department and is responsible to the administration. To become a librarian, it is necessary to have had at least two years of college, plus training in a school approved by the AMA. In order to become registered, the graduate of such a school must pass an examination given by a special board. Upon passing this examination, a certificate of registration is presented, and the person is entitled to use the letters R.R.L. (Registered Record Librarian) following the signature. A technical assistant, however, may be an Accredited Record Technician (A.R.T.). The training for this job classification is a special course at approved schools or an approved correspondence course and an examination. The Accredited Record Technician is responsible for such tasks as reviewing charts for completeness, coding operations and diseases, compiling statistics (including census statistics), and tabulating data for research. The medical assistant is usually the transcriber, typing all medical reports, which may include operative, X-ray, and pathology reports.

Project 66
Transcribing Histories and Physicals

Shortly after admission, every patient has a history taken and gets a physical examination. Your instructor will dictate two complete histories and physicals for you to transcribe. Use the forms on WP 103 and WP 105. Put the data for both patients in a folder labeled "Hospital."

Radiology Department

In large hospitals, the radiology department has its own medical assistant. Duties may include scheduling procedures for outpatients as well as inpatients, greeting patients, assisting them with dressing or undressing, com-

CHAPTER 17: MEDICAL SPECIALTIES 163

pleting request and charge forms, giving directions and instructions, filing, and transcribing radiology reports.

Project 67
Transcribing X-Ray Reports

The radiologist "reads" and dictates reports on all X rays taken in the hospital. Your instructor will provide X-ray dictation for you to transcribe. Use the forms on WP 107 and WP 109.

Operating Room The operating room assistant has no patient contact. This position involves scheduling all operative procedures to be performed in the operating suites. Telephone calls may be made to surgeons to confirm or change the operating time. The assistant may also telephone a nursing station to tell them to give the preoperative medication, send the patient to surgery, or give a message changing the time of the operation. The operative report dictated by the surgeon after the operation may be transcribed in this department rather than in the medical records department.

Project 68
Transcribing Operative Reports

Upon completion of surgery, the surgeon dictates the operative notes describing the procedure. This dictation will be provided by your instructor. Use the forms on WP 111 and WP 113.

Pathology In a large laboratory there are many positions for a medical assistant. There will be little or no patient contact. The size of the department determines the duties performed. A hospital pathologist does not have a personal secretary;

Martin Bough/Studios, Inc.

therefore, correspondence, lecture materials for teaching, research articles, and telephone communications will be carried out by the department assistant. In addition, the pathologist will dictate reports on specimens coming into the laboratory. Specimens may include bone marrow biopsy, blood morphology, semen for fertility studies, vaginal smears for legal cases, operative specimens, and cadavers for autopsy. Dictated reports are transcribed in duplicate, triplicate, and even quadruplicate so each doctor on the case will receive a copy for office records. Other tasks to perform will be filing, placing reports in patients' charts, delivering reports to nursing stations, and typing procedures and policies for laboratory manuals.

Project 69
Transcribing Pathology (Tissue) Reports

The pathologist dictates as the biopsy is being performed. Your instructor will furnish the dictation from a pathology department. Use the forms on WP 115 and WP 117.

Patient Education — Many hospitals have a department for assisting patients with questions and problems. The educator is usually a nurse who has had additional training in explaining medical concepts and procedures to patients. This position will offer contact with patients. Patients will telephone with specific questions about their illnesses. The assistant will not answer these questions but will relay the call to the educator or take a message for the educator to return the call. Information may be dispensed over the telephone, through the mail, or through special audiovisual programs and discussion.

Social Services — Social worker and chaplain services may be combined in one department. There may be more contact with patients via the telephone than in person. Patients may inquire about nursing homes, insurance coverage, Medicare, home visits, counseling, transportation, tutors for the homebound, and legal assistance. The social worker or chaplain may dictate reports after visiting and counseling a patient. After transcribing the report, the assistant will send a copy to the physician and furnish one for the hospital inpatient's chart. The assistant may become involved in arranging meetings, visitations, or any of the services offered by the department.

Physical Medicine Department — This medical assistant performs a variety of tasks and has contact with inpatients and outpatients. The assistant schedules procedures such as hot packs, whirlpool treatments, and exercises; greets patients; and gives directions. An aide is present to assist the patient. Both the physiatrist and physical therapist may dictate reports to be transcribed and placed on the patient's chart.

PERSONAL DEVELOPMENT PROJECTS

TOPICS FOR DISCUSSION 1. Children in the waiting room may demand a special approach. Exchange ideas on how to keep them occupied; how to discipline them; how to handle crying or screaming; how to deal with parents accompanying the children.

2. Discuss the advantages and disadvantages of working in a hospital and working for a specialist.

ROLE PLAYING 1. Mrs. Burns telephones and asks what services are performed by the hospital's social service department.

2. Mr. Burman from United Medical Supplies has stopped at the clinic. He asks to see Dr. Taylor to show him a new laryngoscope. You know that Dr. Taylor is not interested in viewing or purchasing the instrument.

18

Medical Assistant, Clinical

The certification program of the AAMA provides for two categories: medical assistant, clinical; and medical assistant, administrative. The subjects covered in this text so far represent the tasks performed by assistants in the latter category. The medical assistant, clinical, must be specially trained in procedures needed to assist the doctor in the examination and treatment of patients. These duties were formerly performed almost exclusively by nurses. Today, the specially trained medical assistant may perform them in many doctors' offices. This assistant is a graduate of a college or vocational school where he or she learned clinical office procedures and basic laboratory and X-ray work.

This chapter is addressed to the medical assistant who takes a position where the doctor, an office nurse, or a technician usually attends to clinical matters but where the assistant may occasionally be expected to assist. Various procedures are therefore briefly discussed to acquaint the assistant with some of the elementary routine of a medical practice. No attempt is made to offer instruction in any of these procedures. For more extensive information, the sources listed in the Reference Section will be helpful.

STERILIZATION

Because of the constant danger of infection, certain appliances and instruments used in the examination and treatment of patients must be sterilized; that is, they must be exposed to prolonged heat or chemical solutions that will kill bacteria that are adhering to them. There is some confusion in the use of terms such as *sterile, antiseptic,* and *disinfectant.* These terms are often used interchangeably, but they definitely are not interchangeable. Correct definitions are given below.

> *Antiseptic:* Anything that prevents the growth of microorganisms. (An antiseptic may arrest growth without actually killing the microorganism; therefore, it is not the same thing as a germicide or a bactericide.)
>
> *Aseptic:* Free from all pathogens.
>
> *Bactericide:* Capable of destroying bacteria.
>
> *Disinfectant:* Anything that destroys pathogenic microorganisms, but usually not spores.
>
> *Germicide:* Capable of destroying germs.
>
> *Pathogenic:* Capable of producing a disease.
>
> *Sterile:* Free of all living microorganisms.

METHODS OF STERILIZATION

Boiling water, chemical or cold solutions, and steam under pressure are still in use as sterilization methods, although many equipment items are now disposable.

Boiling

This is a popular method of sterilization. Most equipment has an automatic control that interrupts the current as soon as the water has evaporated, which is a safety measure.

The boiling method may be used for all dull instruments, syringes, needles, soft-rubber goods, glassware, and enamelware. Items must be clean when placed in the sterilizer. They should be cleansed with cold water and washed in warm soapy water. All stains should be removed. A stiff brush should be used on instruments with teeth. All jointed instruments should be separated or unclasped. A syringe should not be boiled with the plunger inside, as this may cause the syringe to break. Care must be taken to see that air pockets do not form under cup-shaped objects; they should be placed on their sides.

Sterilizing time may vary according to material. After an instrument has been sterilized, it must be removed with a sterile forceps and placed on a sterile field for immediate use.

Chemical or Cold Sterilization

These solutions are rapid in action, not injurious to the skin, and noncorrosive to instruments. Follow directions given with the solutions regarding strength and length of time for immersion. The chemical solution is poured into a container and instruments are placed in solution, usually for 15 to 20 minutes.

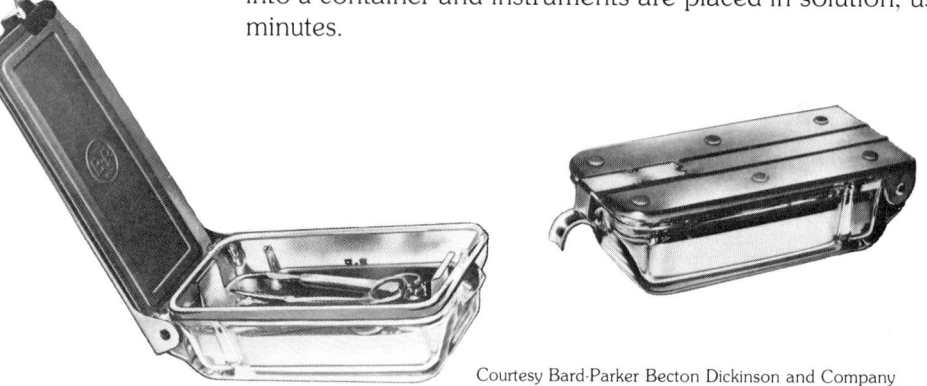

Courtesy Bard-Parker Becton Dickinson and Company

Cold sterilization is the method of choice for all sharp instruments, since boiling dulls the edges of knives or scissors.

Steam Under Pressure, or Autoclave

Surgeons usually employ this method, and it is used in all hospitals. The apparatus, called an autoclave, consists of a sterilizing chamber surrounded by pipes, valves, a pressure gauge, a safety valve, and a thermometer. It works on the same principle as a pressure cooker. Articles to be sterilized are packaged in towels or muslin and placed in the autoclave. Each package should be clearly marked for identification. The length of time needed for sterilization will vary with the content of the package and the pressure in the chamber. Instructions must be followed to assure sterilization.

Disposable Equipment

With the development of plastics and new fibers that are durable, unbreakable, and resistant to heat and chemicals, a large variety of medical equipment is now available that is presterilized, packaged in sterile containers, and discarded after use. The advantages of disposable equipment include convenience, minimizing the risk of infection, and saving of time. Cost compares favorably with the expense of maintaining standard equipment. Use of disposable equipment has become the method of choice. Gloves, ear and nose specula, catheterization trays, blood lancets, tubing, suture-removing kits, and different types of trays are available as disposable items. Disposable items that are not necessarily sterile include towels, sheets, and gowns.

EXAMINATION

Examination of a patient varies according to the patient's complaint. It may be a general examination from head to foot, a neurologic examination, or a local examination of any part of the body. The doctor may examine the

CHAPTER 18: MEDICAL ASSISTANT, CLINICAL 167

patient by *inspection* (visual observation), *palpation* (using the hand to outline the size of an organ, to discover tumors, and to feel chest vibrations), *percussion* (tapping with the fingers to determine the density of parts), and *auscultation* (listening to heartbeat and respiration). The physician may also use instruments designed to examine specific organs.

Basic physical examinations should include the entire body—openings, pelvic region, abdomen, breasts, chest, heart, skin, joints, muscles, nerve reactions, and vital signs. Routine instruments for a physical examination include the following:

Stethoscope	Flashlight
Blood pressure apparatus	Otoscope
Tongue blades	Ophthalmoscope
Tuning fork	Percussion hammer
Vaginal speculum	Plastic gloves
Slides	

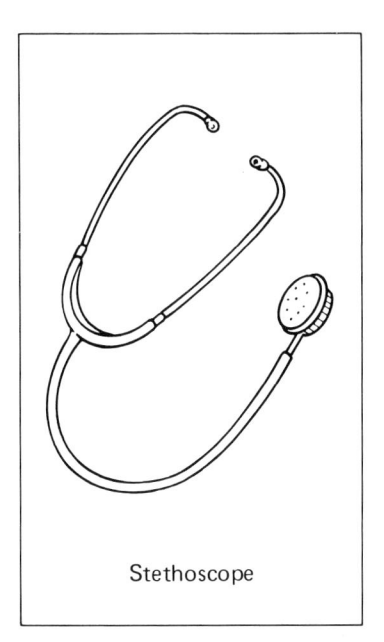

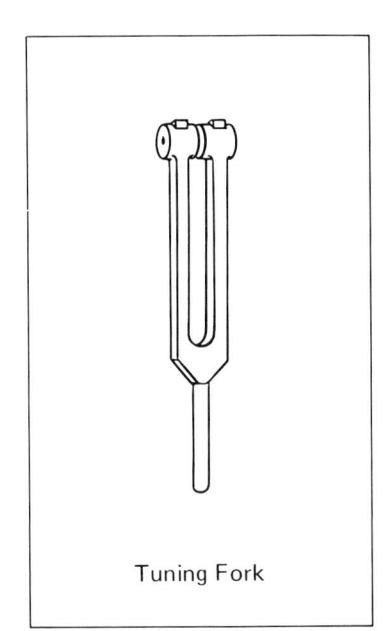

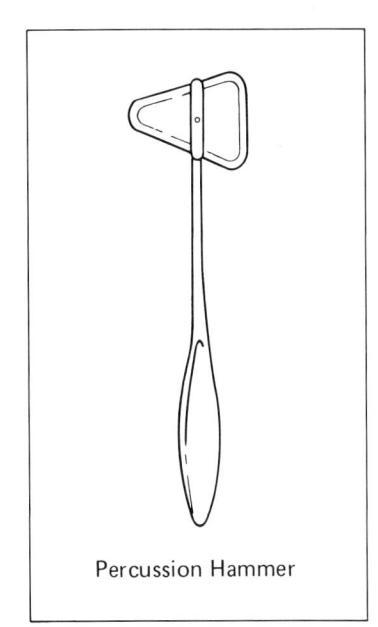

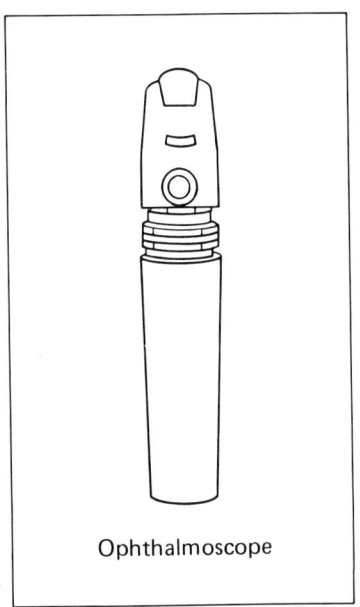

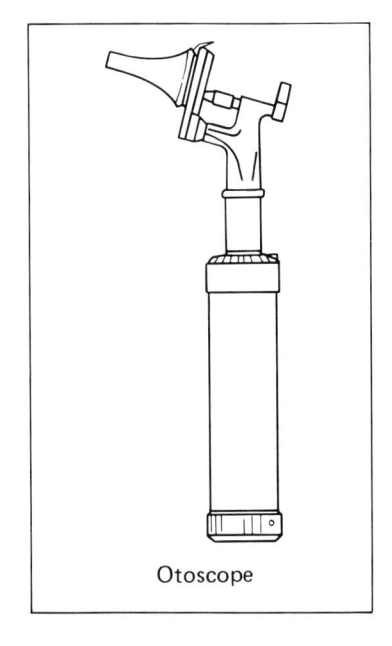

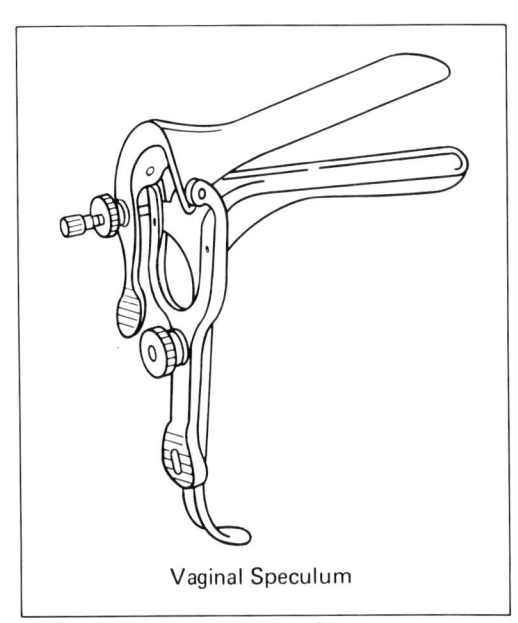

Stethoscope

Tuning Fork

Percussion Hammer

Ophthalmoscope

Otoscope

Vaginal Speculum

The duties of the assistant consist of preparing the patient for the examination, having all instruments and materials in readiness, and assisting as necessary during the examination. The assistant may be asked to perform some of the tests, such as checking the weight, height, pulse, respiration, temperature, and blood pressure. Much of the doctor's time is saved if the assistant can ascertain these data before the doctor starts the examination. The specialty of the doctor, as well as the condition of the patient, will determine what tests the assistant will perform. It should not take long for the assistant to learn what information to obtain from the patient prior to the doctor's examination.

Preparing the Patient

Preparation of a patient for examination depends on the type of examination to be performed and on the sex of the patient. Patients should be exposed as little as possible. A gown or sheet should be given to the patient, along with instructions about disrobing. For a general examination, all clothes must be removed. For a pelvic examination, women sometimes need to undress only from the waist down. For a chest, shoulder, or arm examination, it may be necessary to remove the outer garments, and underwear can usually be slipped off the shoulder.

It may be necessary to assist the patient with undressing, especially if he or she is handicapped by disease or injury. In the case of a fractured arm, the sleeve of the healthy arm is removed first. In dressing, the injured arm is covered first. The examination usually begins with the patient sitting on the table facing the doctor.

Some standard positions in which patients are examined are shown in the illustration below.

Sim's Position Posterior View

Knee-Chest Position

Lithotomy Position

Trendelenburg Position

Measuring Height and Weight

Height is measured with the patient in stocking feet. Most scales have an attachment for recording height. Tape measures are used for infants' length, as well as for circumference of head and chest. If weight is an important factor in diagnosis and treatment, it is wise to suggest that the patient wear the same amount of clothing for each succeeding visit.

Taking Pulse and Respiration

Before taking the pulse, the patient's arm should be placed in a comfortable position. The pulse is measured over the radial artery. The figure entered on the record represents the number of pulse beats per minute. The average rate is between 70 and 80 beats a minute; fluctuations may occur and be considered normal for that individual. Rate, rhythm, and character (faint or strong) should be noted.

Normal respiration rate is about 18 to 20 inhalations a minute. Respirations may be short, deep, rasping, labored, or irregular, and such characteristics must be noted on the record. Counting of respirations should be done by continuing to hold the patient's wrist as if still taking the pulse, but counting the movements of the chest. It is important that the patient remain completely relaxed. Any realization by the patient that respirations are being watched will alter the normal rhythm of breathing.

Taking Temperature

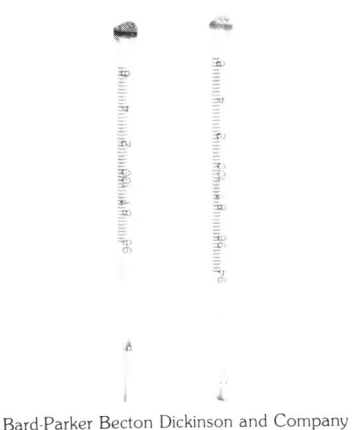

Three common methods are in use for measuring temperature: oral, axillary, and rectal. In the oral method, the thermometer is placed under the patient's tongue and left there for 3 to 5 minutes. The oral method should not be used with small children, if a patient cannot keep the lips closed, or if the patient is confused.

The axillary method is seldom used because it is not very accurate. The thermometer is placed in the armpit, and the arm is placed over the chest to hold the thermometer in place. After 5 minutes, a reading is taken.

Rectal temperatures are taken when the oral method is contraindicated. Rectal thermometers should be lubricated with oil, jelly, or soap.

Before a thermometer is used, it must be shaken down so that the mercury column is below 96 degrees Fahrenheit or 37 degrees centigrade. After use, the thermometer must be wiped clean and placed in an antiseptic solution. It must not be held under hot water. Oral and rectal thermometers are kept in separate containers.

Bard-Parker Becton Dickinson and Company

Measuring Blood Pressure

Blood pressure is the force exerted on an arterial wall as the heart contracts, forcing the blood out of the heart into arteries. The taking of a patient's blood pressure is a routine procedure in practically every examination. A special blood-pressure apparatus is used. An assistant will need practice

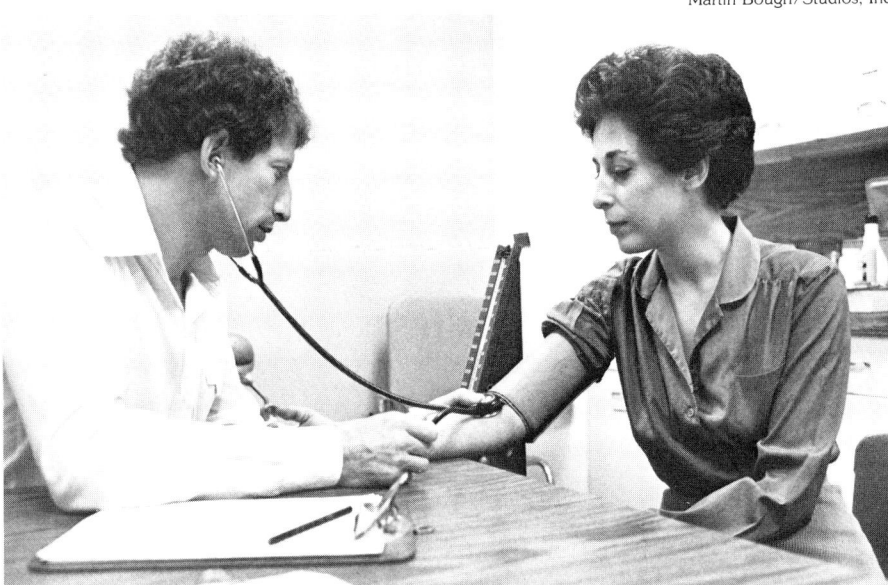

Martin Bough/Studios, Inc.

before becoming proficient in using the equipment and obtaining a blood-pressure reading. An average blood pressure would be recorded as 120/80, indicating the systolic and the diastolic pressure.

Temperature, pulse, respiration, and blood-pressure readings are called the patient's vital signs.

DIAGNOSTIC TESTS

The doctor today has many different methods of testing the patient in order to practice good medicine.

Laboratory Specimens

Most medical examinations include some laboratory tests. Tests may be done for the following reasons: as a diagnostic aid, to indicate general physical condition, to verify a diagnosis, or as a guide for treatment. Specimens may be obtained from many sources: ears, nose, throat, wounds, rectum, vagina, and so forth. They may consist of bone marrow, vomitus, tissue, urine, blood, spinal fluid, feces, sputum, vaginal smears, and semen.

Many doctors have their own laboratories, though they may be small ones, in order to do routine examinations. For more complicated tests—for instance, the Rh test, prothrombin time, fasting blood sugar (FBS), or Wassermann—a fully equipped laboratory is required. Patients are sent to a clinical or hospital laboratory for such examinations. It probably will be the assistant's duty to write out the name and address of the laboratory for the patient, or even to make the appointment.

If the doctor has a laboratory in the office, some educational training in routine laboratory procedures must be obtained before the assistant can perform these tests. An office assistant without specific training may be of assistance in collecting specimens, preparing slides, and helping with some of the tests.

The laboratory assistant must realize the importance of being absolutely accurate, honest, and reliable. Responsibilities would include explaining the "right" procedure to the "right" patient, obtaining the specimen requested, properly labeling the specimen, and delivering or testing the specimen. Great care should be taken in the handling of needles, instruments used, the specimen itself, and any contaminated material.

Electrocardiograph

The electrocardiograph is an instrument that makes it possible to measure the extremely fine currents of the heart muscle by registering them on special paper. From this record, the physician can form an opinion as to the condition of the heart muscle, how well it functions, and the nervous impulses. The tracing produced, called an electrocardiogram, is abbreviated ECG (or EKG). It is usually taken while the patient is in a supine position. The position must be noted in the patient's record. Careful instruction and training, practice with the particular apparatus in the office, and knowledge of the anatomy of the heart are all important to the assistant taking electrocardiograms.

Courtesy Computer Instruments Corporation

X Ray and Fluoroscopy

If the doctor has an X-ray machine for diagnostic purposes, a trained X-ray technician will do the work. Under no circumstances should the assistant touch an X-ray machine until given instructions. The patient may need assistance, however. Patients who are to have head X rays must remove their dentures and hairpins. The assistant should instruct the patient to remove any metallic objects, such as jewelry or watches, from that part of the body which is to be X-rayed. Pictures should not be taken through clothing.

X rays constitute a potential danger, and they may lead to sterility in those exposed to them too frequently or without protection. Although the assistant may stay in the X-ray room while the picture is being taken, a lead apron should be worn.

The X-ray films are considered the doctor's records and do not have to be delivered to the patient, even if the patient has paid for them. It is customary, however, to lend the films to other physicians upon their written request.

The fluoroscope is a part of an X-ray apparatus. It permits the observation of internal organs and their functions. No untrained person should attempt to handle a fluoroscope.

Project 70 Identifying X-Ray Procedures

On WP 119 is a list of X-ray procedures. Next to the procedures, write the organs or body areas that are involved with each X ray. Be specific in your answers.

TREATMENTS

After the doctor has completed the examination and has made the diagnosis, treatment is prescribed. This may consist of a prescription for medication, instructions in dietary and general hygienic regime, or treatments to be administered at the doctor's office.

Medication

The duties of the medical assistant include the storage and sometimes the dispensing or administering of medicines. Administration of medications would include the oral method, injections, irrigations, and inhalations. Medications are classified by their effect; familiarity with these categories will help to develop the strong sense of responsibility that is necessary for anyone handling drugs. It would go beyond the scope of this book to list all the different types of drugs, but this information may be obtained from books in any reference library.

It is enough to say here that the medical assistant should never dispense or administer any drug whatsoever without specific instructions from the doctor. Because of the danger involved in making a mistake, the assistant should have additional education and training in pharmacology before administering medications.

Minor Operations

Minor operations are those procedures which can be carried out in the doctor's office under local anesthesia. (Local anesthesia means the deadening of sensation in the immediate area only.) Minor surgery includes the removal of warts and ingrown toenails, the incision and drainage of boils, vasectomies, and similar operations.

Appointments should be arranged so there will be no interruptions during the operation. All surgery involves potential risk. The physician may request a written consent signed by the patient before beginning the procedure. The assistant will have to learn about sterile procedure before assisting with operations.

Other sterile procedures include irrigations, catheterizations, repair of lacerations, insertions of intrauterine devices, and removal of sutures.

ASSISTING THE DOCTOR

Basically, the role of the medical assistant in examinations, treatments, and minor surgery is threefold:

1. Preparing the instruments and materials needed. It is especially important to make sure that everything is at hand.
2. Preparing the patient, both physically and mentally. This includes positioning and draping as well as reassuring the patient.
3. Assisting the doctor as necessary.

PERSONAL DEVELOPMENT PROJECTS

TOPICS FOR DISCUSSION 1. Invite a nurse to discuss the following:
  a. Blood pressure and hypertension
  b. Thermometer reading and fevers
  c. Taking pulses and respirations
  d. Proper techniques of obtaining a urine specimen
  e. X-ray preparations

2. Discuss the different duties of the medical assistant, clinical, and the medical assistant, administrative. Which duties are common to both? Which kind of medical assistant would you prefer to be?

ROLE PLAYING 1. Dr. Taylor asks you for a patient's chart. You gave it to him yesterday.
2. Mrs. Bates telephones to say that her bill has been submitted to an insurance company and that she will not pay anything on the bill until she is reimbursed. (The bill is now 3 months old.)

Simulation 5

Today you will begin your fifth and last two-day simulation in Dr. Taylor's office. The days will be Wednesday, December 3, and Friday, December 5.

PROCEDURES Review the general directions on pages 74-75 for handling simulations. Follow the same procedures for Day 1 and Day 2 as you did in other simulations.

MATERIALS YOU WILL NEED

Appointment Book

Card File

Supplies Folder
All the usual supplies

Day 1 Folder	Source
Incoming letter from Dr. Taylor	WP 121
Manuscript	WP 123-127
Medicare (Kellogg)	WP 129
Daily journal December 3	WP 131
Checks from Marion Wellman, Gail Hayes, Jill Grimes, and John Bachman	WP 209-211

Day 2 Folder

Daily journal December 5	WP 133
Blue Cross-Blue Shield form	WP 135
Checks from Carl Logan and Ellen Goldberg	WP 211

Patients' Charts
The following patients' charts (folders) should contain the items given below:

Patients' Charts	Source
Bachman, Joseph	
Ledger card	Project 36
Clinical data sheet	Project 15
Letter to Dr. Gonzalez	Simulation 4
Letter to Dr. Gonzalez	Project 15
Bachmann, Paul	
Ledger card, updated	Simulation 3
Clinical data sheet, updated	Project 32
House call slip	Project 12
Message	Simulation 1
Berndt, Stanley	
Ledger card, updated	Simulation 4
Clinical data sheet, updated	Simulation 4
Collection letter	Project 37
Appointment card	Simulation 2
Message	Simulation 3
Receipt	Simulation 4
Berquist, Rebecca	
Ledger card	Project 36
Clinical data sheet, updated	Simulation 4
Message	Simulation 4
Burnett, Jane	
Ledger card, updated	Simulation 4
OB form, updated	Simulation 4
Letter rescheduling appointment	Simulation 3
Letter about fees	Project 35
Records release and letter to Dr. Kaplan	Simulation 1
Patient introduction slip	Project 13
Appointment card	Simulation 1
Message	Simulation 3
Receipt	Simulation 4
Curtiss, Lois	
Ledger card, updated	Simulation 4
Clinical data sheet, updated	Simulation 3
House call slip	Project 31
Message	Simulation 3
Check	Simulation 4
Goldberg, Ellen	
Ledger card, updated	Simulation 4

Patients' Charts	Source
Clinical data sheet, updated	Simulation 3
Medicare form	Project 40
Message	Project 17
Receipt	Simulation 3
Check	Simulation 4
Grazzini, Mario	
Ledger card	Project 36
Clinical data sheet	Project 25
Messages—2	Simulation 1
Grebowski, Paul	
Ledger card	Project 36
Clinical data sheet	Project 25
Letter to Dr. Williams	Simulation 4
Letter rescheduling appointment	Simulation 1
Message	Simulation 2
Grimes, Jill	
Ledger card, updated	Simulation 3
Clinical data sheet, updated	Simulation 2
Letter to Dr. Margaret Whitman	Simulation 4
Letter to Dr. Margaret Whitman	Simulation 2
Health insurance claim form	Project 38
Card with Dr. Whitman's address	Simulation 2
Appointment card	Simulation 1
Hayes, Gail	
Ledger card, updated	Simulation 4
Clinical data sheet, updated	Simulation 4
Patient introduction slip	Project 32
Receipt	Simulation 3
Appointment card	Simulation 3
Kellogg, Alice	
Ledger card, updated	Simulation 3
Clinical data sheet, updated	Simulation 4
Message	Simulation 4
Message	Simulation 2
Message	Simulation 1
Knutson, Karen	
Ledger card	Project 36
Clinical data sheet	Project 25
Message	Simulation 2
Leslie, Sheila	
Ledger card, updated	Simulation 4
Clinical data sheet, updated	Simulation 3
Appointment card	Simulation 2
Message	Simulation 3
Check	Simulation 4
Logan, Carl	
Ledger card, updated	Simulation 4
Clinical data sheet, updated	Simulation 4
Medicare form	Simulation 3
Receipt	Simulation 4
Message	Simulation 3
Malinsky, William	
Ledger card, updated	Simulation 4
Clinical data sheet, updated	Simulation 4
Appointment card	Simulation 2
Appointment card	Simulation 3

Patients' Charts	Source
Message	Simulation 2
Receipt	Simulation 3
McKinley, Sharon	
Ledger card, updated	Simulation 4
Clinical data sheet, updated	Simulation 4
Messages—3	Simulation 3
Receipt	Simulation 4
Perez, Manuel	
Ledger card, updated	Simulation 4
Clinical data sheet, updated	Simulation 4
Patient introduction slip	Simulation 2
Message	Simulation 1
Letter to Dr. Andrews	Simulation 1
Letter to Dr. Andrews	Simulation 4
Provost, Janis	
Ledger card, updated	Simulation 4
Clinical data sheet, updated	Simulation 2
Letter to Dr. Lillian Bradford	Simulation 4
Letter to Dr. Lillian Bradford	Simulation 2
Blue Cross–Blue Shield form	Project 39
Check	Simulation 4
Stephens, Jason	
Ledger card, updated	Simulation 4
Clinical data sheet, updated	Simulation 4
Letter to Industrial Commission	Simulation 4
Workers' compensation reports	Simulation 4
Workers' compensation progress report	Project 41
Stillman, Marlene	
Ledger card	Simulation 2
Clinical data sheet, updated	Simulation 2
Patient introduction slip	Simulation 2
Message	Simulation 1
Wellman, Marion	
Ledger card, updated	Simulation 3
Clinical data sheet, updated	Simulation 3
Appointment card	Simulation 1
Appointment card	Project 11
Appointment card	Simulation 2
Message	Simulation 2
Whitfall, Martin	
Ledger card	Project 36
Clinical data sheet	Project 32
Patient introduction slip	Project 32

Miscellaneous Folder
Letters:

American Family Physician	Project 61
Dr. Stanley F. Anderson	Simulation 1
Dr. Allen Jones	Simulation 2
Journal of Family Practice	Project 61
Dr. Scott McIntosh	Project 10
Medical Supplies Service	Project 53
Dr. Louise Merryweather	Project 27
Dr. Milton Monroe	Project 62

PART 6: SPECIALIZATION IN MEDICINE

Miscellaneous Folder	Source
Fee Schedule	Simulation 4
Procedures and diagnoses numbers	Simulation 4
Procedures manual	Projects 49 and 51
"Loving Hands"	Project 59
Messages:	
Mrs. Taylor	Simulation 1
Mrs. Bateson	Simulation 1

Financial Records Folder

Daily journals	Project 42
Daily journals	Simulation 3
Daily journals	Simulation 4
Monthly summary sheet, updated	Simulation 3
Deposit slip	Project 44
Deposit slip	Simulation 3
Deposit slip	Simulation 4
Checks	Project 45
Bank statement	Project 46
Petty cash voucher	Project 47
Check	Project 47
Salary check	Project 48
Employee earnings record	Project 48

Local Medical Society Meetings Folder

Announcement	Project 54
Agenda	Project 55
Letter to Dr. Cassini	Project 56
Letter to Langdon Hotel	Project 56
Minutes of the meeting	Project 57
Letter to Dr. Watson, including Dr. Taylor's biographical sketch	Project 58

Travel Folder

Letter changing reservations	Project 63
Itinerary	Project 64
Letter to Dr. Milton Monroe	Project 28

Hospital Folder

History and physical—2	Project 66
Roentgen report—2	Project 67
Operative report—2	Project 68
Tissue report—2	Project 69

If you have not completed all the projects and do not have all these records set up in advance, talk with your instructor.

MEDICAL TERMINOLOGY

_____ abortion

_____ amniocentesis

_____ amniotic fluid

_____ cesarean section

_____ colostrum

_____ congenital

_____ ectopic pregnancy

_____ effacement

_____ embryo

_____ episiotomy

_____ fetus

_____ fontanel

_____ gestation

_____ gravida

_____ hydramnios

_____ lochia

_____ meconium

_____ neonatal

_____ phenylketonuria

_____ puerperium

_____ quickening

_____ secundines

_____ toxemia

_____ vernix caseosa

7
Facing the Future

19

Your Job-Hunting Campaign

As a graduate of this course, you will have learned to perform all the basic duties required for an office position. Getting the right job and being successful in it demand a specialized knowledge of job-hunting techniques in addition to your technical skills.

Opportunities as a professionally trained medical office assistant are manifold. You may find that the medical field does not appeal to you; or you may hear of an opening in a different type of organization. Since this book is devoted to the medical field, it is hoped you will select a career in medicine upon graduation.

FINDING THE RIGHT JOB

The decision as to what kind of job to look for is an important one, and you should give careful consideration to the steps involved in choosing the kind of work you want.

Most employers prefer experienced personnel, especially in top positions, and hire beginners only for those jobs that may seem less desirable. The beginner must obtain experience before qualifying for top positions, so think twice before turning down a job that does not seem to be exactly what you want. Think of a job as a definite task or duty, a career as a progression of jobs.

Medical Fields and Working Environments

It is important that you select a field of medicine and a working environment in which you are interested and for which you feel well suited. The list of opportunities in Chapter 1 should be studied carefully again. If your inclination to enter one field or work in a certain environment is particularly strong, set your goal accordingly.

New York University

Project 71
Choosing a Working Environment

In Project 2, you made a decision about the types of working environment you might choose. Consider what you have learned. Write a brief statement affirming your original choices, or describing your choices now if there has been a change. Type the information on plain paper.

Other Considerations

There are several factors to consider when looking for a job. It is advisable to be certain about the locality in which you wish to work. It would be foolish to accept an otherwise tempting job offer only to find after a few weeks that the office is too far from home or the transportation is difficult. Leaving any job after a short time does not look good on your record.

Consider the working hours. Not every medical assistant works from 9 to 5; there are many good jobs requiring irregular schedules. This may mean your social life will be curtailed and that the trip from office to home will be made when transportation is more difficult.

Of course, salary is an important factor in selecting a job. You may be satisfied with a lower salary if the medical specialty is one in which you are particularly interested. A company that offers a number of fringe benefits such as an extensive medical and dental plan, educational tuition refund plans, and free parking may offer a lower salary than another employer. However, you may feel that the fringe benefits offset the low salary. (Remember, you don't have to pay income taxes on fringe benefits.) But before you make a quick decision about salary, it is advisable to compute the salary you will need. Will you live at home, share an apartment with a roommate, or live alone? How much will it cost you to get to your job? Will you need a car, or is public transportation available? Will you have to pay local and state income taxes in addition to federal income taxes and FICA deductions? All these factors, and more, will be a part of your decision to accept or reject a job offer based on salary.

Project 72
Making a Personal Budget

Use WP 137 as a guide in computing your weekly or monthly and yearly expenses. Your total expenses will give you an estimate of the income you will need. Your instructor will assist you in projecting gross income from the net earnings you will need to have.

JOB SOURCES

Jobs must be searched out. Don't wait until after graduation to start looking. Begin your job hunting at least a month or two before graduation, unless you are planning to take a vacation. Some sources open to you are listed here:

1. The school placement bureau may be able to help you.
2. Your own doctor or a colleague of your doctor may have an opening.
3. Tell your friends that you are looking for a job. Their doctors may also be looking for assistants.
4. The classified advertisements in newspapers or professional publications are a good source. Openings will be found under *G* for "Gal/Guy Friday," *M* for "Medical," *R* for "Receptionist," and *S* for "Secretary." Whether you write or telephone, promptness is essential.

Martin Bough/Studios, Inc.

5. Employment agencies, some specializing in medical personnel only, are listed in the telephone directory and the classified ads. Commercial agencies may charge the applicant a fee upon acceptance of a job. When you file an application, be sure you understand the agency's terms. Other employment agencies are sponsored by the city and state.

Project 73
Interpreting Advertisements

Scan the classified ads in a daily newspaper for positions you might like. Using a sheet of plain white paper, copy all abbreviations you encounter and define them.

YOUR RÉSUMÉ No matter what avenue of job hunting you choose, it will be necessary to present your record of qualifications, training, and experience. This record is called a résumé, or personal data sheet. Your résumé should contain the information listed below. The object is to present your qualifications as logically, concisely, and interestingly as possible.

Résumés should be typed. Use plain white paper and provide sufficient spacing to create a neat, pleasing appearance.

Personal Data Personal data should include name, address, telephone number, and (optional) social security number.

CHAPTER 19: YOUR JOB-HUNTING CAMPAIGN 179

Education List college, business school, extension courses, high school, names and locations of schools, degrees or citations received, and so forth. Dates of attendance or graduation are optional.

Experience Every job, even if only after-hour, summer, or volunteer work, should be mentioned. Include name and address of employer, dates of employment, and salary.

Special Interests Extracurricular activities such as serving as a class officer, editing a school paper, working in the school office, volunteer work in church or community, or special interests that might have a bearing on your application may be listed. Do not list hobbies such as tennis or dancing, which have no relationship to your work.

References Names, addresses, and telephone numbers of at least three people (not relatives) should be provided as references. Use the business address and telephone number if the person is employed. Remember never to give a

---

RESUME   MARY DONNELLY
                                          2589 South Pulaski Road
                                          Chicago, IL 60623
                                          (312) 555-2256

Position Desired: Medical Assistant

EDUCATION

Chicago Vocational Technical Institute, Chicago, IL 60623.
Graduated with Medical Assistant diploma in January 1980.
Subjects studied in the one-year program included:

   Shorthand and Transcription
   Medical Terminology
   Medical Office Procedures
   English
   Anatomy and Physiology
   Accounting
   Medical Typing
   Psychology
   Communications

Center High School, 2989 West 24th Boulevard, Chicago, IL 60623.
General academic curriculum. Graduated in June 1978.

EXPERIENCE

Secretarial: July 1978 to January 1980, Dr. J. J. Bradon, 5691 South Princeton Avenue, Chicago, IL 60621. Full-time from July 1978 to January 1979; part-time while attending Chicago Vocational.

INTERESTS AND ACTIVITIES

Riley Community Hospital: Volunteer nurse's aide; two afternoons weekly, 1976-1978.

Chicago Vocational Technical Institute, Editor, CVTI News, 1979-1980.

REFERENCES

   Upon request.

reference without first obtaining permission from the individual. References may be omitted from the résumé, but you should have them available should the employer request them on an application blank or during an interview.

Project 74
Preparing Your Résumé

Prepare a personal résumé that you will be able to use when applying for a position. After typing the résumé, prepare copies in order to be able to give each potential employer a copy.

THE LETTER OF APPLICATION

The résumé must be accompanied by a letter of application. This letter may be the first impression of you that the employer receives.

The letter should be typed, not handwritten. Include the return address above the date. If possible, address the letter to the person who will be doing the hiring. Limit the letter to three or four paragraphs and one page only. The first paragraph should state your purpose for writing. The next paragraph should give your qualifications, and the last paragraph should request an interview. Keep a carbon copy for your file. Sign the letter in blue or black ink. Don't forget the enclosure notation.

Here is an example of how an application letter might read:

> Dear Dr. Winthrop:
>
> Please consider this letter an application for the position as medical assistant advertised in today's *Times*.
>
> In two weeks I shall graduate from Chicago Vocational Technical Institute after completing a 12-month course for medical assistants, and I believe that I am qualified to fill the opening you offer.
>
> The enclosed résumé will give you detailed information about my education and experience.
>
> May I have the opportunity of talking with you? I am free after 3:30 on weekdays and any time on Saturdays. If you do call my home, there is someone who will take a message if I am in school.
>
> Sincerely,
> Mary Donnelly

Enclosure

Project 75
Writing Application Letters

Using the advertisements from Project 73 or others selected from your local newspaper, write three letters of application. Make up names and addresses to which you will address the letters. In the letters, ask for an interview. Enclose a copy of your résumé. Use plain paper.

APPLICATION FORMS

When you apply for a position, you may receive an application form in reply. This form may be your first introduction to an employer; therefore, it too must make a good impression. The employer will consider neatness, ability to follow directions, and qualifications. Complete the form carefully, typed if possible, and return it promptly.

The information requested will be similar to that contained in your personal résumé. Be brief, but do not omit any vital information, and do not leave blanks. Where a question does not apply to you, draw a short line through (or type two hyphens in) the reply blank to indicate that you have read the item. Use the current date.

CHAPTER 19: YOUR JOB-HUNTING CAMPAIGN   181

Project 76
Completing an Application Form

A sample application form will be found on WP 139. Complete the form.

THE INTERVIEW

The purpose of your résumé and letter of application is to secure an interview. The purpose of the interview is to secure the job. When you receive an invitation for an interview, you can face the interviewer with the assurance that someone is truly interested in talking with you.

Prepare for your interview thoroughly. Remember that cleanliness, neatness, and good grooming are important. Their lack cannot be covered up, no matter how attractive your clothes.

Select a simple outfit in which you look well and feel comfortable. The day of the interview is not the time to try out a new outfit, experiment with a different hair style, or wear new shoes for the first time. Wear conservative clothes and suitable accessories. Your shoes should be polished. Women's handbags should not be overflowing, nor should a man's suit pockets be bulging. Do not take anyone with you to the interview.

Allow plenty of time to reach your destination. If you do not know the transportation facilities or the neighborhood, it is a good idea to take the time a day before the interview to make the complete trip.

Take your credentials with you: résumé, diplomas, certificates attesting to your skills, social security card. Take a notebook, a pen and pencil, an eraser, and possibly a small dictionary if you have trouble with spelling. Be prepared to take employment tests.

If you are asked to take a shorthand or typing test, be grateful for the opportunity to demonstrate your skills. The interviewer will expect a certain amount of nervousness, but remind yourself that the test will probably be no more difficult than the many you have successfully taken at school—and may actually be easier.

When you are called into the interviewer's office, wait to be asked to sit. Smile and say "Good morning" or "Good afternoon." Shake hands, if offered to do so. Never put anything on the interviewer's desk.

Let the interviewer take the initiative and ask questions. It is better to answer as completely as possible, rather than to reply with a simple yes or no, but don't monopolize the conversation. Remember that the interviewer is interested in finding out what kind of person you are and learning about your qualifications and your outside interests. Be courteous and friendly, not timid or aggressive. The interviewer may ask why you left your last job.

Martin Bough/Studios, Inc.

Some interviewers use an evaluation sheet to record their impressions of an applicant. The interviewer is trying to evaluate attitudes. He or she will want to determine whether the applicant shows an interest in people; likes doing things for others; and has poise, tact, and self-confidence. The interviewer will note if the applicant appears cheerful, talks articulately but not too much, expresses a thought well, has a pleasing voice and personality, and has sufficient maturity for the job. Other factors of interest to the interviewer will be whether the applicant seems emotionally stable, has not changed jobs too often, seems eager to obtain this position, has shown initiative through schoolwork or after-school jobs, and looks neat and well-groomed.

When the interviewer has finished questioning you, it is your turn to ask questions about anything pertinent to the job: working hours, salary, vacations, chance of advancement, your responsibilities. Show an interest in the work itself, rather than the monetary or fringe benefits.

THE LETTER OF THANKS

In addition to thanking the interviewer for seeing you, you may choose to write a letter of thanks after you return home. This is another way of showing you are interested in the position.

If you want the job, a thank-you letter is an important part of your total application. If you do not receive a reply to your letter within a reasonable length of time, it is permissible to telephone to ask whether or not a decision has been made. If the interviewer has suggested that you telephone within a certain length of time or on a specific date to learn the decision, be sure to do so.

Here is a sample letter of thanks:

> Dear Dr. Winthrop:
>
> Thank you for giving me so much time today to discuss the medical assistant position in your office.
>
> After thinking over the requirements as you outlined them and reviewing my own qualifications and interests, I feel quite sure that I could perform the work to your satisfaction.
>
> I hope that you will give me the opportunity of proving my ability to you.
>
> Sincerely,
> Mary Donnelly

THE LETTER OF REGRET

In thinking over the interview and reviewing the pros and cons of the position, you may not be sure that you would like to work in that particular office. There are a number of important considerations in any job, not the least of which is the personality of the doctor. In addition to professional qualifications and the area of specialization, much of which the doctor will reveal to you during the interview, there should be a mutual liking and respect. Doctors reveal a great deal about the kind of employer they will be when they interview you by telling something of their work, their patients, and their expectations of the medical assistant.

If you have any qualms about accepting the position—or even if you simply want time to think it over—do not tell the interviewer that you would like the job and then write in your thank-you letter that you have changed your mind. It is far better to say frankly that you would like a day or two to think it over and discuss the position with your family. The interviewer will appreciate your sincerity. However, you must follow up the interview with a letter of thanks and an explanation of why you do not think the position is right for you.

Project 77
Writing Follow-Up Letters

Assume that you were given interviews for each of the openings for which you applied. Write three letters, the first refusing a job because it is too far to travel, the second refusing another job because the salary is too low, and the third saying that you would very much like to have the job and hope to be accepted. Use plain paper for all three letters and type envelopes for each.

PERSONAL DEVELOPMENT PROJECTS

TOPICS FOR DISCUSSION 1. Compare positions, responsibilities, and salaries for medical assistants in your area.
2. Discuss questions that an interviewer may and may not ask a potential employee.
3. Discuss whether or not it is ethical to accept a job advertised as permanent on a temporary basis while you are waiting for a really good position to come along.
4. Discuss the advantages of visiting potential employers in person rather than telephoning to ask if any positions are available.

ROLE PLAYING 1. Make a telephone call asking if an office has any openings.
2. Make a telephone call to a place of employment that has advertised for a job, and set an appointment for an interview.

20
Preparing for Advancement

Finally, the big day arrives. You have ceased being a student and have become a medical assistant. This is a giant step indeed. Instead of paying tuition for your training, you are now being paid for your office skills, your work, and your time. This places a decided responsibility on you.

THE FIRST JOB

As soon as you have been hired, take the time to study the medical terms of the particular specialty with which your work will be involved.

The first day on your first full-time job is probably the most exciting and, at the same time, the most frightening one, although there is really no reason to be nervous. Your employer has had beginners before and is prepared to be understanding. In most instances, an employer will try to ease a new employee into the job. If you should arrive during a rush period, any assistance you can give will be appreciated.

Your preparation for the first day of work should be similar to that for the interview. Go to the office looking your best, and be appropriately dressed. Familiarize yourself with the physical layout of the offices, waiting rooms, examination rooms, typing areas—whatever setup applies to your particular job. Find out about closets, lockers, rest rooms, and lunchrooms. Become acquainted with your desk, typewriter, files, and telephone system.

If there are other employees, introduce yourself to your co-workers if your employer is unable to do so. Make an effort to remember names and positions. Be pleasant and friendly, but do not push yourself into the company of your co-workers; wait until you are invited to join them.

Although you should be prepared and able to carry out practically any task that may be asked of you, the preference of your employer is the deciding factor of how letters should be written, appointments made, and records kept. Pay close attention to instructions, making notes if necessary. Ask questions when the employer has finished talking. If you feel that you know a better way to perform a task, wait until you have established yourself as an efficient and capable employee; then make your suggestions.

Observe everything that goes on in your new office. No two offices or doctors follow the same routine. In order for you to succeed, you must convince your employer that you are completely dependable. This means that you will carry out instructions without fail. Your first sign of success will be when the doctor stops checking what you have done and takes for granted that you have followed instructions. The next step is when you are given responsibility for certain tasks, and still another signal of success is when your opinion is asked.

MOVING AHEAD

Once you have learned all the ropes of office routine, you will find that a little initiative on your part will earn you a promotion or a more promising position elsewhere.

Preparing for Promotion

Your chances for promotion in the medical world vary greatly. If you have accepted a job in a pharmaceutical house, the succession may lead from receptionist to stenographer to executive secretary to department supervisor. If you work in a one-doctor office, the chances for promotion are somewhat different.

Before giving financial advancement, the doctor must be able to rely absolutely on the assistant's ability to assume more and more of the office responsibility. The more the assistant can do without supervision, the more time the doctor has for patients, and, consequently, the greater the income. Appreciation will be expressed to the assistant as a salary increase.

If you wish to grow in such a job, it is necessary to evaluate the doctor's interests, the practice, and the specialty. Go to a medical library and look up journals devoted to that specialty. There may be many technical passages that you do not understand, but you will gradually learn the vocabulary. You will learn the names of the different pathological conditions treated in this specialty. Treatments, procedures, and drugs that you should recognize by name will be mentioned. Look up definitions of words you do not know.

If it is your ambition to become an executive secretary in a group practice or clinic, become familiar with every department and with the organization's basic operation. Offer to help different people with their work in order to learn different aspects of the practice. Then, when such a position is open, you will be justified in applying for it.

If you would like to become a medical assistant, clinical, offer to learn and help with examinations and procedures. Show your interest, and do not be afraid to put in extra time. If you learn of an evening course, take it.

Remember that the sure way, and probably the only way, to earn promotion is to observe these rules:

> Do excellent work on every task assigned to you.
>
> Make your superior feel that you can be depended on unconditionally.
>
> Always be prompt, do not overstay your breaks, and put in a full day's work.

Demonstrate interest, initiative, and ingenuity.
Use good judgment when faced with a decision.
Be cheerful when the work is heavy and the hours long.
Be cooperative and pitch in to help others.
Practice those skills you may not be using in your job.
Study the specialty and let the doctor know you are doing so.
Offer to do extra work in the particular field you enjoy.

Going Up the Ladder Besides earning a promotion in the job you are holding, there are many opportunities to proceed to another and better job. If you would like to work in one of the specialties described in Chapter 17, study this specialty, and map out a campaign to acquaint specialists in that field with your qualifications.

Personal Advancement In addition to moving ahead in your career, you will want to develop your personality as a whole. Part of your leisure time should be devoted to this goal. It is a fact that personality can be improved with a sincere desire to do so and steady application to a definite plan. There are many courses in personal development given in colleges, vocational schools, the YMCA and YWCA, and similar institutions.

Continue your education. Experts predict that in order to keep up with our society's fast pace, adults will have to take refresher courses or study new areas affecting their employment all their lives. Certainly this is true in the medical profession, where one must constantly keep up to date.

Do not expect to finish your learning program. If you have an inquiring mind and an alert personality, you will want to learn new things as long as you live. You will find that the more you learn, the easier it is to study new things, and the more fun it is. An additional and priceless bonus is meeting people who have the same interests and different ones as well. These friendships will broaden your outlook and add zest to your life. You will derive satisfaction, contentment, and a feeling of accomplishment from your continuing education.

Michael Weisbrot and Family

Project 78
Reevaluating Yourself

In Project 4 you assessed your strengths and weaknesses. Remove the self-evaluation sheet from your personal folder. Rate yourself in Column 3. On the back of the sheet, indicate the extent to which you think you have improved. Indicate those areas still needing improvement.

PREPARING FOR CERTIFICATION

The official recognition represented by the initials CMA after your name will assure your future employer that you have a solid background of theoretical and practical training in your profession. Whenever there is an opening available in any specialized field, the medical assistant who is a Certified Medical Assistant will be given special consideration.

Candidates for certification are required to pass the basic certification examination. When it is passed, a Certified Medical Assistant (CMA) certificate is issued. Candidates for specialty examinations must pass the basic certification examination before specialty certification is granted.

Most of the subjects required for the Certified Medical Assistant, Administrative, (CMA-A) certificate have been covered in this textbook. In addition, a knowledge of anatomy, pathological conditions, diagnostic procedures, surgical procedures, and medical terminology is required.

An important section in the examination is the one dealing with human relations; that is, the personal adjustment of the assistant to employer, patients, callers, and co-workers. The examination questions present problem situations, and the applicant is asked to resolve the problem.

Information regarding membership and application for the examination should be addressed to the American Association of Medical Assistants, Inc., One East Wacker Drive, Suite 1510, Chicago, IL 60601, by January 1 for the examination given on the first Friday in June of that year. Upon receipt of an application, the Association will send to the applicant a kit containing suggested reference material, a study outline, and a list of places where the examinations will be given. Also, rules governing payment of fees, cancellations, and repeating examinations are provided.

Applicants who fail to pass the basic certification examination are offered the opportunity of taking the examination again. Specialty examinations may also be repeated. Additional fees are required.

PERSONAL DEVELOPMENT PROJECTS

TOPICS FOR DISCUSSION 1. Discuss ways one person influences another person. Try one method on a friend or family member and relate experiences to classmates.

2. List ways employees waste time. Assume you are a supervisor. How could you correct these problems?

3. Devise a list of qualities upon which to evaluate the performance of an entry-level medical assistant, administrative. Discuss these qualities in small groups or with the entire class.

ROLE PLAYING 1. You have been promoted to office manager, responsible for eight employees. Role-play the following situations:
   a. Speak with an employee who is habitually late to work.
   b. Explain that the task of collecting samples is being transferred from the secretary to the new nurse.

2. The medical assistant brings a personal problem to you—the medical assistant's parents asked the assistant to move out of the family dwelling.

3. A newly hired clinical assistant insists upon preparing notes for the clinical data sheet her way instead of the way Dr. Taylor wants them to be done. You had explained Dr. Taylor's preferences to her when she was hired.

Reference Section

Addressing Envelopes

In order to ensure fast processing of mail, the United States Postal Service has issued guidelines for addressing envelopes. Although the placement of copy may vary somewhat, the following directions will meet the Postal Service's guidelines.

The address block should be single-spaced (regardless of the number of lines in the address) and should be typed in block style. The city, state, and ZIP Code should appear on one line. One space should separate the state from the ZIP Code.

On a large (No. 10) envelope, start the address block on line 14, about 45 spaces from the left edge. On a small (No. 6¾) envelope or on postal cards, begin the address block on line 12, about 22 spaces from the left edge. If the envelope does not contain a preprinted return address, begin the return address block on line 3, about 5 spaces from the left edge.

On-arrival directions such as attention lines and *Personal* or *Confidential* notations should be typed on line 9 (or at least three lines below the return address). Every word should begin with a capital letter, and the entire notation should be underscored. The attention line may also be typed on the second line of the address block, as in the illustration below.

Mailing directions such as SPECIAL DELIVERY should be typed in all-capital letters on line 9. The notation should end about 5 spaces from the right edge of the envelope. (If using oversized stamps, type the mailing directions a few lines lower.)

States in an address may be spelled out in full, or the standard abbreviations may be used, or the new two-letter abbreviations created for the ZIP Codes may be used. Follow the preference of your employer. If your employer has no preference, the two-letter abbreviations are recommended. This is particularly true if you live and work in an area that has already begun using the new nine-digit ZIP Codes. A table giving the standard and the new two-letter state abbreviations appears below. Two-letter abbreviations for U.S. possessions and Canadian provinces are also given.

STATES

Standard	New	Standard	New
Ala.	AL	Mont.	MT
Alaska	AK	Nebr.	NE
Ariz.	AZ	Nev.	NV
Ark.	AR	N.H.	NH
Calif.	CA	N.J.	NJ
Colo.	CO	N. Mex.	NM
Conn.	CT	N.Y.	NY
Del.	DE	N.C.	NC
D.C.	DC	N. Dak.	ND
Fla.	FL	Ohio	OH
Ga.	GA	Okla.	OK
Hawaii	HI	Oreg.	OR
Idaho	ID	Pa.	PA
Ill.	IL	R.I.	RI
Ind.	IN	S.C.	SC
Iowa	IA	S. Dak.	SD
Kans.	KS	Tenn.	TN
Ky.	KY	Tex.	TX
La.	LA	Utah	UT
Maine	ME	Vt.	VT
Md.	MD	Va.	VA
Mass.	MA	Wash.	WA
Mich.	MI	W. Va.	WV
Minn.	MN	Wis.	WI
Miss.	MS	Wyo.	WY
Mo.	MO		

```
Warren Taylor, M.D.
2235 South Ridgeway Avenue
Chicago, Illinois 60623


Confidential                                        CERTIFIED


              Central Medical Plaza
              Attention Greta Eklund, M.D.
              3399 South Sawyer Avenue
              Chicago, IL 60623
```

U.S. POSSESSIONS

Guam	GU
Puerto Rico	PR
Virgin Islands	VI

For addresses that will be imprinted by means of an address plate or computerized equipment, type the lines in all-capital letters, and do not use punctuation:

```
CENTRAL MEDICAL PLAZA
ATTENTION GRETA EKLUND MD
3399 SOUTH SAWYER AVENUE
CHICAGO IL 60623
```

CANADIAN PROVINCES

Alberta	AB	Nova Scotia	NS
British Columbia	BC	Ontario	ON
Labrador	LB	Prince Edward Island	PE
Manitoba	MB	Quebec	PQ
New Brunswick	NB	Saskatchewan	SK
Newfoundland	NF	Yukon Territory	YT
Northwest Territories	NT		

Letter Styles

Letters should be typed in the style preferred by the employer. A letterhead may look better with one style than with another. Some commonly accepted styles of punctuation and arrangement on the page are shown below and on page 190.

Blocked style, standard punctuation.

Full-blocked style, open punctuation.

190 REFERENCE SECTION

Warren Taylor, M.D.
2235 South Ridgeway Avenue
Chicago, IL 60623
(312) 555-6022

July 7, 19--

Mrs. Jane Thompson
1058 West 63d Place
Chicago, IL 60621

HOSPITAL RESERVATION

The Riverview Hospital has a private room available for you on Monday, July 21. Your surgery will be scheduled for the following morning. Report to the hospital by three o'clock on Monday.

Please notify us by July 14 if this is not satisfactory, and other arrangements will be made.

(Ms.) Molly Benson

MOLLY BENSON - MEDICAL ASSISTANT

Simplified style, open punctuation.

Warren Taylor, M.D.
2235 South Ridgeway Avenue
Chicago, IL 60623
(312) 555-6022

August 15, 19--

Mrs. Annette Blake
5687 South Princeton Avenue
Chicago, IL 60621

Dear Mrs. Blake

Because of a change in the hospital's operating schedule, Johnny's tonsillectomy has been postponed until Thursday, August 21, at 10 a.m.

Please admit Johnny to the hospital by 3 p.m. on Wednesday.

Sincerely

(Ms.) Molly Benson

Molly Benson
Medical Assistant

Blocked style, open punctuation.

Warren Taylor, M.D.
2235 South Ridgeway Avenue
Chicago, IL 60623
(312) 555-6022

September 5, 19--

Dr. Ethan Hershey
4366 Maple Avenue
Baltimore, MD 21227

Dear Dr. Hershey:

Enclosed is the report that was inadvertently omitted from Dr. Taylor's letter of September 2.

I hope this has not inconvenienced you.

Sincerely,

(Ms.) Molly Benson

Molly Benson
Medical Assistant

Enclosure

Full-blocked style, standard punctuation.

Medical Abbreviations

In writing medical reports, patients' histories, and prescriptions, certain abbreviations are commonly employed. The medical assistant must be familiar with these abbreviations. Some of the more widely used abbreviations follow. They are divided into the categories in which they fall—prescriptions, diseases, lab terms, and so forth.

PRESCRIPTION OR TREATMENT

Abbreviation	Meaning
aa	equal parts of each
ac	before meals
ad lib	as desired
a.m.	morning
bid	twice a day
cc	cubic centimeter
c̄	with
disc.	discontinue
dr	dram
g	gram
gr	grain
h	hour
hs	at bedtime
IM	intramuscular
IV	intravenous
kg	kilogram
L	liter
mcg	microgram (also expressed as μg)
mEq	milliequivalent
mg	milligram
mL	milliliter (replacing cc)
NPO	nothing by mouth
OD	right eye
OS	left eye
oz	ounce
pc	after meals
per os	by mouth
p.m.	afternoon
prn	as needed
q	every
qd	every day
qh	every hour
q2h	every two hours
qod	every other day
qid	four times a day
s̄	without
ss	one-half
stat	immediately
tbsp	tablespoon
tid	three times a day
tsp	teaspoon

DISEASES

Abbreviation	Meaning
ASHD	arteriosclerotic heart disease
Ca	carcinoma
CHF	congestive heart failure
CVA	cerebrovascular accident
FX	fracture
GC	gonorrhea (gonococcus)
MI	myocardial infarction
PID	pelvic inflammatory disease
URI	upper respiratory infection
VD	venereal disease

OPERATIVE PROCEDURES*

Abbreviation	Meaning
D & C	dilatation & curettage
I & D	incision & drainage
Pap	Papanicolaou (Pap) smear
T & A	tonsillectomy and adenoidectomy
TUR	transurethral resection

LABORATORY AND X-RAY TERMS

Abbreviation	Meaning
BMR	basal metabolic rate
BUN	blood urea nitrogen
CBC	complete blood count
DIFF	differential blood count
ECG (EKG)	electrocardiogram
EEG	electroencephalogram
EMG	electromyogram
Hct	hematocrit
Hgb	hemoglobin
hpf	high-power field
IVP	intravenous pyelogram
lab	laboratory
PBI	protein-bound iodine
PT	prothrombin time†
RBC	red blood count
ESR	erythrocyte sedimentation rate
UA	urinalysis
WBC	white blood count

PHYSICAL EXAMINATION

Abbreviation	Meaning
BP	blood pressure
CC	chief complaint
CV	cardiovascular
DTR	deep tendon reflex

* Not included are colloquial expressions such as "cysto" for *cystoscopy* and "procto" for *proctoscopy*.
† Also referred to as "pro time."

PHYSICAL EXAMINATION (Continued)

Abbreviation	Meaning	Abbreviation	Meaning
Dx	diagnosis	MH	marital history
EENT	eye-ear-nose-throat	N & V	nausea and vomiting
EOM	extraocular movement	P & A	percussion and auscultation
FH	family history	PE	physical examination
GI	gastrointestinal	PMH	past medical history
GU	genitourinary	PMI	point of maximal impulse
GYN	gynecological	R/O	rule out
H & P	history and physical	ROM	range of motion
Ht.	height	ROS	review of systems
Hx	history	TM	tympanic membrane
LKS	liver-kidney-spleen	TPR	temperature-pulse-respiration
LLQ	left lower quadrant	WD	well-developed
LMP	last menstrual period	WN	well-nourished
LUQ	left upper quadrant	wt.	weight

Metrics

COMMON UNITS OF MEASUREMENT

Customary

12 inches (in)	=	1 foot (ft)
3 feet	=	1 yard (yd)
1,760 yards	=	1 mile (mi)
5,280 feet	=	1 mile (mi)
16 ounces (oz)	=	1 pound (lb)
100 pounds	=	1 hundredweight (cwt)
200 hundredweight	=	1 ton
2,000 pounds	=	1 ton

Metric

10 millimeters (mm)	=	1 centimeter (cm)
100 centimeters	=	1 meter (m)
1,000 millimeters	=	1 meter (m)
1,000 meters	=	1 kilometer (km)
10 milligrams (mg)	=	1 centigram (cg)
100 centigrams	=	1 gram (g)
1,000 milligrams	=	1 gram
1,000 grams	=	1 kilogram (kg)

APPROXIMATE CONVERSIONS

Customary to Metric

1 ounce	=	28.35	grams
1 pound	=	0.45	kilograms
1 inch	=	2.54	centimeters *or*
		25.4	millimeters
1 foot	=	30.48	centimeters
1 yard	=	0.914	meters *or*
		91.44	centimeters
1 mile	=	1.609	kilometers

Metric to Customary

1 gram	=	0.035	ounce
1 kilogram	=	2.205	pounds
1 millimeter	=	0.035	ounce
1 centimeter	=	0.39	inch
1 meter	=	39.37	inches *or*
		3.28	feet *or*
		1.09	yards
1 kilometer	=	0.62	miles

STATIONERY SIZES (ALL CONVERSIONS APPROXIMATE)

Customary

Index card: 5" × 3" (127 × 76 mm)
Baronial: 5½" × 8½" (140 × 216 mm)
Monarch: 7¼" × 10½" (184 × 267 mm)
Official: 8" × 10½" (203 × 267 mm)
Standard: 8½" × 11" (216 × 279 mm)
Legal: 8½" × 13" (216 × 330 mm) *or*
     8½" × 14" (216 × 356 mm)

Metric

No metric equivalent size
A5: 148 × 210 mm (5⅞" × 8¼")
No metric equivalent size
No metric equivalent size
A4: 210 × 297 mm (8¼" × 11⅜")
No metric equivalent size

ENVELOPE SIZES

Customary	Metric
No. 10: 9½″ × 4⅛″ (241 × 105 mm)	DL: 220 × 110 mm (8⅝″ × 4⅜″)
No. 6¾: 6½″ × 3⅝″ (165 × 92 mm)	C7/6: 162 × 81 mm (6⅜″ × 3⅛″)
Postal card: 5½″ × 3½″ (140 × 89 mm)	No metric equivalent size

Conversion Tables

TEMPERATURE

Centigrade Degrees	Fahrenheit Degrees	Centigrade Degrees	Fahrenheit Degrees
50	122	36	96.8
45	113	35.5	95.9
44	111.2	35	95
43	109.4	34	93.2
42	107.6	33	91.4
41	105.8	32	89.6
40.5	104.9	31	87.8
40	104	30	86
39.5	103.1		
39	102.2		
38.5	101.3		
38	100.4		
37.5	99.5		
37	98.6		
36.5	97.7		

To change degrees Fahrenheit to degrees centigrade, subtract 32 from the Fahrenheit reading and multiply the result by 0.555.

To change centigrade degrees to Fahrenheit degrees, multiply the centigrade reading by 1.8 and add 32 to the result.

LIQUID MEASURES

Apothecary	Metric	Apothecary	Metric
1 pint (16 fl oz)	480 cc	1 fl dr	4 cc
12 fl oz	360 cc	16 minims	1 cc
4 fl oz	120 cc	10 minims	0.6 cc
3⅜ fl oz	100 cc	5 minims	0.3 cc
1 fl oz	30 cc	1⅝ minims	0.1 cc
6 fl dr	24 cc	1 minim	0.06 cc

WEIGHT

Apothecary	Metric	Apothecary	Metric
1 ounce	30 grams	¾ grain	50 milligrams
1 dram	4 grams	⅔ grain	45 milligrams
15 grains	1 gram	½ grain	32 milligrams
7½ grains	0.5 gram	⅜ grain	24 milligrams
5 grains	0.32 gram	⅓ grain	22 milligrams
4 grains	0.25 gram	¼ grain	16 milligrams
3 grains	0.2 gram	⅛ grain	8 milligrams
2 grains	0.13 gram	1/10 grain	6.5 milligrams
1½ grains	0.1 gram	1/64 grain	1 milligram
1 grain	65 milligrams	1/100 grain	0.65 milligram

SOLUTIONS

Prescribed Strength	Amount of Crude Drug	Fluid to Be Added
1:1000	1 teaspoonful	to 1 gallon
1:1000	15 drops	to 1 quart
1/10 of 1 percent	15 drops	to 1 quart
1:500	2 teaspoonfuls	to 1 gallon
1:500	30 drops	to 1 quart
1/5 of 1 percent	30 drops	to 1 quart
1:200	5 teaspoonfuls	to 1 gallon
1:200	1¼ teaspoonfuls	to 1 quart
½ of 1 percent	1¼ teaspoonfuls	to 1 quart
1:100 (1 percent)	2½ teaspoonfuls	to 1 quart
1:50 (2 percent)	5 teaspoonfuls	to 1 quart
1:25 (4 percent)	2½ tablespoonfuls	to 1 quart
1:20 (5 percent)	3 tablespoonfuls	to 1 quart

HOUSEHOLD MEASURES

1 drop	=	1 minim	1 teacupful	=	4 fluidounces or 120 cc
1 teaspoonful	=	1 dram or 4 cc	1 tumblerful	=	8 fluidounces or 240 cc
1 tablespoonful	=	4 drams or 16 cc	12 tablespoonfuls	=	1 cup (powder)
1 wineglassful	=	2 fluidounces or 60 cc	16 tablespoonfuls	=	1 cup (liquid)

Reading References

ADMINISTRATIVE SKILLS

Eckersley-Johnson, Anna L. (ed.), *Webster's Secretarial Handbook,* G. & C. Merriam Company, Springfield, Mass., 1976.

Fowler, Henry W., *A Dictionary of Modern English Usage,* 2d ed., revised by Sir Ernest Gowers, Oxford University Press, New York, 1965.

Hanna, J. Marshall, Estelle L. Popham, and Rita Sloan Tilton, *Secretarial Procedures and Administration,* 7th ed., South-Western Publishing Company, Cincinnati, 1978.

Hutchinson, Lois Irene, *Standard Handbook for Secretaries,* 8th ed., McGraw-Hill Book Company, New York, 1969.

Nicholson, Margaret, *Practical Style Guide for Authors and Editors,* Holt, Rinehart and Winston, Inc., New York, 1970.

Place, Irene, Edward E. Byers, and Elaine F. Uthe, *Executive Secretarial Procedures,* 5th ed., Gregg Division, McGraw-Hill Book Company, New York, 1980.

Sabin, William A., *The Gregg Reference Manual,* 5th ed., Gregg Division, McGraw-Hill Book Company, New York, 1977.

Siegfried, W., *Typing Medical Forms,* McGraw-Hill Book Company, New York, 1969.

Webster's Collegiate Thesaurus, G. & C. Merriam Company, Springfield, Mass., 1976.

Webster's Medical Speller, G. & C. Merriam Company, Springfield, Mass., 1975.

Webster's Third New International Dictionary, G. & C. Merriam Company, Springfield, Mass., 1976.

Willeford, George, *Medical Word Finder,* 2d ed., Prentice-Hall, Inc., Englewood Cliffs, N.J., 1976.

ADVANCEMENT

Bittel, Lester R., *What Every Supervisor Should Know: The Basics of Supervisory Management,* 4th ed., Gregg Division, McGraw-Hill Book Company, New York, 1980.

Chapman, Elwood N., *Your Attitude is Showing,* 3d ed., Science Research Associates, Inc., Palo Alto, 1977.

Diekelmann, Nancy L., and Martin M. Broadwell, *The New Hospital Supervisor,* Addison-Wesley Publishing Company, Reading, Mass., 1977.

Miller, Lawrence M., *Behavior Management: The New Science of Managing People at Work,* John Wiley & Sons, Inc., New York, 1978.

Milliken, Mary Elizabeth, *Understanding Human Behavior,* Delmar Publishing, Albany, N.Y., 1974.

Preston, Paul, and Thomas W. Zimmerer, *Management for Supervisors,* Prentice-Hall, Inc., Englewood Cliffs, N.J., 1978.

Strauss, George, and Leonard R. Sayles, *Personnel: The Human Problems of Management,* 3d ed., Prentice-Hall, Inc., Englewood Cliffs, N.J., 1972.

CLINICAL PROCEDURES

Anthony, Catherine P., and Irene B. Alyn, *Structure and Function of the Body,* 5th ed., The C. V. Mosby Company, St. Louis, 1976.

DeCoursey, Russell, *The Human Organism,* 5th ed., McGraw-Hill Book Company, New York, 1980.

Dennis, Robert L., and Jean M. Doyle, *The Complete Handbook for Medical Secretaries and Assistants,* Little, Brown and Company, Boston, 1978.

Frederick, Portia M., and Mary E. Kinn, *The Medical Office Assistant: Administrative and Clinical,* 4th ed., W. B. Saunders Company, Philadelphia, 1974.

French, Ruth M., *Nurse's Guide to Diagnostic Procedures,* 5th ed., McGraw-Hill Book Company, New York, 1980.

Garb, Solomon, *Laboratory Tests in Common Use,* 6th ed., Springer Publishing, New York, 1976.

Hardy, Clyde, and Nancy Martin, *Your Role as a Medical Assistant,* Medical Economics Co., Oradell, N.J., 1974.

Henderson, John, *Emergency Medical Guide,* 4th ed., McGraw-Hill Book Company, New York, 1978.

Matin, N., and H. Cotton, *Aid for the Medical Assistant,* Medical Economics Co., Oradell, N.J., 1975.

Purtilo, Ruth, *Health Professional-Patient Interaction,* 2d ed., W. B. Saunders Company, Philadelphia, 1978.

Sherman, Jacques L., Jr., and Sylvia Kleimer Fields (eds.), *Guide to Patient Evaluation,* 3d ed., Medical Examination Publishing Company, Flushing, N.Y., 1978.

Skydell, Barbara, and Anne S. Crowder, *Diagnostic Procedures: A Reference for Health Practitioners and a Guide for Patient Counseling,* Little, Brown and Company, Boston, 1975.

Wallach, Jacques B., *Interpretation of Diagnostic Tests: A Handbook Synopsis of Laboratory Medicine,* 3d ed., Little, Brown and Company, Boston, 1978.

FINANCIAL RECORDS

American Medical Association, *Business Side of Medical Practice,* American Medical Association, Chicago, 1977.

Brock, Horace R., Charles E. Palmer, Red C. Archer, and John E. Binnion, *College Accounting for Secretaries,* Gregg Division, McGraw-Hill Book Company, New York, 1971.

Sarner, Harvey, and Herbert C. Lassiter, *Insurance for the Doctor*, W. B. Saunders Company, Philadelphia, 1967.
Walker, Arthur, J. Kenneth Roach, and J. Marshall Hanna, *How to Use Adding and Calculating Machines*, 4th ed., Gregg Division, McGraw-Hill Book Company, New York, 1979.
Wigge, Barton, and Merle Wood, *Payroll Systems and Procedures*, Gregg Division, McGraw-Hill Book Company, New York, 1970.
Wilson, John, *How to Get Paid for What You've Earned*, Medical Economics Co., Oradell, N.J., 1974.

INTERPERSONAL RELATIONS

Carenza, Edward C., *Pediatricks*, Medical Economics Co., Oradell, N.J., 1974.
Dennis, Lorraine B., *Psychology of Human Behavior for Nurses*, 3d ed., W. B. Saunders Company, Philadelphia, 1967.
Halloran, Jack, *Applied Human Relations: An Organizational Approach*, Prentice-Hall, Englewood Cliffs, N.J., 1978.
Lair, Jess, and Jacqueline Lair, *Hey, God, What Should I Do Now?* Fawcett World Library, 1978.
——, *I Ain't Much Baby, But I'm All I've Got*, Fawcett World Library, 1978.
Laird, Donald A., Eleanor C. Laird, Rosemary T. Fruehling, and W. Porter Swift, *Psychology: Human Relations and Motivation*, 5th ed., McGraw-Hill Book Company, New York, 1975.
Likert, Rensis, and Jane Gibson Likert, *New Ways of Managing Conflict*, McGraw-Hill Book Company, New York, 1976.
Milliken, Mary Elizabeth, *Understanding Human Behavior*, Delmar Publishing, Albany, N.Y., 1974.

MEDICAL RECORDS

Alcazar, Carol C., *Medical Typist's Guide for Histories and Physicals*, 2d ed., Medical Examination Publishing Company, Flushing, N.Y., 1974.
International Classification of Diseases, 9th edition, *Clinical Modification* (ICD-9-CM), Commission on Professional and Hospital Activities, Ann Arbor, 1978.
Moritz, Alan R., and Morris R. Crawford, *Handbook of Legal Medicine*, 4th ed., The C. V. Mosby Company, St. Louis, 1975.
Smith, Genevieve Long, and Phyllis E. Davis, *Medical Terminology: A Programmed Text*, 4th ed., John Wiley & Sons, Inc., New York, 1980.
Springer, Eric (ed.), *Automated Medical Records and the Law*, Aspen Systems, Germantown, Md., 1971.

RECORDS MANAGEMENT

Johnson, Mina M., and Norman F. Kallans, *Records Management*, South-Western Publishing Company, Cincinnati, 1974.
Kahn, Gilbert, Theodore Yerian, and Jeffrey R. Stewart, *Filing Systems and Records Management*, 3d ed., Gregg Division, McGraw-Hill Book Company, New York, 1981.
Longest, Beaufort B., Jr., *Management Practices for the Health Professional*, Reston Publishing Company, Reston, Va., 1976.
Place, Irene, and E. L. Popham, *Filing and Records Management*, Prentice-Hall, Englewood Cliffs, N.J., 1966.

Index

Abbreviations
   medical, 16, 191–192
   postal, 188–189
Abstracts of journal articles, 142
Accident insurance, 98, 109
Accounting (see Billing; Financial records)
Accuracy, importance of, 10
Address, change of, 130
Administrative medical assistants, 2–4, 9
Admitting offices, hospital, 161–162
Agencies
   bill collection by, 94
   employment, 178
Agendas for medical society meetings, 137; illus.
Allergy, 157
Alphabetic filing, 58–60
American Association of Medical Assistants (AAMA), 9, 186
American Hospital Association, 141
American Medical Association (AMA), 18–19, 101, 135, 146
Anesthesia, local, 171
Announcement cards, 130; illus.
Answering services and machines, 55
Antiseptic, meaning of, 165
Apothecary-metric equivalents, 193
Appearance (see Career qualifications, appearance)
Application forms and letters, 180
Appointment books, 30–31, 33, 111; illus., 31, 33
Appointment cards, 36; illus.
Appointments, 30–37
   cancellation of, 35
   during doctor's absence, 151–152
   fixed, 31–33
   and hospital rounds, 37
   irregular, 34–35
   for new patients, 32
   next, 36
   and out-of-office calls, 36–37
   scheduling of, 31–36
Area codes for long-distance calls, 54
Armed services
   career opportunities in, 6
   health care (CHAMPUS) in, 107–108
Aseptic, meaning of, 165
Assault and battery, 23
Assignment of benefits, 100
Associations, professional (see also Medical societies)
   American Association of Medical Assistants (AAMA), 9, 186
   American Hospital Association, 141
   American Medical Association (AMA), 18–19, 101, 135, 146
   Certified Professional Secretaries (CPS), 8
   Future Secretaries Association (FSA), 9
   National Secretaries Association (NSA), 8
   Society of Professional Business Consultants, 126
Autoclaves, 166

Bactericide, meaning of, 165
Banking procedures, 115–119
   checks (see Checks)
   statements, 117–119; illus., 117, 118
Bibliographies in journal articles, 145
Billing
   arranging for payment, 86–89, 100, 111
   collecting accounts, 93–94, 111
   computerized, 92, 111
   determining fees (see Fees, doctors')
   procedures for, 128
   recording transactions, 89–92
Biographical directories, use of, 148
Biopsy reports, 83
Blood pressure, taking of, 169–170
Blue Cross and Blue Shield, 88, 103–104
   claim form, 103; illus.
Board of Medical Examiners, 21
Boiling, sterilization by, 165–166
Bookkeeping (see Billing; Financial records)
Business records, filing of, 57
Business world, career opportunities in, 7

Canadian provinces, abbreviations, 189
Canceled checks, 64, 87, 117–118
Canceling of appointments, 35
Carbon copies of letters, 73
Card catalogs in libraries, 141; illus.
Card files, 57–58; illus., 57
Cardiology, 158
Career opportunities, 2, 4–9, 176–178
   armed services, 6
   business world, 7
   clinics, 5, 165
   dentists' offices, 5
   doctors' offices, 5
   foundations, 6
   free-lance, 7
   group practice, 5
   hospitals, 5
   institutions, 6
   insurance companies, 6–7
   laboratories, 7, 163–164
   Medicare, 7
   prepaid medical care and hospitalization plans, 6–7
   public health departments, 6
   publishing, 7
   research, 8
   teaching, 7
Career qualifications, 10–16
   appearance, 13–14
      cosmetics, 13
      grooming, 13
      street clothes, 14
      uniforms, 13
   personal attributes, 10–12
      accuracy, 10
      courtesy, 39, 48–49
      criticism, acceptance of, 12
      dependability, 10
      kindness, 12

Career qualifications, personal attributes (continued)
      punctuality, 10
      sympathy, 12
      tact, 12
      thoroughness, 11–12
   professional conduct, 14–16, 19–20 (see also Medical ethics)
      confidentiality, 15–16, 19–20
      familiarity, avoidance of, 15
      maturity, 16
      serenity, 14
   secretarial skills, 16
Carriers, insurance policy, 99
Case histories (see Medical histories)
Cash payments, 87, 114–116
   receipts for, 87; illus.
Centigrade, conversion to Fahrenheit, 193
Certification as medical assistant, 9, 186
Certified mail, 67–68
Certified Medical Assistant (CMA), 9, 186
Certified Professional Secretaries (CPS), 8
CHAMPUS (Civilian Health and Medical Program of the Uniformed Services), 107–108
   claim form, 107; illus.
Charge slips, 90; illus.
Charges (see Fees, doctors')
Charts, patients' (see Medical histories; Medical records; Medical reports)
Checks
   canceled, 64, 87, 117–118
   deposit of, 115–116
   endorsements for, 115; illus.
   forged, 117
   outstanding, 118
   payment of fees by, 87, 114–116
   payroll, 121
   signing of, 117
   and statement reconciliation, 117–119
   stubs, 116–117; illus., 116
   traveler's, 151
   writing of, 116–117; illus., 116
Chemical sterilization, 166; illus.
Chiropractic medicine, 161
Civilian Health and Medical Program of the Uniformed Services (CHAMPUS), 107–108
Claim forms, health insurance, 101–103, 106–108; illus., 102, 103, 106, 107, 108
Classified advertisements, 177
Cleaning supplies, 133
Clinical data sheets, 78–81; illus., 81
Clinical medical assistants, 3–4, 9, 165–171
Clinics
   assisting doctors in, 171
   career opportunities in, 5, 165
   diagnostic tests in, 170–171
   examinations in, 166–170
   sterilization methods in, 165–166
   treatments in, 171
Coding of files, 63
Coinsurance, 100

Cold sterilization, 166; *illus.*
Collection of accounts, 93–94, 111
Computer-based retrieval systems for medical literature, 142
Computerized billing, 92, 111
Conduct, professional (*see* Career qualifications, professional conduct; Medical ethics)
Confidentiality, need for, 15–16, 19–20
Consent forms, 23
Consultants, medical management, 126–127
Contracts
  breach of, 24
  insurance policy, 99
Conversion tables, 193–194
  household measures, 194
  liquid measures, 193
  solutions, 194
  temperature, 193
  weight, 193
Coordination of benefits, 100
Correspondence (*see* Letters; Mail)
Cosmetics, use of, 13
Court, doctors in, 25–26
Courtesy, need for, 39, 48–49
Coverage, insurance policy, 99
Credit, arrangements for, 88–89
Criticism, acceptance of, 12
Cross-reference sheets, 58
Cross-referencing of files, 63
Current Procedural Terminology (AMA), 101
"Customary" fees, 100

Daily earnings records (*see* Daily journals)
Daily journals, 110–112; *illus.*, 112
Daily routine, 127
Damage suits, 25–26
Daysheets (*see* Daily journals)
Deductible disbursements, 114
Deductibles, insurance policy, 99–100
Deductions, tax, 120–121
Dental office, career opportunities in, 5
Dependability, importance of, 10
Deposit tickets for cash and checks, 115–116; *illus.*, 115
Dermatology, 158
Desks, medical assistants', 130–131
Diagnosis, 78
Diagnostic filing, 61
Diagnostic tests
  electrocardiograph, 83, 170; *illus.*, 170
  fluoroscopy, 170–171
  laboratory specimens, 170
  X ray, 170–171
Dictation machines, 72–73
Dictionaries, use of, 147
Dietary regimens, 171
Diplomates, 161
Directories
  biographical, 148
  telephone, 53–54
Disability insurance, 98, 109
Diseases, classifications of, 101
Disinfectant, meaning of, 165
Disposable equipment, use of, 166
Doctors
  absence of, 151–152
  announcement cards sent by, 130; *illus.*
  appointments with (*see* Appointments)
  bags used by, 131
  in court, 25–26
  earnings and income of, 89
  education of, 157

Doctors (*continued*)
  familiarity with, 15
  fees of (*see* Fees, doctors')
  hospital affiliations of, 128
  as lecturers, 139–140
  licensing of, 21–22, 127, 157
  listed in office procedures manual, 127
  medical ethics and medical law concerning (*see* Medical ethics; Medical law)
  office of, career opportunities in, 5
  responsibilities of, 19–20
  as specialists, 157
Double-entry accounting systems, 110
Drafts, manuscript, 142–143
  proofreader's marks for, *illus.*, 142
Drug and medicine reference books, use of, 148
Duplicating equipment, 73–74; *illus.*, 74

Editing of journal articles, 145–146
Electrocardiographs, 83, 170
Emergencies
  recognizing, 46
  telephone calls regarding, 37, 51
Employment (*see* Career opportunities; Job advancement; Job hunting)
Employment agencies, 178
Endocrinology, 158
Endorsements for checks, 115; *illus.*
Envelopes
  addressing, 188–189; *illus.*, 188
  sizes, 193
Equipment (*see* Supplies)
Estates, collection from, 94
Ethics (*see* Medical ethics)
Etiquette, professional, 19, 88
Examinations, patients', 166–170
  blood pressure, 169–170
  height and weight, 169
  instruments for, 167; *illus.*
  positioning patients for, 168; *illus.*
  pulse, 169
  respiration, 169
  temperature, 169
Express mail, 68

Fahrenheit, conversion to centigrade, 193
Family medicine, 157
Fees, doctors' (*see also* Billing)
  adjustments of, 88
  discussions of, 85–86
  and health insurance, 88, 100
  schedules for, 85
FICA (social security) taxes, 120–121
File cabinets, 57; *illus.*
Filing
  equipment and supplies, 57–58; *illus.*, 57
    card files, 57; *illus.*
    cross-reference sheets, 58
    file cabinets, 57; *illus.*
    folders, 58
    labels, 58
    microfilming and microfiche, 57–58
    out guides, 58
  of health insurance claim forms, 101–102
  methods, 58–62, 131
    alphabetic, 58–60
    geographic, 60
    numeric, 61
    phonetic, 62
    subject, 61
  procedures, 62–63, 128

Filing, procedures (*continued*)
    coding, 63
    cross-referencing, 63
    follow-up, 63
    indexing, 63
    releasing, 63
    sorting, 63
    transferring, 63
  of records of incoming calls, 51–52
  retention and destruction, 63–64
    canceled checks, 64
    insurance policies, 64
    medical histories, 63
    personal records, 64
    receipts for equipment, 64
  supplies needed for, 57–58
  types of records, 56–57
    business and financial, 57
    correspondence, medical or general, 56
    patient, 57
Financial records (*see also* Billing; Checks)
  accounting systems, 110–111
  banking procedures, 115–119
  charges and payments by patients, 89–92
  daily journals, 110–112; *illus.*, 112
  during doctor's absence, 151
  filing of, 57
  health insurance claim forms, 100–103, 106–108
  journals, daily, 110–112
  patients' ledgers, 90–91, 110, 111; *illus.*, 91
  payroll and taxes, 9, 120–121
  petty cash, 119–120
    register of, 119–120; *illus.*, 119
    voucher for, 119; *illus.*
  preparing, 111–114
  summary sheets, monthly and yearly, 111–114; *illus.*, 113, 114
Flashlights, use of, 167
Fluoroscopy, 170–171
Folders, file, 58
Follow-up files, 63
Footnotes in journal articles, 144
Forms, samples of, in office procedures manual, 129
Foundations, career opportunities in, 6
Free-lance work, career opportunities in, 7
Funeral homes, keeping list of, 129
Future Secretaries Association (FSA), 9

Gastroenterology, 158
Geographic filing, 60
Germicide, meaning of, 165
Good Samaritan Acts, 24
Grooming, importance of, 13
Group insurance, 99
Group practice, career opportunities in, 5
Gynecology, 158

Headings
  in journal articles, 144
  in medical records, 77, 81; *illus.*, 81
  in minutes, 138; *illus.*
Health insurance (*see* Insurance)
Health Insurance Claim Form, 101–102; *illus.*, 102
Health Insurance Council (HIC), 101
Height, taking of, 169
Hippocratic oath, 17–18
Histories (*see* Medical histories)
Hospital assistants, 161–164
Hospital Literature Index, 141

INDEX

Hospitalization insurance (see Insurance)
Hospitals
  admitting office, 161–162
  career opportunities in, 5
  and doctors' appointments, 37
  listed in office procedures manual, 128
  medical record department, 162
  operating room, 163
  pathology, 163–164
  patient education, 164
  physical medicine department, 164
  radiology department, 162–163
  social services, 164
Hotel reservations, making, 149
House visits
  and appointments, 36–37
  fees for, 86
  forms for, illus., 37
Household measure equivalents, 194
Hygienic regimens, 171

Identification cards, health insurance, 101
Illustrations in journal articles, 144
Immunization records, 83
Income taxes, 89, 120–121
Index Medicus, 61, 141
Indexes, consulting and preparing, 146
Indexing of files, 63
Institutions, career opportunities in, 5
Instruments
  examination, 167; illus.
  sterilization of, 165–166
Insurance
  accident, 98, 109
  Blue Cross and Blue Shield, 88, 103–104
  CHAMPUS, 107–108
  claim forms for, 101–103, 106–108; illus., 102, 103, 106, 107, 108
  coinsurance, 100
  disability, 98, 109
  group, 99
  health and hospitalization, 98–109
    and billing, 88, 100
    information needed for, 100–102
    plans, 103–109
    terminology of, 99–100
    types of, 98
  major medical, 98
  malpractice, 22–23
  Medicaid, 106–107
  medical, 98, 105–106
  Medicare (see Medicare)
  outpatient, 98
  policy retention, 64
  procedures for, 128–129
  surgical, 98
  workers' compensation, 108–109
Insurance companies, career opportunities in, 6–7
Insured mail, 68
Internal medicine, 158
International Classification of Diseases, 101
Interviews, job, 181–182
Itemized bills, 91–92; illus., 91
Itineraries, 150–151; illus., 150

Job advancement, 183–186
  first job, 183–184
  preparing for certification, 186
  promotion, 184–185
Job hunting, 176–182
  application forms, 180

Job hunting (continued)
  finding right job, 176–177
  interviews, 181–182
  letters of application, 180
  letters of regret, 182
  letters of thanks, 182
  résumés, 178–180; illus., 179
  sources for jobs, 177–178
Journal of the American Medical Association, 135, 146
Journals, medical, 65, 135 (see also Professional reports)

Kindness, need for, 12

Labels for file folders, 58
Laboratories
  career opportunities in, 7, 163–164
  findings from, 83, 170
  list of, in office, 130
  specimens for, 170
Laundry, 133
Law (see Medical law)
Lectures at medical society meetings, 139–140
Ledgers
  cards, 111
  general, 110–111
  patients', 90–91, 110, 111; illus., 91
Letters (see also Mail)
  appearance of, 69
  of application, 180
  collection by, 93
  correspondence, medical or general, 56
  dispatching, 68–69
  envelopes, 188–189, 193; illus., 188
  incoming, 65
  making copies of, 73–74
  from medical assistant, 71–72
  outgoing, 68–69
  personal, 65
  of referral, 42–43
  style of, 70–71, 189–190; illus., 189, 190
  of thanks or regret, 182
  using dictation and transcription machines, 72–73
Liability (see Professional liability)
Libraries, use of, 141–142
Licenses
  listed in office procedures manual, 127
  medical, 21
  narcotic, 21–22
  renewal of, 127
  for specialists, 157
Liquid measure equivalents, 193
Long-distance telephone calls, 54

Machines, office, 55, 72–74, 129
Mail, 64–69, 152 (see also Letters)
  classifications, 67
  during doctor's absence, 152
  equipment and supplies, 67
  incoming, 65
  outgoing, 66–69
  postal services, 67–68
  samples received by, 65
  sending bills by, 87–88, 93
  and telegrams, 69
Mailgrams, 69
Maintenance of office, 132–134
Major medical insurance, 98

Malpractice insurance, 22–23
Manuscripts (see Professional reports)
Maturity, need for, 16
Medicaid, 106–107
Medical assistants
  administrative, 2–4, 9
  certification of, 9, 186
  clinical, 3–4, 9, 165–171
  desks of, 130–131
  in hospital, 161–164
  job advancements (see Job advancement)
  job hunting (see Job hunting)
  opportunities for (see Career opportunities)
  personality of, 10–12
  professional associations for, 8–9
  professional conduct of, 14–16
  qualifications of (see Career qualifications)
  responsibilities of, 19–20
Medical ethics, 17–21 (see also Professional conduct)
  assistants' responsibilities, 19–20
  etiquette of, 19
  Hippocratic oath, 17–18
  patients' rights, 20–21
  principles of, 18–19
Medical histories
  forms for, 79–81; illus., 79, 80, 81
  microfilming, 63
  retention of, 63
  taking of, 77–78
Medical insurance, 98, 105–106
Medical journals (see Journals, medical)
Medical law, 21–26
  doctors in court, 25–26
  Medical Practice Acts, 21–22
  professional liability (see Professional liability)
Medical licenses (see Licenses)
Medical management consultants, 126–127
Medical Practice Acts, 21–22
Medical record departments in hospitals, 162
Medical records
  content of, 77–78
  forms for, 79–81; illus., 79, 80, 81
  health insurance claim forms, 101–103, 106–108; illus., 102, 103, 106, 107, 108
  obtaining clinical data, 79
  protecting and preserving, 63–64, 84
  release of, 19; illus.
  and reports, 82–84; illus., 82
Medical reports
  in doctors' offices, 82–84; illus., 82
  in hospitals, 162–164
Medical samples, 65
Medical secretaries (see Medical assistants)
Medical societies (see also Associations, professional)
  listed in office procedures manual, 128
  meetings of, 65, 136–139
  papers presented at, 139–140
  types and functions of, 135–136
Medical specialties (see Specialists)
Medical supplies, 133–134, 166
Medical terminology, understanding of, 16
Medicare
  career opportunities in, 7
  claim form, illus., 106
  hospitalization insurance, 104–105
  Medicaid, 106–107
  medical insurance, 105–106
  procedures for, 129

INDEX

Medications, 171
 apothecary-metric equivalents, 193
 drug and medicine reference books, 148
MEDLARS computer bank, 142
Meetings (see Medical societies)
Messages, telephone, 51–52
Metric-apothecary equivalents, 193
Metric system, 192–193
Microfilming and microfiche, 57–58
Minutes of medical society meetings, 138–139; illus., 138
Money orders, 115

Narcotic licenses, 21–22
National Library of Medicine, 141–142
National Secretaries Association (NSA), 8
Neurology, 158
Numeric filing, 61
Nurses, keeping list of, 130
Nursing homes, keeping list of, 130

Obstetrics, 158
Office hours, 33
Office management
 assistants' desks, 130–131
 cleaning and laundry, 133
 doctors' bags, 130
 filing system methods (see Filing)
 and machines used in office, 55, 72–74, 129
 maintenance, 132–134
 and medical management consultants, 126–127
 organization, 130–131
 and outside services, 129–130
 procedures manual for, 127–129
 public relations in, 2
 route slips, 46
 safety guidelines, 133
 supplies (see Supplies)
 waiting room, 132
Oncology, 158
Open shelf filing system, 57
Operating rooms, hospital, 163
Ophthalmology, 158–159
Ophthalmoscopes, 167; illus.
Opportunities (see Career opportunities)
Optometry, 160
Orthopedics, 159
Osteopathy, 161
Otorhinolaryngology (ENT), 159
Otoscopes, 167; illus.
Out guides for filing, 58
Out-of-office calls (see House visits)
Outpatient insurance, 98
Outside services, 129–130

Papers presented at medical society meetings, 139–140
Passports, obtaining, 149
Pathogenic, meaning of, 165
Pathology, 159, 163–164
Patients
 assistant-patient relationships, 12, 43–46
 billing of (see Billing)
 daily list of, 36
 determining competency of, 26
 difficult, 44–45
 education of, 164
 examining (see Examinations, patients')
 financial status of, 45–46, 86, 106–107

Patients (continued)
 first visits of, 32, 39–41, 61
 histories of (see Medical histories)
 new, 32, 39–41, 61
 physician-patient relationships, 22
 preparation of, 168; illus.
 reception of, 38–43
 records of (see Financial records; Medical records)
 referral of, 42–43, 129–130
 rights of, 20–21
 routine, 44
 selection of, 20
Patients' ledgers, 90–91, 110, 111; illus., 91
Payroll procedures
 checks, 121
 records of, 120–121; illus., 121
 taxes, 120–121
Pediatrics, 159
Pegboard accounting systems, 111; illus.
Percussion hammers, 167; illus.
Personal appearance (see Career qualifications, personal appearance)
Personal attributes (see Career qualifications, personal attributes)
Personnel records, 120–121, 128; illus., 121
Petty cash, 119–120
 register of, 119–120; illus., 119
 voucher for, 119; illus.
Pharmacies, keeping list of, 130
Phonetic filing, 62
Photocopies of letters, 73–74
Physical medicine, 160, 164
Physical therapists, keeping list of, 130
Physicians (see Doctors)
Placement bureaus, school, 177
Plastic gloves, use of, 167
Podiatrists, keeping list of, 130
Policies, health insurance (see Insurance)
Positioning of patients for examination, 168; illus.
Possessions, U.S., abbreviations, 188
Postal services (see Letters; Mail)
Premiums, insurance policy, 99
Prepaid medical care and hospitalization plans, career opportunities in, 6–7
Preparation of patients for examination, 168; illus.
Privileged communications, 23–24
Problem-oriented medical record (POMR) format, 80–81
Procedures manuals, office, 127–129
Proctology, 160
Professional associations (see Associations, professional; Medical societies)
Professional conduct (see Career qualifications, professional conduct; Medical ethics)
Professional liability, 22–25 (see also Medical law)
 assault and battery, 23
 breach of contract, 24
 consent, 24
 Good Samaritan Acts, 24
 malpractice, 22–23
 physician-patient relationships, 22
 privileged communications, 23–24
 safeguards against suits, 25
 slander, 24
 statute of limitations, 24
Professional reports, 140–148
 editing manuscripts, 145–146
 and medical journals, 146–147
 preparing manuscripts, 142–145

Professional reports (continued)
 researching and assembling information, 140–142
 use of reference and resource works, 147–148
Prognosis, 78
Progress reports, 78
Promotion, job, 184–185
Promptness, importance of, 10, 48–49
Proofreading of journal articles, 145–146
Providers, health care, 99
Psychiatry, 160
Public health departments
 career opportunities in, 6
 information disclosed to, 20
Public relations in doctors' offices, 2
Publishing, career opportunities in, 7
Pulse, taking of, 169
Punctuality, importance of, 10

Qualifications (see Career qualifications)
Quotations in journal articles, 144

Radiology, 160, 162–163
"Reasonable" fees, 100
Receipts
 for cash payments, 87; illus.
 retention of, 64, 151
Reception of patients, 38–43
Records management (see Billing; Filing; Financial records; Medical records; Personnel records)
Reference and resource works, use of, 147–148, 195–196
Referral of patients, 42–43, 129–130
Registered mail, 67
Release of information
 in doctors' files, 63
 for health insurance, 100; illus.
 for medical records, 19; illus.
Renewal of licenses, 127
Reports
 medical (see Medical reports)
 professional (see Professional reports)
 progress, 78
 sent to doctors during absence, 152
Reprints of journal articles, 147
Research
 career opportunities in, 8
 publication of, 140–142
Respiration, taking of, 169
Résumés, 178–180; illus., 179
Retention and destruction of files, 63–64
Retirement funds, 9
Return receipt mail, 68
Rights of patients, 20–21
Rotary files, 57; illus.
Route slips, 46
Routine, daily, 127
Routine patients, 44

Safety guidelines, 133
Scales, use of, 169
Scheduling
 of appointments, 31–35
 fee schedules, 85
Secretarial associations (see Associations, professional)
Secretarial reference books, use of, 148
Secretarial skills, 16
Serenity, need for, 14

INDEX

Single-entry accounting systems, 110
Slander, 24
Slides, microscope, 167
Social security (FICA) taxes, 120–121
Social services, 129–130, 164
Society of Professional Business Consultants, 126
Solutions, tables for, 194
Sorting of files, 63
Special delivery mail, 67
Special handling mail, 68
Specialists
   branches of medical practice, 157–161
   diplomates, 161
   doctors as, 157
   and hospital assistants, 161–164
   list of, kept in office, 130
Specimens, laboratory, 170
States (U.S.), abbreviations, 188
Stationery supplies
   kinds needed, 67
   sizes, 192–193
Statute of limitations
   collection of accounts, 94
   malpractice suits, 24
Steam and pressure, sterilization by, 166
Sterile, meaning of, 165
Sterilization methods, 165–166
Stethoscopes, 167; *illus.*
Street clothes, wearing of, 14
Subject filing, 61
Subscribers, insurance policy, 99
Subscriptions, medical journal, 146
Suits, 25–26
   damage, 25–26
   safeguards against, 25
Summary sheets, monthly and yearly, 111–114; *illus.*, 113, 114
Superbills, 90
Supplies
   cleaning and maintenance, 133
   for duplicating, 73–74
   filing, 57–58, 65
   listed in office procedures manual, 129
   for mailing, 67
   medical, 133–134
      disposable, 166
   receipts for, 64
   stationery, 67, 192–193
Surgery, 160, 163, 171

Surgical insurance, 98
Switchboards, telephone, 55
Sympathy, need for, 12

Tables, conversion (*see* Conversion tables)
Tact, importance of, 12
Taxes
   and availability of financial records, 110
   earnings versus income, 89
   FICA (social security), 120–121
   income, 89, 120–121
   travel expenses as business deductions, 151
   withholding, 120–121
Teaching, career opportunities in, 7
Telegrams, 69
Telephone procedures
   answering services and machines, 55
   collection of bills, 94
   directory, use of, 53–54
   discussing fees, 86
   during doctor's absence, 152
   emergency calls, 37, 51
   how to answer, 48–49
   importance of, 47–48
   incoming calls, 49–52, 55
   long-distance calls, 54
   messages, 51–52
   outgoing calls, 53–54
   promptness and courtesy, 48–49
   recording incoming calls, 51–52, 55
   screening incoming calls, 49–51
   switchboards, 55
   verification of information, 49
Temperature
   conversion tables for, 193
   taking of, 169
Thermometers, 169; *illus.*
Thesauruses, use of, 147
Third-party liability and fee payment, 89
Thoroughness, need for, 11–12
"Tickler files," 57, 63
Tongue blades, 167
Transcription machines, 72–73
Transferring of files, 63
Transportation reservations, making, 148–149
Travel arrangements, 148–151
   financial, 151
   hotel reservations, 149

Travel arrangements (*continued*)
   itineraries, 150–151; *illus.*, 150
   passports, 149
   transportation reservations, 148–149
Traveler's checks, 151
Treatments
   medications, 171
   minor operations, 171
Tuning forks, 167; *illus.*

UCR (usual, customary, and reasonable) fees, 100
Uniformed services medical benefits, 107–108
Uniforms, wearing of, 13
United States and possessions, abbreviations, 188
Universal (Uniform) Claim Form, 101–102; *illus.*, 102
Urology, 160
"Usual" fees, 100

Vaginal speculums, 167; *illus.*
Vertical filing systems, 57; *illus.*
Visitors in doctors' offices, 39
Visits by doctors (*see* House visits)
Vital signs, 170

Waiting room, maintenance of, 132
Weight
   conversion tables for, 193
   taking of, 169
Withholding taxes, 120–121
Workers' compensation insurance, 108–109
   claim form, 108–109; *illus.*, 108
Write-it-once accounting systems (*see* Pegboard accounting systems)
Written communications (*see* Letters; Mail)

X rays
   as diagnostic test, 170–171
   films and reports, 82
   and radiology, 160, 162–163

ZIP Codes, use of, 188

Working Papers

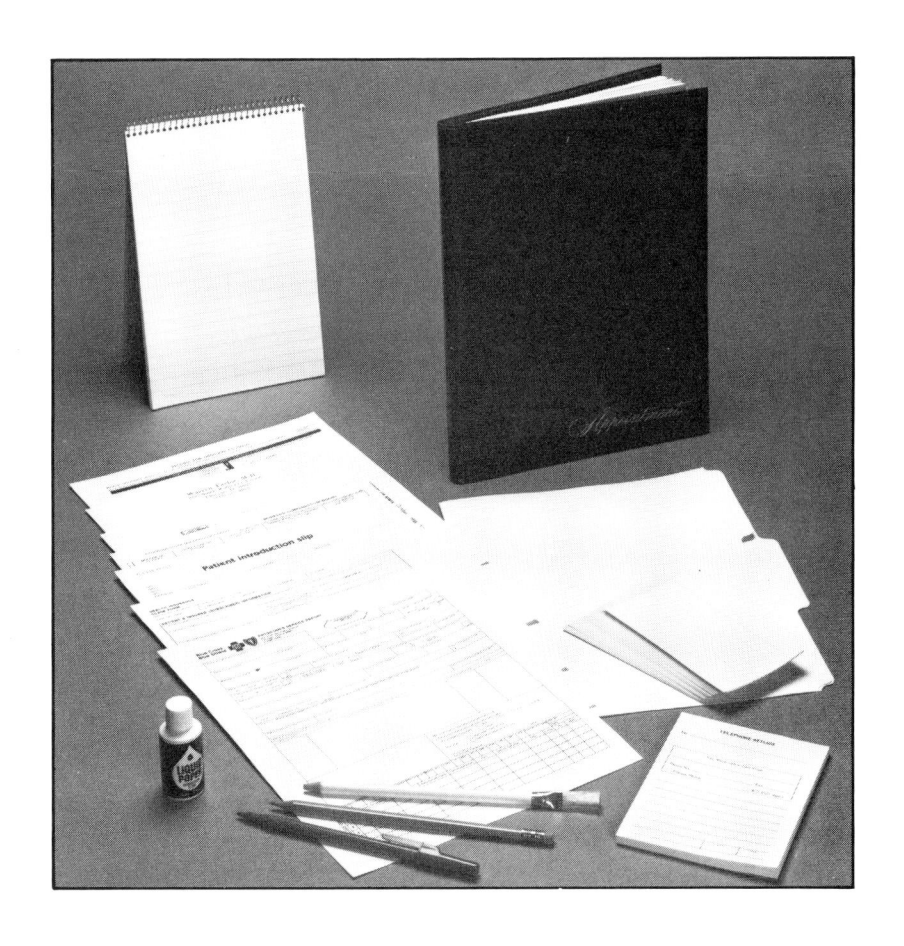

CREDITS

WP 3-19: courtesy Sheaffer Eaton Division of Textron Inc.

WP 23, 25, 29, 39, 41, 47, 51, 63, 65, 67, 75-81, 93, 95, 131, 133, 153 (bottom), 159-187: courtesy Little Press, Inc.

WP 33: courtesy SCM Histacount Corporation

WP 53: courtesy Medical Arts Press, Minneapolis, Minnesota 55427

WP 55, 135: courtesy Blue Cross and Blue Shield of Illinois

WP 59, 61, 97: courtesy Workers' Compensation Board of New York

from OCTOBER 16

NOVEMBER

S	M	T	W	T	F	S
						1
2	3	4	5	6	7	8
9	10	11	12	13	14	15
16	17	18	19	20	21	22
23/30	24	25	26	27	28	29

Thursday, Oct. 16 290	Friday, Oct. 17 291	Saturday, Oct. 18 292
8	8	8
8:15	8:15	8:15
8:30	8:30	8:30
8:45	8:45	8:45
9	9	9
9:15	9:15	9:15
9:30	9:30	9:30
9:45	9:45	9:45
10	10	10
10:15	10:15	10:15
10:30	10:30	10:30
10:45	10:45	10:45
11	11	11
11:15	11:15	11:15
11:30	11:30	11:30
11:45	11:45	11:45
12	12	12
12:15	12:15	12:15
12:30	12:30	12:30
12:45	12:45	12:45
1	1	1
1:15	1:15	1:15
1:30	1:30	1:30
1:45	1:45	1:45
2	2	2
2:15	2:15	2:15
2:30	2:30	2:30
2:45	2:45	2:45
3	3	3
3:15	3:15	3:15
3:30	3:30	3:30
3:45	3:45	3:45
4	4	4
4:15	4:15	4:15
4:30	4:30	4:30
4:45	4:45	4:45
5	5	5
5:15	5:15	5:15
5:30	5:30	5:30
5:45	5:45	5:45
6	6	6
6:15	6:15	6:15
6:30	6:30	6:30
6:45	6:45	**Sunday, Oct. 19** 293
7	7	
7:15	7:15	
7:30	7:30	
7:45	7:45	
8	8	
8:15	8:15	
8:30	8:30	
8:45	8:45	
9	9	
9:15	9:15	
9:30	9:30	
9:45	9:45	

AT·A·GLANCE®

WP 5

OCTOBER

S	M	T	W	T	F	S
			1	2	3	4
5	6	7	8	9	10	11
12	13	14	15	16	17	18
19	20	21	22	23	24	25
26	27	28	29	30	31	

WEEK AT A GLANCE

from **OCTOBER 20**

Monday, Oct. 20 294	Tuesday, Oct. 21 295	Wednesday, Oct. 22 296
8	8	8
8 15	8 15	8 15
8 30	8 30	8 30
8 45	8 45	8 45
9	9	9
9 15	9 15	9 15
9 30	9 30	9 30
9 45	9 45	9 45
10	10	10
10 15	10 15	10 15
10 30	10 30	10 30
10 45	10 45	10 45
11	11	11
11 15	11 15	11 15
11 30	11 30	11 30
11 45	11 45	11 45
12	12	12
12 15	12 15	12 15
12 30	12 30	12 30
12 45	12 45	12 45
1	1	1
1 15	1 15	1 15
1 30	1 30	1 30
1 45	1 45	1 45
2	2	2
2 15	2 15	2 15
2 30	2 30	2 30
2 45	2 45	2 45
3	3	3
3 15	3 15	3 15
3 30	3 30	3 30
3 45	3 45	3 45
4	4	4
4 15	4 15	4 15
4 30	4 30	4 30
4 45	4 45	4 45
5	5	5
5 15	5 15	5 15
5 30	5 30	5 30
5 45	5 45	5 45
6	6	6
6 15	6 15	6 15
6 30	6 30	6 30
6 45	6 45	6 45
7	7	7
7 15	7 15	7 15
7 30	7 30	7 30
7 45	7 45	7 45
8	8	8
8 15	8 15	8 15
8 30	8 30	8 30
8 45	8 45	8 45
9	9	9
9 15	9 15	9 15
9 30	9 30	9 30
9 45	9 45	9 45

from **OCTOBER 23**

NOVEMBER
S M T W T
2 3 4 5
9 10 11
16 17 1
23 30 24

Thursday, Oct. 23 297	Friday, Oct. 24 298	Saturday, Oct. 25 299
8	8	8
8 15	8 15	8 15
8 30	8 30	8 30
8 45	8 45	8 45
9	9	9
9 15	9 15	9 15
9 30	9 30	9 30
9 45	9 45	9 45
10	10	10
10 15	10 15	10 15
10 30	10 30	10 30
10 45	10 45	10 45
11	11	11
11 15	11 15	11 15
11 30	11 30	11 30
11 45	11 45	11 45
12	12	12
12 15	12 15	12 15
12 30	12 30	12 30
12 45	12 45	12 45
1	1	1
1 15	1 15	1 15
1 30	1 30	1 30
1 45	1 45	1 45
2	2	2
2 15	2 15	2 15
2 30	2 30	2 30
2 45	2 45	2 45
3	3	3
3 15	3 15	3 15
3 30	3 30	3 30
3 45	3 45	3 45
4	4	4
4 15	4 15	4 15
4 30	4 30	4 30
4 45	4 45	4 45
5	5	5
5 15	5 15	5 15
5 30	5 30	5 30
5 45	5 45	5 45
6	6	6
6 15	6 15	6 15
6 30	6 30	6 30
6 45	6 45	**Sunday, Oct. 26** 300
7	7	
7 15	7 15	
7 30	7 30	
7 45		
8		
8 15		
8 45		
9		
9 15		
9 30		
9 45		

AT·A·GLANCE®

OCTOBER

S	M	T	W	T	F	S
			1	2	3	4
5	6	7	8	9	10	11
12	13	14	15	16	17	18
19	20	21	22	23	24	25
26	27	28	29	30	31	

WEEK-AT-A-GLANCE

from **OCTOBER 27**

Monday, Oct. 27 301	Tuesday, Oct. 28 302	Wednesday, Oct. 29 303
8	8	8
8 15	8 15	8 15
8 30	8 30	8 30
8 45	8 45	8 45
9	9	9
9 15	9 15	9 15
9 30	9 30	9 30
9 45	9 45	9 45
10	10	10
10 15	10 15	10 15
10 30	10 30	10 30
10 45	10 45	10 45
11	11	11
11 15	11 15	11 15
11 30	11 30	11 30
11 45	11 45	11 45
12	12	12
12 15	12 15	12 15
12 30	12 30	12 30
12 45	12 45	12 45
1	1	
1 15	1 15	
1 30	1 30	
1 45	1 45	
2	2	
2 15	2 15	
2 30	2 30	
2 45	2 45	
3	3	
3 15	3 15	
3 30	3 30	
3 45	3 45	
4	4	
4 15	4 15	
4 30	4 30	
4 45	4 45	
5		
5 15		
5 30		
5 45		
6	6	
6 15	6 15	
6 30	6 30	
6 45	6 45	
7	7	
7 15	7 15	
7 30	7 30	
7 45	7 45	
8	8	
8 15	8 15	
8 30	8 30	
8 45		
9		
9 15		
9 30		
9 45		

from **NOVEMBER 6**

DECEMBER
S	M	T	W	T	F	S
	1	2	3	4	5	6
7	8	9	10	11	12	13
14	15	16	17	18	19	20
21	22	23	24	25	26	27
28	29	30	31			

Thursday, Nov. 6 311

- 8
- 8.15
- 8.30
- 8.45
- 9
- 9.15
- 9.30
- 9.45
- 10
- 10.15
- 10.30
- 10.45
- 11
- 11.15
- 11.30
- 11.45
- 12
- 12.15
- 12.30
- 12.45
- 1
- 1.15
- 1.30
- 1.45
- 2
- 2.15
- 2.30
- 2.45
- 3
- 3.15
- 3.30
- 3.45
- 4
- 4.15
- 4.30
- 4.45
- 5
- 5.15
- 5.30
- 5.45
- 6
- 6.15
- 6.30
- 6.45
- 7
- 7.15
- 7.30
- 7.45
- 8
- 8.15
- 8.30
- 8.45
- 9
- 9.15
- 9.30
- 9.45

Friday, Nov. 7 312

- 8
- 8.15
- 8.30
- 8.45
- 9
- 9.15
- 9.30
- 9.45
- 10
- 10.15
- 10.30
- 10.45
- 11
- 11.15
- 11.30
- 11.45
- 12
- 12.15
- 12.30
- 12.45
- 1
- 1.15
- 1.30
- 1.45
- 2
- 2.15
- 2.30
- 2.45
- 3
- 3.15
- 3.30
- 3.45
- 4
- 4.15
- 4.30
- 4.45
- 5
- 5.15
- 5.30
- 5.45
- 6
- 6.15
- 6.30
- 6.45
- 7
- 7.15
- 7.30
- 7.45
- 8
- 8.15
- 8.30
- 8.45
- 9
- 9.15
- 9.30
- 9.45

Saturday, Nov. 8 313

- 8
- 8.15
- 8.30
- 8.45
- 9
- 9.15
- 9.30
- 9.45
- 10
- 10.15
- 10.30
- 10.45
- 11
- 11.15
- 11.30
- 11.45
- 12
- 12.15
- 12.30
- 12.45
- 1
- 1.15
- 1.30
- 1.45
- 2
- 2.15
- 2.30
- 2.45
- 3
- 3.15
- 3.30
- 3.45
- 4
- 4.15
- 4.30
- 4.45
- 5
- 5.15
- 5.30
- 5.45
- 6
- 6.15
- 6.30

Sunday, Nov. 9 314

AT·A·GLANCE®

WP 11

WEEK AT A GLANCE

NOVEMBER

S	M	T	W	T	F	S
						1
2	3	4	5	6	7	8
9	10	11	12	13	14	15
16	17	18	19	20	21	22
23/30	24	25	26	27	28	29

from **NOVEMBER 10**

Monday, Nov. 10 — 315	Tuesday, Nov. 11 — 316	Wednesday, Nov. 12 — 317
8	8 VETERANS DAY	8
8 15	8 15	8 15
8 30	8 30	8 30
8 45	8 45	8 45
9	9	9
9 15	9 15	9 15
9 30	9 30	9 30
9 45	9 45	9 45
10	10	10
10 15	10 15	10 15
10 30	10 30	10 30
10 45	10 45	10 45
11	11	11
11 15	11 15	11 15
11 30	11 30	11 30
11 45	11 45	11 45
12	12	12
12 15	12 15	12 15
12 30	12 30	12 30
12 45	12 45	12 45
1	1	1
1 15	1 15	1 15
1 30	1 30	1 30
1 45	1 45	1 45
2	2	2
2 15	2 15	2 15
2 30	2 30	2 30
2 45	2 45	2 45
3	3	3
3 15	3 15	3 15
3 30	3 30	3 30
3 45	3 45	3 45
4	4	4
4 15	4 15	4 15
4 30	4 30	4 30
4 45	4 45	4 45
5	5	5
5 15	5 15	5 15
5 30	5 30	5 30
5 45	5 45	5 45
6	6	6
6 15	6 15	6 15
6 30	6 30	6 30
6 45	6 45	6 45
7	7	7
7 15	7 15	7 15
7 30	7 30	7 30
7 45	7 45	7 45
8	8	8
8 15	8 15	8 15
8 30	8 30	8 30
8 45	8 45	8 45
9	9	9
9 15	9 15	9 15
9 30	9 30	9 30
9 45	9 45	9 45

from **NOVEMBER 13**

WEEK-AT-A-GLANCE

DECEMBER
S	M	T	W	T	F	S
	1	2	3	4	5	6
7	8	9	10	11	12	13
14	15	16	17	18	19	20
21	22	23	24	25	26	27
28	29	30	31			

Thursday, Nov. 13 318	**Friday, Nov. 14** 319	**Saturday, Nov. 15** 320
8	8	8
8.15	8.15	8.15
8.30	8.30	8.30
8.45	8.45	8.45
9	9	9
9.15	9.15	9.15
9.30	9.30	9.30
9.45	9.45	9.45
10	10	10
10.15	10.15	10.15
10.30	10.30	10.30
10.45	10.45	10.45
11	11	11
11.15	11.15	11.15
11.30	11.30	11.30
11.45	11.45	11.45
12	12	12
12.15	12.15	12.15
12.30	12.30	12.30
12.45	12.45	12.45
1	1	1
1.15	1.15	1.15
1.30	1.30	1.30
1.45	1.45	1.45
2	2	2
2.15	2.15	2.15
2.30	2.30	2.30
2.45	2.45	2.45
3	3	3
3.15	3.15	3.15
3.30	3.30	3.30
3.45	3.45	3.45
4	4	4
4.15	4.15	4.15
4.30	4.30	4.30
4.45	4.45	4.45
5	5	5
5.15	5.15	5.15
5.30	5.30	5.30
5.45	5.45	5.45
6	6	6
6.15	6.15	6.15
6.30	6.30	6.30
6.45	6.45	**Sunday, Nov. 16** 321
7	7	
7.15	7.15	
7.30	7.30	
7.45	7.45	
8	8	
8.15	8.15	
8.30	8.30	
8.45	8.45	
9	9	
9.15	9.15	
9.30	9.30	
9.45	9.45	

AT-A-GLANCE®

WP 13

NOVEMBER

S	M	T	W	T	F	S
						1
2	3	4	5	6	7	8
9	10	11	12	13	14	15
16	17	18	19	20	21	22
23/30	24	25	26	27	28	29

WEEK AT A GLANCE

from **NOVEMBER 17**

Monday, Nov. 17 322	Tuesday, Nov. 18 323	Wednesday, Nov. 19 324
8	8	8
8 15	8 15	8 15
8 30	8 30	8 30
8 45	8 45	8 45
9	9	9
9 15	9 15	9 15
9 30	9 30	9 30
9 45	9 45	9 45
10	10	10
10 15	10 15	10 15
10 30	10 30	10 30
10 45	10 45	10 45
11	11	11
11 15	11 15	11 15
11 30	11 30	11 30
11 45	11 45	11 45
12	12	12
12 15	12 15	12 15
12 30	12 30	12 30
12 45	12 45	12 45
1	1	1
1 15	1 15	1 15
1 30	1 30	1 30
1 45	1 45	1 45
2	2	2
2 15	2 15	2 15
2 30	2 30	2 30
2 45	2 45	2 45
3	3	3
3 15	3 15	3 15
3 30	3 30	3 30
3 45	3 45	3 45
4	4	4
4 15	4 15	4 15
4 30	4 30	4 30
4 45	4 45	4 45
5	5	5
5 15	5 15	5 15
5 30	5 30	5 30
5 45	5 45	5 45
6	6	6
6 15	6 15	6 15
6 30	6 30	6 30
6 45	6 45	6 45
7	7	7
7 15	7 15	7 15
7 30	7 30	7 30
7 45	7 45	7 45
8	8	8
8 15	8 15	8 15
8 30	8 30	8 30
8 45	8 45	8 45
9	9	9
9 15	9 15	9 15
9 30	9 30	9 30
9 45	9 45	9 45

from NOVEMBER 20

DECEMBER
S	M	T	W	T	F	S
	1	2	3	4	5	6
7	8	9	10	11	12	13
14	15	16	17	18	19	20
21	22	23	24	25	26	27
28	29	30	31			

Thursday, Nov. 20
- 10:30 Sharon McKinley – recheck ↓
- 2:30 Manuel Perez – recheck ↓
- 3 Jason Stephens – recheck ↓
- 4 Carl Logan – recheck ↓

Friday, Nov. 21

Saturday, Nov. 22

Sunday, Nov. 23

WP 15

NOVEMBER

S	M	T	W	T	F	S
						1
2	3	4	5	6	7	8
9	10	11	12	13	14	15
16	17	18	19	20	21	22
23/30	24	25	26	27	28	29

WEEK AT A GLANCE

from **NOVEMBER 24**

Monday, Nov. 24 329

8
8.15
8.30
8.45
9
9.15
9.30
9.45
10
10.15
10.30
10.45
11
11.15
11.30
11.45
12
12.15
12.30
12.45
1
1.15
1.30
1.45
2
2.15
2.30
2.45
3
3.15
3.30
3.45
4
4.15
4.30
4.45
5
5.15
5.30
5.45
6
6.15
6.30
6.45
7
7.15
7.30
7.45
8
8.15
8.30
8.45
9
9.15
9.30
9.45

Tuesday, Nov. 25 330

8
8.15
8.30
8.45
9
9.15
9.30
9.45
10
10.15
10.30
10.45
11
11.15
11.30
11.45
12
12.15
12.30
12.45
1
1.15
1.30
1.45
2
2.15
2.30
2.45
3
3.15
3.30
3.45
4
4.15
4.30
4.45
5
5.15
5.30
5.45
6
6.15
6.30
6.45
7
7.15
7.30
7.45
8
8.15
8.30
8.45
9
9.15
9.30
9.45

Wednesday, Nov. 26 331

8
8.15
8.30
8.45
9
9.15
9.30
9.45
10
10.15
10.30
10.45
11
11.15
11.30
11.45
12
12.15
12.30
12.45
1
1.15
1.30
1.45
2
2.15
2.30
2.45
3
3.15
3.30
3.45
4
4.15
4.30
4.45
5
5.15
5.30
5.45
6
6.15
6.30
6.45
7
7.15
7.30
7.45
8
8.15
8.30
8.45
9
9.15
9.30
9.45

from **NOVEMBER 27**

DECEMBER
S	M	T	W	T	F	S
	1	2	3	4	5	6
7	8	9	10	11	12	13
14	15	16	17	18	19	20
21	22	23	24	25	26	27
28	29	30	31			

WEEK AT A GLANCE

Thursday, Nov. 27 332	**Friday, Nov. 28** 333	**Saturday, Nov. 29** 334
8 THANKSGIVING DAY	8	8
8.15	8.15	8.15
8.30	8.30	8.30
8.45	8.45	8.45
9	9	9
9.15	9.15	9.15
9.30	9.30	9.30
9.45	9.45	9.45
10	10	10
10.15	10.15	10.15
10.30	10.30	10.30
10.45	10.45	10.45
11	11	11
11.15	11.15	11.15
11.30	11.30	11.30
11.45	11.45	11.45
12	12	12
12.15	12.15	12.15
12.30	12.30	12.30
12.45	12.45	12.45
1	1	1
1.15	1.15	1.15
1.30	1.30	1.30
1.45	1.45	1.45
2	2	2
2.15	2.15	2.15
2.30	2.30	2.30
2.45	2.45	2.45
3	3	3
3.15	3.15	3.15
3.30	3.30	3.30
3.45	3.45	3.45
4	4	4
4.15	4.15	4.15
4.30	4.30	4.30
4.45	4.45	4.45
5	5	5
5.15	5.15	5.15
5.30	5.30	5.30
5.45	5.45	5.45
6	6	6
6.15	6.15	6.15
6.30	6.30	6.30
6.45	6.45	**Sunday, Nov. 30** 335
7	7	
7.15	7.15	
7.30	7.30	
7.45	7.45	
8	8	
8.15	8.15	
8.30	8.30	
8.45	8.45	
9	9	
9.15	9.15	
9.30	9.30	
9.45	9.45	AT-A-GLANCE®

WP 17

DECEMBER

S	M	T	W	T	F	S
	1	2	3	4	5	6
7	8	9	10	11	12	13
14	15	16	17	18	19	20
21	22	23	24	25	26	27
28	29	30	31			

WEEK AT A GLANCE

from **DECEMBER 1**

Monday, Dec. 1 — 336	Tuesday, Dec. 2 — 337	Wednesday, Dec. 3 — 338
8	8	8 HANUKAH
8.15	8.15	8.15
8.30	8.30	8.30
8.45	8.45	8.45
9	9	9
9.15	9.15	9.15
9.30	9.30	9.30
9.45	9.45	9.45
10	10	10
10.15	10.15	10.15
10.30	10.30	10.30
10.45	10.45	10.45
11	11	11
11.15	11.15	11.15
11.30	11.30	11.30
11.45	11.45	11.45
12	12	12
12.15	12.15	12.15
12.30	12.30	12.30
12.45	12.45	12.45
1	1	1
1.15	1.15	1.15
1.30	1.30	1.30
1.45	1.45	1.45
2	2	2
2.15	2.15	2.15
2.30	2.30	2.30
2.45	2.45	2.45
3	3	3
3.15	3.15	3.15
3.30	3.30	3.30
3.45	3.45	3.45
4	4	4
4.15	4.15	4.15
4.30	4.30	4.30
4.45	4.45	4.45
5	5	5
5.15	5.15	5.15
5.30	5.30	5.30
5.45	5.45	5.45
6	6	6
6.15	6.15	6.15
6.30	6.30	6.30
6.45	6.45	6.45
7	7	7
7.15	7.15	7.15
7.30	7.30	7.30
7.45	7.45	7.45
8	8	8
8.15	8.15	8.15
8.30	8.30	8.30
8.45	8.45	8.45
9	9	9
9.15	9.15	9.15
9.30	9.30	9.30
9.45	9.45	9.45

from **DECEMBER 4**

JANUARY
S	M	T	W	T	F	S
				1	2	3
4	5	6	7	8	9	10
11	12	13	14	15	16	17
18	19	20	21	22	23	24
25	26	27	28	29	30	31

Thursday, Dec. 4 339	Friday, Dec. 5 340	Saturday, Dec. 6 341
8	8	8
8.15	8.15	8.15
8.30	8.30	8.30
8.45	8.45	8.45
9	9	9
9.15	9.15	9.15
9.30	9.30	9.30
9.45	9.45	9.45
10	10	10
10.15	10.15	10.15
10.30	10.30	10.30
10.45	10.45	10.45
11	11	11
11.15	11.15	11.15
11.30	11.30	11.30
11.45	11.45	11.45
12	12	12
12.15	12.15	12.15
12.30	12.30	12.30
12.45	12.45	12.45
1	1	1
1.15	1.15	1.15
1.30	1.30	1.30
1.45	1.45	1.45
2	2	2
2.15	2.15	2.15
2.30	2.30	2.30
2.45	2.45	2.45
3	3	3
3.15	3.15	3.15
3.30	3.30	3.30
3.45	3.45	3.45
4	4	4
4.15	4.15	4.15
4.30	4.30	4.30
4.45	4.45	4.45
5	5	5
5.15	5.15	5.15
5.30	5.30	5.30
5.45	5.45	5.45
6	6	6
6.15	6.15	6.15
6.30	6.30	6.30
6.45	6.45	**Sunday, Dec. 7** 342
7	7	
7.15	7.15	
7.30	7.30	
7.45	7.45	
8	8	
8.15	8.15	
8.30	8.30	
8.45	8.45	
9	9	
9.15	9.15	
9.30	9.30	
9.45	9.45	

AT·A·GLANCE®

WP 19

DECEMBER

S	M	T	W	T	F	S
	1	2	3	4	5	6
7	8	9	10	11	12	13
14	15	16	17	18	19	20
21	22	23	24	25	26	27
28	29	30	31			

WEEK AT A GLANCE

from **DECEMBER 8**

Monday, Dec. 8 — 343	Tuesday, Dec. 9 — 344	Wednesday, Dec. 10 — 345
8	8	8
8:15	8:15	8:15
8:30	8:30	8:30
8:45	8:45	8:45
9	9	9
9:15	9:15	9:15
9:30	9:30	9:30
9:45	9:45	9:45
10	10	10
10:15	10:15	10:15
10:30	10:30	10:30
10:45	10:45	10:45
11	11	11
11:15	11:15	11:15
11:30	11:30	11:30
11:45	11:45	11:45
12	12	12
12:15	12:15	12:15
12:30	12:30	12:30
12:45	12:45	12:45
1	1	1
1:15	1:15	1:15
1:30	1:30	1:30
1:45	1:45	1:45
2	2	2
2:15	2:15	2:15
2:30	2:30	2:30
2:45	2:45	2:45
3	3	3
3:15	3:15	3:15
3:30	3:30	3:30
3:45	3:45	3:45
4	4	4
4:15	4:15	4:15
4:30	4:30	4:30
4:45	4:45	4:45
5	5	5
5:15	5:15	5:15
5:30	5:30	5:30
5:45	5:45	5:45
6	6	6
6:15	6:15	6:15
6:30	6:30	6:30
6:45	6:45	6:45
7	7	7
7:15	7:15	7:15
7:30	7:30	7:30
7:45	7:45	7:45
8	8	8
8:15	8:15	8:15
8:30	8:30	8:30
8:45	8:45	8:45
9	9	9
9:15	9:15	9:15
9:30	9:30	9:30
9:45	9:45	9:45

Warren Taylor, M.D.
2235 South Ridgeway Avenue
Chicago, IL 60623
(312) 555-6022

PLEASE PRINT

Patient introduction slip

MR.
MRS.
MISS
MS.

PATIENT   LAST NAME   FIRST NAME   MIDDLE

SOCIAL SECURITY NUMBER   DATE OF BIRTH   AGE   DRIVER'S LICENSE NO.

ADDRESS   STREET   Apt. #   CITY   STATE   ZIP

HOME PHONE   SEX   MARITAL STATUS   REFERRED BY

EMPLOYED BY   EMPLOYER'S ADDRESS   OCCUPATION   BUS. PHONE

SPOUSE'S NAME   EMPLOYED BY   EMPLOYER'S ADDRESS   BUS. PHONE

CHILDREN'S NAME(S):   BIRTH DATE(S)

SPOUSE'S OCCUPATION

NEAREST FRIEND OR RELATIVE   RELATIONSHIP TO PATIENT   PHONE

MEDICAL INSURANCE INFORMATION

COMPANY   SUBSCRIBER NO.   POLICY NO.   COMPANY   SUBSCRIBER NO.   POLICY NO.

MEDICAID NO.   MEDICARE NO.

WORKERS' COMPENSATION   NAME OF COMPANY

ADDRESS OF COMPANY   COMPANY PHONE   TREATMENT AUTHORIZED BY:

RESPONSIBLE PARTY

PLEASE COMPLETE THE SECTION BELOW IF SOMEONE OTHER THAN THE PATIENT IS RESPONSIBLE FOR THE BILL:

NAME   ADDRESS   CITY   STATE   ZIP CODE

HOME PHONE   RELATIONSHIP TO PATIENT   OCCUPATION

EMPLOYER   EMPLOYER'S ADDRESS   CITY   STATE   ZIP CODE

SIGNATURE OF PATIENT OR LEGAL GUARDIAN

LITTLE PRESS, INC., MPLS. 55423

WP 23

NAME	Joseph Bachman	TELEPHONE 555-7400 S X M__ W__ D__
ADDRESS	704 North Sawyer Avenue, Chicago, IL 60624	

REFERRED BY		ADDRESS
AGE 34 BIRTH DATE 2/17/--		INSURANCE CONTRACT NO. BCBS
RELIGION	OCCUPATION Lawyer	EMPLOYER Moes, Moes & Mathey

DATE		CHG.
10/1	CC: Allergy	
	SUBJECTIVE: Sneezing, runny nose, watery eyes, bothersome for several months. Takes antihistamines and decongestants for relief.	
	OBJECTIVE: Conjunctivitis, rhinorrhea, generalized urticaria.	
	ASSESSMENT: Allergy.	
	PLAN: 1. Nasal smear positive for eosinophils. 2. Refer to allergist for evaluation and treatment.	

LITTLE PRESS, INC., MPLS. 55423

NAME _____ TELEPHONE _____ S___ ___W___D___

ADDRESS _____

_____

REFERRED BY _____ ADDRESS _____

AGE _____ BIRTH DATE _____ INSURANCE CONTRACT NO. _____

RELIGION _____ OCCUPATION _____ EMPLOYER _____

DATE		CHG.

LITTLE PRESS, INC., MPLS. 55423

WP 29

Dr. Stanley F. Anderson
340 Chestnut Street
San Francisco, CA 94133

    I would like to invite you to stay with me during the week of October 19 while you are visiting Chicago. Please let me know your flight number and arrival time and I'll meet you at the airport.

    I look forward to seeing you again.

GYNECOLOGY

CASE NO. _____ PATIENT'S NAME _____
ADDRESS _____ INSURANCE _____ DATE _____
TEL. NO. _____ REFERRED BY _____ OCCUPATION _____ AGE _____ S.M.W.D. _____

FAMILY HISTORY _____

PERSONAL HISTORY _____

PRESENT AILMENT: _____
MENSTRUATION: FIRST AT AGE _____ DAYS INTERVENING _____ DAYS DURATION _____ AMOUNT _____ PAINS _____
LAST PERIOD _____ AMENORRHEA _____ MENORRHAGIA _____ DYSMENORRHEA _____ MENOPAUSE _____
VAGINAL DISCHARGE: COLOR _____ CHARACTER _____ AMOUNT _____
VESICLE SYMPTOMS: _____
GASTRO-INTESTINAL SYMPTOMS: _____

OBSTETRICAL RECORD

	DATE	AT TERM	MONTH MIS-CARRIAGE	MONTH PRE-MATURE	MONTH STILL BORN	PREGNANCY COMPLI-CATED	DELIVERY OPERATIVE	MULTIPLE	MONTHS BREAST FED	WEIGHT AT BIRTH	REMARKS
1											
2											
3											
4											

PHYSICAL EXAMINATION: TEMP. ____ PULSE ____ RESP. ____ B.P. ____ WT. ____ HT. ____
HEART *no (m)* LUNGS *clear to A+P* LIVER *not palp* SPLEEN *not palp*
ABDOMEN *no tenderness or masses*
BREASTS: SECRETING *ō* PAINFUL *ō* DISTENDED *ō* SKIN REDDENED *ō*
NIPPLES: CRACKED *ō* ERECT *ō* FLAT ✓ INVERTED *ō*

LOWER EXTREMITIES *no varices or edema* REFLEXES *physiological*
PERINEUM: FIRM ✓ LACERATED _____ ANUS: HEMORRHOIDS *ō* FISSURE *ō*
VULVA: URETHRAL ORIFICE, INFLAMED *ō* RELAXED *ō* LEAKAGE *ō*
VAGINA: SECRETION _____ RELAXED *ō* CYSTOCELE *ō* RECTOCELE *ō*
CERVIX: LENGTH *ō* THICKNESS *ō* LACERATIONS *ō* ENDOCERVICITIS *minor erosion*
UTERUS: POSITION *anteflexed* MOBILITY *normal* CONSISTENCY *+ Hegar*
SIZE *1½ × normal* TUMORS *none*
RIGHT ADNEXA *normal* LEFT ADNEXA *normal*
UTERO-SACRAL LIGAMENTS *clean*

REMARKS: _____

LABORATORY: _____

SYMBOLS: ✓ NORMAL _____ ABNORMAL (UNDERLINE WORD)
DEGREE OF ABNORMALITY: X XX XXX

WP 33

DIAGNOSIS:_____

TREATMENT:

DATE			SUBSEQUENT VISITS AND FINDINGS	ACCOUNT RECORD		
MO.	DAY	YR.		CHARGE	PAID	BALANCE

Jason Stephens: The examination was on October 7. <u>Subjective</u>: Fell off a ladder while taking down a high bookshelf. Pain in right upper arm. <u>Objective</u>: Bruises on torso, hip, and thigh. Upper arm swollen. <u>Assessment</u>: X rays revealed fractured right humerus, midshaft, nondisplaced. <u>Plan</u>: 1. Arm was sugar-tong splinted and strapped to the body. 2. Patient told to avoid using the arm, but encouraged to move hand and fingers. 3. Aspirin for pain. 4. Return to the office in one week.

Marion Wellman: I did a complete physical on 10/14. <u>Problem</u>: Persistent lobar pneumonia. <u>Subjective</u>: She had right middle lobe pneumonia. Was treated with penicillin and was considered well enough to discontinue medication on the twelfth day. However, temperature continues to rise about 2° every afternoon. <u>Objective</u>: Appears pale and fatigued. HEENT: Negative. Neck: No nervous distention. Thyroid is normal and midline. Chest: Normal excursion; symmetrical. Cardiac: Tachycardia at 96; regular sinus rhythm without murmur or S_3. Lungs: Dullness and decreased breath sounds over right middle lobe. No fremitus noted. Rest of lungs clear. Abdomen: No liver or spleen palpable. Abdomen, soft with normal bowel sounds. Remainder of exam, normal. Assessment: Most likely etiology is pneumococcal and medication was stopped too soon. Plan: 1. Sputum culture. 2. IM penicillin 600,000 Units stat. 3. Recheck in one week. 4. To enter convalescent home.

Ellen Goldberg: I did a complete physical exam on 10/1. CC: Enlargement of abdomen for past six months. PMH: Measles at 9, tonsils and adenoids removed at 12. Periods began when 12, q 28-30 days, lasting 5-6 days with slight pain. One pregnancy, full term, normal spontaneous delivery. Personal History: Uses alcohol and tobacco moderately. Sleeps 8-9 hours. Likes walking, reading, movies. Has had no serious illness. Married 10 years, husband died. Married again 16 years ago. No pregnancies. No brothers; one sister living and well; mother died at 56 of carcinoma of breast; father is living and well. No serious illnesses in family except mother's cancer. Exam: BP, 130/90. Weight, 145 pounds. Height: 5'5". Appears in good health, slightly overweight. Skin: No icterus or spider nevi. EENT: No arcus. PERLA: Fundi, normal. Chest: Breasts, benign and pendulous. Heart, regular sinus rhythm without murmur or rub. Lungs, clear to A & P. Abdomen: Firm, tender mass R L Q. No organomegaly. Pelvic: Mass in right ovary or upper uterine segment. Diagnosis: Probably ovarian tumor. Plan: Surgery to remove tumor recommended. Surgical risk, good. Surgery scheduled at University Hospital on October 7.

PLEASE PRINT

Patient introduction slip

MR.
MRS.
(MISS)
MS.

PATIENT: HAYES, GAIL
LAST NAME / FIRST NAME / MIDDLE

SOCIAL SECURITY NUMBER:
DATE OF BIRTH: 8/13/—
AGE: 25
DRIVER'S LICENSE NO.:

ADDRESS: 5632 S. Princeton Ave.
STREET / Apt. # / CITY: Chicago / STATE: IL / ZIP: 60621

HOME PHONE: 555-8241
SEX: F
MARITAL STATUS: Single
REFERRED BY:

EMPLOYED BY: Fabric Outlet
EMPLOYER'S ADDRESS: 6399 N. Seeley Ave.
OCCUPATION: Salesclerk
BUS. PHONE: 555-6230

SPOUSE'S NAME:
EMPLOYED BY:
EMPLOYER'S ADDRESS:
BUS. PHONE:

CHILDREN'S NAME(S):
BIRTH DATE(S):

SPOUSE'S OCCUPATION:

NEAREST FRIEND OR RELATIVE: George Hayes
RELATIONSHIP TO PATIENT: brother
PHONE: 555-1502

MEDICAL INSURANCE INFORMATION

COMPANY: None
SUBSCRIBER NO. / POLICY NO. / COMPANY / SUBSCRIBER NO. / POLICY NO.

MEDICAID NO.:
MEDICARE NO.:

WORKERS' COMPENSATION:
NAME OF COMPANY:

ADDRESS OF COMPANY:
COMPANY PHONE:
TREATMENT AUTHORIZED BY:

RESPONSIBLE PARTY

PLEASE COMPLETE THE SECTION BELOW IF SOMEONE OTHER THAN THE PATIENT IS RESPONSIBLE FOR THE BILL:

NAME / ADDRESS / CITY / STATE / ZIP CODE

HOME PHONE / RELATIONSHIP TO PATIENT / OCCUPATION

EMPLOYER / EMPLOYER'S ADDRESS / CITY / STATE / ZIP CODE

SIGNATURE OF PATIENT OR LEGAL GUARDIAN: Gail Hayes

LITTLE PRESS, INC., MPLS. 55423

WP 39

PLEASE PRINT

Patient introduction slip

(MR.) / MRS. / MISS / MS.

PATIENT LAST NAME: WHITFALL   FIRST NAME: MARTIN   MIDDLE:

SOCIAL SECURITY NUMBER: 473-04-0000   DATE OF BIRTH: 11/23/—   AGE: 38   DRIVER'S LICENSE NO.:

ADDRESS STREET: 1303 South 55th Avenue   Apt. #:   CITY: Chicago   STATE: IL   ZIP: 60650

HOME PHONE: 555-5331   SEX: M   MARITAL STATUS: Married   REFERRED BY:

EMPLOYED BY: Clearwater Concrete Prod.   EMPLOYER'S ADDRESS: 2859 No. Sayre Ave.   OCCUPATION: Laborer   BUS. PHONE: 555-3720

SPOUSE'S NAME: Elsie   EMPLOYED BY: housewife   EMPLOYER'S ADDRESS: BUS. PHONE:

CHILDREN'S NAME(S):   BIRTH DATE(S):

SPOUSE'S OCCUPATION:

NEAREST FRIEND OR RELATIVE: RELATIONSHIP TO PATIENT: PHONE:

MEDICAL INSURANCE INFORMATION

COMPANY: None   SUBSCRIBER NO.:   POLICY NO.:   COMPANY: SUBSCRIBER NO.:   POLICY NO.:

MEDICAID NO.:   MEDICARE NO.:

WORKERS' COMPENSATION: NAME OF COMPANY:

ADDRESS OF COMPANY: COMPANY PHONE: TREATMENT AUTHORIZED BY:

RESPONSIBLE PARTY

PLEASE COMPLETE THE SECTION BELOW IF SOMEONE OTHER THAN THE PATIENT IS RESPONSIBLE FOR THE BILL:

NAME: ADDRESS: CITY: STATE: ZIP CODE:

HOME PHONE: RELATIONSHIP TO PATIENT: OCCUPATION:

EMPLOYER: EMPLOYER'S ADDRESS: CITY: STATE: ZIP CODE:

SIGNATURE OF PATIENT OR LEGAL GUARDIAN: Martin Whitfall

LITTLE PRESS, INC., MPLS. 55423

WP 41

FEE SCHEDULE Center

New Patient:

    Brief Visit (OVB) $35

    Extended visit (OVE) $45

Established patients:

    Routine limited office visit (OVR) $15

    Extended office visit (OVE) ~~$15~~ $20   chest X ray $25

    Complete physical exam $50   Lumbar spine X ray $45

    House call (HC) $50   AP spine X ray $55

    Hospital visit (HV) $20   Ultrasound $18

    consultation $60 unless dictated

    ECG ~~$30~~ $45

    Emergency Room Call $30

Throat culture $12   Cortisone injection $8.50

Urine culture $12   Penicillin injection

sputum culture $12   1.2 CR Bicillin $10.00

Urinalysis $15   600,000 CR Bicillin $8.50

Injection – depends on kind   Lasix injection $5.75

Laboratory

    Pap smear $15

    WBC and Differential $15

OB Care: $500 # delivery only

           $575 # delivery, newborn care, six-week checkup

           $625 # delivery, newborn care, circumcision, six-week checkup

<u>Note</u>: Dr. Taylor's offices are in a clinic that has its own laboratory, and therefore each doctor in the clinic bills patients for lab charges. Some tests can only be done at the University Hospital laboratory, which bills the patients directly.

Dr. Allen Jones
33 East 63 Street
New York, NY 10021

Dear Dr. J.

In the last issue of American Journal of ~~Gastrology~~ Biology, I read your article on ~~about~~ the use of fiberoptic duodenoscopy on the gastrointestinal tract. This is a subject that is of great interest to gastroenterologists, & I am therefore wondering whether you would be willing to speak to the local med. staff at one of our meetings.

I am a member of the Program Committee and I would be happy to make the necessary arrangements. Please let me know your answer as soon as possible.

W.J.

Patient introduction slip

PLEASE PRINT

MR. / MRS. / MISS / MS.

PATIENT: Stillman, Marlene

SOCIAL SECURITY NUMBER: 434-52-6593
DATE OF BIRTH: 12/2/—
AGE: 54
DRIVER'S LICENSE NO.: none

ADDRESS: 2920 West 24th Blvd., Chicago, IL 60623

HOME PHONE: 555-2029
SEX: Female
MARITAL STATUS: Divorced
REFERRED BY:

EMPLOYED BY: Self-employed
EMPLOYER'S ADDRESS:
OCCUPATION: Seamstress
BUS. PHONE: Same

SPOUSE'S NAME:
EMPLOYED BY:
EMPLOYER'S ADDRESS:
BUS. PHONE:

CHILDREN'S NAME(S):
BIRTH DATE(S):

SPOUSE'S OCCUPATION:

NEAREST FRIEND OR RELATIVE: Alisa Bowmann
RELATIONSHIP TO PATIENT: daughter
PHONE: 555-2247

MEDICAL INSURANCE INFORMATION

COMPANY: None

MEDICAID NO.:
MEDICARE NO.:

WORKERS' COMPENSATION:
NAME OF COMPANY:

ADDRESS OF COMPANY:
COMPANY PHONE:
TREATMENT AUTHORIZED BY:

RESPONSIBLE PARTY

PLEASE COMPLETE THE SECTION BELOW IF SOMEONE OTHER THAN THE PATIENT IS RESPONSIBLE FOR THE BILL:

NAME:
ADDRESS:
CITY:
STATE:
ZIP CODE:

HOME PHONE:
RELATIONSHIP TO PATIENT:
OCCUPATION:

EMPLOYER:
EMPLOYER'S ADDRESS:
CITY:
STATE:
ZIP CODE:

SIGNATURE OF PATIENT OR LEGAL GUARDIAN: Marlene Stillman

LITTLE PRESS, INC., MPLS. 55423

WP 47

Sharon McKinley OVE 10/21

CC: Abdominal pain

Subjective: For the past two years has had frequent nausea after eating. Worse recently, with severe upper abdominal pain.

PMH: Measles at age 10; mumps at 12. No other childhood diseases. Appendectomy at age 18. No allergies. No meds. No smoking or alcohol.

FH: Married 21 years and has one boy, 18. Father died at age 64 of malignancy of liver and colon. Mother, 65, living and well.

Objective: All pertinent findings localized to abdomen. Remainder of exam, normal.

Abdomen: Tenderness right epigastrium. Worse on deep breathing. No palpable masses.

Assessment: Probable acute cholecystitis or duodenal ulcer.

Plan:
1. Outpatient cholecystogram.
2. OP SMA profile to rule out liver dysfunction.
3. OP upper GI series.

PLEASE PRINT

Patient introduction slip

~~MR.~~
~~MRS.~~
~~MISS~~
~~MS.~~

PATIENT: Perez, Manuel
LAST NAME / FIRST NAME / MIDDLE

SOCIAL SECURITY NUMBER: 434-91-4288
DATE OF BIRTH: 10/4/—
AGE: 32
DRIVER'S LICENSE NO.:

ADDRESS: 1207
STREET: South 56th Avenue
Apt. #:
CITY: Chicago
STATE: Illinois
ZIP: 60650

HOME PHONE: 555-4274
SEX: Male
MARITAL STATUS: Married
REFERRED BY: Dr. Alan Andrews

EMPLOYED BY: Wyman's Cargo
EMPLOYER'S ADDRESS: 6269 South Ridge Ave.
OCCUPATION: Janitor
BUS. PHONE: 555-7020

SPOUSE'S NAME: Alice
EMPLOYED BY: —
EMPLOYER'S ADDRESS: —
BUS. PHONE: —

CHILDREN'S NAME(S):
BIRTH DATE(S):

SPOUSE'S OCCUPATION:

NEAREST FRIEND OR RELATIVE: Alice Perez
RELATIONSHIP TO PATIENT: Wife
PHONE: 555-4274

MEDICAL INSURANCE INFORMATION

COMPANY: Insurance with Wyman's Cargo
SUBSCRIBER NO.:
POLICY NO.:
COMPANY:
SUBSCRIBER NO.:
POLICY NO.:

MEDICAID NO.:
MEDICARE NO.:

WORKERS' COMPENSATION:
NAME OF COMPANY:

ADDRESS OF COMPANY:
COMPANY PHONE:
TREATMENT AUTHORIZED BY:

RESPONSIBLE PARTY

PLEASE COMPLETE THE SECTION BELOW IF SOMEONE OTHER THAN THE PATIENT IS RESPONSIBLE FOR THE BILL:

NAME / ADDRESS / CITY / STATE / ZIP CODE

HOME PHONE / RELATIONSHIP TO PATIENT / OCCUPATION

EMPLOYER / EMPLOYER'S ADDRESS / CITY / STATE / ZIP CODE

SIGNATURE OF PATIENT OR LEGAL GUARDIAN: Manuel Perez

LITTLE PRESS, INC., MPLS. 55423

WP 51

HEALTH INSURANCE
CLAIM FORM

READ INSTRUCTIONS BEFORE COMPLETING OR SIGNING THIS FORM

TYPE OR PRINT ☐ MEDICARE ☐ MEDICAID ☐ CHAMPUS ☐ OTHER

PATIENT & INSURED (SUBSCRIBER) INFORMATION

1. PATIENT'S NAME (First name, middle initial, last name)	2. PATIENT'S DATE OF BIRTH	3. INSURED'S NAME (First name, middle initial, last name)
4. PATIENT'S ADDRESS (Street, city, state, ZIP code)	5. PATIENT'S SEX — MALE ☐ FEMALE ☐	6. INSURED'S I.D. No. or **MEDICARE No.** (Include any letters)
	7. PATIENT'S RELATIONSHIP TO INSURED — SELF ☐ SPOUSE ☐ CHILD ☐ OTHER ☐	8. INSURED'S GROUP NO. (Or Group Name)
9. OTHER HEALTH INSURANCE COVERAGE — Enter Name of Policyholder and Plan Name and Address and Policy or Medical Assistance Number	10. WAS CONDITION RELATED TO: A. PATIENT'S EMPLOYMENT — YES ☐ NO ☐ B. AN AUTO ACCIDENT — YES ☐ NO ☐	11. INSURED'S ADDRESS (Street, city, state, ZIP code)
12. PATIENT'S OR AUTHORIZED PERSON'S SIGNATURE (Read back before signing) I Authorize the Release of any Medical Information Necessary to Process this Claim and Request Payment of MEDICARE/CHAMPUS Benefits Either to Myself or to the Party Who Accepts Assignment Below. SIGNED *Jill Grimes* DATE 10/21/—		13. I AUTHORIZE PAYMENT OF MEDICAL BENEFITS TO UNDERSIGNED PHYSICIAN OR SUPPLIER FOR SERVICE DESCRIBED BELOW. SIGNED (Insured or Authorized Person)

PHYSICIAN OR SUPPLIER INFORMATION

14. DATE OF:	ILLNESS (FIRST SYMPTOM) OR INJURY (ACCIDENT) OR PREGNANCY (LMP)	15. DATE FIRST CONSULTED YOU FOR THIS CONDITION	16. HAS PATIENT EVER HAD SAME OR SIMILAR SYMPTOMS? YES ☐ NO ☐
17. DATE PATIENT ABLE TO RETURN TO WORK	18. DATES OF TOTAL DISABILITY FROM THROUGH	DATES OF PARTIAL DISABILITY FROM THROUGH
19. NAME OF REFERRING PHYSICIAN		20. FOR SERVICES RELATED TO HOSPITALIZATION GIVE HOSPITALIZATION DATES ADMITTED DISCHARGED
21. NAME & ADDRESS OF FACILITY WHERE SERVICES RENDERED (If other than home or office)		22. WAS LABORATORY WORK PERFORMED OUTSIDE YOUR OFFICE? YES ☐ NO ☐ CHARGES

23. DIAGNOSIS OR NATURE OF ILLNESS OR INJURY. RELATE DIAGNOSIS TO PROCEDURE IN COLUMN D BY REFERENCE TO NUMBERS 1, 2, 3, ETC. OR DX CODE

1.
2.
3.
4.

24. A DATE OF SERVICE	B* PLACE OF SERVICE	C PROCEDURE CODE (IDENTIFY:) FULLY DESCRIBE PROCEDURES, MEDICAL SERVICES OR SUPPLIES FURNISHED FOR EACH DATE GIVEN (EXPLAIN UNUSUAL SERVICES OR CIRCUMSTANCES)	D DIAGNOSIS CODE	E CHARGES	F

25. SIGNATURE OF PHYSICIAN OR SUPPLIER (Read back before signing) SIGNED DATE	26. ACCEPT ASSIGNMENT (GOVERNMENT CLAIMS ONLY) (SEE BACK) YES ☐ NO ☐ 30. YOUR SOCIAL SECURITY NO.	27. TOTAL CHARGE	28. AMOUNT PAID	29. BALANCE DUE
32. YOUR PATIENT'S ACCOUNT NO.	33. YOUR EMPLOYER I.D. NO.	31. PHYSICIAN'S OR SUPPLIER'S NAME, ADDRESS, ZIP CODE & TELEPHONE NO. I.D. NO.

*PLACE OF SERVICE CODES

- 1 — (IH) — INPATIENT HOSPITAL
- 2 — (OH) — OUTPATIENT HOSPITAL
- 3 — (O) — DOCTOR'S OFFICE
- 4 — (H) — PATIENT'S HOME
- 5 — DAY CARE FACILITY (PSY)
- 6 — NIGHT CARE FACILITY (PSY)
- 7 — (NH) — NURSING HOME
- 8 — (SNF) — SKILLED NURSING FACILITY
- 9 — AMBULANCE
- O — (OL) — OTHER LOCATIONS
- A — (IL) — INDEPENDENT LABORATORY
- B — OTHER MEDICAL/SURGICAL FACILITY

#1A9390 — Medical Arts Press, Mpls., Mn. 55427

APPROVED BY AMA COUNCIL ON MEDICAL SERVICE 6-74

WP 53

HEALTH INSURANCE CLAIM FORM

MEDICARE PAYMENTS: If the patient cannot write, have him sign by mark (X) and have a witness sign in item 12. If the patient cannot sign by mark, another person may sign, showing his relationship and indicating on the reverse of the form why the patient could not sign. A patient's signature requests that payment be made and authorizes release of medical information necessary to pay the claim. If item 9 is completed, the patient's signature authorizes releasing of the information to the insurer or agency shown. In assigned cases, the physician agrees to accept the charge determination of the Medicare carrier as the full charge, and the patient is responsible only for the deductible, coinsurance, and noncovered services. Coinsurance and the deductible are based upon the charge determination of the carrier, if this is less than the charge submitted.

MEDICAID PAYMENTS: I hereby agree to keep such records as are necessary to disclose fully the extent of services provided to individuals under the state's Title XIX plan and to furnish information regarding any payments claimed for providing such services as the state agency may request. I further agree to accept, as payment in full, the amount paid by the Medicaid program for those claims submitted for payment under that program, with the exception of authorized deductibles and coinsurance.

SIGNATURE OF PHYSICIAN (OR SUPPLIER): I certify that the services listed above were medically indicated and necessary to the health of this patient and were personally rendered by me or under my personal direction.

NOTICE: Anyone who misrepresents or falsifies essential information to receive payment from federal funds requested by this form may upon conviction be subject to fine and imprisonment under applicable federal laws.

Blue Cross Blue Shield

PHYSICIAN'S SERVICE REPORT
233 North Michigan Avenue
Chicago, Illinois 60601
312/661-4200

FOR RECIPROCITY USE ONLY

Group and Member ID Number	Patient Number
Patient's Last Name / First Name / Patient's Sex / Patient's Age / Patient's Birth Date / Patient's Marital Status: Married □ Single □	
Member's Last Name / First Name / Member's Address Street / City / State / Zip	

Patient's Relationship to Member
1—Self 2—Spouse 3—Dependent

Member's Sex | Member's Employer Name | If Accident/Emergency Date: Time:

Is This a Work-Related Case?
0—No 1—Yes 2—Unknown

Where Was Service Rendered?
1—Hospital Inpatient 3—Office
2—Hospital Outpatient 4—Other

Specify if "Other" | Hosp. Admission Date | Discharge Date

Name and Location of Hospital

Is the Patient Covered Under Other Health Insurance?
0—No 2—Unknown
1—Yes 3—Medicare

If Yes, Name and Location Other Insurance Company | Policy Holder's Name | Policy Number

Laboratory/Pathology Services Performed
1—Office 2—Independent Lab 3—Hospital

Name and Address of Lab | Amt. Charged by Lab $

Diagnosis (Place primary diagnosis first, verbal description with ICDA Code, please give LMP date if OB related)

Was Surgery Also Performed? | If Yes, By Whom | Were You the Surgical Assistant?

Name and Address of Referring Physician

SERVICE DATE	DESCRIPTION/PROCEDURE/ANESTHESIA TIME	CPT PROCEDURE CODE	FEE

My Total Fee for the Described Service(s) is $ _____
I Personally Performed the Services Described.
I am a Legally Qualified: □ M.D. □ D.O. □ D.D.S. □ D.P.M.
□ Other:
This Fee: □ HAS been paid to me.
□ HAS NOT been paid to me.
Physician's or Authorized Signature: _____ Date: _____

FOR BS USE ONLY

PLAN CODE	NO.SER.	PAYEE	M.MD.	PT.EX.	CODER	PRO.CD.	COST	MEM.	M/S	S.SEX	IP	MED.	BC	MM	TOB	DB	WP	P/S	Contract Eff. Date	VER. BY
																				DATE

S. NO.	PTR	DATE OF SERVICE	DIAG. CODE	PROCEDURE CODE	PHYSICIAN'S FEE	V-D-U	END OF SERVICE	TIME	E. PTS.	TS	DESC.
1											
2											
3											
4											
5											

BS-11 Rev. 1-78

WP 55

REQUEST FOR MEDICARE PAYMENT

MEDICAL INSURANCE BENEFITS—SOCIAL SECURITY ACT (See Instructions on Back—**Type or Print Information**)

Form Approved
OMB No.
72-R0730

NOTICE—Anyone who misrepresents or falsifies essential information requested by this form may upon conviction be subject to fine and imprisonment under Federal Law.

PART I—PATIENT TO FILL IN ITEMS 1 THROUGH 6 ONLY

Copy from YOUR OWN HEALTH INSURANCE CARD (See example on back)

1 Name of patient (First name, Middle initial, Last name)

2 Health insurance claim number (Include all letters) ☐ Male ☐ Female

3 Patient's mailing address | City, State, ZIP code | Telephone Number

4 Describe the illness or injury for which you received treatment (Always fill in this item if your doctor does not complete Part II below) | Was your illness or injury connected with your employment? ☐ Yes ☐ No

5 If any of your medical expenses will be or could be paid by another insurance organization or government agency (including FEHB), show below.
Name and address of organization or agency | Policy or Identification Number

Note: If you **Do Not** want information about this Medicare claim released to the above upon its request, check (X) the following block ☐

6 I authorize any holder of medical or other information about me to release to the Social Security Administration or its intermediaries or carriers any information needed for this or a related Medicare claim. I permit a copy of this authorization to be used in place of the original, and request payment of medical insurance benefits either to myself or to the party who accepts assignment below.

Signature of patient (See instructions on reverse where patient is unable to sign) | Date signed

SIGN HERE ▶ *Ellen Goldberg* | 10/20/—

PART II—PHYSICIAN OR SUPPLIER TO FILL IN 7 THROUGH 14

7
A. Date of each service	B. Place of service (*See Codes below)	C. Fully describe surgical or medical procedures and other services or supplies furnished for each date given / Procedure Code	D. Nature of illness or injury requiring services or supplies (diagnosis)	E. Charges (If related to unusual circumstances explain in 7C)	Leave Blank
				$	

8 Name and address of physician or supplier (Number and street, city, State, ZIP code) | Telephone No. | **9** Total charges $
| | Physician or supplier code | **10** Amount paid $
| | | **11** Any unpaid balance due $

12 Assignment of patient's bill
▶ ☐ I accept assignment (See reverse) ☐ I do not accept assignment.

13 Show name and address of person or facility which furnished service (if other than your own office or patient's home)

14 Signature of physician or supplier (A physician's signature certifies that a physician's services were personally rendered by the physician or under the physician's personal direction) | Date signed

*O—Doctor's Office   H—Patient's Home (If portable X-ray services, identify the supplier)   SNF—Skilled Nursing Facility   OL—Other Locations
IL—Independent Laboratory   IH—Inpatient Hospital   OH—Outpatient Hospital   NH—Nursing Home

FORM **SSA 1490** (11-75)

Department of Health, Education, and Welfare
Social Security Administration

WP 57

HOW TO FILL OUT YOUR MEDICARE FORM
There are two ways that Medicare can help pay your doctor bills

One way is for Medicare to pay your doctor.—If you and your doctor agree, Medicare will pay the doctor directly. This is the assignment method. You do not submit any claim; the doctor does. All you do is fill out Part I of this form and leave it with your doctor. Under this method the doctor agrees to accept the charge determination of the Medicare carrier as the full charge for covered services; you are responsible for the deductible, coinsurance, and non-covered services. Please read Your Medicare Handbook to help you understand about the deductible and coinsurance.

The other way is for Medicare to pay you.—Medicare can also pay you directly—before or after you have paid your doctor. If you submit the claim yourself, fill out Part I and ask your doctor to fill out Part II. If you have an itemized bill from the doctor, you may submit it rather than have the doctor complete Part II. (This form, with Part I completed by you, may be used to send in several itemized bills from different doctors and suppliers.) Bills should show who furnished the services, **the patient's name and number,** dates of services, where the services were furnished, a description of the services, and charges for each separate service. It is helpful if the diagnosis is also shown. Then mail itemized bills and this form to the address shown in the upper left-hand corner. If no address is shown there, use the address listed in Your Medicare Handbook—or get advice from any social security office.

Notice: It is important to keep a record of your claim in case you ever want to inquire about it. Before you send it in, write down the date you mailed it, the services you received, the date and charge for each, and the name of the doctor or supplier who performed the services. Have this information available when you inquire about a claim.

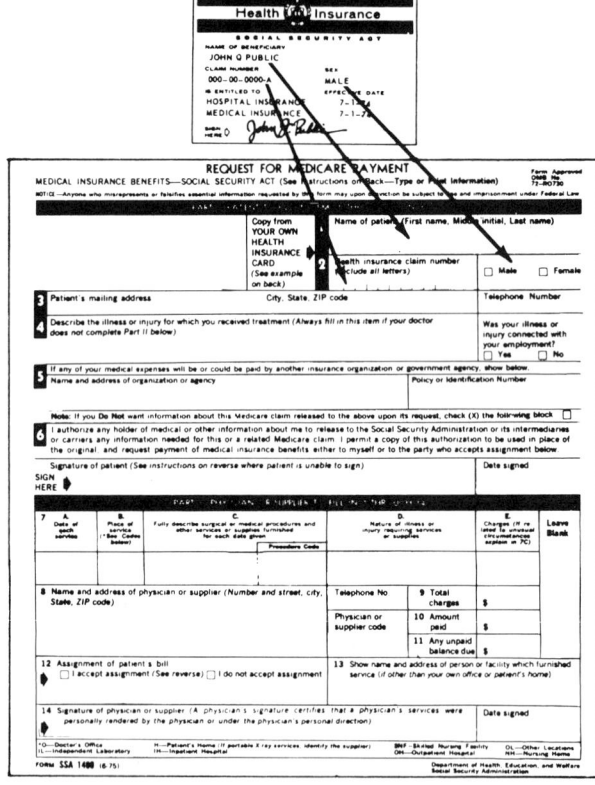

SOME THINGS TO NOTE IN FILLING OUT PART I
(Your doctor will fill out Part II.)

1 & 2 Copy the name and number and indicate your sex exactly as shown on your health insurance card. Include the letters at the end of the number.

3 Enter your mailing address and telephone number, if any.

4 Describe your illness or injury. Be sure to check one of the two boxes.

5 If you have other health insurance or expect a welfare agency to pay part of the expenses, complete item 5.

6 Be sure to sign your name. If you cannot write your name, sign by mark (X), and have the signature witnessed. The witness's signature and address must also be shown in item 6.

If you are filing the claim for a Medicare beneficiary, in item 6 enter the patient's name and write "By", sign your name and enter your address in this space, show your relationship to the patient, and explain why the patient cannot sign. (If the patient has died, the survivor should contact any social security office for information on what to do.)

IMPORTANT NOTES FOR PHYSICIANS AND SUPPLIERS

Item 12: In assigned cases the patient is responsible only for the deductible, coinsurance, and non-covered services. Coinsurance and the deductible are based upon the charge determination of the carrier if this is less than the charge submitted.

This form may also be used by a supplier, or by the patient to claim reimbursement for charges by a supplier for services such as the use of an ambulance or medical appliances.

If the physician or supplier does not want Part II information released to the organization named in item 5, the physician or supplier should write "No further release" in item 7C following the description of services.

COLLECTION AND USE OF MEDICARE INFORMATION

We are authorized by the Social Security Administration to ask you for information needed in the administration of the Medicare program. Social Security's authority to collect information is in section 205(a), 1872 and 1875 of the Social Security Act. as amended.

The information we obtain to complete your Medicare claim is used to identify you and to determine your eligibility. It is also used to decide if the services and supplies you received are covered by Medicare and to insure that proper payment is made.

The information may also be given to other providers of services, carriers, intermediaries, medical review boards, and other organizations as necessary to administer the Medicare program. For example, it may be necessary to disclose information about the Medicare benefits you have used to a hospital or doctor.

With one exception, which is discussed below, there are no penalties under social security law for refusing to supply information. However, failure to furnish information regarding the medical services rendered or the amount charged would prevent payment of the claim. Failure to furnish any other information, such as name or claim number, would delay payment of the claim.

It is mandatory that you tell us if you are being treated for a work related injury so we can determine whether workmen's compensation will pay for the treatment. Section 1877(a)(3) of the Social Security Act provides criminal penalties for withholding this information.

☆U.S.GPO:1976-0-211-071/50

WORKMEN'S COMPENSATION BOARD

ATTENDING PHYSICIAN'S 48-HOUR REPORT

PLEASE PRINT OR TYPE — INCLUDE ZIP CODE IN ALL ADDRESSES — CLAIMANT'S SS # MUST BE ENTERED BELOW

WCB CASE NO. (If Known)	CARRIER CASE NO. (If Known)	DATE OF INJURY AND TIME	ADDRESS WHERE INJURY OCCURRED (City, Town or Village)	SOCIAL SECURITY NUMBER
		10/7/-- 10:30 a.m.	1442 N. Pulaski Road Chicago, IL 60651	336-72-5225

INJURED PERSON	NAME: Jason Stephens	AGE: 51	ADDRESS: 712 N. Ridgeway Ave. Chicago, IL 60624	APT. NO.
EMPLOYER	Abbott Memorial Library		1442 N. Pulaski Rd., Chicago, IL 60651	
INSURANCE CARRIER	Nelson Casualty, Limited		878 N. Sawyer Ave., Chicago, IL 60624	

HISTORY

1. State how injury occurred and give source of this information. (If claim is for *occupational disease*, include occupational history and date of onset of related symptoms).

   Patient states that he fell off a ladder while taking down a high bookshelf. Has pain in right upper arm.

2. Is there a history of unconsciousness? YES [ ] NO [x] If "Yes," for how long? ____ Were X-Rays taken? YES [x] NO [ ]

3. Was patient hospitalized? YES [ ] NO [x] If "Yes," state name and address of hospital:

4. Was patient previously under the care of another physician for this injury? YES [ ] NO [x] If "Yes," enter his name and address, and reason for transfer under "Remarks" (Item 10).

DIAGNOSIS

5. Describe nature and extent of injury or disease and specify *all* parts of body involved:

   Subjective: Pain in upper arm. Objective: Bruises on torso, hip, and thigh. Upper arm swollen. Assessment: X rays revealed fractured right humerus, midshaft, nondisplaced.

TREATMENT

6. Nature of treatment: Arm sugar-tong splinted and strapped to the body. Avoid use of arm.

   Date of your first treatment: 10/7/--

   If treatment is continuing, estimate its duration. Six weeks

   If treatment is not continuing, is this your final report? YES [ ] NO [ ] If "Yes," state date of last treatment:

DISABILITY

7. May the injury result in permanent restriction, total or partial loss of function of a part or member, or permanent facial, head or neck disfigurement? YES [ ] NO [x]

8. Is patient working? YES [ ] NO [x] Is patient disabled? YES [x] NO [ ] If "Yes," estimate duration of disability: Six weeks

CAUSAL RELATION

9. In your opinion, was the occurrence described above the competent producing cause of the injury and disability (if any) sustained? YES [x] NO [ ]

REMARKS

10. Enter here additional information of value, requests for authorization, etc.:

11. Medical testimony is occasionally required. If your testimony should be necessary in this case, please indicate the days of the week (and hours) most convenient to you for this purpose: ____

Dated 10/8/--	Typed or Printed Name of Attending Physician: Warren Taylor, M.D.	Address: 2235 S. Ridgeway Ave. Chicago, IL 60623
WCB Rating Code: SJ	WCB Authorization No. 381075	Telephone No. 555-6022	Written Signature of Attending Physician: *Warren Taylor, M.D.*

C-48 (12-73)

ANSWER ALL QUESTIONS. AVOID USE OF INDEFINITE TERMS
See Reverse Side

WP 59

IMPORTANT

TO THE ATTENDING PHYSICIAN

1. Reports on *this form must be filed within 48 hours* after you first render treatment in a workmen's compensation case or a volunteer firemen's benefit case. Use Form C-4 (or C-5 if filed by an ophthalmologist) for subsequent reports.

    Please ask your patient for his Workmen's Compensation Board Case Number and the Insurance Carrier's Case Number, if they are known to him, and show these numbers on your reports, in the spaces provided.

    File the signed original of this report directly with (1) CHAIRMAN, WORKMEN'S COMPENSATION BOARD at the office of the district in which the accident occurred and file a signed copy with (2) the INSURANCE CARRIER, if known, or the EMPLOYER.

2. The Law provides that no claim for medical or surgical treatment shall be valid and enforceable unless the physician furnishes the employer (or insurance carrier) and the Chairman with a preliminary notice (C-48) of injury and treatment within 48 hours following first treatment, and within 15 days thereafter a more complete report (C-4 or C-5), and subsequent thereto progress reports (C-4 or C-5) at intervals of 22 days or less, with a final report (C-4 or C-5) upon termination of treatment.

3. This form must be signed personally by the attending physician and must contain his authorization certificate number and code letters. If the patient is hospitalized, it may be signed by a licensed physician to whom the treatment of the case has been assigned as a member of the attending staff of the hospital.

4. **CHANGE OF ATTENDING PHYSICIAN:** The rules of the Chairman provide that "a physician authorized to treat workmen's compensation cases, when requested to supersede another physician, must, before beginning treatment of such patient, make reasonable effort to communicate with the attending physician to ascertain the patient's condition. The superseding physician must also advise the attending physician of the name of the person who has requested him to assume care of the case and state the reason therefor. If the second physician cannot contact the attending physician, and the claimant's condition requires immediate treatment, the said physician should advise the doctor previously in attendance within 48 hours that he now has the patient in his care. The preceding physician shall supply the succeeding physician with a complete history of the case."

5. **AUTHORIZATION FOR CONTINUED MEDICAL CARE:** When it is necessary to engage the services of a specialist, consultant, or surgeon, or to provide for physiotherapeutic procedures or x-ray examination costing more than $75, or special diagnostic laboratory tests costing more than $35, the physician must secure authorization from the employer, the insurance company, or the Chairman. Such authorization may be requested on this form under item 10. If authorization is not forthcoming or is not denied within five working days, or if a denial of authorization is not justified medically or otherwise, the special services required for the patient's welfare should be proceeded with on the ground that authorization has been unreasonably withheld. Such authorization is not required in an emergency under the provisions of Section 13-a (5).

6. **PENALTY FOR FALSE REPRESENTATION:** If for the purpose of obtaining any benefit or payment under the provisions of the Workmen's Compensation or Volunteer Firemen's Benefit Laws, or for the purpose of influencing any determinations regarding any benefit or payment under the provisions of these laws, either for himself or any other person, any person willfully makes a false statement or representation, he shall be guilty of a misdemeanor.

C-48 Reverse (12-73)

ATTENDING PHYSICIAN'S PROGRESS REPORT   **WORKERS' COMPENSATION BOARD**

DO NOT USE THIS FORM UNLESS YOU INITIALLY FILED A FIRST REPORT (C-48)

PLEASE PRINT OR TYPE

WCB CASE NO. (If Known)	CARRIER CASE NO. (If Known)	DATE OF INJURY AND TIME	ADDRESS WHERE INJURY OCCURRED (City, Town or Village)	CLAIMANT'S SOC. SEC. NO.

INJURED PERSON	(First Name) (Middle Initial) (Last Name)	AGE	ADDRESS	APT. NO.
EMPLOYER				
INSURANCE CARRIER				

MESSAGE TO DOCTOR — THIS REPORT MUST BE FILED AT INTERVALS OF 22 DAYS OR LESS DURING CONTINUING TREATMENT. SEND ORIGINAL TO WORKERS' COMPENSATION BOARD AND COPY TO INSURANCE CARRIER.
FAILURE TO FILE REPORTS ON TIME MAY RESULT IN YOUR BILL BEING INVALIDATED.

PLEASE COMPLETE THIS FORM IN FULL

THIS IS A (CHECK ONE): ☐ PROGRESS REPORT   ☐ FINAL REPORT

1. DATE(S) OF EXAMINATION ON WHICH REPORT IS BASED   WHEN WILL PATIENT BE SEEN AGAIN?

2. AT TIME OF LAST EXAMINATION
   (a) HAS PATIENT RETURNED TO WORK? ☐ YES ☐ NO   IF "YES" DATE RESUMED REGULAR WORK _____   DATE RESUMED LIMITED WORK _____

   (b) IS PATIENT DISABLED? ☐ YES ☐ NO   If "Yes" check one: ☐ Total disability ☐ Partial disability   ESTIMATE LENGTH OF DISABILITY   Totally disabled until _____   Partially disabled until _____

   NOTE: IF ABLE TO WORK PLEASE ADVISE PATIENT TO CONTACT EMPLOYER.

3. DESCRIBE SUBJECTIVE COMPLAINTS AND PHYSICAL FINDINGS WHEN EXAMINED

4. DESCRIBE TREATMENT RENDERED SINCE LAST REPORT AND PLANNED FUTURE TREATMENT

★ 5. IS AUTHORIZATION FOR SPECIAL SERVICES REQUESTED? (SEE ITEM 3 ON REVERSE) ☐ YES ☐ NO

6. (a) WAS THE OCCURRENCE DESCRIBED IN YOUR INITIAL FORM C-48 THE COMPETENT PRODUCING CAUSE OF THE INJURY AND DISABILITY (IF ANY) SUSTAINED? ☐ YES ☐ NO
   (b) DID YOU FILE AN INITIAL REPORT (FORM C-48) STATING HOW THE INJURY OCCURRED? ☐ YES ☐ NO   IF "NO" ATTACH FORM C-48 TO THIS REPORT

7. MAY THE INJURY RESULT IN PERMANENT RESTRICTION, TOTAL OR PARTIAL LOSS OF FUNCTION OF A PART OR MEMBER, OR PERMANENT FACIAL, HEAD OR NECK DISFIGUREMENT? ☐ YES ☐ NO   IF "YES" DESCRIBE

8. WAS PATIENT HOSPITALIZED SINCE LAST REPORT? IF SO, WHAT HOSPITAL AND WHEN? ☐ YES ☐ NO

9. (a) ANY FACTORS DELAYING RECOVERY? IF "YES" DESCRIBE ☐ YES ☐ NO
   (b) IS MEDICAL AND/OR VOCATIONAL REHABILITATION INDICATED? IF "YES" GIVE DETAILS ☐ YES ☐ NO
   (c) IF "YES" HAS REFERRAL BEEN MADE? (GIVE DETAILS) ☐ YES ☐ NO

10. ENTER HERE ADDITIONAL PERTINENT INFORMATION, WORK LIMITATIONS, IF ANY, ETC.

Dated	Typed or Printed Name of Attending Physician	Address
WCB Rating Code	WCB Authorization No.	Telephone No.	Written Signature of Attending Physician (Facsimile Not Accepted)

C-4 (11-78)   SEE REVERSE SIDE FOR SPECIAL INSTRUCTIONS

WP 61

IMPORTANT
TO THE ATTENDING PHYSICIAN

1. Progress reports on this form must be filed within 17 days after you first render treatment in a workers' compensation case or a volunteer firemen's benefit case, and thereafter at intervals of 22 days or less during continuing treatment. When patient is seen less frequently, file forms as of date of examination. This form is also to be used for a final report upon termination of treatment.
   THIS FORM IS NOT TO BE USED UNLESS AN INITIAL REPORT (FORM C-48) WAS PREVIOUSLY FILED.

   Please ask your patient for his Workers' Compensation Board Case Number and the Insurance Carrier's Case Number, if they are known to him, and show these numbers on your reports, in the spaces provided.

   File the signed original of this report directly with (1) CHAIRMAN, WORKERS' COMPENSATION BOARD in the district office serving the county in which the accident occurred and file a signed copy with (2) the INSURANCE CARRIER, if known, or the EMPLOYER.

2. This form must be <u>signed personally</u> by the attending physician and must contain his authorization certificate number and code letters. If the patient is hospitalized, it may be signed by a licensed physician to whom the treatment of the case has been assigned as a member of the attending staff of the hospital. A FACSIMILE SIGNATURE IS NOT ACCEPTABLE.

3. <u>**AUTHORIZATION FOR SPECIAL SERVICES:**</u> When it is necessary for the attending physician to engage the services of a specialist, consultant, or a surgeon, or to provide for X-ray examinations or physiotherapeutic or other procedures costing more than $75 or to provide for special diagnostic laboratory tests costing more than $35, he must request and secure authorization from the employer or insurance carrier or the Chairman, as follows:

    a. Telephone the employer or insurance carrier, explain the need for the special services, and request the necessary authorization.

    b. Confirm the request in writing, setting forth the medical necessity for the special services.

    c. The employer or insurance carrier may have the patient examined within four (4) working days of the request for authorization, if the patient is hospitalized, or within twenty-one (21) calendar days if the patient is not hospitalized.

    d. If authorization or denial is not forthcoming within the four working days if the patient is hospitalized, or within the twenty-one calendar days if the patient is not hospitalized, notify the nearest office of the Workers' Compensation Board.

    SUCH AUTHORIZATION IS NOT REQUIRED IN AN EMERGENCY UNDER THE PROVISIONS OF SECTION 13-a (5).

    In cases in which the claimant's physician prescribes a surgical appliance or dental treatment or denture, the physician should notify the employer or carrier of the need for such appliance or dental aid, and direct the claimant to the employer or carrier for the purpose of securing authorization for the purchase of such appliance or dental aid before the same is furnished to the claimant by the appliance dealer or dentist.

4. <u>**PENALTY FOR FALSE REPRESENTATION:**</u> Any person who wilfully makes a false statement or representation on this form shall be guilty of a misdemeanor.

THE WORKERS' COMPENSATION BOARD EMPLOYS AND SERVES THE HANDICAPPED WITHOUT DISCRIMINATION.

C-4 Reverse (11-78)

DAILY JOURNAL

DATE October 21, 19— SHEET NO. 79

RECEIPT NUMBER	DATE	DESCRIPTION-CODE	CHARGE	PAYMENT	BALANCE	PREVIOUS BALANCE	NAME
1							
2							
3							
4							
5							
6							
7							
8							
9							
10							
11							
12							
13							
14							
15							
16							
17							
32							
33							
34							TOTALS

Column A	Column B	Column C	Column D

◆ ALL RECEIPTS MUST BE IN NUMERICAL ORDER

PROOF OF POSTING
COLUMN D TOTAL $ _____
"PLUS" COLUMN A TOTAL $ _____
SUB TOTAL $ _____
"MINUS" COL. B TOTAL $ _____
EQUALS COLUMN C TOTAL $ _____

ACCOUNTS RECEIVABLE CONTROL
PREVIOUS BALANCE $ 2530.25
"PLUS" COLUMN A $ _____
SUB TOTAL $ _____
"MINUS" COL. B TOTAL $ _____
PRESENT ACC'TS REC. BALANCE $ _____

DAILY CASH SUMMARY
OPENING CASH ON HAND AT BEGINNING OF DAY $ _____
CASH RECEIVED DURING DAY $ _____
TOTAL $ _____

FORM NO. 210-1

LITTLE PRESS, INC., MPLS. 55423

WP 63

DAILY JOURNAL

DATE *October 22*, 19— SHEET NO. *80*

RECEIPT NUMBER	DATE	DESCRIPTION-CODE	CHARGE	PAYMENT	BALANCE	PREVIOUS BALANCE	NAME
1							
2							
3							
4							
5							
6							
7							
8							
9							
10							
11							
12							
13							
14							
15							
16							
17							
...							
32							
33							
34							
TOTALS			Column A	Column B	Column C	Column D	

◄ ALL RECEIPTS MUST BE IN NUMERICAL ORDER

PROOF OF POSTING

COLUMN D TOTAL $ _____
"PLUS" COLUMN A TOTAL $ _____
SUB TOTAL $ _____
"MINUS" COL. B TOTAL $ _____
EQUALS COLUMN C TOTAL $ _____

ACCOUNTS RECEIVABLE CONTROL

PREVIOUS BALANCE $ _____
"PLUS" COLUMN A $ _____
SUB TOTAL $ _____
"MINUS" COL. B TOTAL $ _____
PRESENT ACCTS REC. BALANCE $ _____

DAILY CASH SUMMARY

OPENING CASH ON HAND AT BEGINNING OF DAY $ _____
CASH RECEIVED DURING DAY $ _____
TOTAL $ _____

LITTLE PRESS, INC., MPLS. 55423

FORM NO. 210-1

SUMMARY FOR MONTH October YEAR 19___

MONTHLY SUMMARY SHEET — PART A

Month _____ Year _____

DAY OF MONTH	CHARGES (COLUMN "A")	PAYMENTS (COLUMN "B")	MISCELLANEOUS SUMMARIES
1	70 00	25 00	
2	—	—	
3	—	75 00	
4	—	—	
5	—	—	
6	—	116 25	
7	1,725 00	100 00	
8	—	—	
9	50 00	—	
10	—	—	
11	—	—	
12	—	—	
13	—	—	
14	314 50	—	
15	30 00	—	
16	178 50	35 00	
17	—	100 00	
18	—	—	
19	—	—	
20	20 00	25 00	
21			
22			
23			
24			
25			
26			
27			
28			
29			
30			
31			
TOTAL FOR MONTH			
BROUGHT FORWARD	45,540 25	44,921 75	
GRAND TOTAL			

SUMMARY OF EXPENSE (From Reverse Side)

	AMOUNT
DRUGS AND PROFESSIONAL SUPPLIES	
LAB EXPENSE	
SALARIES	
OFFICE RENT AND MAINTENANCE	
LAUNDRY SERVICE	
ELECTRICITY, GAS, WATER	
TELEPHONE	
DUES AND MEETINGS	
OFFICE EXPENSES (SUPPLIES, ETC.)	
PROFESSIONAL INSURANCE	
BUSINESS TAXES	
INTEREST PAID	
ENTERTAINMENT	
TOTAL FOR PRESENT MONTH	
FORWARDED FROM PREVIOUS MONTH	15,182 31
GRAND TOTAL	

MONTHLY BALANCES

For The Present Month
- TOTAL RECEIPTS (COL. B)
- TOTAL EXPENSE
- NET EARNINGS

For The Year To Date
- GRAND TOTAL RECEIPTS
- GRAND TOTAL EXPENSE
- NET EARNINGS

ACCOUNTS RECEIVABLE (FROM LAST DAY SHEET OF THE MONTH) $ _____

CHECKED BY _____

FORM NO. SUM. 1231-A   PRINTED IN U.S.A. LITTLE PRESS, INC., MINNEAPOLIS, MINN.

ACCRA FORM

WP 67

EXPENDITURES FOR THE MONTH

DRUGS AND PROFESSIONAL SUPPLIES			SALARIES			DUES AND MEETINGS			ENTERTAINMENT			OTHER	
DAY	ITEM	AMOUNT	DAY	ITEM	AMOUNT	DAY	ITEM	AMOUNT	DAY	ITEM	AMOUNT	DAY	ITEM	AMOUNT
TOTAL														

LAB EXPENSE — TOTAL

OFFICE RENT AND UPKEEP — TOTAL

LAUNDRY SERVICE — TOTAL

ELECTRICITY, GAS, WATER — TOTAL

TELEPHONE — TOTAL

TOTAL

OFFICE EXPENSES (SUPPLIES, ETC.) — TOTAL

PROFESSIONAL INSURANCE — TOTAL

BUSINESS TAXES — TOTAL

INTEREST PAID — TOTAL

TOTAL

NONPROFESSIONAL EXPENSES — SOURCE — TOTAL — AMOUNT

NONPROFESSIONAL RECEIPTS — DESCRIBE — TOTAL — AMOUNT

ALL TOTALS TO BE TRANSFERRED TO PART A

MONTHLY SUMMARY SHEET   PART B   Month _____   Year _____

FORM NO. SUM. 1231-B

First National Bank
Chicago, IL 60623

STATEMENT OF
ACCOUNT NUMBER

242 027720

CLOSING DATE   ITEMS

10/24   8

WARREN TAYLOR, M.D.
2235 SOUTH RIDGEWAY AVENUE
CHICAGO, IL 60623

PERSONAL CHECKING ACCOUNT STATEMENT

BEGINNING BALANCE	(+) TOTAL CREDITS	(—) TOTAL DEBITS	(—) SERVICE CHARGE	(=) NEW BALANCE
1,745.65	666.25	1,061.72		1,350.18

CHECKS & OTHER DEBITS	DEPOSITS & OTHER CREDITS	DATE	BALANCE
	25.00	10/1	1,770.65
500.00	75.00	10/3	1,345.65
	116.25	10/6	1,461.90
	100.00	10/7	1,561.90
35.50		10/10	1,526.40
100.00			1,426.40
255.75		10/15	1,170.65
	35.00	10/16	1,205.65
24.32	100.00	10/17	1,281.33
65.90			1,215.43
55.25	25.00	10/20	1,185.18
25.00		10/21	1,160.18
	190.00	10/22	1,350.18

SYMBOLS

AD = LOAN ADVANCE   CM = CREDIT MEMO   LS = LIST POSTED   RI = RETURN ITEM
BV = BACK VALUE   DM = DEBIT MEMO   OD = OVERDRAFT   SC = SERVICE CHARGE
C = CORRECTION   IP = INSTALMENT LOAN PAYMENT   PY = PAYMENT TO LOAN

WP 69

CHANGE OF ADDRESS ORDER

TO CHANGE YOUR ADDRESS PLEASE COMPLETE THIS FORM;

THEN CUT ALONG DOTTED LINE AND MAIL OR BRING TO THE BANK

NEW ADDRESS:

NUMBER
AND STREET _____

CITY _____ STATE AND ZIP CODE _____ NEW PHONE NUMBER _____

DATE _____ CUSTOMER'S SIGNATURE _____

OUTSTANDING CHECKS

NUMBER	AMOUNT	
TOTAL		

TO RECONCILE YOUR STATEMENT AND CHECKBOOK

1. DEDUCT FROM YOUR CHECKBOOK BALANCE ANY SERVICE OR OTHER CHARGE ORIGINATED BY THE BANK. THESE CHARGES WILL BE IDENTIFIED BY SYMBOLS AS SHOWN ON FRONT.

2. ARRANGE ENDORSED CHECKS BY DATE OR NUMBER AND CHECK THEM OFF AGAINST THE STUBS IN YOUR CHECKBOOK.

3. LIST IN THE OUTSTANDING CHECKS SECTION AT THE LEFT ANY CHECKS ISSUED BY YOU AND NOT YET PAID BY US.

TO RECONCILE YOUR STATEMENT AND CHECKBOOK

LAST BALANCE SHOWN ON STATEMENT		
PLUS: DEPOSITS AND CREDITS MADE AFTER DATE OF LAST ENTRY ON STATEMENT.		
SUBTOTAL		
MINUS: OUTSTANDING CHECKS		
BALANCE: WHICH SHOULD AGREE WITH YOUR CHECKBOOK		

INDIVIDUAL EMPLOYEE'S EARNINGS RECORD

Name Janet Owen
Address 301 Hickory Ave.
City Chicago, IL 60622
Telephone 555-2130

Social Security No. 095-27-3821
Marital Status Single
No. of Allowances 1
Birthdate 5/19/—

Position Medical Assistant
Monthly Rate _____
Weekly Rate _____
Overtime Rate _____

Period Ending	Hours Worked	Gross Earnings			Deductions						Net Pay	Accumulated Earnings (Gross)
		Regular	Overtime	Total	FICA	Federal Withholding	State Withholding	City Withholding	Insurance	Other	Total		

WP 71

SINGLE Persons — BIWEEKLY Payroll Period

And the wages are—		And the number of withholding allowances claimed is→										
At least	But less than	0	1	2	3	4	5	6	7	8	9	10 or more
		The amount of income tax to be withheld shall be—											

At least	But less than	0	1	2	3	4	5	6	7	8	9	10 or more
$0	$54	$0	$0	$0	$0	$0	$0	$0	$0	$0	$0	$0
54	56	.10	0	0	0	0	0	0	0	0	0	0
56	58	.40	0	0	0	0	0	0	0	0	0	0
58	60	.70	0	0	0	0	0	0	0	0	0	0
60	62	1.00	0	0	0	0	0	0	0	0	0	0
62	64	1.30	0	0	0	0	0	0	0	0	0	0
64	66	1.60	0	0	0	0	0	0	0	0	0	0
66	68	1.90	0	0	0	0	0	0	0	0	0	0
68	70	2.20	0	0	0	0	0	0	0	0	0	0
70	72	2.50	0	0	0	0	0	0	0	0	0	0
72	74	2.80	0	0	0	0	0	0	0	0	0	0
74	76	3.10	0	0	0	0	0	0	0	0	0	0
76	78	3.40	0	0	0	0	0	0	0	0	0	0
78	80	3.70	0	0	0	0	0	0	0	0	0	0
80	82	4.00	0	0	0	0	0	0	0	0	0	0
82	84	4.30	0	0	0	0	0	0	0	0	0	0
84	86	4.60	0	0	0	0	0	0	0	0	0	0
86	88	4.90	0	0	0	0	0	0	0	0	0	0
88	90	5.20	0	0	0	0	0	0	0	0	0	0
90	92	5.50	0	0	0	0	0	0	0	0	0	0
92	94	5.80	0	0	0	0	0	0	0	0	0	0
94	96	6.10	.30	0	0	0	0	0	0	0	0	0
96	98	6.40	.60	0	0	0	0	0	0	0	0	0
98	100	6.70	.90	0	0	0	0	0	0	0	0	0
100	102	7.00	1.20	0	0	0	0	0	0	0	0	0
102	104	7.30	1.50	0	0	0	0	0	0	0	0	0
104	106	7.60	1.80	0	0	0	0	0	0	0	0	0
106	108	7.90	2.10	0	0	0	0	0	0	0	0	0
108	110	8.20	2.40	0	0	0	0	0	0	0	0	0
110	112	8.50	2.70	0	0	0	0	0	0	0	0	0
112	114	8.80	3.00	0	0	0	0	0	0	0	0	0
114	116	9.10	3.30	0	0	0	0	0	0	0	0	0
116	118	9.40	3.60	0	0	0	0	0	0	0	0	0
118	120	9.70	3.90	0	0	0	0	0	0	0	0	0
120	124	10.10	4.30	0	0	0	0	0	0	0	0	0
124	128	10.70	4.90	0	0	0	0	0	0	0	0	0
128	132	11.40	5.50	0	0	0	0	0	0	0	0	0
132	136	12.10	6.10	.40	0	0	0	0	0	0	0	0
136	140	12.80	6.70	1.00	0	0	0	0	0	0	0	0
140	144	13.60	7.30	1.60	0	0	0	0	0	0	0	0
144	148	14.30	7.90	2.20	0	0	0	0	0	0	0	0
148	152	15.00	8.50	2.80	0	0	0	0	0	0	0	0
152	156	15.70	9.10	3.40	0	0	0	0	0	0	0	0
156	160	16.40	9.70	4.00	0	0	0	0	0	0	0	0
160	164	17.20	10.30	4.60	0	0	0	0	0	0	0	0
164	168	17.90	11.00	5.20	0	0	0	0	0	0	0	0
168	172	18.60	11.70	5.80	0	0	0	0	0	0	0	0
172	176	19.30	12.40	6.40	.60	0	0	0	0	0	0	0
176	180	20.00	13.10	7.00	1.20	0	0	0	0	0	0	0
180	184	20.80	13.80	7.60	1.80	0	0	0	0	0	0	0
184	188	21.50	14.60	8.20	2.40	0	0	0	0	0	0	0
188	192	22.20	15.30	8.80	3.00	0	0	0	0	0	0	0
192	196	22.90	16.00	9.40	3.60	0	0	0	0	0	0	0
196	200	23.60	16.70	10.00	4.20	0	0	0	0	0	0	0
200	210	24.90	18.00	11.10	5.30	0	0	0	0	0	0	0
210	220	26.70	19.80	12.90	6.80	1.00	0	0	0	0	0	0
220	230	28.50	21.60	14.70	8.30	2.50	0	0	0	0	0	0
230	240	30.30	23.40	16.50	9.80	4.00	0	0	0	0	0	0
240	250	32.10	25.20	18.30	11.30	5.50	0	0	0	0	0	0
250	260	33.90	27.00	20.10	13.10	7.00	1.20	0	0	0	0	0

(Continued on next page)

WP 73

SINGLE Persons — BIWEEKLY Payroll Period

And the wages are —		And the number of withholding allowances claimed is —										
At least	But less than	0	1	2	3	4	5	6	7	8	9	10 or more
		The amount of income tax to be withheld shall be —										
$260	$270	$35.80	$28.80	$21.90	$14.90	$8.50	$2.70	$0	$0	$0	$0	$0
270	280	37.90	30.60	23.70	16.70	10.00	4.20	0	0	0	0	0
280	290	40.00	32.40	25.50	18.50	11.60	5.70	0	0	0	0	0
290	300	42.10	34.20	27.30	20.30	13.40	7.20	1.40	0	0	0	0
300	320	45.30	37.20	30.00	23.00	16.10	9.50	3.70	0	0	0	0
320	340	49.50	41.40	33.60	26.60	19.70	12.80	6.70	.90	0	0	0
340	360	53.70	45.60	37.50	30.20	23.30	16.40	9.70	3.90	0	0	0
360	380	57.90	49.80	41.70	33.80	26.90	20.00	13.10	6.90	1.20	0	0
380	400	62.10	54.00	45.90	37.80	30.50	23.60	16.70	9.90	4.20	0	0
400	420	67.10	58.20	50.10	42.00	34.10	27.20	20.30	13.30	7.20	1.40	0
420	440	72.30	62.40	54.30	46.20	38.10	30.80	23.90	16.90	10.20	4.40	0
440	460	77.50	67.50	58.50	50.40	42.30	34.40	27.50	20.50	13.60	7.40	1.60
460	480	82.70	72.70	62.70	54.60	46.50	38.50	31.10	24.10	17.20	10.40	4.60
480	500	87.90	77.90	67.90	58.80	50.70	42.70	34.70	27.70	20.80	13.90	7.60
500	520	93.10	83.10	73.10	63.10	54.90	46.90	38.80	31.30	24.40	17.50	10.60
520	540	98.30	88.30	78.30	68.30	59.10	51.10	43.00	34.90	28.00	21.10	14.20
540	560	103.70	93.50	83.50	73.50	63.50	55.30	47.20	39.10	31.60	24.70	17.80
560	580	109.70	98.70	88.70	78.70	68.70	59.50	51.40	43.30	35.20	28.30	21.40
580	600	115.70	104.20	93.90	83.90	73.90	63.90	55.60	47.50	39.40	31.90	25.00
600	620	121.70	110.20	99.10	89.10	79.10	69.10	59.80	51.70	43.60	35.60	28.60
620	640	127.70	116.20	104.60	94.30	84.30	74.30	64.30	55.90	47.80	39.80	32.20
640	660	133.70	122.20	110.60	99.50	89.50	79.50	69.50	60.10	52.00	44.00	35.90
660	680	140.00	128.20	116.60	105.10	94.70	84.70	74.70	64.70	56.20	48.20	40.10
680	700	146.80	134.20	122.60	111.10	99.90	89.90	79.90	69.90	60.40	52.40	44.30
700	720	153.60	140.60	128.60	117.10	105.50	95.10	85.10	75.10	65.10	56.60	48.50
720	740	160.40	147.40	134.60	123.10	111.50	100.30	90.30	80.30	70.30	60.80	52.70
740	760	167.20	154.20	141.10	129.10	117.50	106.00	95.50	85.50	75.50	65.50	56.90
760	780	174.00	161.00	147.90	135.10	123.50	112.00	100.70	90.70	80.70	70.70	61.10
780	800	180.80	167.80	154.70	141.60	129.50	118.00	106.50	95.90	85.90	75.90	65.90
800	820	187.60	174.60	161.50	148.40	135.50	124.00	112.50	101.10	91.10	81.10	71.10
820	840	194.40	181.40	168.30	155.20	142.10	130.00	118.50	106.90	96.30	86.30	76.30
840	860	201.20	188.20	175.10	162.00	148.90	136.00	124.50	112.90	101.50	91.50	81.50
860	880	208.30	195.00	181.90	168.80	155.70	142.60	130.50	118.90	107.40	96.70	86.70
880	900	216.10	201.80	188.70	175.60	162.50	149.40	136.50	124.90	113.40	101.90	91.90
900	920	223.90	208.90	195.50	182.40	169.30	156.20	143.20	130.90	119.40	107.80	97.10
920	940	231.70	216.70	202.30	189.20	176.10	163.00	150.00	136.90	125.40	113.80	102.30
940	960	239.50	224.50	209.50	196.00	182.90	169.80	156.80	143.70	131.40	119.80	108.30
960	980	247.30	232.30	217.30	202.80	189.70	176.60	163.60	150.50	137.40	125.80	114.30
980	1,000	255.10	240.10	225.10	210.10	196.50	183.40	170.40	157.30	144.20	131.80	120.30
1,000	1,020	262.90	247.90	232.90	217.90	203.30	190.20	177.20	164.10	151.00	137.90	126.30
1,020	1,040	270.70	255.70	240.70	225.70	210.70	197.00	184.00	170.90	157.80	144.70	132.30
1,040	1,060	278.50	263.50	248.50	233.50	218.50	203.80	190.80	177.70	164.60	151.50	138.50
1,060	1,080	286.30	271.30	256.30	241.30	226.30	211.30	197.60	184.50	171.40	158.30	145.30
1,080	1,100	294.10	279.10	264.10	249.10	234.10	219.10	204.40	191.30	178.20	165.10	152.10
1,100	1,120	301.90	286.90	271.90	256.90	241.90	226.90	211.90	198.10	185.00	171.90	158.90
1,120	1,140	309.70	294.70	279.70	264.70	249.70	234.70	219.70	204.90	191.80	178.70	165.70
1,140	1,160	317.50	302.50	287.50	272.50	257.50	242.50	227.50	212.50	198.60	185.50	172.50
1,160	1,180	325.30	310.30	295.30	280.30	265.30	250.30	235.30	220.30	205.40	192.30	179.30
1,180	1,200	333.10	318.10	303.10	288.10	273.10	258.10	243.10	228.10	213.10	199.10	186.10
1,200	1,220	340.90	325.90	310.90	295.90	280.90	265.90	250.90	235.90	220.90	205.90	192.90
1,220	1,240	348.70	333.70	318.70	303.70	288.70	273.70	258.70	243.70	228.70	213.70	199.70
1,240	1,260	356.50	341.50	326.50	311.50	296.50	281.50	266.50	251.50	236.50	221.50	206.50
1,260	1,280	364.30	349.30	334.30	319.30	304.30	289.30	274.30	259.30	244.30	229.30	214.30
1,280	1,300	372.10	357.10	342.10	327.10	312.10	297.10	282.10	267.10	252.10	237.10	222.10
1,300	1,320	379.90	364.90	349.90	334.90	319.90	304.90	289.90	274.90	259.90	244.90	229.90
		39 percent of the excess over $1,320 plus —										
$1,320 and over		383.80	368.80	353.80	338.80	323.80	308.80	293.80	278.80	263.80	248.80	233.80

DAILY JOURNAL

DATE October 28   SHEET NO. _____

RECEIPT NUMBER	DATE	DESCRIPTION-CODE	CHARGE	PAYMENT	BALANCE	PREVIOUS BALANCE	NAME
1	10/28	Check		50 00			Paul Bochmann
2	10/28	Check		25 00			Jill Grimes

Deposit Slip

DEPOSITED IN
First National Bank
THIS DEPOSIT ACCEPTED UNDER AND SUBJECT TO THE PROVISIONS OF THE UNIFORM COMMERCIAL CODE.

DATE October 28, 19—

Warren Taylor, M.D.
2235 South Ridgeway Avenue
Chicago, IL 60623

12 FNB 42
OCT 28

⑆0710⑈0052 24⑆0277201⑈

	DOLLARS	CENTS
Cash	50	00
Checks — list separately 1	25	00
2		
3		
4		
5		
6		
7		
8	75	00

◀ ALL RECEIPTS MUST BE IN NUMERICAL ORDER

PROOF OF POSTING

COLUMN D TOTAL $ _____
"PLUS" COLUMN A TOTAL $ _____
SUB TOTAL $ _____
"MINUS" COL. B TOTAL $ _____
EQUALS COLUMN C TOTAL $ _____

Column A	Column B	Column C	Column D

TOTALS

ACCOUNTS RECEIVABLE CONTROL

PREVIOUS BALANCE $ 2894.25
"PLUS" COLUMN A $ _____
SUB TOTAL $ _____
"MINUS" COL. B TOTAL $ _____
PRESENT ACC'TS REC. BALANCE $ _____

DAILY CASH SUMMARY

OPENING CASH ON HAND AT BEGINNING OF DAY $ _____
CASH RECEIVED DURING DAY $ _____
TOTAL $ _____

FORM NO. 210-1

LITTLE PRESS, INC., MPLS. 55423

WP 75

DAILY JOURNAL

DATE October 29   SHEET NO. _____

RECEIPT NUMBER	DATE	DESCRIPTION-CODE	CHARGE	PAYMENT	BALANCE	PREVIOUS BALANCE	NAME
558	10/29			50 25			Stanley Berndt
559	10/29			50 00			Marion Wellman
3							
4							
5							
6							
7							
8							
9							
10							
11							
12							
13							
14							
15							
16							
17							
32							
33							
34							
			Column A	Column B	Column C	Column D	TOTALS

➤ ALL RECEIPTS MUST BE IN NUMERICAL ORDER

PROOF OF POSTING

COLUMN D TOTAL $ _____
"PLUS" COLUMN A TOTAL $ _____
SUB TOTAL $ _____
"MINUS" COL. B TOTAL $ _____
EQUALS COLUMN C TOTAL $ _____

ACCOUNTS RECEIVABLE CONTROL

PREVIOUS BALANCE $ _____
"PLUS" COLUMN A $ _____
SUB TOTAL $ _____
"MINUS" COL. B TOTAL $ _____
PRESENT ACC'TS REC. BALANCE $ _____

DAILY CASH SUMMARY

OPENING CASH ON HAND AT BEGINNING OF DAY $ _____
CASH RECEIVED DURING DAY $ _____
TOTAL $ _____

FORM NO. 210-1

LITTLE PRESS, INC., MPLS. 55423

WP 77

DAILY JOURNAL

DATE October 30   SHEET NO. _____

RECEIPT NUMBER	DATE	DESCRIPTION-CODE	CHARGE	PAYMENT	BALANCE	PREVIOUS BALANCE	NAME
1							
2							
3							
4							
5							
6							
7							
8							
9							
10							
11							
12							
13							
14							
15							
16							
17							
32							
33							
34							
TOTALS			Column A	Column B	Column C	Column D	

◀ ALL RECEIPTS MUST BE IN NUMERICAL ORDER

PROOF OF POSTING

COLUMN D TOTAL $ _____
"PLUS" COLUMN A TOTAL $ _____
SUB TOTAL $ _____
"MINUS" COL. B TOTAL $ _____
EQUALS COLUMN C TOTAL $ _____

ACCOUNTS RECEIVABLE CONTROL

PREVIOUS BALANCE $ _____
"PLUS" COLUMN A $ _____
SUB TOTAL $ _____
"MINUS" COL. B TOTAL $ _____
PRESENT ACC'TS REC. BALANCE $ _____

DAILY CASH SUMMARY

OPENING CASH ON HAND AT BEGINNING OF DAY $ _____
CASH RECEIVED DURING DAY $ _____
TOTAL $ _____

FORM NO. 210-1

LITTLE PRESS, INC., MPLS. 55423

WP 79

DAILY JOURNAL

DATE October 31   SHEET NO. _____

RECEIPT NUMBER	DATE	DESCRIPTION-CODE	CHARGE	PAYMENT	BALANCE	PREVIOUS BALANCE	NAME
1							
2							
3							
4							
5							
6							
7							
8							
9							
10							
11							
12							
13							
14							
15							
16							
17							
32							
33							
34							
			Column A	Column B	Column C	Column D	TOTALS

◆ ALL RECEIPTS MUST BE IN NUMERICAL ORDER

PROOF OF POSTING

COLUMN D TOTAL $ _____
"PLUS" COLUMN A TOTAL $ _____
SUB TOTAL $ _____
"MINUS" COL. B TOTAL $ _____
EQUALS COLUMN C TOTAL $ _____

ACCOUNTS RECEIVABLE CONTROL

PREVIOUS BALANCE $ _____
"PLUS" COLUMN A $ _____
SUB TOTAL $ _____
"MINUS" COL. B TOTAL $ _____
PRESENT ACC'TS REC. BALANCE $ _____

DAILY CASH SUMMARY

OPENING CASH ON HAND AT BEGINNING OF DAY $ _____
CASH RECEIVED DURING DAY $ _____
TOTAL $ _____

FORM NO. 210-1

LITTLE PRESS, INC., MPLS. 55423

REQUEST FOR MEDICARE PAYMENT

MEDICAL INSURANCE BENEFITS—SOCIAL SECURITY ACT (See Instructions on Back—**Type or Print Information**)

Form Approved
OMB No.
72-RO730

NOTICE—Anyone who misrepresents or falsifies essential information requested by this form may upon conviction be subject to fine and imprisonment under Federal Law.

PART I—PATIENT TO FILL IN ITEMS 1 THROUGH 6 ONLY

Copy from YOUR OWN HEALTH INSURANCE CARD (See example on back)

1 Name of patient (First name, Middle initial, Last name)
Carl Logan

2 Health insurance claim number (Include all letters)
0,5,0,0,1,4,7,4,8,A

☒ Male   ☐ Female

3 Patient's mailing address — City, State, ZIP code
729 N. Wolcott Ave., Chicago, IL 60622

Telephone Number
555-2365

4 Describe the illness or injury for which you received treatment (Always fill in this item if your doctor does not complete Part II below)

Was your illness or injury connected with your employment?
☐ Yes ☒ No

5 If any of your medical expenses will be or could be paid by another insurance organization or government agency (including FEHB), show below.

Name and address of organization or agency | Policy or Identification Number

Note: If you **Do Not** want information about this Medicare claim released to the above upon its request, check (X) the following block ☐

6 I authorize any holder of medical or other information about me to release to the Social Security Administration or its intermediaries or carriers any information needed for this or a related Medicare claim. I permit a copy of this authorization to be used in place of the original, and request payment of medical insurance benefits either to myself or to the party who accepts assignment below.

Signature of patient (See instructions on reverse where patient is unable to sign)
SIGN HERE ▶ *Carl Logan*

Date signed
10/30/—

PART II—PHYSICIAN OR SUPPLIER TO FILL IN 7 THROUGH 14

7
A. Date of each service	B. Place of service (*See Codes below)	C. Fully describe surgical or medical procedures and other services or supplies furnished for each date given / Procedure Code	D. Nature of illness or injury requiring services or supplies (diagnosis)	E. Charges (If related to unusual circumstances explain in 7C)	Leave Blank
				$	

8 Name and address of physician or supplier (Number and street, city, State, ZIP code)

Telephone No.

Physician or supplier code

9 Total charges $
10 Amount paid $
11 Any unpaid balance due $

12 Assignment of patient's bill
▶ ☐ I accept assignment (See reverse) ☐ I do not accept assignment.

13 Show name and address of person or facility which furnished service (if other than your own office or patient's home)

14 Signature of physician or supplier (A physician's signature certifies that a physician's services were personally rendered by the physician or under the physician's personal direction)

Date signed

*O—Doctor's Office   H—Patient's Home (If portable X-ray services, identify the supplier)   SNF—Skilled Nursing Facility   OL—Other Locations
IL—Independent Laboratory   IH—Inpatient Hospital   OH—Outpatient Hospital   NH—Nursing Home

FORM SSA 1490 (11-75)

Department of Health, Education, and Welfare
Social Security Administration

WP 83

HOW TO FILL OUT YOUR MEDICARE FORM
There are two ways that Medicare can help pay your doctor bills

One way is for Medicare to pay your doctor.—If you and your doctor agree, Medicare will pay the doctor directly. This is the assignment method. You do not submit any claim; the doctor does. All you do is fill out Part I of this form and leave it with your doctor. Under this method the doctor agrees to accept the charge determination of the Medicare carrier as the full charge for covered services; you are responsible for the deductible, coinsurance, and non-covered services. Please read Your Medicare Handbook to help you understand about the deductible and coinsurance.

The other way is for Medicare to pay you.—Medicare can also pay you directly—before or after you have paid your doctor. If you submit the claim yourself, fill out Part I and ask your doctor to fill out Part II. If you have an itemized bill from the doctor, you may submit it rather than have the doctor complete Part II. (This form, with Part I completed by you, may be used to send in several itemized bills from different doctors and suppliers.) Bills should show who furnished the services, **the patient's name and number,** dates of services, where the services were furnished, a description of the services, and charges for each separate service. It is helpful if the diagnosis is also shown. Then mail itemized bills and this form to the address shown in the upper left-hand corner. If no address is shown there, use the address listed in Your Medicare Handbook—or get advice from any social security office.

Notice: It is important to keep a record of your claim in case you ever want to inquire about it. Before you send it in, write down the date you mailed it, the services you received, the date and charge for each, and the name of the doctor or supplier who performed the services. Have this information available when you inquire about a claim.

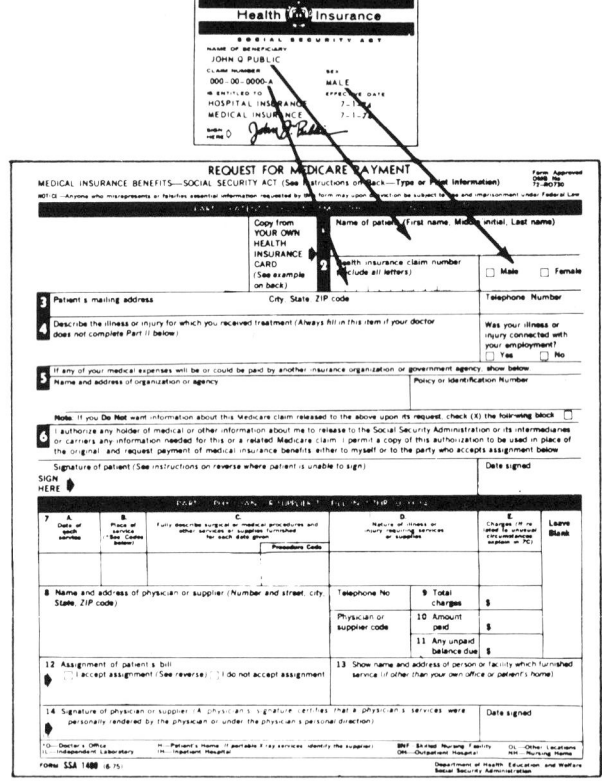

SOME THINGS TO NOTE IN FILLING OUT PART I
(Your doctor will fill out Part II.)

1 & 2 Copy the name and number and indicate your sex exactly as shown on your health insurance card. Include the letters at the end of the number.

3 Enter your mailing address and telephone number, if any.

4 Describe your illness or injury. Be sure to check one of the two boxes.

5 If you have other health insurance or expect a welfare agency to pay part of the expenses, complete item 5.

6 Be sure to sign your name. If you cannot write your name, sign by mark (X), and have the signature witnessed. The witness's signature and address must also be shown in item 6.
If you are filing the claim for a Medicare beneficiary, in item 6 enter the patient's name and write "By", sign your name and enter your address in this space, show your relationship to the patient, and explain why the patient cannot sign. (If the patient has died, the survivor should contact any social security office for information on what to do.)

IMPORTANT NOTES FOR PHYSICIANS AND SUPPLIERS

Item 12: In assigned cases the patient is responsible only for the deductible, coinsurance, and non-covered services. Coinsurance and the deductible are based upon the charge determination of the carrier if this is less than the charge submitted.
This form may also be used by a supplier, or by the patient to claim reimbursement for charges by a supplier for services such as the use of an ambulance or medical appliances.
If the physician or supplier does not want Part II information released to the organization named in item 5, the physician or supplier should write "No further release" in item 7C following the description of services.

COLLECTION AND USE OF MEDICARE INFORMATION

We are authorized by the Social Security Administration to ask you for information needed in the administration of the Medicare program. Social Security's authority to collect information is in section 205(a), 1872 and 1875 of the Social Security Act, as amended.
The information we obtain to complete your Medicare claim is used to identify you and to determine your eligibility. It is also used to decide if the services and supplies you received are covered by Medicare and to insure that proper payment is made.
The information may also be given to other providers of services, carriers, intermediaries, medical review boards, and other organizations as necessary to administer the Medicare program. For example, it may be necessary to disclose information about the Medicare benefits you have used to a hospital or doctor.
With one exception, which is discussed below, there are no penalties under social security law for refusing to supply information. However, failure to furnish information regarding the medical services rendered or the amount charged would prevent payment of the claim. Failure to furnish any other information, such as name or claim number, would delay payment of the claim.
It is mandatory that you tell us if you are being treated for a work related injury so we can determine whether workmen's compensation will pay for the treatment. Section 1877(a)(3) of the Social Security Act provides criminal penalties for withholding this information.

☆U.S. GPO:1976-0-211-071/50

Minutes of the meeting of the Chicago Medical Society held at 8 p.m. on November 13 at the Langdon Hotel.

Members present: Drs. Brian Jones, Warren Taylor, Patricia Perez, Ira Atkins, Noel Allen, Julia Barclay, Cynthia Murphy, James O'Connor, Stella Black, Carl Swenson.

Reading of minutes of previous meeting waived.

Treasurer read financial statement of past year, reporting cash on hand as $2,567.99. Presented budget for coming year, which estimates income from dues as $1,800 and expenditures as $2,500.

Chairperson of Membership Committee reported that 11 members had joined the Society and that 3 applications for membership were on file, to be voted on under new business.

Chairperson of Program Committee outlined plans for the next six meetings. Subjects to be discussed are: 1) pancreatitis, a place for conservative management; 2) ventricular ectopy versus aberrancy; 3) pneumonia, etiologic agents; 4) common dermatologic problems of the feet; 5) ultrasonography for placental imaging; and 6) duodenal examination by fiberoptics. An informal discussion followed and the chairman was instructed to work out more definite plans in accordance with (over) suggestions made in the discussion.

An increase in membership dues from $75 to $100 annually was proposed. No final action was taken.

The three names of the applicants for membership were offered for consideration: all were elected unanimously, and the secretary was instructed to notify each new member.

The meeting was adjourned, upon motion, at 10:45.

Recording Secretary ――――
President ――――

In care and assesment of a neonate's medical needs and nutritional equivalents, the pediatricians and nursery personnel of our hospital institutions have done an outstanding job. With the sophistocated technologic advances in the intensive care approach to the newborn, mortality and morbidity are continually on the decline.

Infections are less and less of a problem; cardiac surgical intervention in the young infants is accomplished daily with less risk. There have truly been more strides in past 10 years than ever before.

"Loving hands," a program of instructional massage for mothers and their new borns is offered as a simple, realistic, inexpensive way to promote early bonding between parent and child. Research now relates to this and confirms that touch and closeness enhance growth and development of newborns particularly premature and sick infants.

ITINERARY

Warren Taylor, M.D.   November 19--

(Chicago, Phoenix, San Diego)

Friday, November 21

(Chicago-Phoenix)

    6:30 p.m., CST   Depart Chicago, O'Hare International, Western Airlines, first class, nonstop flight 164. Dinner.

    8:15 p.m., MST   Arrive Phoenix, Sky Harbor International.

    Accommodation: Mrs. Janis Boeker (sister-in-law), 785 West Sherman Avenue, Phoenix, AZ 85007.

Saturday, November 29

(Phoenix-San Diego)

    11:30 a.m., MST   Depart Phoenix, Sky Harbor International, Western Airlines, coach, nonstop flight 281. Snack.

    12:05 p.m., PST   Arrive San Diego, Charles Lindbergh Field.

    Accommodation: San Diego Heights Hotel, 11199 Berry Knoll, San Diego, CA 92126.

Wednesday, December 3

(San Diego-Chicago)

    4:05 p.m., PST   Depart San Diego, Charles Lindbergh Field, Western Airlines, first class, nonstop flight 192. Dinner.

    10:05 p.m., CST   Arrive Chicago, O'Hare International.

National Medical Society Convention
Address: San Diego Heights Hotel, 11199 Berry Knoll, San Diego, CA 92126

Sunday, November 30

    3 - 5 p.m.   Registration. Main Lobby.

    7:30 p.m.   Opening dinner session with guests. Ambassador Room. (Tickets with airplane reservations.)

Monday, December 1

    8:30 a.m.   General business meeting.

    9:30 a.m.   Coffee; exhibits.

    10:00 a.m.   Presentation: Long-Distance Nurturing of the Family Bond. *John Stoight, M.D., Seattle.* Green Room.

    12:30 p.m.   Lunch with Dean Issacs, M.D., at Lamp Liter, *San Diego Heights Hotel.*

    2:00 p.m.   Panel discussion: Pulmonary Function in Young Smokers. Drs. Lawrence Polend, Galen Becker, Erick Brantford, and Pat Gilman. Talman Room.

    3:15   Exhibits; coffee.

    4:00 p.m.   Presentation: Bronchodilator Therapy & Arterial Blood Gases. *Jerry Stoeker, M.D., St. Paul.* Green Room.

    6:30 p.m.   Central Board Meeting. Dinner. Blue Lounge.

Tuesday, Dec. 2

    8:30 a.m.   Presentation: The Developmentally Disabled Child. David Crossman, M.D., *Phoenix. Talman Room.*

    10:15 a.m.   Exhibits; coffee.

    11:00 a.m.   Presentation: Cerebral Revascularization. Thomas Loming, M.D., Newark. Roosevelt Suite.

    2:00 p.m.   Panel discussion: Detection of Ventricular Ectopy. Drs. Joshua Jonet, Kevin Smithe, Daniel Bloomer, Ed Scanlon. Roosevelt Suite.

    6:30   Dinner at Maxim's with Mrs. Taylor. (Reservations made.)

Wed., Dec. 3

    8:30   General session. Ambassador Room.
    10:15   Exhibits; coffee
    11:00   Presentation: Cardiorespiratory Effects of Flexible Fiberoptic Bronchoscopy. Leonard Westman, M.D., Chicago. Talman Room.

    12:30   Ending session dinner. Daisy Ballroom.

DAILY JOURNAL

DATE November 20 SHEET NO. _____

RECEIPT NUMBER	DATE	DESCRIPTION-CODE	CHARGE	PAYMENT	BALANCE	PREVIOUS BALANCE	NAME
1							
2							
3							
4							
5							
6							
7							
8							
9							
10							
11							
12							
13							
14							
15							
16							
17							
...							
32							
33							
34							

◆ ALL RECEIPTS MUST BE IN NUMERICAL ORDER

PROOF OF POSTING

COLUMN D TOTAL $ _____
"PLUS" COLUMN A TOTAL $ _____
SUB TOTAL $ _____
"MINUS" COL. B TOTAL $ _____
EQUALS COLUMN C TOTAL $ _____

Column A	Column B	Column C	Column D

TOTALS

ACCOUNTS RECEIVABLE CONTROL

PREVIOUS BALANCE $ 3440.75
"PLUS" COLUMN A $ _____
SUB TOTAL $ _____
"MINUS" COL. B TOTAL $ _____
PRESENT ACC'TS REC. BALANCE $ _____

DAILY CASH SUMMARY

OPENING CASH ON HAND AT BEGINNING OF DAY $ _____
CASH RECEIVED DURING DAY $ _____
TOTAL $ _____

FORM NO. 210-1

LITTLE PRESS, INC., MPLS. 55423

WP 93

DAILY JOURNAL

DATE November 21 SHEET NO. _____

RECEIPT NUMBER	DATE	DESCRIPTION-CODE	CHARGE	PAYMENT	BALANCE	PREVIOUS BALANCE	NAME
1							
2							
3							
4							
5							
6							
7							
8							
9							
10							
11							
12							
13							
14							
15							
16							
17							
32							
33							
34							

	Column A	Column B	Column C	Column D
TOTALS				

◆ ALL RECEIPTS MUST BE IN NUMERICAL ORDER

PROOF OF POSTING

COLUMN D TOTAL $ _____
"PLUS" COLUMN A TOTAL $ _____
SUB TOTAL $ _____
"MINUS" COL. B TOTAL $ _____
EQUALS COLUMN C TOTAL $ _____

ACCOUNTS RECEIVABLE CONTROL

PREVIOUS BALANCE $ _____
"PLUS" COLUMN A $ _____
SUB TOTAL $ _____
"MINUS" COL. B TOTAL $ _____
PRESENT ACC'TS REC. BALANCE $ _____

DAILY CASH SUMMARY

OPENING CASH ON HAND AT BEGINNING OF DAY $ _____
CASH RECEIVED DURING DAY $ _____
TOTAL $ _____

FORM NO. 210-1

LITTLE PRESS, INC., MPLS. 55423

WP 95

ATTENDING PHYSICIAN'S PROGRESS REPORT   **WORKERS' COMPENSATION BOARD**

DO NOT USE THIS FORM UNLESS YOU INITIALLY FILED A FIRST REPORT (C-48)

PLEASE PRINT OR TYPE

WCB CASE NO. (If Known)	CARRIER CASE NO. (If Known)	DATE OF INJURY AND TIME	ADDRESS WHERE INJURY OCCURRED (City, Town or Village)	CLAIMANT'S SOC. SEC. NO.

INJURED PERSON	(First Name) (Middle Initial) (Last Name)	AGE	ADDRESS	APT. NO.
EMPLOYER				
INSURANCE CARRIER				

MESSAGE TO DOCTOR

THIS REPORT MUST BE FILED AT INTERVALS OF 22 DAYS OR LESS DURING CONTINUING TREATMENT. SEND ORIGINAL TO WORKERS' COMPENSATION BOARD AND COPY TO INSURANCE CARRIER.

FAILURE TO FILE REPORTS ON TIME MAY RESULT IN YOUR BILL BEING INVALIDATED.

PLEASE COMPLETE THIS FORM IN FULL

THIS IS A (CHECK ONE): ☐ PROGRESS REPORT   ☐ FINAL REPORT

1. DATE(S) OF EXAMINATION ON WHICH REPORT IS BASED   WHEN WILL PATIENT BE SEEN AGAIN?

2. AT TIME OF LAST EXAMINATION
   (a) HAS PATIENT RETURNED TO WORK? ☐ YES ☐ NO   IF "YES" DATE RESUMED REGULAR WORK _____ DATE RESUMED LIMITED WORK _____
   (b) IS PATIENT DISABLED? ☐ YES ☐ NO   If "Yes" check one: ☐ Total disability ☐ Partial disability   ESTIMATE LENGTH OF DISABILITY   Totally disabled until _____ Partially disabled until _____
   NOTE: IF ABLE TO WORK PLEASE ADVISE PATIENT TO CONTACT EMPLOYER.

3. DESCRIBE SUBJECTIVE COMPLAINTS AND PHYSICAL FINDINGS WHEN EXAMINED

4. DESCRIBE TREATMENT RENDERED SINCE LAST REPORT AND PLANNED FUTURE TREATMENT

★ 5. IS AUTHORIZATION FOR SPECIAL SERVICES REQUESTED? (SEE ITEM 3 ON REVERSE) ☐ YES ☐ NO

6. (a) WAS THE OCCURRENCE DESCRIBED IN YOUR INITIAL FORM C-48 THE COMPETENT PRODUCING CAUSE OF THE INJURY AND DISABILITY (IF ANY) SUSTAINED? ☐ YES ☐ NO
   (b) DID YOU FILE AN INITIAL REPORT (FORM C-48) STATING HOW THE INJURY OCCURRED? ☐ YES ☐ NO   IF "NO" ATTACH FORM C-48 TO THIS REPORT

7. MAY THE INJURY RESULT IN PERMANENT RESTRICTION, TOTAL OR PARTIAL LOSS OF FUNCTION OF A PART OR MEMBER, OR PERMANENT FACIAL, HEAD OR NECK DISFIGUREMENT? ☐ YES ☐ NO   IF "YES" DESCRIBE

8. WAS PATIENT HOSPITALIZED SINCE LAST REPORT? IF SO, WHAT HOSPITAL AND WHEN? ☐ YES ☐ NO

9. (a) ANY FACTORS DELAYING RECOVERY? IF "YES" DESCRIBE ☐ YES ☐ NO
   (b) IS MEDICAL AND/OR VOCATIONAL REHABILITATION INDICATED? IF "YES" GIVE DETAILS ☐ YES ☐ NO
   (c) IF "YES" HAS REFERRAL BEEN MADE? (GIVE DETAILS) ☐ YES ☐ NO

10. ENTER HERE ADDITIONAL PERTINENT INFORMATION, WORK LIMITATIONS, IF ANY, ETC.

Dated	Typed or Printed Name of Attending Physician	Address	
WCB Rating Code	WCB Authorization No.	Telephone No.	Written Signature of Attending Physician (Facsimile Not Accepted)

C-4 (11-78)   SEE REVERSE SIDE FOR SPECIAL INSTRUCTIONS

WP 97

IMPORTANT
TO THE ATTENDING PHYSICIAN

1. Progress reports on this form must be filed within 17 days after you first render treatment in a workers' compensation case or a volunteer firemen's benefit case, and thereafter at intervals of 22 days or less during continuing treatment. When patient is seen less frequently, file forms as of date of examination. This form is also to be used for a final report upon termination of treatment.
   THIS FORM IS NOT TO BE USED UNLESS AN INITIAL REPORT (FORM C-48) WAS PREVIOUSLY FILED.

   Please ask your patient for his Workers' Compensation Board Case Number and the Insurance Carrier's Case Number, if they are known to him, and show these numbers on your reports, in the spaces provided.

   File the signed original of this report directly with (1) CHAIRMAN, WORKERS' COMPENSATION BOARD in the district office serving the county in which the accident occurred and file a signed copy with (2) the INSURANCE CARRIER, if known, or the EMPLOYER.

2. This form must be <u>signed personally</u> by the attending physician and must contain his authorization certificate number and code letters. If the patient is hospitalized, it may be signed by a licensed physician to whom the treatment of the case has been assigned as a member of the attending staff of the hospital. A FACSIMILE SIGNATURE IS NOT ACCEPTABLE.

3. **<u>AUTHORIZATION FOR SPECIAL SERVICES</u>:** When it is necessary for the attending physician to engage the services of a specialist, consultant, or a surgeon, or to provide for X-ray examinations or physiotherapeutic or other procedures costing more than $75 or to provide for special diagnostic laboratory tests costing more than $35, he must request and secure authorization from the employer or insurance carrier or the Chairman, as follows:

   a. Telephone the employer or insurance carrier, explain the need for the special services, and request the necessary authorization.

   b. Confirm the request in writing, setting forth the medical necessity for the special services.

   c. The employer or insurance carrier may have the patient examined within four (4) working days of the request for authorization, if the patient is hospitalized, or within twenty-one (21) calendar days if the patient is not hospitalized.

   d. If authorization or denial is not forthcoming within the four working days if the patient is hospitalized, or within the twenty-one calendar days if the patient is not hospitalized, notify the nearest office of the Workers' Compensation Board.

   SUCH AUTHORIZATION IS NOT REQUIRED IN AN EMERGENCY UNDER THE PROVISIONS OF SECTION 13-a (5).

   In cases in which the claimant's physician prescribes a surgical appliance or dental treatment or denture, the physician should notify the employer or carrier of the need for such appliance or dental aid, and direct the claimant to the employer or carrier for the purpose of securing authorization for the purchase of such appliance or dental aid before the same is furnished to the claimant by the appliance dealer or dentist.

4. **<u>PENALTY FOR FALSE REPRESENTATION</u>:** Any person who wilfully makes a false statement or representation on this form shall be guilty of a misdemeanor.

THE WORKERS' COMPENSATION BOARD EMPLOYS AND SERVES THE HANDICAPPED WITHOUT DISCRIMINATION.

C-4 Reverse (11-78)

Procedures	Diagnoses
automated CBC	MI
Hgb (colormetric)	rheumatic heart disease
WBC	contact dermatitis
pro time	epistaxis
routine ECG	otitis media
routine UA	tonsillitis
glucose: blood	diabetes mellitus
simple I & D of abscess	appendicitis
removal of foreign body (external) eye	headache
	cholecystitis
AP + lat. lumbar spine Xray	pneumonia
scoliosis spine Xray	emphysema
humerus Xray	cholelithiasis
PA + lat. chest Xray	infectious mono
profile of 12 blood chemistry tests	hyperthyroidism
	hypothyroidism
	conjunctivitis NEC

Specialty	Specialist	Patient Problem
family medicine		
internal medicine		
cardiology		
dermatology		
endocrinology		
neurology		
gastroenterology		
gynecology		
obstetrics		
urology		
ophthalmology		
oncology		
otorhinolaryngology		
pediatrics		
physical medicine		
proctology		
radiology		
general surgery		
chest surgery		
neurosurgery		
orthopedic surgery		
plastic surgery		

Patient _____ Hospital No. _____ Date _____

Referring Physician _____

HISTORY AND PHYSICAL

WP 103

Patient _____ Hospital No. _____ Date _____

Referring Physician _____

HISTORY AND PHYSICAL

Patient _____ Hospital No. _____ Date _____

Referring Physician _____

DEPARTMENT OF RADIOLOGY / ROENTGEN REPORT

WP 107

Patient _____ Hospital No. _____ Date _____

Referring Physician _____

DEPARTMENT OF RADIOLOGY / ROENTGEN REPORT

WP 109

Patient _____ Hospital No. _____ Date _____

Surgeon _____ 1st Asst. _____ 2d Asst. _____

Operation Began _____ Ended _____ Anesthesia _____

Referring Physician _____ Specimen to Lab _____

PREOPERATIVE DIAGNOSIS:

POSTOPERATIVE DIAGNOSIS:

OPERATIVE PROCEDURE:

OPERATIVE REPORT

WP 111

Patient _____ Hospital No. _____ Date _____

Surgeon _____ 1st Asst. _____ 2d Asst. _____

Operation Began _____ Ended _____ Anesthesia _____

Referring Physician _____ Specimen to Lab _____

PREOPERATIVE DIAGNOSIS:

POSTOPERATIVE DIAGNOSIS:

OPERATIVE PROCEDURE:

OPERATIVE REPORT

WP 113

Patient _____ Hospital No. _____ Date _____

Referring Physician _____

DEPARTMENT OF PATHOLOGY / TISSUE REPORT

WP 115

Patient _____ Hospital No. _____ Date _____

Referring Physician _____

DEPARTMENT OF PATHOLOGY / TISSUE REPORT

WP 117

These X-ray procedures yield pictures of what organs or body areas?

barium enema _____

cholecystogram _____

IVP (intravenous pyelogram) _____

KUB _____

cerebral angiogram _____

AP chest _____

GI series _____

cholangiogram _____

barium swallow _____

Water's projection _____

mammogram _____

femoral arteriogram _____

ventriculogram _____

pneumoencephalogram _____

_____

arthrogram _____

WP 119

December 1, 19--

Dear Miss Owen,

    I will be back in the office on December 5 as planned. I would appreciate not having any patients scheduled before 10:30. I will need time to review the week's activities and to get ready for the residents again.

    I am going to submit my article "Loving Hands" to JAMA for publication. Type the article in manuscript style. Please also write a letter for my signature to accompany the manuscript asking JAMA if they will publish the article.

    Also, type some sample forms for me. I will need samples of release of information, consent forms, release from physical activity for students, and an announcement card for opening a new medical practice. I will be showing these samples to the residents next week. Keep a copy in our own procedures manual.

    See you on the 5th.

Warren Taylor

LOVING HANDS - A Page From the Past

In the care and assessment of a neonate's medical needs and nutritional equivalents, the pediatricians and nursery personnel of our hospital institutions have done an outstanding job. With the sophisticated technologic advances in the intensive care approach to the newborn, mortality and morbidity are continually on the decline. Infections are less and less of a problem; cardiac surgical intervention in the young infants is daily accomplished with less risk. There have truly been more strides in the past ten years than ever before.

We have paid a price for these advances. There is almost no attention given to the thousands of babies who need none of these modern medical miracles, yet they enter this world and are treated just the same as the severely distressed infant. We detach them from what they need most--the closeness of the mother---and put them in plastic boxes, under bright lights, and in sterile nurseries. What a pity! We have missed that critical moment when the bonding of the mother and child has been relegated to a lesser role--we have overlooked the importance of the emotional needs of the infant and mother.

How do you go about this coalescing the best of the new and the old? One simple way is to allow the baby to remain with the mother in close skin-to-skin contact after birth until the baby enters the quiescent stage before going to the nursery if rooming in is not an option.

Another simple method is to encourage maternal stroking and touching. Its amazing how tense and unsure of themselves some mothers are, particularly the primiparas. But actually it could almost be expected since we do nothing to educate people on how to be parents-- only what to expect from the birthing process, the labor, and the delivery.

[5] It seems some mothers, and again usually first-time mothers, need permission to hold their babies close, reassurance that they are doing it correctly and only then are they able to relax and enjoy this miracle that has been created within their own body. Thus it becomes not only appropriate but necessary that these women be led back into the nurturing and bonding process by a class demonstration of infant massage--a class in "Loving Hands."

Many things can be emphasized duing this special time, all aimed at producing a feeling of security for the mother and relaxed contentment of the baby. Emphasis is placed on positioning, with the "en face" position being preferred. The mother is told that any massage routine she finds easiest for her is okay--there is no one way. Areas of anatomy are discussed and they are encouraged to feel the soft spot in the skull and the nipple engorgement that frequently is noted on newborns. They are encouraged to enlist the father in the massaging practice and have him become an emotion provider early in the child's life.

What about outcomes? It has been documented that premature babies will gain quicker, grow faster, develop intellectually at an accelerated pace if fondled, cuddled, talked to, or stroked. I can see a difference at two weeks and certainly by the 2-month checkup. These babies are alert, quietly relaxed, usually enjoy being touched and palpated. The most amazing thing is the eye contact and lack of jerky, startled muscular movements. And the mothers and fathers are so much more attentive and playful with the child during the exam--no signs of indifference or detachment. It's exciting--these infants starting life with such a solid secure emotional basis--only time will tell us what kind of impact society will have on them.

WP 125

5) You say these parents might have been just as good, just as attentive and supportive without the massage classes? Perhaps, or maybe it was the class that partly brought them to this level of commitment, who knows? Is it of any real importance so long as the baby is the benefactor?

SUMMARY

"Loving Hands", a program of instructional massage for mothers and their newborns is offered as a realistic, simple, inexpensive way to promote early bonding between parent and child. Research now confirms that touch and closeness enhance growth and development of newborns, particularly premature and sick infants.

REQUEST FOR MEDICARE PAYMENT

MEDICAL INSURANCE BENEFITS—SOCIAL SECURITY ACT (See Instructions on Back—**Type or Print Information**)

Form Approved
OMB No. 72-R0730

NOTICE—Anyone who misrepresents or falsifies essential information requested by this form may upon conviction be subject to fine and imprisonment under Federal Law.

PART I—PATIENT TO FILL IN ITEMS 1 THROUGH 6 ONLY

Copy from YOUR OWN HEALTH INSURANCE CARD (See example on back)

1 Name of patient (First name, Middle initial, Last name)

2 Health insurance claim number (Include all letters)

1 22 4 77 6 97 B

☐ Male ☐ Female

3 Patient's mailing address — City, State, ZIP code — Telephone Number

4 Describe the illness or injury for which you received treatment (Always fill in this item if your doctor does not complete Part II below)

Was your illness or injury connected with your employment? ☐ Yes ☐ No

5 If any of your medical expenses will be or could be paid by another insurance organization or government agency (including FEHB), show below.
Name and address of organization or agency — Policy or Identification Number

Note: If you **Do Not** want information about this Medicare claim released to the above upon its request, check (X) the following block ☐

6 I authorize any holder of medical or other information about me to release to the Social Security Administration or its intermediaries or carriers any information needed for this or a related Medicare claim. I permit a copy of this authorization to be used in place of the original, and request payment of medical insurance benefits either to myself or to the party who accepts assignment below.

Signature of patient (See instructions on reverse where patient is unable to sign)

SIGN HERE ▶ *Alice Kellogg*

Date signed: 11/29/—

PART II—PHYSICIAN OR SUPPLIER TO FILL IN 7 THROUGH 14

7 A. Date of each service	B. Place of service (*See Codes below)	C. Fully describe surgical or medical procedures and other services or supplies furnished for each date given / Procedure Code	D. Nature of illness or injury requiring services or supplies (diagnosis)	E. Charges (If related to unusual circumstances explain in 7C)	Leave Blank
				$	

8 Name and address of physician or supplier (Number and street, city, State, ZIP code)

Telephone No.	**9** Total charges	$
Physician or supplier code	**10** Amount paid	$
	11 Any unpaid balance due	$

12 Assignment of patient's bill
▶ ☐ I accept assignment (See reverse) ☐ I do not accept assignment.

13 Show name and address of person or facility which furnished service (if other than your own office or patient's home)

14 Signature of physician or supplier (A physician's signature certifies that a physician's services were personally rendered by the physician or under the physician's personal direction)

Date signed

*O—Doctor's Office   H—Patient's Home (If portable X-ray services, identify the supplier)   SNF—Skilled Nursing Facility   OL—Other Locations
IL—Independent Laboratory   IH—Inpatient Hospital   OH—Outpatient Hospital   NH—Nursing Home

FORM SSA 1490 (11-75)

Department of Health, Education, and Welfare
Social Security Administration

WP 129

HOW TO FILL OUT YOUR MEDICARE FORM
There are two ways that Medicare can help pay your doctor bills

One way is for Medicare to pay your doctor.—If you and your doctor agree, Medicare will pay the doctor directly. This is the assignment method. You do not submit any claim; the doctor does. All you do is fill out Part I of this form and leave it with your doctor. Under this method the doctor agrees to accept the charge determination of the Medicare carrier as the full charge for covered services; you are responsible for the deductible, coinsurance, and non-covered services. Please read Your Medicare Handbook to help you understand about the deductible and coinsurance.

The other way is for Medicare to pay you.—Medicare can also pay you directly—before or after you have paid your doctor. If you submit the claim yourself, fill out Part I and ask your doctor to fill out Part II. If you have an itemized bill from the doctor, you may submit it rather than have the doctor complete Part II. (This form, with Part I completed by you, may be used to send in several itemized bills from different doctors and suppliers.) Bills should show who furnished the services, **the patient's name and number,** dates of services, where the services were furnished, a description of the services, and charges for each separate service. It is helpful if the diagnosis is also shown. Then mail itemized bills and this form to the address shown in the upper left-hand corner. If no address is shown there, use the address listed in Your Medicare Handbook—or get advice from any social security office.

Notice: It is important to keep a record of your claim in case you ever want to inquire about it. Before you send it in, write down the date you mailed it, the services you received, the date and charge for each, and the name of the doctor or supplier who performed the services. Have this information available when you inquire about a claim.

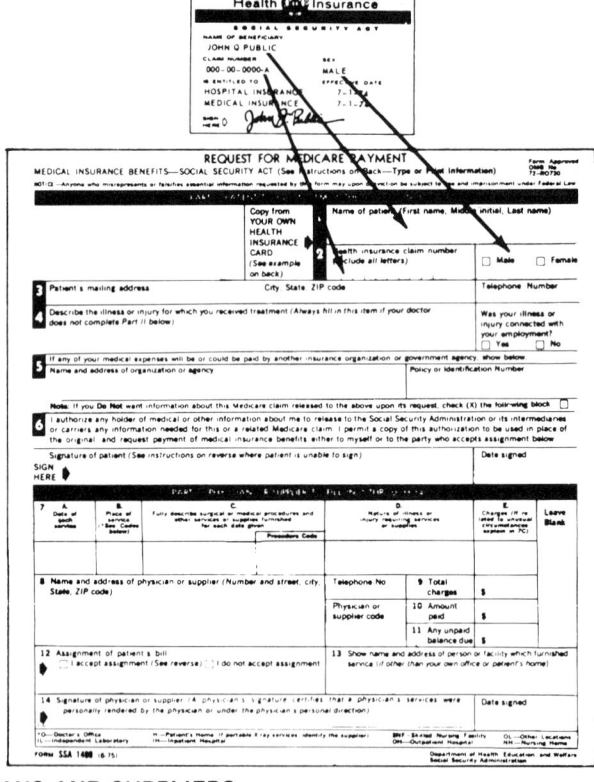

SOME THINGS TO NOTE IN FILLING OUT PART I
(Your doctor will fill out Part II.)

1 & 2 Copy the name and number and indicate your sex exactly as shown on your health insurance card. Include the letters at the end of the number.

3 Enter your mailing address and telephone number, if any.

4 Describe your illness or injury. Be sure to check one of the two boxes.

5 If you have other health insurance or expect a welfare agency to pay part of the expenses, complete item 5.

6 Be sure to sign your name. If you cannot write your name, sign by mark (X), and have the signature witnessed. The witness's signature and address must also be shown in item 6.
If you are filing the claim for a Medicare beneficiary, in item 6 enter the patient's name and write "By", sign your name and enter your address in this space, show your relationship to the patient, and explain why the patient cannot sign. (If the patient has died, the survivor should contact any social security office for information on what to do.)

IMPORTANT NOTES FOR PHYSICIANS AND SUPPLIERS

Item 12: In assigned cases the patient is responsible only for the deductible, coinsurance, and non-covered services. Coinsurance and the deductible are based upon the charge determination of the carrier if this is less than the charge submitted.
This form may also be used by a supplier, or by the patient to claim reimbursement for charges by a supplier for services such as the use of an ambulance or medical appliances.
If the physician or supplier does not want Part II information released to the organization named in item 5, the physician or supplier should write "No further release" in item 7C following the description of services.

COLLECTION AND USE OF MEDICARE INFORMATION

We are authorized by the Social Security Administration to ask you for information needed in the administration of the Medicare program. Social Security's authority to collect information is in section 205(a), 1872 and 1875 of the Social Security Act. as amended.
The information we obtain to complete your Medicare claim is used to identify you and to determine your eligibility. It is also used to decide if the services and supplies you received are covered by Medicare and to insure that proper payment is made.
The information may also be given to other providers of services, carriers, intermediaries, medical review boards, and other organizations as necessary to administer the Medicare program. For example, it may be necessary to disclose information about the Medicare benefits you have used to a hospital or doctor.
With one exception, which is discussed below, there are no penalties under social security law for refusing to supply information. However, failure to furnish information regarding the medical services rendered or the amount charged would prevent payment of the claim. Failure to furnish any other information, such as name or claim number, would delay payment of the claim.
It is mandatory that you tell us if you are being treated for a work related injury so we can determine whether workmen's compensation will pay for the treatment. Section 1877(a)(3) of the Social Security Act provides criminal penalties for withholding this information.

☆U.S. GPO:1976-0-211-071/50

DAILY JOURNAL

DATE *December 3*   SHEET NO. _____

RECEIPT NUMBER	DATE	DESCRIPTION-CODE	CHARGE	PAYMENT	BALANCE	PREVIOUS BALANCE	NAME
1							
2							
3							
4							
5							
6							
7							
8							
9							
10							
11							
12							
13							
14							
15							
16							
17							
32							
33							
34							

◀ ALL RECEIPTS MUST BE IN NUMERICAL ORDER

PROOF OF POSTING

COLUMN D TOTAL $ _____
"PLUS" COLUMN A TOTAL $ _____
SUB TOTAL $ _____
"MINUS" COL. B TOTAL $ _____
EQUALS COLUMN C TOTAL $ _____

Column A	Column B	Column C	Column D

TOTALS

ACCOUNTS RECEIVABLE CONTROL

PREVIOUS BALANCE $ *4719.75*
"PLUS" COLUMN A $ _____
SUB TOTAL $ _____
"MINUS" COL. B TOTAL $ _____
PRESENT ACC'TS REC. BALANCE $ _____

DAILY CASH SUMMARY

OPENING CASH ON HAND AT BEGINNING OF DAY $ _____
CASH RECEIVED DURING DAY $ _____
TOTAL $ _____

FORM NO. 210-1

LITTLE PRESS, INC., MPLS. 55423

WP 131

DAILY JOURNAL

DATE December 5   SHEET NO. _____

RECEIPT NUMBER	DATE	DESCRIPTION-CODE	CHARGE	PAYMENT	BALANCE	PREVIOUS BALANCE	NAME
1							
2							
3							
4							
5							
6							
7							
8							
9							
10							
11							
12							
13							
14							
15							
16							
17							
32							
33							
34							
		TOTALS	Column A	Column B	Column C	Column D	

◄ ALL RECEIPTS MUST BE IN NUMERICAL ORDER

PROOF OF POSTING

COLUMN D TOTAL $ _____
"PLUS" COLUMN A TOTAL $ _____
SUB TOTAL $ _____
"MINUS" COL. B TOTAL $ _____
EQUALS COLUMN C TOTAL $ _____

ACCOUNTS RECEIVABLE CONTROL

PREVIOUS BALANCE $ _____
"PLUS" COLUMN A $ _____
SUB TOTAL $ _____
"MINUS" COL. B TOTAL $ _____
PRESENT ACC'TS REC. BALANCE $ _____

DAILY CASH SUMMARY

OPENING CASH ON HAND AT BEGINNING OF DAY $ _____
CASH RECEIVED DURING DAY $ _____
TOTAL $ _____

FORM NO. 210-1

LITTLE PRESS, INC., MPLS. 55423

WP 133

Blue Cross Blue Shield

PHYSICIAN'S SERVICE REPORT
233 North Michigan Avenue
Chicago, Illinois 60601
312/661-4200

FOR RECIPROCITY USE ONLY

Group and Member ID Number		Patient Number

Patient's Last Name	First Name	Patient's Sex	Patient's Age	Patient's Birth Date	Patient's Marital Status: Married ☐ Single ☐

Member's Last Name	First Name	Member's Address	Street	City	State	Zip

Patient's Relationship to Member: 1—Self 2—Spouse 3—Dependent	Member's Sex	Member's Employer Name	If Accident/Emergency Date: Time:

Is This a Work-Related Case? 0—No 1—Yes 2—Unknown	Where Was Service Rendered? 1—Hospital Inpatient 2—Hospital Outpatient 3—Office 4—Other	Specify if "Other"	Hosp. Admission Date	Discharge Date

Name and Location of Hospital	Is the Patient Covered Under Other Health Insurance? 0—No 2—Unknown 1—Yes 3—Medicare

If Yes, Name and Location Other Insurance Company	Policy Holder's Name	Policy Number

Laboratory/Pathology Services Performed 1—Office 2—Independent Lab 3—Hospital	Name and Address of Lab	Amt. Charged by Lab $

Diagnosis (Place primary diagnosis first, verbal description with ICDA Code, please give LMP date if OB related)

Was Surgery Also Performed?	If Yes, By Whom	Were You the Surgical Assistant?

Name and Address of Referring Physician

SERVICE DATE	DESCRIPTION/PROCEDURE/ANESTHESIA TIME	CPT PROCEDURE CODE	FEE

My Total Fee for the Described Service(s) is $ _____

I Personally Performed the Services Described.

I am a Legally Qualified: ☐ M.D. ☐ D.O. ☐ D.D.S. ☐ D.P.M. ☐ Other:

This Fee: ☐ HAS been paid to me.
☐ HAS NOT been paid to me.

Physician's or Authorized Signature: _____ Date: _____

FOR BS USE ONLY

PLAN CODE	NO.SER.	PAYEE	M.MD.	PT.EX.	CODER	PRO.CD.	COST	MEM.	M/S	S.SEX	IP	MED.	BC	MM	TOB	DB	WP	P/S	Contract Eff. Date	VER. BY / DATE

S. NO.	PTR	DATE OF SERVICE	DIAG. CODE	PROCEDURE CODE	PHYSICIAN'S FEE	V-D-U	END OF SERVICE	TIME	E. PTS.	TS	DESC.
1											
2											
3											
4											
5											

BS-11 Rev. 1-78

WP 135

EXPENSES	WEEKLY	MONTHLY	YEARLY
Rent			
Food			
Utilities (gas, oil, electricity)			
Telephone			
Clothing			
Laundry			
Medical and dental			
Hair and cosmetic supplies			
Recreation			
Gifts			
Contributions (religious and charitable)			
Life insurance			
Car payments			
Car insurance			
Car license			
Car gasoline			
Car maintenance			
Public transportation/parking			
Miscellaneous			

Yearly expenses _____

÷ 12

Monthly expenses _____

Weekly expenses _____

× 4.3

Total _____

Monthly salary _____

Take-home pay _____

WP 137

APPLICATION FOR EMPLOYMENT

Name _____ Date _____

Address _____
              (Street)   (City)   (ZIP Code)

Telephone _____ Social Security No. _____

What position are you applying for? _____

Interested in: Temporary work _____ Full-time _____ Part-time _____ Salary desired _____

Nature of any physical defects _____

Recent illnesses _____ Date of last physical exam _____

EDUCATIONAL HISTORY

Education	School Name and Address	Major Subject	Years Attended/Degree
High School			
Business or Vocational School			
College or University			
Evening or Correspondence School			

Give details of any other educational training _____
_____

Why do you feel qualified for the position for which you are applying? _____
_____

PREVIOUS EMPLOYMENT
(Last employment first)

Dates	Name and Address of Employer	Position and Salary	Reason for Leaving

WP 139

Last Name _____ First Name _____ Address _____

Phone # _____ City _____ State _____ Zip _____

INTRO I

#1. Final Exam _____
#2. Quiz Average
#1= _____ #2= _____ #3= _____
(drop lowest quiz grade)

PROCEDURES:
1. Ad/Ch _____ Wt _____
2. Ht & Wt Worksheet _____
3. Baby Worksheet _____
4. Wt _____ Ch _____ Lgth _____

PROCEDURES COMPLETED   Yes _____ No _____

NUMBER AVERAGE _____
LETTER AVERAGE _____

Date _____

Signature _____

INTRO II

#1. Final Exam _____
#2. Quiz Average
#1= _____ #2= _____ #3= _____
(drop lowest quiz grade)

PROCEDURES:
1. Temp. _____ 2. Pulse _____
3. Resp. _____ 4. B/P _____
5. Vital Sign Sheet _____

PROCEDURES COMPLETED   Yes _____ No _____

NUMBER AVERAGE _____
LETTER AVERAGE _____

Date _____

Signature _____

INTRO III

#1. Final Exam _____
#2. Quiz Average
#1= _____ #2= _____ #3= _____
(drop lowest quiz grade)

PROCEDURES:
1. Use of Phone
   Incoming _____ Hold _____
   Av. Line _____ On Hold _____
2. Take Phone Message _____

PROCEDURES COMPLETED   Yes _____ No _____

NUMBER AVERAGE _____
LETTER AVERAGE _____

Date _____

Signature _____

TELEPHONE MESSAGE

To: _____

You Received a Call From:
_____
Phone No. _____ Ext. _____
☐ Please Phone   ☐ Will Call Again

_____
_____
_____
_____
_____
_____

TAKEN BY	DATE	TIME

TELEPHONE MESSAGE

To: _____

You Received a Call From:
_____
Phone No. _____ Ext. _____
☐ Please Phone   ☐ Will Call Again

_____
_____
_____
_____
_____
_____

TAKEN BY	DATE	TIME

TELEPHONE MESSAGE

To: _____

You Received a Call From:
_____
Phone No. _____ Ext. _____
☐ Please Phone   ☐ Will Call Again

_____
_____
_____
_____
_____
_____

TAKEN BY	DATE	TIME

TELEPHONE MESSAGE

To: _____

You Received a Call From:
_____
Phone No. _____ Ext. _____
☐ Please Phone   ☐ Will Call Again

_____
_____
_____
_____
_____
_____

TAKEN BY	DATE	TIME

WP 141

TELEPHONE MESSAGE

To: _____

You Received a Call From:
_____
Phone No. _____ Ext. _____
☐ Please Phone ☐ Will Call Again

_____
_____
_____
_____
_____
_____

TAKEN BY	DATE	TIME

TELEPHONE MESSAGE

To: _____

You Received a Call From:
_____
Phone No. _____ Ext. _____
☐ Please Phone ☐ Will Call Again

_____
_____
_____
_____
_____
_____

TAKEN BY	DATE	TIME

TELEPHONE MESSAGE

To: _____

You Received a Call From:
_____
Phone No. _____ Ext. _____
☐ Please Phone ☐ Will Call Again

_____
_____
_____
_____
_____
_____

TAKEN BY	DATE	TIME

TELEPHONE MESSAGE

To: _____

You Received a Call From:
_____
Phone No. _____ Ext. _____
☐ Please Phone ☐ Will Call Again

_____
_____
_____
_____
_____
_____

TAKEN BY	DATE	TIME

WP 143

TELEPHONE MESSAGE

To: _____

You Received a Call From:
_____
Phone No. _____ Ext. _____
☐ Please Phone   ☐ Will Call Again

_____
_____
_____
_____
_____
_____

TAKEN BY	DATE	TIME

TELEPHONE MESSAGE

To: _____

You Received a Call From:
_____
Phone No. _____ Ext. _____
☐ Please Phone   ☐ Will Call Again

_____
_____
_____
_____
_____
_____

TAKEN BY	DATE	TIME

TELEPHONE MESSAGE

To: _____

You Received a Call From:
_____
Phone No. _____ Ext. _____
☐ Please Phone   ☐ Will Call Again

_____
_____
_____
_____
_____
_____

TAKEN BY	DATE	TIME

TELEPHONE MESSAGE

To: _____

You Received a Call From:
_____
Phone No. _____ Ext. _____
☐ Please Phone   ☐ Will Call Again

_____
_____
_____
_____
_____
_____

TAKEN BY	DATE	TIME

WP 145

TELEPHONE MESSAGE

To: _____

You Received a Call From:
_____
Phone No. _____ Ext. _____
☐ Please Phone   ☐ Will Call Again

_____
_____
_____
_____
_____

TAKEN BY	DATE	TIME

TELEPHONE MESSAGE

To: _____

You Received a Call From:
_____
Phone No. _____ Ext. _____
☐ Please Phone   ☐ Will Call Again

_____
_____
_____
_____
_____

TAKEN BY	DATE	TIME

TELEPHONE MESSAGE

To: _____

You Received a Call From:
_____
Phone No. _____ Ext. _____
☐ Please Phone   ☐ Will Call Again

_____
_____
_____
_____
_____

TAKEN BY	DATE	TIME

TELEPHONE MESSAGE

To: _____

You Received a Call From:
_____
Phone No. _____ Ext. _____
☐ Please Phone   ☐ Will Call Again

_____
_____
_____
_____
_____

TAKEN BY	DATE	TIME

WP 147

TELEPHONE MESSAGE

To: _____

You Received a Call From:
_____
Phone No. _____ Ext. _____
☐ Please Phone   ☐ Will Call Again

_____
_____
_____
_____
_____
_____

TAKEN BY	DATE	TIME

TELEPHONE MESSAGE

To: _____

You Received a Call From:
_____
Phone No. _____ Ext. _____
☐ Please Phone   ☐ Will Call Again

_____
_____
_____
_____
_____
_____

TAKEN BY	DATE	TIME

TELEPHONE MESSAGE

To: _____

You Received a Call From:
_____
Phone No. _____ Ext. _____
☐ Please Phone   ☐ Will Call Again

_____
_____
_____
_____
_____
_____

TAKEN BY	DATE	TIME

TELEPHONE MESSAGE

To: _____

You Received a Call From:
_____
Phone No. _____ Ext. _____
☐ Please Phone   ☐ Will Call Again

_____
_____
_____
_____
_____
_____

TAKEN BY	DATE	TIME

WP 149

TELEPHONE MESSAGE

To: _____

You Received a Call From:
_____
Phone No. _____ Ext. _____
☐ Please Phone   ☐ Will Call Again

_____
_____
_____
_____
_____
_____

TAKEN BY	DATE	TIME

TELEPHONE MESSAGE

To: _____

You Received a Call From:
_____
Phone No. _____ Ext. _____
☐ Please Phone   ☐ Will Call Again

_____
_____
_____
_____
_____
_____

TAKEN BY	DATE	TIME

TELEPHONE MESSAGE

To: _____

You Received a Call From:
_____
Phone No. _____ Ext. _____
☐ Please Phone   ☐ Will Call Again

_____
_____
_____
_____
_____
_____

TAKEN BY	DATE	TIME

TELEPHONE MESSAGE

To: _____

You Received a Call From:
_____
Phone No. _____ Ext. _____
☐ Please Phone   ☐ Will Call Again

_____
_____
_____
_____
_____
_____

TAKEN BY	DATE	TIME

WP 151

TELEPHONE MESSAGE

To: _____

You Received a Call From:
_____
Phone No. _____ Ext. _____
☐ Please Phone   ☐ Will Call Again

_____
_____
_____
_____
_____

TAKEN BY	DATE	TIME

RECORDS RELEASE

DATE _____

TO _____ DOCTOR OR HOSPITAL _____ ADDRESS _____

I HEREBY AUTHORIZE AND REQUEST YOU TO RELEASE TO _____ DOCTOR OR HOSPITAL _____ ADDRESS _____ THE COMPLETE RECORDS IN YOUR POSSESSION, CONCERNING MY ILLNESS AND/OR TREATMENT DURING THE PERIOD FROM _____ TO _____

SIGNED _____ (PATIENT OR NEAREST RELATIVE)

WITNESS _____ RELATIONSHIP _____

FORM NO. 119   LITTLE PRESS, INC.

TELEPHONE MESSAGE

To: _____

You Received a Call From:
_____
Phone No. _____ Ext. _____
☐ Please Phone   ☐ Will Call Again

_____
_____
_____
_____
_____

TAKEN BY	DATE	TIME

RECORDS RELEASE

DATE _____

TO _____ DOCTOR OR HOSPITAL _____ ADDRESS _____

I HEREBY AUTHORIZE AND REQUEST YOU TO RELEASE TO _____ DOCTOR OR HOSPITAL _____ ADDRESS _____ THE COMPLETE RECORDS IN YOUR POSSESSION, CONCERNING MY ILLNESS AND/OR TREATMENT DURING THE PERIOD FROM _____ TO _____

SIGNED _____ (PATIENT OR NEAREST RELATIVE)

WITNESS _____ RELATIONSHIP _____

FORM NO. 119   LITTLE PRESS, INC.

WP 153

TELEPHONE MESSAGE

To: Dr. Taylor

You Received a Call From:
LAB

Phone No. _____ Ext. _____
☐ Please Phone ☐ Will Call Again
☐ Returned Your Call ☐ Urgent

Marion Wellman — 10/14
Sputum, negative.

TAKEN BY: JO
DATE: 10/20
TIME:

DATE: 10/14/19
PATIENT: Lois Curtis
ADDRESS:
CHARGE TO:
ADDRESS:

APPETITE: good
TEMP: 101 R
PULSE:
RESP:
SLEEP:
BLOOD PRESSURE:
BOWELS:

SYMPTOMS: Ordinary cold. Runny nose. Cough. Mother gave 3 gr. aspirin + juice but no change x 3. Now has earache.

DIAGNOSIS: O: Rt. tympanic membrane inflamed. Nasal tissue swollen. Purulent postnasal discharge. Chest clear. No adenopathy. A: Rt. otitis media. P: Ampicillin

TREATMENT: 125 mgm qid. Decongestant qid. Humidity. Recheck one week.

No. _____ Amount _____

PETTY CASH VOUCHER

_____ 19 ___

For _____

Charge to _____

Approved by   Received by
_____   _____

No. _____ Amount _____

PETTY CASH VOUCHER

_____ 19 ___

For _____

Charge to _____

Approved by   Received by
_____   _____

WP 155

THINGS TO DO TODAY

DATE _____

✓	☐

1 Balance daily journals.
2 Bring ledger cards up to date.
3 Check calendar for next week.
4 Make up deposit slip for payments
5 received yesterday.
6
7
8
9
10
11
12
13
14
15
16
17
18
19
20

DATE _____ 19 ___
PATIENT _____
ADDRESS _____
CHARGE TO _____
ADDRESS _____

APPETITE _____ SLEEP _____ BOWELS _____
TEMP. _____ PULSE _____ RESP. _____ BLOOD PRESSURE _____
SYMPTOMS _____
DIAGNOSIS _____
TREATMENT _____

DATE _____ 19 ___
PATIENT _____
ADDRESS _____
CHARGE TO _____
ADDRESS _____

APPETITE _____ SLEEP _____ BOWELS _____
TEMP. _____ PULSE _____ RESP. _____ BLOOD PRESSURE _____
SYMPTOMS _____
DIAGNOSIS _____
TREATMENT _____

WARREN TAYLOR, M.D.
2235 SOUTH RIDGEWAY AVENUE
CHICAGO, IL 60623

TELEPHONE
312-555-6022

1 _____
2 _____
3 _____
4 _____
5 _____

LITTLE PRESS, INC., MPLS. 55423

NO.	DATE	DESCRIPTION — CODE	CHARGE	PAYMENT	CURRENT BALANCE

PLEASE PAY LAST FIGURE IN THIS COLUMN ◄

BP—Blood Pressure
BS—Blood Sugar
CON—Consultation
CP—Complete Physical Exam
ECG—Electrocardiogram
ER—Emergency Room Call
HC—House Call
HV—Hospital Visit
HGB—Hemoglobin
INJ—Injection
IOA—Insurance on Account
LAB—Laboratory
MIS—Miscellaneous
OVB—Office Visit, Brief
OVE—Office Visit, Extended
OVR—Office Visit, Routine
PS—Pap Smear with Physical
PEPS—Pelvic Exam & Pap Smear
ROA—Rec'd on Account
SPE—Short Physical Exam
TC—Throat Culture
UA—Urinalysis-Chem. or Full

WARREN TAYLOR, M.D.
2235 SOUTH RIDGEWAY AVENUE
CHICAGO, IL 60623

TELEPHONE
312-555-6022

1 _____
2 _____
3 _____
4 _____
5 _____

LITTLE PRESS, INC., MPLS. 55423

NO.	DATE	DESCRIPTION — CODE	CHARGE	PAYMENT	CURRENT BALANCE

PLEASE PAY LAST FIGURE IN THIS COLUMN ◄

BP—Blood Pressure
BS—Blood Sugar
CON—Consultation
CP—Complete Physical Exam
ECG—Electrocardiogram
ER—Emergency Room Call
HC—House Call
HV—Hospital Visit
HGB—Hemoglobin
INJ—Injection
IOA—Insurance on Account
LAB—Laboratory
MIS—Miscellaneous
OVB—Office Visit, Brief
OVE—Office Visit, Extended
OVR—Office Visit, Routine
PS—Pap Smear with Physical
PEPS—Pelvic Exam & Pap Smear
ROA—Rec'd on Account
SPE—Short Physical Exam
TC—Throat Culture
UA—Urinalysis-Chem. or Full

WP 159

WARREN TAYLOR, M.D.
2235 SOUTH RIDGEWAY AVENUE
CHICAGO, IL 60623

TELEPHONE
312-555-6022

NO.	DATE	DESCRIPTION — CODE	CHARGE	PAYMENT	CURRENT BALANCE

LITTLE PRESS, INC., MPLS. 55423

PLEASE PAY LAST FIGURE IN THIS COLUMN ◀

BP—Blood Pressure
BS—Blood Sugar
CON—Consultation
CP—Complete Physical Exam
ECG—Electrocardiogram
ER—Emergency Room Call
HC—House Call
HV—Hospital Visit

HGB—Hemoglobin
INJ—Injection
IOA—Insurance on Account
LAB—Laboratory
MIS—Miscellaneous
OVB—Office Visit, Brief
OVE—Office Visit, Extended

OVR—Office Visit, Routine
PS—Pap Smear with Physical
PEPS—Pelvic Exam & Pap Smear
ROA—Rec'd on Account
SPE—Short Physical Exam
TC—Throat Culture
UA—Urinalysis-Chem. or Full

WARREN TAYLOR, M.D.
2235 SOUTH RIDGEWAY AVENUE
CHICAGO, IL 60623

TELEPHONE
312-555-6022

NO.	DATE	DESCRIPTION — CODE	CHARGE	PAYMENT	CURRENT BALANCE

LITTLE PRESS, INC., MPLS. 55423

PLEASE PAY LAST FIGURE IN THIS COLUMN ◀

BP—Blood Pressure
BS—Blood Sugar
CON—Consultation
CP—Complete Physical Exam
ECG—Electrocardiogram
ER—Emergency Room Call
HC—House Call
HV—Hospital Visit

HGB—Hemoglobin
INJ—Injection
IOA—Insurance on Account
LAB—Laboratory
MIS—Miscellaneous
OVB—Office Visit, Brief
OVE—Office Visit, Extended

OVR—Office Visit, Routine
PS—Pap Smear with Physical
PEPS—Pelvic Exam & Pap Smear
ROA—Rec'd on Account
SPE—Short Physical Exam
TC—Throat Culture
UA—Urinalysis-Chem. or Full

WP 161

WARREN TAYLOR, M.D.
2235 SOUTH RIDGEWAY AVENUE
CHICAGO, IL 60623

TELEPHONE
312-555-6022

1 _____
2 _____
3 _____
4 _____
5 _____

LITTLE PRESS, INC., MPLS. 55423

NO.	DATE	DESCRIPTION — CODE	CHARGE	PAYMENT	CURRENT BALANCE

PLEASE PAY LAST FIGURE IN THIS COLUMN ◀

BP—Blood Pressure
BS—Blood Sugar
CON—Consultation
CP—Complete Physical Exam
ECG—Electrocardiogram
ER—Emergency Room Call
HC—House Call
HV—Hospital Visit

HGB—Hemoglobin
INJ—Injection
IOA—Insurance on Account
LAB—Laboratory
MIS—Miscellaneous
OVB—Office Visit, Brief
OVE—Office Visit, Extended

OVR—Office Visit, Routine
PS—Pap Smear with Physical
PEPS—Pelvic Exam & Pap Smear
ROA—Rec'd on Account
SPE—Short Physical Exam
TC—Throat Culture
UA—Urinalysis-Chem. or Full

WARREN TAYLOR, M.D.
2235 SOUTH RIDGEWAY AVENUE
CHICAGO, IL 60623

TELEPHONE
312-555-6022

1 _____
2 _____
3 _____
4 _____
5 _____

LITTLE PRESS, INC., MPLS. 55423

NO.	DATE	DESCRIPTION — CODE	CHARGE	PAYMENT	CURRENT BALANCE

PLEASE PAY LAST FIGURE IN THIS COLUMN ◀

BP—Blood Pressure
BS—Blood Sugar
CON—Consultation
CP—Complete Physical Exam
ECG—Electrocardiogram
ER—Emergency Room Call
HC—House Call
HV—Hospital Visit

HGB—Hemoglobin
INJ—Injection
IOA—Insurance on Account
LAB—Laboratory
MIS—Miscellaneous
OVB—Office Visit, Brief
OVE—Office Visit, Extended

OVR—Office Visit, Routine
PS—Pap Smear with Physical
PEPS—Pelvic Exam & Pap Smear
ROA—Rec'd on Account
SPE—Short Physical Exam
TC—Throat Culture
UA—Urinalysis-Chem. or Full

WP 163

WARREN TAYLOR, M.D.
2235 SOUTH RIDGEWAY AVENUE
CHICAGO, IL 60623

TELEPHONE
312-555-6022

NO	DATE	DESCRIPTION — CODE	CHARGE	PAYMENT	CURRENT BALANCE

LITTLE PRESS, INC., MPLS. 55423

PLEASE PAY LAST FIGURE IN THIS COLUMN ◀

BP — Blood Pressure
BS — Blood Sugar
CON — Consultation
CP — Complete Physical Exam
ECG — Electrocardiogram
ER — Emergency Room Call
HC — House Call
HV — Hospital Visit

HGB — Hemoglobin
INJ — Injection
IOA — Insurance on Account
LAB — Laboratory
MIS — Miscellaneous
OVB — Office Visit, Brief
OVE — Office Visit, Extended

OVR — Office Visit, Routine
PS — Pap Smear with Physical
PEPS — Pelvic Exam & Pap Smear
ROA — Rec'd on Account
SPE — Short Physical Exam
TC — Throat Culture
UA — Urinalysis-Chem. or Full

WARREN TAYLOR, M.D.
2235 SOUTH RIDGEWAY AVENUE
CHICAGO, IL 60623

TELEPHONE
312-555-6022

NO	DATE	DESCRIPTION — CODE	CHARGE	PAYMENT	CURRENT BALANCE

LITTLE PRESS, INC., MPLS. 55423

PLEASE PAY LAST FIGURE IN THIS COLUMN ◀

BP — Blood Pressure
BS — Blood Sugar
CON — Consultation
CP — Complete Physical Exam
ECG — Electrocardiogram
ER — Emergency Room Call
HC — House Call
HV — Hospital Visit

HGB — Hemoglobin
INJ — Injection
IOA — Insurance on Account
LAB — Laboratory
MIS — Miscellaneous
OVB — Office Visit, Brief
OVE — Office Visit, Extended

OVR — Office Visit, Routine
PS — Pap Smear with Physical
PEPS — Pelvic Exam & Pap Smear
ROA — Rec'd on Account
SPE — Short Physical Exam
TC — Throat Culture
UA — Urinalysis-Chem. or Full

WP 165

WARREN TAYLOR, M.D.
2235 SOUTH RIDGEWAY AVENUE
CHICAGO, IL 60623

TELEPHONE
312-555-8022

1 _____
2 _____
3 _____
4 _____
5 _____

LITTLE PRESS, INC., MPLS. 55423

NO.	DATE	DESCRIPTION — CODE	CHARGE	PAYMENT	CURRENT BALANCE

PLEASE PAY LAST FIGURE IN THIS COLUMN ◄

BP — Blood Pressure
BS — Blood Sugar
CON — Consultation
CP — Complete Physical Exam
ECG — Electrocardiogram
ER — Emergency Room Call
HC — House Call
HV — Hospital Visit

HGB — Hemoglobin
INJ — Injection
IOA — Insurance on Account
LAB — Laboratory
MIS — Miscellaneous
OVB — Office Visit, Brief
OVE — Office Visit, Extended

OVR — Office Visit, Routine
PS — Pap Smear with Physical
PEPS — Pelvic Exam & Pap Smear
ROA — Rec'd on Account
SPE — Short Physical Exam
TC — Throat Culture
UA — Urinalysis-Chem. or Full

WARREN TAYLOR, M.D.
2235 SOUTH RIDGEWAY AVENUE
CHICAGO, IL 60623

TELEPHONE
312-555-8022

1 _____
2 _____
3 _____
4 _____
5 _____

LITTLE PRESS, INC., MPLS. 55423

NO.	DATE	DESCRIPTION — CODE	CHARGE	PAYMENT	CURRENT BALANCE

PLEASE PAY LAST FIGURE IN THIS COLUMN ◄

BP — Blood Pressure
BS — Blood Sugar
CON — Consultation
CP — Complete Physical Exam
ECG — Electrocardiogram
ER — Emergency Room Call
HC — House Call
HV — Hospital Visit

HGB — Hemoglobin
INJ — Injection
IOA — Insurance on Account
LAB — Laboratory
MIS — Miscellaneous
OVB — Office Visit, Brief
OVE — Office Visit, Extended

OVR — Office Visit, Routine
PS — Pap Smear with Physical
PEPS — Pelvic Exam & Pap Smear
ROA — Rec'd on Account
SPE — Short Physical Exam
TC — Throat Culture
UA — Urinalysis-Chem. or Full

WP 167

TELEPHONE
312-555-6022

WARREN TAYLOR, M.D.
2235 SOUTH RIDGEWAY AVENUE
CHICAGO, IL 60623

1 _____
2 _____
3 _____
4 _____
5 _____

LITTLE PRESS, INC., MPLS. 55423

NO.	DATE	DESCRIPTION — CODE	CHARGE	PAYMENT	CURRENT BALANCE

PLEASE PAY LAST FIGURE IN THIS COLUMN ◀

BP — Blood Pressure
BS — Blood Sugar
CON — Consultation
CP — Complete Physical Exam
ECG — Electrocardiogram
ER — Emergency Room Call
HC — House Call
HV — Hospital Visit

HGB — Hemoglobin
INJ — Injection
IOA — Insurance on Account
LAB — Laboratory
MIS — Miscellaneous
OVB — Office Visit, Brief
OVE — Office Visit, Extended

OVR — Office Visit, Routine
PS — Pap Smear with Physical
PEPS — Pelvic Exam & Pap Smear
ROA — Rec'd on Account
SPE — Short Physical Exam
TC — Throat Culture
UA — Urinalysis-Chem. or Full

TELEPHONE
312-555-6022

WARREN TAYLOR, M.D.
2235 SOUTH RIDGEWAY AVENUE
CHICAGO, IL 60623

1 _____
2 _____
3 _____
4 _____
5 _____

LITTLE PRESS, INC., MPLS. 55423

NO.	DATE	DESCRIPTION — CODE	CHARGE	PAYMENT	CURRENT BALANCE

PLEASE PAY LAST FIGURE IN THIS COLUMN ◀

BP — Blood Pressure
BS — Blood Sugar
CON — Consultation
CP — Complete Physical Exam
ECG — Electrocardiogram
ER — Emergency Room Call
HC — House Call
HV — Hospital Visit

HGB — Hemoglobin
INJ — Injection
IOA — Insurance on Account
LAB — Laboratory
MIS — Miscellaneous
OVB — Office Visit, Brief
OVE — Office Visit, Extended

OVR — Office Visit, Routine
PS — Pap Smear with Physical
PEPS — Pelvic Exam & Pap Smear
ROA — Rec'd on Account
SPE — Short Physical Exam
TC — Throat Culture
UA — Urinalysis-Chem. or Full

WP 169

WARREN TAYLOR, M.D.
2235 SOUTH RIDGEWAY AVENUE
CHICAGO, IL 60623

TELEPHONE
312-555-6022

1 _____
2 _____
3 _____
4 _____
5 _____

LITTLE PRESS, INC., MPLS. 55423

NO.	DATE	DESCRIPTION – CODE	CHARGE	PAYMENT	CURRENT BALANCE

BP – Blood Pressure
BS – Blood Sugar
CON – Consultation
CP – Complete Physical Exam
ECG – Electrocardiogram
ER – Emergency Room Call
HC – House Call
HV – Hospital Visit

HGB – Hemoglobin
INJ – Injection
IOA – Insurance on Account
LAB – Laboratory
MIS – Miscellaneous
OVB – Office Visit, Brief
OVE – Office Visit, Extended

OVR – Office Visit, Routine
PS – Pap Smear with Physical
PEPS – Pelvic Exam & Pap Smear
ROA – Rec'd on Account
SPE – Short Physical Exam
TC – Throat Culture
UA – Urinalysis-Chem. or Full

PLEASE PAY LAST FIGURE IN THIS COLUMN ◀

WARREN TAYLOR, M.D.
2235 SOUTH RIDGEWAY AVENUE
CHICAGO, IL 60623

TELEPHONE
312-555-6022

1 _____
2 _____
3 _____
4 _____
5 _____

LITTLE PRESS, INC., MPLS. 55423

NO.	DATE	DESCRIPTION – CODE	CHARGE	PAYMENT	CURRENT BALANCE

BP – Blood Pressure
BS – Blood Sugar
CON – Consultation
CP – Complete Physical Exam
ECG – Electrocardiogram
ER – Emergency Room Call
HC – House Call
HV – Hospital Visit

HGB – Hemoglobin
INJ – Injection
IOA – Insurance on Account
LAB – Laboratory
MIS – Miscellaneous
OVB – Office Visit, Brief
OVE – Office Visit, Extended

OVR – Office Visit, Routine
PS – Pap Smear with Physical
PEPS – Pelvic Exam & Pap Smear
ROA – Rec'd on Account
SPE – Short Physical Exam
TC – Throat Culture
UA – Urinalysis-Chem. or Full

PLEASE PAY LAST FIGURE IN THIS COLUMN ◀

WP 171

WARREN TAYLOR, M.D.
2235 SOUTH RIDGEWAY AVENUE
CHICAGO, IL 60623

TELEPHONE
312-555-6022

1 _____
2 _____
3 _____
4 _____
5 _____

LITTLE PRESS, INC., MPLS. 55423

NO.	DATE	DESCRIPTION — CODE	CHARGE	PAYMENT	CURRENT BALANCE

PLEASE PAY LAST FIGURE IN THIS COLUMN ◄

BP—Blood Pressure
BS—Blood Sugar
CON—Consultation
CP—Complete Physical Exam
ECG—Electrocardiogram
ER—Emergency Room Call
HC—House Call
HV—Hospital Visit

HGB—Hemoglobin
INJ—Injection
IOA—Insurance on Account
LAB—Laboratory
MIS—Miscellaneous
OVB—Office Visit, Brief
OVE—Office Visit, Extended

OVR—Office Visit, Routine
PS—Pap Smear with Physical
PEPS—Pelvic Exam & Pap Smear
ROA—Rec'd on Account
SPE—Short Physical Exam
TC—Throat Culture
UA—Urinalysis-Chem. or Full

WARREN TAYLOR, M.D.
2235 SOUTH RIDGEWAY AVENUE
CHICAGO, IL 60623

TELEPHONE
312-555-6022

1 _____
2 _____
3 _____
4 _____
5 _____

LITTLE PRESS, INC., MPLS. 55423

NO.	DATE	DESCRIPTION — CODE	CHARGE	PAYMENT	CURRENT BALANCE

PLEASE PAY LAST FIGURE IN THIS COLUMN ◄

BP—Blood Pressure
BS—Blood Sugar
CON—Consultation
CP—Complete Physical Exam
ECG—Electrocardiogram
ER—Emergency Room Call
HC—House Call
HV—Hospital Visit

HGB—Hemoglobin
INJ—Injection
IOA—Insurance on Account
LAB—Laboratory
MIS—Miscellaneous
OVB—Office Visit, Brief
OVE—Office Visit, Extended

OVR—Office Visit, Routine
PS—Pap Smear with Physical
PEPS—Pelvic Exam & Pap Smear
ROA—Rec'd on Account
SPE—Short Physical Exam
TC—Throat Culture
UA—Urinalysis-Chem. or Full

WP 173

TELEPHONE
312-555-6022

WARREN TAYLOR, M.D.
2235 SOUTH RIDGEWAY AVENUE
CHICAGO, IL 60623

1 _____
2 _____
3 _____
4 _____
5 _____

LITTLE PRESS, INC., MPLS. 55423

NO.	DATE	DESCRIPTION — CODE	CHARGE	PAYMENT	CURRENT BALANCE

BP—Blood Pressure
BS—Blood Sugar
CON—Consultation
CP—Complete Physical Exam
ECG—Electrocardiogram
ER—Emergency Room Call
HC—House Call
HV—Hospital Visit

HGB—Hemoglobin
INJ—Injection
IOA—Insurance on Account
LAB—Laboratory
MIS—Miscellaneous
OVB—Office Visit, Brief
OVE—Office Visit, Extended

OVR—Office Visit, Routine
PS—Pap Smear with Physical
PEPS—Pelvic Exam & Pap Smear
ROA—Rec'd on Account
SPE—Short Physical Exam
TC—Throat Culture
UA—Urinalysis-Chem. or Full

PLEASE PAY LAST FIGURE IN THIS COLUMN ←

TELEPHONE
312-555-6022

WARREN TAYLOR, M.D.
2235 SOUTH RIDGEWAY AVENUE
CHICAGO, IL 60623

1 _____
2 _____
3 _____
4 _____
5 _____

LITTLE PRESS, INC., MPLS. 55423

NO.	DATE	DESCRIPTION — CODE	CHARGE	PAYMENT	CURRENT BALANCE

BP—Blood Pressure
BS—Blood Sugar
CON—Consultation
CP—Complete Physical Exam
ECG—Electrocardiogram
ER—Emergency Room Call
HC—House Call
HV—Hospital Visit

HGB—Hemoglobin
INJ—Injection
IOA—Insurance on Account
LAB—Laboratory
MIS—Miscellaneous
OVB—Office Visit, Brief
OVE—Office Visit, Extended

OVR—Office Visit, Routine
PS—Pap Smear with Physical
PEPS—Pelvic Exam & Pap Smear
ROA—Rec'd on Account
SPE—Short Physical Exam
TC—Throat Culture
UA—Urinalysis-Chem. or Full

PLEASE PAY LAST FIGURE IN THIS COLUMN ←

WP 175

TELEPHONE
312-555-6022

WARREN TAYLOR, M.D.
2235 SOUTH RIDGEWAY AVENUE
CHICAGO, IL 60623

1 _____
2 _____
3 _____
4 _____
5 _____

LITTLE PRESS, INC., MPLS. 55423

NO.	DATE	DESCRIPTION — CODE	CHARGE	PAYMENT	CURRENT BALANCE

PLEASE PAY LAST FIGURE IN THIS COLUMN ◄

BP—Blood Pressure
BS—Blood Sugar
CON—Consultation
CP—Complete Physical Exam
ECG—Electrocardiogram
ER—Emergency Room Call
HC—House Call
HV—Hospital Visit

HGB—Hemoglobin
INJ—Injection
IOA—Insurance on Account
LAB—Laboratory
MIS—Miscellaneous
OVB—Office Visit, Brief
OVE—Office Visit, Extended

OVR—Office Visit, Routine
PS—Pap Smear with Physical
PEPS—Pelvic Exam & Pap Smear
ROA—Rec'd on Account
SPE—Short Physical Exam
TC—Throat Culture
UA—Urinalysis-Chem. or Full

TELEPHONE
312-555-6022

WARREN TAYLOR, M.D.
2235 SOUTH RIDGEWAY AVENUE
CHICAGO, IL 60623

1 _____
2 _____
3 _____
4 _____
5 _____

LITTLE PRESS, INC., MPLS. 55423

NO.	DATE	DESCRIPTION — CODE	CHARGE	PAYMENT	CURRENT BALANCE

PLEASE PAY LAST FIGURE IN THIS COLUMN ◄

BP—Blood Pressure
BS—Blood Sugar
CON—Consultation
CP—Complete Physical Exam
ECG—Electrocardiogram
ER—Emergency Room Call
HC—House Call
HV—Hospital Visit

HGB—Hemoglobin
INJ—Injection
IOA—Insurance on Account
LAB—Laboratory
MIS—Miscellaneous
OVB—Office Visit, Brief
OVE—Office Visit, Extended

OVR—Office Visit, Routine
PS—Pap Smear with Physical
PEPS—Pelvic Exam & Pap Smear
ROA—Rec'd on Account
SPE—Short Physical Exam
TC—Throat Culture
UA—Urinalysis-Chem. or Full

WP 177

WARREN TAYLOR, M.D.
2235 SOUTH RIDGEWAY AVENUE
CHICAGO, IL 60623

TELEPHONE
312-555-6022

1 _____
2 _____
3 _____
4 _____
5 _____

NO.	DATE	DESCRIPTION—CODE	CHARGE	PAYMENT	CURRENT BALANCE

LITTLE PRESS, INC., MPLS. 55423

PLEASE PAY LAST FIGURE IN THIS COLUMN ⬅

BP—Blood Pressure
BS—Blood Sugar
CON—Consultation
CP—Complete Physical Exam
ECG—Electrocardiogram
ER—Emergency Room Call
HC—House Call
HV—Hospital Visit

HGB—Hemoglobin
INJ—Injection
IOA—Insurance on Account
LAB—Laboratory
MIS—Miscellaneous
OVB—Office Visit, Brief
OVE—Office Visit, Extended

OVR—Office Visit, Routine
PS—Pap Smear with Physical
PEPS—Pelvic Exam & Pap Smear
ROA—Rec'd on Account
SPE—Short Physical Exam
TC—Throat Culture
UA—Urinalysis-Chem. or Full

WARREN TAYLOR, M.D.
2235 SOUTH RIDGEWAY AVENUE
CHICAGO, IL 60623

TELEPHONE
312-555-6022

1 _____
2 _____
3 _____
4 _____
5 _____

NO.	DATE	DESCRIPTION—CODE	CHARGE	PAYMENT	CURRENT BALANCE

LITTLE PRESS, INC., MPLS. 55423

PLEASE PAY LAST FIGURE IN THIS COLUMN ⬅

BP—Blood Pressure
BS—Blood Sugar
CON—Consultation
CP—Complete Physical Exam
ECG—Electrocardiogram
ER—Emergency Room Call
HC—House Call
HV—Hospital Visit

HGB—Hemoglobin
INJ—Injection
IOA—Insurance on Account
LAB—Laboratory
MIS—Miscellaneous
OVB—Office Visit, Brief
OVE—Office Visit, Extended

OVR—Office Visit, Routine
PS—Pap Smear with Physical
PEPS—Pelvic Exam & Pap Smear
ROA—Rec'd on Account
SPE—Short Physical Exam
TC—Throat Culture
UA—Urinalysis-Chem. or Full

WP 179

TELEPHONE
312-555-6022

WARREN TAYLOR, M.D.
2235 SOUTH RIDGEWAY AVENUE
CHICAGO, IL 60623

1 _____
2 _____
3 _____
4 _____
5 _____

LITTLE PRESS, INC., MPLS. 55423

NO	DATE	DESCRIPTION — CODE	CHARGE	PAYMENT	CURRENT BALANCE

PLEASE PAY LAST FIGURE IN THIS COLUMN ◀

BP — Blood Pressure
BS — Blood Sugar
CON — Consultation
CP — Complete Physical Exam
ECG — Electrocardiogram
ER — Emergency Room Call
HC — House Call
HV — Hospital Visit

HGB — Hemoglobin
INJ — Injection
IOA — Insurance on Account
LAB — Laboratory
MIS — Miscellaneous
OVB — Office Visit, Brief
OVE — Office Visit, Extended

OVR — Office Visit, Routine
PS — Pap Smear with Physical
PEPS — Pelvic Exam & Pap Smear
ROA — Rec'd on Account
SPE — Short Physical Exam
TC — Throat Culture
UA — Urinalysis-Chem. or Full

TELEPHONE
312-555-6022

WARREN TAYLOR, M.D.
2235 SOUTH RIDGEWAY AVENUE
CHICAGO, IL 60623

1 _____
2 _____
3 _____
4 _____
5 _____

LITTLE PRESS, INC., MPLS. 55423

NO	DATE	DESCRIPTION — CODE	CHARGE	PAYMENT	CURRENT BALANCE

PLEASE PAY LAST FIGURE IN THIS COLUMN ◀

BP — Blood Pressure
BS — Blood Sugar
CON — Consultation
CP — Complete Physical Exam
ECG — Electrocardiogram
ER — Emergency Room Call
HC — House Call
HV — Hospital Visit

HGB — Hemoglobin
INJ — Injection
IOA — Insurance on Account
LAB — Laboratory
MIS — Miscellaneous
OVB — Office Visit, Brief
OVE — Office Visit, Extended

OVR — Office Visit, Routine
PS — Pap Smear with Physical
PEPS — Pelvic Exam & Pap Smear
ROA — Rec'd on Account
SPE — Short Physical Exam
TC — Throat Culture
UA — Urinalysis-Chem. or Full

WP 181

WARREN TAYLOR, M.D.
2235 SOUTH RIDGEWAY AVENUE
CHICAGO, IL 60623

TELEPHONE
312-555-6022

1 _____
2 _____
3 _____
4 _____
5 _____

LITTLE PRESS, INC., MPLS. 55423

NO.	DATE	DESCRIPTION—CODE	CHARGE	PAYMENT	CURRENT BALANCE

PLEASE PAY LAST FIGURE IN THIS COLUMN ◀

BP—Blood Pressure
BS—Blood Sugar
CON—Consultation
CP—Complete Physical Exam
ECG—Electrocardiogram
ER—Emergency Room Call
HC—House Call
HV—Hospital Visit

HGB—Hemoglobin
INJ—Injection
IOA—Insurance on Account
LAB—Laboratory
MIS—Miscellaneous
OVB—Office Visit, Brief
OVE—Office Visit, Extended

OVR—Office Visit, Routine
PS—Pap Smear with Physical
PEPS—Pelvic Exam & Pap Smear
ROA—Rec'd on Account
SPE—Short Physical Exam
TC—Throat Culture
UA—Urinalysis-Chem. or Full

WARREN TAYLOR, M.D.
2235 SOUTH RIDGEWAY AVENUE
CHICAGO, IL 60623

TELEPHONE
312-555-6022

1 _____
2 _____
3 _____
4 _____
5 _____

LITTLE PRESS, INC., MPLS. 55423

NO.	DATE	DESCRIPTION—CODE	CHARGE	PAYMENT	CURRENT BALANCE

PLEASE PAY LAST FIGURE IN THIS COLUMN ◀

BP—Blood Pressure
BS—Blood Sugar
CON—Consultation
CP—Complete Physical Exam
ECG—Electrocardiogram
ER—Emergency Room Call
HC—House Call
HV—Hospital Visit

HGB—Hemoglobin
INJ—Injection
IOA—Insurance on Account
LAB—Laboratory
MIS—Miscellaneous
OVB—Office Visit, Brief
OVE—Office Visit, Extended

OVR—Office Visit, Routine
PS—Pap Smear with Physical
PEPS—Pelvic Exam & Pap Smear
ROA—Rec'd on Account
SPE—Short Physical Exam
TC—Throat Culture
UA—Urinalysis-Chem. or Full

WP 183

WARREN TAYLOR, M.D.
2235 SOUTH RIDGEWAY AVENUE
CHICAGO, IL 60623

TELEPHONE
312-555-8022

1 _____
2 _____
3 _____
4 _____
5 _____

LITTLE PRESS, INC., MPLS. 55423

NO.	DATE	DESCRIPTION — CODE	CHARGE	PAYMENT	CURRENT BALANCE

PLEASE PAY LAST FIGURE IN THIS COLUMN ◆

BP—Blood Pressure
BS—Blood Sugar
CON—Consultation
CP—Complete Physical Exam
ECG—Electrocardiogram
ER—Emergency Room Call
HC—House Call
HV—Hospital Visit

HGB—Hemoglobin
INJ—Injection
IOA—Insurance on Account
LAB—Laboratory
MIS—Miscellaneous
OVB—Office Visit, Brief
OVE—Office Visit, Extended

OVR—Office Visit, Routine
PS—Pap Smear with Physical
PEPS—Pelvic Exam & Pap Smear
ROA—Rec'd on Account
SPE—Short Physical Exam
TC—Throat Culture
UA—Urinalysis-Chem. or Full

WARREN TAYLOR, M.D.
2235 SOUTH RIDGEWAY AVENUE
CHICAGO, IL 60623

TELEPHONE
312-555-8022

1 _____
2 _____
3 _____
4 _____
5 _____

LITTLE PRESS, INC., MPLS. 55423

NO.	DATE	DESCRIPTION — CODE	CHARGE	PAYMENT	CURRENT BALANCE

PLEASE PAY LAST FIGURE IN THIS COLUMN ◆

BP—Blood Pressure
BS—Blood Sugar
CON—Consultation
CP—Complete Physical Exam
ECG—Electrocardiogram
ER—Emergency Room Call
HC—House Call
HV—Hospital Visit

HGB—Hemoglobin
INJ—Injection
IOA—Insurance on Account
LAB—Laboratory
MIS—Miscellaneous
OVB—Office Visit, Brief
OVE—Office Visit, Extended

OVR—Office Visit, Routine
PS—Pap Smear with Physical
PEPS—Pelvic Exam & Pap Smear
ROA—Rec'd on Account
SPE—Short Physical Exam
TC—Throat Culture
UA—Urinalysis-Chem. or Full

WP 185

TELEPHONE
312-555-6022

WARREN TAYLOR, M.D.
2235 SOUTH RIDGEWAY AVENUE
CHICAGO, IL 60623

1 _____
2 _____
3 _____
4 _____
5 _____

LITTLE PRESS, INC., MPLS. 55423

NO	DATE	DESCRIPTION — CODE	CHARGE	PAYMENT	CURRENT BALANCE

PLEASE PAY LAST FIGURE IN THIS COLUMN ◀

BP—Blood Pressure
BS—Blood Sugar
CON—Consultation
CP—Complete Physical Exam
ECG—Electrocardiogram
ER—Emergency Room Call
HC—House Call
HV—Hospital Visit

HGB—Hemoglobin
INJ—Injection
IOA—Insurance on Account
LAB—Laboratory
MIS—Miscellaneous
OVB—Office Visit, Brief
OVE—Office Visit, Extended

OVR—Office Visit, Routine
PS—Pap Smear with Physical
PEPS—Pelvic Exam & Pap Smear
ROA—Rec'd on Account
SPE—Short Physical Exam
TC—Throat Culture
UA—Urinalysis-Chem. or Full

TELEPHONE
312-555-6022

WARREN TAYLOR, M.D.
2235 SOUTH RIDGEWAY AVENUE
CHICAGO, IL 60623

1 _____
2 _____
3 _____
4 _____
5 _____

LITTLE PRESS, INC., MPLS. 55423

NO	DATE	DESCRIPTION — CODE	CHARGE	PAYMENT	CURRENT BALANCE

PLEASE PAY LAST FIGURE IN THIS COLUMN ◀

BP—Blood Pressure
BS—Blood Sugar
CON—Consultation
CP—Complete Physical Exam
ECG—Electrocardiogram
ER—Emergency Room Call
HC—House Call
HV—Hospital Visit

HGB—Hemoglobin
INJ—Injection
IOA—Insurance on Account
LAB—Laboratory
MIS—Miscellaneous
OVB—Office Visit, Brief
OVE—Office Visit, Extended

OVR—Office Visit, Routine
PS—Pap Smear with Physical
PEPS—Pelvic Exam & Pap Smear
ROA—Rec'd on Account
SPE—Short Physical Exam
TC—Throat Culture
UA—Urinalysis-Chem. or Full

WP 187

Appointment Card (×12)

YOUR APPOINTMENT IS _____ AT _____

WARREN TAYLOR, M.D.
2235 South Ridgeway Avenue
Chicago, IL 60623
312/555-6022

THE ABOVE TIME HAS BEEN RESERVED. IF UNABLE TO USE THIS RESERVATION PLEASE NOTIFY THE OFFICE AT WHICH YOUR APPOINTMENT WAS MADE.

WP 189

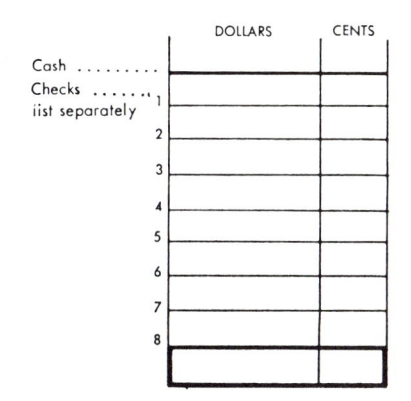

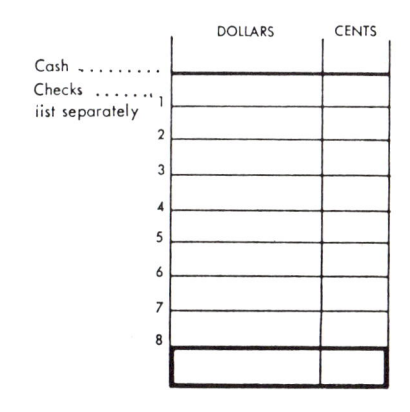

DEPOSITED IN
First National Bank
THIS DEPOSIT ACCEPTED UNDER AND SUBJECT TO THE PROVISIONS OF THE UNIFORM COMMERCIAL CODE.
DATE_____

Warren Taylor, M.D.
2235 South Ridgeway Avenue
Chicago, IL 60623

⑀0710⑀0062 242⑀027720⑀

	DOLLARS	CENTS
Cash		
Checks 1		
list separately 2		
3		
4		
5		
6		
7		
8		

DEPOSITED IN
First National Bank
THIS DEPOSIT ACCEPTED UNDER AND SUBJECT TO THE PROVISIONS OF THE UNIFORM COMMERCIAL CODE.
DATE_____

Warren Taylor, M.D.
2235 South Ridgeway Avenue
Chicago, IL 60623

⑀0710⑀0062 242⑀027720⑀

	DOLLARS	CENTS
Cash		
Checks 1		
list separately 2		
3		
4		
5		
6		
7		
8		

DEPOSITED IN
First National Bank
THIS DEPOSIT ACCEPTED UNDER AND SUBJECT TO THE PROVISIONS OF THE UNIFORM COMMERCIAL CODE.
DATE_____

Warren Taylor, M.D.
2235 South Ridgeway Avenue
Chicago, IL 60623

⑀0710⑀0062 242⑀027720⑀

	DOLLARS	CENTS
Cash		
Checks 1		
list separately 2		
3		
4		
5		
6		
7		
8		

DEPOSITED IN
First National Bank
THIS DEPOSIT ACCEPTED UNDER AND SUBJECT TO THE PROVISIONS OF THE UNIFORM COMMERCIAL CODE.
DATE_____

Warren Taylor, M.D.
2235 South Ridgeway Avenue
Chicago, IL 60623

⑀0710⑀0062 242⑀027720⑀

	DOLLARS	CENTS
Cash		
Checks 1		
list separately 2		
3		
4		
5		
6		
7		
8		

WP 191

DEPOSITED IN
First National Bank
THIS DEPOSIT ACCEPTED UNDER AND SUBJECT TO THE PROVISIONS OF THE UNIFORM COMMERCIAL CODE.
DATE _____

Warren Taylor, M.D.
2235 South Ridgeway Avenue
Chicago, IL 60623

⑇0710⑇0062 242⑇027720⑇

	DOLLARS	CENTS
Cash		
Checks 1		
iist separately		
2		
3		
4		
5		
6		
7		
8		

DEPOSITED IN
First National Bank
THIS DEPOSIT ACCEPTED UNDER AND SUBJECT TO THE PROVISIONS OF THE UNIFORM COMMERCIAL CODE.
DATE _____

Warren Taylor, M.D.
2235 South Ridgeway Avenue
Chicago, IL 60623

⑇0710⑇0062 242⑇027720⑇

	DOLLARS	CENTS
Cash		
Checks 1		
iist separately		
2		
3		
4		
5		
6		
7		
8		

NO. _____ $ _____
DATE _____ 19 ___
TO _____
FOR _____

	DOLLARS	CENTS
BALANCE		
AMT. DEPOSITED		
TOTAL		
AMT. THIS CHECK		
BALANCE		

WARREN TAYLOR, M.D.
2235 South Ridgeway Avenue
Chicago, IL 60623

NO. _____   2–62
                   ―――
                    710

_____ 19 ___

PAY
TO THE
ORDER OF _____ $ _____

_____ DOLLARS

First National Bank
Chicago, IL 60623

⑇0710⑇0062 242⑇027720⑇

NO. _____ $ _____
DATE _____ 19 ___
TO _____
FOR _____

	DOLLARS	CENTS
BALANCE		
AMT. DEPOSITED		
TOTAL		
AMT. THIS CHECK		
BALANCE		

WARREN TAYLOR, M.D.
2235 South Ridgeway Avenue
Chicago, IL 60623

NO. _____   2–62
                   ―――
                    710

_____ 19 ___

PAY
TO THE
ORDER OF _____ $ _____

_____ DOLLARS

First National Bank
Chicago, IL 60623

⑇0710⑇0062 242⑇027720⑇

WP 193

NO. ________ $ ________
DATE ________ 19 ___
TO ________
FOR ________

	DOLLARS	CENTS
BALANCE		
AMT. DEPOSITED		
TOTAL		
AMT. THIS CHECK		
BALANCE		

WARREN TAYLOR, M.D.
2235 South Ridgeway Avenue
Chicago, IL 60623

NO.________ 2–62/710

PAY ________ 19___
TO THE
ORDER OF________ $________

________ DOLLARS

First National Bank
Chicago, IL 60623

⑆0710⑈0062 242⑈027720⑈

NO. ________ $ ________
DATE ________ 19 ___
TO ________
FOR ________

	DOLLARS	CENTS
BALANCE		
AMT. DEPOSITED		
TOTAL		
AMT. THIS CHECK		
BALANCE		

WARREN TAYLOR, M.D.
2235 South Ridgeway Avenue
Chicago, IL 60623

NO.________ 2–62/710

PAY ________ 19___
TO THE
ORDER OF________ $________

________ DOLLARS

First National Bank
Chicago, IL 60623

⑆0710⑈0062 242⑈027720⑈

NO. ________ $ ________
DATE ________ 19 ___
TO ________
FOR ________

	DOLLARS	CENTS
BALANCE		
AMT. DEPOSITED		
TOTAL		
AMT. THIS CHECK		
BALANCE		

WARREN TAYLOR, M.D.
2235 South Ridgeway Avenue
Chicago, IL 60623

NO.________ 2–62/710

PAY ________ 19___
TO THE
ORDER OF________ $________

________ DOLLARS

First National Bank
Chicago, IL 60623

⑆0710⑈0062 242⑈027720⑈

NO. ________ $ ________
DATE ________ 19 ___
TO ________
FOR ________

	DOLLARS	CENTS
BALANCE		
AMT. DEPOSITED		
TOTAL		
AMT. THIS CHECK		
BALANCE		

WARREN TAYLOR, M.D.
2235 South Ridgeway Avenue
Chicago, IL 60623

NO.________ 2–62/710

PAY ________ 19___
TO THE
ORDER OF________ $________

________ DOLLARS

First National Bank
Chicago, IL 60623

⑆0710⑈0062 242⑈027720⑈

| NO. _____ $ _____ |
| DATE _____ 19 ___ |
| TO _____ |
| FOR _____ |

	DOLLARS	CENTS
BALANCE		
AMT. DEPOSITED		
TOTAL		
AMT. THIS CHECK		
BALANCE		

WARREN TAYLOR, M.D.
2235 South Ridgeway Avenue
Chicago, IL 60623

NO. _____   2–62/710

PAY _____ 19 ___
TO THE
ORDER OF _____ $ _____

_____ DOLLARS

First National Bank
Chicago, IL 60623

⑆0710⑆0062 242⑆027720⑆

| NO. _____ $ _____ |
| DATE _____ 19 ___ |
| TO _____ |
| FOR _____ |

	DOLLARS	CENTS
BALANCE		
AMT. DEPOSITED		
TOTAL		
AMT. THIS CHECK		
BALANCE		

WARREN TAYLOR, M.D.
2235 South Ridgeway Avenue
Chicago, IL 60623

NO. _____   2–62/710

PAY _____ 19 ___
TO THE
ORDER OF _____ $ _____

_____ DOLLARS

First National Bank
Chicago, IL 60623

⑆0710⑆0062 242⑆027720⑆

| NO. _____ $ _____ |
| DATE _____ 19 ___ |
| TO _____ |
| FOR _____ |

	DOLLARS	CENTS
BALANCE		
AMT. DEPOSITED		
TOTAL		
AMT. THIS CHECK		
BALANCE		

WARREN TAYLOR, M.D.
2235 South Ridgeway Avenue
Chicago, IL 60623

NO. _____   2–62/710

PAY _____ 19 ___
TO THE
ORDER OF _____ $ _____

_____ DOLLARS

First National Bank
Chicago, IL 60623

⑆0710⑆0062 242⑆027720⑆

| NO. _____ $ _____ |
| DATE _____ 19 ___ |
| TO _____ |
| FOR _____ |

	DOLLARS	CENTS
BALANCE		
AMT. DEPOSITED		
TOTAL		
AMT. THIS CHECK		
BALANCE		

WARREN TAYLOR, M.D.
2235 South Ridgeway Avenue
Chicago, IL 60623

NO. _____   2–62/710

PAY _____ 19 ___
TO THE
ORDER OF _____ $ _____

_____ DOLLARS

First National Bank
Chicago, IL 60623

⑆0710⑆0062 242⑆027720⑆

WP 197

NO. _____ $ _____		
DATE _____ 19 ___	WARREN TAYLOR, M.D.	NO. _____ 2-62/710
TO _____	2235 South Ridgeway Avenue	
FOR _____	Chicago, IL 60623	_____ 19 ___

PAY
TO THE
ORDER OF _____ $ _____

_____ DOLLARS

First National Bank
Chicago, IL 60623

⑆0710⑆0062 242⑆027720⑈

	DOLLARS	CENTS
BALANCE		
AMT. DEPOSITED		
TOTAL		
AMT. THIS CHECK		
BALANCE		

NO. _____ $ _____		
DATE _____ 19 ___	WARREN TAYLOR, M.D.	NO. _____ 2-62/710
TO _____	2235 South Ridgeway Avenue	
FOR _____	Chicago, IL 60623	

PAY _____ 19 ___
TO THE
ORDER OF _____ $ _____

_____ DOLLARS

First National Bank
Chicago, IL 60623

⑆0710⑆0062 242⑆027720⑈

	DOLLARS	CENTS
BALANCE		
AMT. DEPOSITED		
TOTAL		
AMT. THIS CHECK		
BALANCE		

NO. _____ $ _____		
DATE _____ 19 ___	WARREN TAYLOR, M.D.	NO. _____ 2-62/710
TO _____	2235 South Ridgeway Avenue	
FOR _____	Chicago, IL 60623	

PAY _____ 19 ___
TO THE
ORDER OF _____ $ _____

_____ DOLLARS

First National Bank
Chicago, IL 60623

⑆0710⑆0062 242⑆027720⑈

	DOLLARS	CENTS
BALANCE		
AMT. DEPOSITED		
TOTAL		
AMT. THIS CHECK		
BALANCE		

NO. _____ $ _____		
DATE _____ 19 ___	WARREN TAYLOR, M.D.	NO. _____ 2-62/710
TO _____	2235 South Ridgeway Avenue	
FOR _____	Chicago, IL 60623	

PAY _____ 19 ___
TO THE
ORDER OF _____ $ _____

_____ DOLLARS

First National Bank
Chicago, IL 60623

⑆0710⑆0062 242⑆027720⑈

	DOLLARS	CENTS
BALANCE		
AMT. DEPOSITED		
TOTAL		
AMT. THIS CHECK		
BALANCE		

WP 199

| NO. _____ $ _____ |
| DATE _____ 19 ___ |
| TO _____ |
| FOR _____ |

	DOLLARS	CENTS
BALANCE		
AMT. DEPOSITED		
TOTAL		
AMT. THIS CHECK		
BALANCE		

WARREN TAYLOR, M.D.
2235 South Ridgeway Avenue
Chicago, IL 60623

NO. _____   2–62/710

_____ 19 ___

PAY
TO THE
ORDER OF _____ $ _____

_____ DOLLARS

First National Bank
Chicago, IL 60623

⑆0710⑈0062 242⑈027720⑈

| NO. _____ $ _____ |
| DATE _____ 19 ___ |
| TO _____ |
| FOR _____ |

	DOLLARS	CENTS
BALANCE		
AMT. DEPOSITED		
TOTAL		
AMT. THIS CHECK		
BALANCE		

WARREN TAYLOR, M.D.
2235 South Ridgeway Avenue
Chicago, IL 60623

NO. _____   2–62/710

_____ 19 ___

PAY
TO THE
ORDER OF _____ $ _____

_____ DOLLARS

First National Bank
Chicago, IL 60623

⑆0710⑈0062 242⑈027720⑈

No. 560

To _____

Date _____

For _____

Amount _____

_____

No. _____   _____ 19 ___

Received from _____

_____ *Dollars*

FOR _____

$ _____

No. _____

To _____

Date _____

For _____

Amount _____

No. _____   _____ 19 ___

Received from _____

_____ *Dollars*

FOR _____

$ _____

WP 201

No. _____	No. _____	_____ 19 ___
To _____	*Received from* _____	
Date _____	_____ *Dollars*	
For _____	FOR _____	
Amount _____	$ _____	
_____		

No. _____	No. _____	_____ 19 ___
To _____	*Received from* _____	
Date _____	_____ *Dollars*	
For _____	FOR _____	
Amount _____	$ _____	
_____		

No. _____	No. _____	_____ 19 ___
To _____	*Received from* _____	
Date _____	_____ *Dollars*	
For _____	FOR _____	
Amount _____	$ _____	
_____		

No. _____	No. _____	_____ 19 ___
To _____	*Received from* _____	
Date _____	_____ *Dollars*	
For _____	FOR _____	
Amount _____	$ _____	

WP 203

No. _____	No. _____	_____ 19____
To _____	*Received from* _____	
Date _____		
For _____	_____ *Dollars*	
Amount _____	FOR _____	
	$ _____	_____

No. _____	No. _____	_____ 19____
To _____	*Received from* _____	
Date _____		
For _____	_____ *Dollars*	
Amount _____	FOR _____	
	$ _____	_____

No. _____	No. _____	_____ 19____
To _____	*Received from* _____	
Date _____		
For _____	_____ *Dollars*	
Amount _____	FOR _____	
	$ _____	_____

No. _____	No. _____	_____ 19____
To _____	*Received from* _____	
Date _____		
For _____	_____ *Dollars*	
Amount _____	FOR _____	
	$ _____	_____

WP 205

No. _____	No. _____	_____ 19 ____
To _____	*Received from* _____	
Date _____		_____ *Dollars*
For _____	FOR _____	
Amount _____	$ _____	

No. _____	No. _____	_____ 19 ____
To _____	*Received from* _____	
Date _____		_____ *Dollars*
For _____	FOR _____	
Amount _____	$ _____	

ANN CURTISS
1515 North Talman Avenue
Chicago, IL 60622

NO. 115   2-142/710

PAY TO THE ORDER OF __Warren Taylor, M.D.__ $ 30 00/100

__Thirty and 00/100__ ——————— DOLLARS

People's State Bank
Chicago, IL 60622

Ann Curtiss

⑆0710⑆0142 118⑆7443⑈

Lee and Ellen Goldberg
3425 South 61st Avenue
Chicago, IL 60650

NO. 143   2-142/710

PAY TO THE ORDER OF __Warren Taylor, M.D.__ $ 100 00/100

__One hundred and no/100__ ——————— DOLLARS

People's State Bank
Chicago, IL 60622

Ellen Goldberg

⑆0710⑆0142 118⑆8528⑈

WP 207

Joseph Provost
4548 North St. Louis Avenue
Chicago, IL 60625

NO. 70   2-62/710

November 19 19—

PAY TO THE ORDER OF Warren Taylor $107 00/100

One hundred seven and no/100 —————— DOLLARS

First National Bank
Chicago, IL 60623

Joseph Provost

⑈0710⑈0062 0815⑈02249⑈

THOMAS LESLIE
3736 South Pulaski Road
Chicago, IL 60623

NO. 19   2-62/710

November 18 19—

PAY TO THE ORDER OF Warren Taylor, M.D. $89.00/100

Eighty-Nine and 00/100 —————— DOLLARS

First National Bank
Chicago, IL 60623

Thomas Leslie

⑈0710⑈0062 242⑈046580⑈

Marion Wellman
13405 South School Avenue
Chicago, IL 60627

NO. 196   2-62/710

December 2 19--

PAY TO THE ORDER OF Dr. Warren Taylor $75 00/100

Seventy-five and 00/100 —————— DOLLARS

First National Bank
Chicago, IL 60623

Marion Wellman

⑈0710⑈0062 202⑈056232⑈

Gail Hayes
5632 South Princeton Avenue
Chicago, IL 60621

NO. 22   2-155/710

December 1 19--

PAY TO THE ORDER OF Warren Taylor, M.D. $112.50

One Hundred Twelve and 50/100 —————— DOLLARS

Chicago Bank
Chicago, IL 60621

Gail Hayes

⑈0710⑈0155 262⑈025592⑈

WP 209

Jill Grimes
5664 South Ross Avenue
Chicago, IL 60621

NO. 287   2-62/710

December 1 19--

PAY TO THE ORDER OF Warren Taylor, M.D. $ 50 00/100

Fifty and 00/100 ———————————————— DOLLARS

First National Bank
Chicago, IL 60623

Jill Grimes

⑆0710⑆0062 232⑆095465⑈

JOHN BACHMANN
5503 South Perry Avenue
Chicago, IL 60621

NO. 111   2-155/710

December 1 19--

PAY TO THE ORDER OF Warren Taylor, M.D. $ 30 00/100

Thirty and 00/100 ———————————————— DOLLARS

Chicago Bank
Chicago, IL 60621

John Bachmann

⑆0710⑆0155 262⑆052100⑈

Carl Logan
729 North Wolcott Avenue
Chicago, IL 60622

NO. 82   2-62/710

December 3 19--

PAY TO THE ORDER OF Warren Taylor, M.D. $ 50 00

Fifty dollars and 00/100 cents ———————— DOLLARS

First National Bank
Chicago, IL 60623

Carl Logan

⑆0710⑆0062 202⑆884430⑈

Lee and Ellen Goldberg
3425 South 61st Avenue
Chicago, IL 60650

NO. 213   2-142/710

December 3 19--

PAY TO THE ORDER OF Warren Taylor, M.D. $ 1000 00/100

One thousand and 00/100 ———————————— DOLLARS

People's State Bank
Chicago, IL 60622

Ellen Goldberg

⑆0710⑆0142 118⑆8528⑈